THE RELIGIOUS BELIEFS
OF AMERICA'S FOUNDERS

AMERICAN POLITICAL THOUGHT

Wilson Carey McWilliams and Lance Banning
Founding Editors

THE RELIGIOUS BELIEFS OF AMERICA'S FOUNDERS

Reason, Revelation, and Revolution

Gregg L. Frazer

University Press of Kansas

© 2012 by the University Press of Kansas
All rights reserved

Published by the University Press of Kansas (Lawrence, Kansas 66045),
which was organized by the Kansas Board of Regents and is operated
and funded by Emporia State University, Fort Hays State University,
Kansas State University, Pittsburg State University, the University of
Kansas, and Wichita State University

Library of Congress Cataloging-in-Publication Data

Frazer, Gregg L.
The religious beliefs of America's founders : reason, revelation, and revolution /
Gregg L. Frazer.
p.   cm. — (American political thought)
Includes bibliographical references and index.
ISBN 978-0-7006-1845-3 (alk. paper)
1. Founding Fathers of the United States—Religious life. 2. Religion and politics—
United States—History—18th century. 3. United States—Religion—To 1800.
4. Theism—United States. 5. Rationalism. 6. United States—Church history—
18th century. I. Title.
BL2525.F74 2012
200.92'273—dc23
2012005819

British Library Cataloguing-in-Publication Data is available.
Printed in the United States of America

10 9 8 7 6 5 4 3 2 1

The paper used in this publication is recycled and contains 30 percent
postconsumer waste. It is acid free and meets the minimum requirements
of the American National Standard for Permanence of Paper for Printed
Library Materials Z39.48-1992.

TO MY PARENTS,
LOWELL AND SHIRLEY FRAZER,
FOR EVERYTHING

CONTENTS

PREFACE

As I sat in a convention hall about thirty years ago listening to the authors of *The Light and the Glory* make a severely flawed case that America was founded as a Christian nation, I decided that someone should write a comprehensive, accurate account of the religious beliefs of the American Founders. My frustration with the lack of an accurate record grew each time someone passed me a video by Christian America advocate David Barton. Representatives of the other extreme were just as exasperating in their inaccuracy. People such as Americans United for Separation of Church and State spokesman Barry Lynn tried to make the equally flawed case that the Founders were rank secularists who wanted to completely separate religion from the public realm. I saw both sides as clearly wrong and as interested parties who were willing to manipulate the historical record in support of their agendas. The Supreme Court regularly compounded the problem by interpreting the Establishment Clause on the basis of the historically spurious "wall of separation" notion. All of this compelled me to consider taking on the project myself. I felt increasingly driven to set the record straight. The interest of my colleague Joseph Bessette encouraged me to finally put decades of research into written form.

Any historian worth the label has a desire to correct the historical record when it is in error. And any student of politics knows, as did the Founders, that those who win the battle of ideas generally determine policy. My purpose in writing this book spans both disciplines and includes both motives. I want to get the history right. More than that, though, I want to force extremists on the Left and on the Right to make the case for their vision of what America should be on its own merits, without hijacking the fame of the Founders and without holding their reputations hostage to causes of which they would not approve. Since the Founders are not here to defend themselves in person, this book is an attempt to allow them to defend themselves through the written record of their words.

My first goal was to try to discover from their own testimony what the key Founders actually said that they believed—as opposed to making assumptions based on mere denominational affiliation. My second goal was to trace to the extent possible the effect that their religious beliefs had upon their political actions and, consequently, on the Founding of America. A third goal was to explicate the arguments made by patriotic preachers in

support of the American Revolution and to demonstrate the affinity between the beliefs expressed by the religious leaders and those of the political
leaders. Finally, I wanted to suggest a possible solution to the twenty-first-
century argument over the relationship between church and state by show-
casing the approach taken by the nation's key Founders. This last goal was
born out of my conviction that the Founders best understood how government can and should promote and support religion while affording maximum religious liberty.

Pursuit of the first goal led to the conclusion that the expressed beliefs of
the key Founders did not fit within any established categories, which in turn
led me to develop a name for their belief system: *theistic rationalism.* Chapter 1 introduces the concept of theistic rationalism, distinguishes it from
Christianity and from deism, and lays out today's dispute over the religious
views of the Founders. Chapter 2 traces the origins of theistic rationalism
by reviewing the beliefs of those clergymen and religious philosophers who
most heavily influenced the key Founders and the preachers who supported
the Revolution. In chapter 3, I explain the importance of the education of
eighteenth-century ministers and analyze the content of their sermons in
support of revolution and republicanism. Chapters 4 through 7 provide in-
depth analysis of the expressed religious beliefs of eight men who arguably
were the most influential Founders. Although John Adams was affiliated
with a Congregational church and is regularly categorized as a Christian,
the evidence presented in chapter 4 makes him the clearest representative of
theistic rationalism. Thomas Jefferson and Benjamin Franklin are routinely
placed at the other end of the spectrum as deists, but that designation does
not stand up to scrutiny, as revealed in chapter 5. Chapter 6 explores several
fundamental beliefs of theistic rationalism in the words and actions of four
prominent framers of the Constitution: Gouverneur Morris, James Wilson,
James Madison, and Alexander Hamilton. The religious beliefs of the famously taciturn George Washington are unearthed in chapter 7, where he
is shown to be neither Christian nor deist but a theistic rationalist as well.
The book concludes in chapter 8 with a look at how the theistic rationalism
of the key Founders and many patriotic preachers impacted the American
Founding and left a legacy in American civil religion. Special attention is
paid to the Declaration of Independence and the Constitution, as I suggest a
proper understanding of the religious elements and aspects of both.

A fundamental and necessary assumption of this work is that the key
Founders believed what they said and said what they believed—unless the
context gives us some reason to doubt that. We cannot evaluate and draw
conclusions about what individuals believed if we cannot generally trust

what they said that they believed. Otherwise, we decide in advance what they must have believed and then interpret all evidence according to that agenda, dismissing any evidence to the contrary. Unfortunately, that has been the standard approach of most of those in the Christian America and secular camps.

That said, certain types of sources are generally more reliable than others. It is my conviction that private correspondence, diary entries, and personal memoranda are the most reliable sources because an author is freest to use candor when there is no threat of public disapproval. The fact that some, such as Thomas Jefferson, tried desperately to retrieve their letters to keep them from public view supports this conviction. The bulk of the evidence presented here concerning the beliefs of the key Founders comes from private writings. The least reliable sources are those produced for public political consumption and designed to gain public approval. Public pronouncements, public speeches, and public proclamations must be viewed carefully, with attention to possible ulterior motives. That does not mean that they are useless but rather that one must be circumspect in the treatment and consideration of them. Where clergy are concerned, I take their sermons to be reliable conduits for their sincere views—especially the published versions. Where jurists or philosophers are concerned, their lectures unrelated to specific cases and their treatises would appear to be reliable.

In the chapters that follow, I take expressions of belief to be genuine unless there is some contextual reason to doubt them. On a number of occasions, I will point out such instances and suggest ulterior motives that should, perhaps, shape our understanding of a given statement or document.

I am grateful for the interest, encouragement, and input of many faculty colleagues at The Master's College. Special appreciation goes to my mentor and sounding board, John Stead, and to John Hotchkiss and Grant Horner, who willingly answered many questions of style and word choice. I am indebted to John Hughes for a reduced teaching load and a timely sabbatical during which the principal part of the manuscript was written. I also wish to acknowledge Peg Westphalen and Grace Bater for innumerable interlibrary loan acquisitions.

Through the evolution of this work, Ralph Rossum offered support, encouragement, and a number of helpful suggestions. Charles Kesler posed critical and difficult questions, pushing me to greater clarity and to a tighter line of argument. Joseph Bessette provided guiding wisdom, his usual attention to detail, and valuable advice in pursuing publication. I am greatly indebted to him for his painstaking efforts and for his friendship. It is an honor to have these eminent scholars approve my work.

Speaking of eminent scholars, Thomas Pangle read the original version of the manuscript and offered very helpful, detailed recommendations for revision, clarification, and readability. Russell Muirhead read the revised manuscript and provoked some restructuring, polishing, and focused improvements. By his permission, a few sentences in the final text are his. The final version is much improved as a result of their recommendations; their enthusiasm for the book was encouraging and made publication possible. Director Fred Woodward orchestrated the project for the University Press of Kansas, and his insights and suggestions throughout the process were invaluable.

I also wish to thank the University of Notre Dame Press for granting me permission to include material revised from "Alexander Hamilton, Theistic Rationalist," in *The Forgotten Founders on Religion and Public Life*, edited by Daniel L. Dreisbach, Mark David Hall, and Jeffry H. Morrison and published in 2009, in chapters 1 and 6 of this book.

Finally, I want to thank my daughters, Kaci, Kelli, and Kari, for sharing their daddy with an office for many years and my wife, Leanne, for her amazing selfless support and encouragement. I cannot adequately express my appreciation to her.

I

Theistic Rationalism Introduced

A Creed which should be acceptable to all good and reasonable men.
                                                          Basil Willey

THE FOUNDERS OF THE UNITED STATES believed that ideas have consequences. Some of the most important and powerful ideas held by men and women concern religion or religious belief. Because they are so important and powerful, religious ideas inevitably influence political thought and practice. That was certainly true with respect to the American Founding. The Founders were religious men who believed that religion was a crucial support for free societies. Yet even though religious ideas played a significant role in the Founding era, a profound misapprehension of those ideas pervades twenty-first-century America. Thomas Pangle, distinguished scholar of American political thought, wrote what serves as a virtual commission for this book when he observed: "What is needed is a more sustained attempt at interpreting the few greatest Founders in their own terms and spirit."[1] This book aims to meet precisely that need.

It is tempting for some to go beyond what the Founders actually said about their religious beliefs by speculating more generally about those beliefs and about their spiritual lives—if only because we want to "know them" and because there is so much we would like to know that they did not speak to. And so—from sympathy or affection or curiosity—we fill in their silences and speak for them when they refuse to speak for themselves. But this is a mistake, one that is more likely to distort our understanding of the Founders than deepen it. That the mistake is all the more tempting when some wish to recruit the Founders to their side in contemporary disputes is all the more reason to avoid it. This book resists the temptation to speak for the Founders: it does not suppose that we can know more than they revealed. The problem today is that we are so invested in the Founders that, in an effort to agree with them, we too often make them agree with us. In the process, we lose sight of what they actually said and wrote. This is particularly the case with their religion. One side wants to see the Founders as forerunners of today's secularists who prize a "wall of separation" between church and state. Another side wants to show that the Founders

I

intended the United States to be a Christian nation built upon Christian and, specifically, biblical principles. Amid this, the danger is that we will not see past our own attachments to entertain the Founders accurately, on their own terms. This book seeks to allow the key Founders to speak for themselves so that we can understand their religious beliefs on their own terms. Although "cherry-picking" or a convenient perusal of the evidence could supply material in support of either view, a comprehensive study reveals that neither of the prevailing views is correct. The political theology of the American Founding era was neither Christianity nor deism. The prevailing political theology of the American Founding era was *theistic rationalism.*

The "secular" camp is represented in the academic community by the majority of historians and political scientists. Many prominent names are closely associated with this view, including Charles Beard, Vernon Parrington, Louis Hartz, Adrienne and Gustav Koch, Gordon Wood, Walter Berns, Wilson Carey McWilliams, and Robert Goldwin. Their arguments range from economic determinism to the march of secularism to Lockean consensus to entrenchment in the Enlightenment to outright opposition to religion to stark cynicism on the part of the Founders. The secular school of thought has been extremely influential on university campuses because it accords well with the secularism taught in other disciplines and because members of its intended audience *want* to believe that it is true, as it coincides with the type of society and culture they prefer.

A number of interest groups and organizations in the public eye are also members of the secular camp. They raise money and support by declaring the irreligion of those who founded the country, by extolling the virtues of a wholly secular republic, and by warning of danger in the growing power of those who contend for religious influence in politics. Included in this group are the American Civil Liberties Union, People for the American Way, and Americans United for Separation of Church and State. Their influence depends on the extent to which they can raise the specter of fundamentalist theocracy in America. Their sensitivity on this issue was exemplified by their near hysteria over the nomination of John Ashcroft as attorney general. Ashcroft was grilled by members of the Judiciary Committee over his (accurate) quotation of a religious slogan from the Revolutionary period: "No King but King Jesus."[2] It was difficult to tell whether the secularists were more upset about the quote itself or about the fact that Ashcroft made the remark at a fundamentalist Christian college.

The "Christian America" camp is not well represented in the academic community. For the most part, historians or political scientists who hold this view teach at sectarian colleges or at colleges specifically created to promulgate the view, such as Patrick Henry College. The academic arenas in which the Christian America view holds a dominant position are the Christian school and home school movements. Most of those who are published and influential in this group, however, are either lawyers or pastors, not historians. Thus, there are no prominent historians or political scientists to mention in connection with the Christian America camp, but one book and one individual deserve mention. On the heels of the American Bicentennial celebration, Peter Marshall and David Manuel's *The Light and the Glory* was published and inspired a revival of the Christian America view. It became the classic text of that camp. Its historiography is abominable; it is a collection of speculations, suppositions, personal musings, and "insights" with little or no proof or documentation for extraordinary claims. Nonetheless, it remains very influential. The most prolific of the Christian America proponents is David Barton. Barton has created an entire organization, called Wallbuilders, to promote his views and to market his voluminous material.

The Christian America camp has its main influence in the evangelical Christian subculture. Prominent pastors, particularly those with television programs, effectively propagate the message to willing listeners. D. James Kennedy even established the Center for Reclaiming America as an "outreach" of his church. In addition to books and school curricula, videotapes and DVDs have been a most effective means of disseminating this view. Interest groups, publishing companies, legal services, tour group companies, lecture circuits, and colleges have all been established to promote the Christianization of the American Founding.

The Christian America camp is very active politically, and adherents have organized in order to "take back America" from the secularists and return the nation to its "biblical foundations." The Christian Coalition and numerous grassroots organizations work to elect Christians to political office across the country. They will not be satisfied until professing Christians occupy the strategic offices of the land and promote biblical policies, as they believe the Founding Fathers did. In other words, their utopian goal is to create exactly the kind of society warned against by the secularists. The Christian America view has found a huge and trusting audience among those who feel alienated by the cultural and political changes in America and who *want* to believe that the view is accurate.

Both the secular and Christian America schools of thought, then, are warmly received by their intended audiences. Consequently, there is little motivation to investigate the evidence and to make an independent analysis. This book presents the results of such an independent analysis and finds both views wanting. In addition to receptive audiences, the political and cultural groups organized around these two views have one other thing in common: they both base much of what they claim on what they believe to be the political theology of the American Founders. This book demonstrates that both of these camps err in their view of the Founders' political theology.

It is worth noting that a third school of thought exists concerning the political theology of the American Founding. This perspective is not nearly as popular as the Christian America view or as widely accepted in the academic community as the secular view, but it is much closer to being correct than either of the others. This third view might be called the "balanced" view. It recognizes a significant degree of impact on the Founders from both secular and Christian influences. Alan Heimert's *Religion and the American Mind* and Alice Baldwin's *The New England Clergy and the American Revolution* are the definitive works of this camp. Historians Mark Noll, Nathan Hatch, and George Marsden and political scientists Thomas Pangle and Michael Zuckert have done fine work in this area. Yet none has done a comprehensive study of the religious beliefs of the key Founders or made the theoretical connection between the religious and political leadership of the Founding era.

Pangle's remarks in *The Spirit of Modern Republicanism* about the political theology of the Founders are essentially correct, but he ends the discussion just as he whets the appetite of the reader. His analysis culminates in a series of probing questions:

> But the question remains whether the moral and political understanding of men like Franklin, Madison, Jefferson, Wilson, and Hamilton can be adequately interpreted as a continuation of the Christian tradition. . . . Was Christianity the dominant or defining element in their thinking? Or were they not rather engaged in an attempt to exploit and transform Christianity in the direction of a liberal rationalism? Does their "Christianity" not look more plausible to us only because they succeeded so well in their project of changing the heart and soul of Christianity?[3]

Pangle's incisive questions go to the core of the dispute over the political theology of the American Founding and serve as a call for a study such as this.

Why would the key Founders be interested in trying to change or shape religious opinion? Sidney Mead suggests that "societies create their concepts of the attributes and character of the god they worship in the likeness of the pressing practical problems of their time and place."[4] For the key Founders and a number of ministers, the Christian God—the God of the Bible—was inadequate for their political needs. That God did not grant religious freedom, He claimed to be the sole source of governmental authority, He neither granted nor recognized natural rights, and He preferred faith and obedience to moralism.[5] To meet their needs, they constructed a god and a belief system more to their liking. In particular, liberal democratic and republican theory significantly shaped religious belief in eighteenth-century America and contributed to the construction of a new belief system—theistic rationalism. That belief system, in turn, provided fertile soil in which to plant the American experiment. It furnished the basis for the toleration, diversity, and emphasis on rights and morality that lie at the heart of the American political culture. As one embarks upon a study of the political theology of the American Founding era, it is critical to recognize that the god of the theistic rationalists was not the God of the Puritans in the previous century. Although, as Stephen Marini notes, a form of religious liberalism informed by the Enlightenment "supplied a powerful theological and philosophical foundation for the cosmopolitan republican culture of the 1780s,"[6] it was not deism, either.

POLITICAL THEOLOGY AT THE FOUNDING: THEISTIC RATIONALISM

Many scholars who study the period have concluded that political and religious thought were not nearly as differentiated in the Founding era as modern sensibilities or modern thinking would make them. Henry May explains that men of that period, regardless of their religious persuasion, "seldom thought about any branch of human affairs without referring consciously to some general beliefs about the nature of the universe and man's place in it, and about human nature itself." Religious historian Nathan Hatch complains that the modern penchant for compartmentalization has hindered understanding of the Founding era. He argues that modern scholars struggle to make sense of "the surprisingly undifferentiated thinking" of men of the late eighteenth century and to "bring together conceptual worlds that for the Revolutionary generation never were separate."[7]

The realms of religion and politics were inextricably linked for the Founding generation. That may be why courses in moral philosophy were centerpieces of university education. John Witherspoon, for instance, exerted a profound influence over a generation of prominent figures through his course in moral philosophy at Princeton. It is also, perhaps, the reason that Benjamin Franklin and others expended so much effort in the search for the essentials of religion to which "all good men" could agree. It was important to them because religion and politics "are very closely intertwined components of the human search for order."[8]

Because of the intimate connection between religion and politics, monumental political events and ideas necessarily produced considerable religious changes. Sydney Ahlstrom observes that the politics of the Founding era "accelerated the advance of Enlightenment philosophy, natural theology, and secularized thought," which, in turn, "contributed to theological transformation." Because the biblical God does not specifically or exclusively favor liberal democratic thought,[9] the changes and transformations to which Ahlstrom refers were movements away from Christianity and the Bible and toward a belief system that harmonized with the spirit of the age.

Most obvious was the revolt against Calvinism, which was abandoned by many at the time of the Revolution because it was viewed as inconsistent with the Revolutionary emphasis on liberty. Each of the so-called five points of Calvinism offended liberal democratic sensibilities. Eventually, many deemed the tenets of Calvinism to be irrational, making those who had rejected them feel further justified. As Cushing Strout contends, "Tocqueville's emphasis on the Puritan roots of the Revolution does less than justice to the rationalist anti-Calvinists who led it." George Willis Cooke connects the Calvinist doctrine of decrees with divine right of kings and Arminianism with the people's claim to the right to rule.[10] In doing so, he demonstrates another reason that Calvinism had to go.

In eighteenth-century America, *Arminianism* was "the technical term for democracy in religion" and was characterized by "toleration, free inquiry, the use of reason, [and] democratic methods in church and state."[11] For example, Arminians criticized the practice of distinguishing between communicant and noncommunicant members and labeled such distinctions "undemocratic" or "illiberal." The term itself stemmed from a theological position that contrasted sharply with Calvinist conceptions of the relationship between God and man. In particular, it was a denial of the doctrine of original sin and an affirmation of man's ability to save himself through "a continuous rational process of self-dedication." Arminians viewed man as a "free agent" who "worked out his own salvation and suffered his just deserts."[12] Clearly, this view fit more easily with republican ideas than did Calvinism.

A more subtle change was the convenient reinterpretation of Scripture. Thus, since the Bible never promotes political liberty, passages extolling *spiritual* liberty and freedom from sin were commandeered and pressed into service in support of *political* freedom and the Revolutionary cause. And as will be discussed in chapters 2 and 3, the quintessential passage demanding subjection to governing authority (Romans 13) was turned on its head to support rebellion. Furthermore, in order to support and justify the American cause, the history of Israel was rewritten. Theistic rationalists read concern for political liberty and republican self-government into the accounts of premonarchical Israel.[13] This abuse of the history of Israel will be addressed in chapter 3, but a few observations by Robert Kraynak are appropriate here to illustrate the desire of theistic rationalists to move away from Christianity and a plenary view of Scripture to revelation of their own choosing and interpretation.

First, as Kraynak points out, "the biblical covenant is undemocratic: God is not bound by the covenant and keeps His promises solely out of His own divine self-limitation." Second, "there is nothing voluntary or consensual about the biblical covenant; and the most severe punishments are threatened by God for disobedience." Third, "insofar as the covenant with Israel sanctions specific forms of government, the main ones are illiberal and undemocratic," including patriarchy, theocracy, and kingships established by divine right. Fourth, "the Bible shows that God delivers the people from slavery in Egypt and supports national liberation, not for the purpose of enjoying their political and economic rights, but for the purpose of putting on the yoke of the law in the polity of Moses." Fifth, "the content of the divine law revealed to Moses consists, in the first place, of the Ten Commandments rather than the Ten Bill of Rights, commanding duties to God, family, and neighbors rather than establishing protections for personal freedom." Sixth and finally, the combined judicial, civil, ceremonial, and dietary laws imposed on the people "regulate all aspects of religious, personal, and social life."[14] The history of Israel, therefore, had to be radically rewritten to provide support for the demands of political liberty and for republican self-government.

Various strategies were employed to inculcate Whig and republican ideas into acceptable religious forms. In the quarter century leading up to the Revolution, roughly half of American books and pamphlets discussed politics from a religious perspective. In the 1770s, the vast majority of sermons addressed the political crisis from the Whig point of view. By the time of the Revolution, republican ideas were for many an article of faith.[15] Steven

Keillor aptly describes radical Whig ideology as "political Protestantism." Theistic rationalists, though no longer strictly religious Protestants, were political Protestants and could, consequently, use familiar and socially acceptable language. Radical Whig republicanism "offered underlying parallels to Protestant Christianity," and that reassured the theistic rationalists that "they had jettisoned only religious dogmas and were otherwise following tried and true paths." For example, both republicans and Christians stressed virtue, but republicans meant political virtue, whereas Christians meant biblical morality. Although the theistic rationalists tried to make republican virtue equivalent to Christian morality, "republican virtue was embedded in a worldview that was Greco-Roman, rationalist, egalitarian, antiauthoritarian and basically non-Christian." Similarly, one could confuse republican concern about the lust for power with the Christian belief in human depravity.[16]

A number of scholars have identified and discussed the belief system I call theistic rationalism, but none have examined it in a comprehensive fashion or recognized that it was the predominant political theology of the Founding era. Some have encountered it in connection with their study of the key Founders and others in their study of influential preachers; some have suggested its political significance. No one, however, has made the connection between all three. To place the remainder of this study in context, it is important to review scholarly observations of rational religion in eighteenth-century America.

Establishing the larger context, Basil Willey noted that the religious conflicts of the sixteenth and seventeenth centuries set the stage for the eighteenth by "calling in doubt all the points of the faith, and reducing them to the level of controversy." As a result, said Willey, "a desire arose during the seventeenth century to formulate a creed which should be acceptable to all good and reasonable men."[17] That desire was eventually satisfied in the eighteenth century by theistic rationalism. In his discussion of what I am calling theistic rationalism, Conrad Wright said that "it was so widely accepted, across denominational lines, that one might justly call it the great ecumenical theology of its age." He elsewhere described it as "virtually the orthodox theology of the Age of Reason." According to Wright, it was "far more sharply defined, prevalent, and significant than any of our scholars . . . have ever intimated." In fact, he described it as "all-pervasive." In clarifying to what he was referring, Wright noted that "we should of course keep it in mind that we are not talking about a sect, or a denomination, or similar special group. The term refers to a position in a scheme of logical classification of ideas, not to a sociological entity."[18] In other words, theistic rationalism was a belief system not identified with any particular religion or church structure.

Wright offered an explanation for the lack of general awareness of theistic rationalism: "It is certainly satisfying—at any rate, for pedagogues—to be able to contrast Deism with Puritanism, the Enlightenment with Christian orthodoxy, Benjamin Franklin with Jonathan Edwards, the eighteenth century with the seventeenth." However, said Wright, "the choice was not simply between Natural Religion and Christian orthodoxy, but . . . there was a viable middle way, which was widely accepted in the American colonies." Furthermore, he essentially called for this book when he suggested, "There is a magic about names; and if there is an entity without a common name, we fail to recognize that it exists. I would even go so far as to argue that the fact that Deism has long had an accepted name, while the other kind of rationalism . . . has not, helps to explain why the latter has been so readily overlooked as a separate, distinct, and vigorous tradition in this country."[19] I submit *theistic rationalism* as the name to finally bring recognition to this belief system.

Although scholars use different terms for this belief system (as demonstrated earlier) and stress different elements of it, there is essential agreement that the American experiment was begun "through a combination of the ideas of the Enlightenment and the ideals of the Christian religion."[20] For instance, Henry May argued that Protestantism and the Enlightenment were the two main "clusters of ideas" critical to an understanding of eighteenth-century America. Indeed, according to May, the "relation between these two major idea systems is basic to the understanding of eighteenth-century America." May discovered that Enlightenment thought was "often inextricably mixed with Christian ideas," and he concluded that eighteenth-century man did not think either Enlightenment thought or Christianity "express[ed] the whole truth about human nature."[21] Although the latter remark is overstated, it is certainly true that the eighteenth-century men in this study held that view.

According to Robert Kraynak, these men of the Enlightenment "did not so much call for the abolition of religion as for the transformation of religion into something more reasonable" that "discarded" many fundamental elements of Christianity "while preserving a set of core convictions grounded on reason rather than on revelation or Scripture."[22] Kraynak surveyed a number of "rational religions" that emerged in response to this call. One of them was "Theism, which saw God as the Supreme Governor who not only created the universe but also actively and continuously intervenes in it, directing the lives of men and nations, judging their actions, and

administering rewards and punishments in this life and the next."[23] This is
the God of theistic rationalism.

Following his survey of rational religions, Kraynak concluded:

> What all of these movements have in common is the belief that religion
> can be preserved in the modern age of Enlightenment only by rational-
> izing and simplifying it to include the belief in a rational morality of
> universal benevolence that requires religious toleration, human free-
> dom, and scientific progress. Nearly all other doctrines of traditional
> Judaism and Christianity . . . were to be discarded as irrational relics of
> a less enlightened age which modern people, especially educated people,
> have outgrown.[24]

Kraynak then identified "some of the most important figures" of the eighteenth century as "public or private adherents of rational religion," including Franklin, Jefferson, Washington, Adams, and Madison.[25]

Prominent scholars of American religious history have recognized that a
new belief system was created with Enlightenment rationalism and Christianity as its building blocks. Sidney Mead acknowledged that "the main cur-
rents of thought among the intellectuals" came to theological agreement "at
the expense of discarding the keystone of the orthodox Christian arch—the
Bible as the one and only revelation of God for the guidance of mankind to
'salvation' through Jesus Christ, truly God, truly human, and only Savior."
Furthermore, "the new breed of intellectuals presumed to be rational beside, beyond, or without the Scriptures, and in doing so they created a new
religion."[26] Mead was quick to note that they were not atheists but "'infidels' in the precise sense the term then conveyed, in that they rejected the
orthodox Christian premises: that the Bible was the only revelation of God
to man, and that Jesus was Deity."[27] According to Cushing Strout, "The
secular leaders, participants in the Enlightenment's culture of liberal political philosophy, Newtonian science, and classical humanism, still preserved
residual connections with Christianity, even when they attacked specific
Christian dogmas and practices. Their Christian allies also thought of themselves as friends of the secular ideology of social contract and the natural
rights of man. The two groups were symbiotically related."[28] Strout came
close to recognizing that many in the two groups actually shared the same
belief system, but he saw it as simply a "mutually advantageous alliance."
Speaking of the secular leaders, he argued that, among others, Madison,
Jefferson, Franklin, and Adams had "a shared conception of 'enlightened'
religion, purified of the corruptions they believed the historic faiths had

made in the simple truth."[29] Here, again, is the emphasis on simplicity implied by Willey's comments on the search for a widely acceptable creed and identified as characteristic of the period by Kraynak. Strout also recognized that their belief system was something unique when he observed that "the rationalist statesmen did not believe in the traditional Christian religions, but they did have a religion of their own, neither cynical, deistical, nor fundamentalist in any exact sense."[30]

In his classic *Religious History of the American People,* Sydney Ahlstrom attested to the development of a new belief system, calling it "a distinct form of Enlightenment theology."[31] He said, "There emerged a recognizable type of 'enlightened' Christianity," and he delineated its characteristics.[32] Those characteristics meshed quite well with theistic rationalism. According to Ahlstrom, "'Natural religion' flourished in alliance with 'revealed religion' in the theology of many Christian rationalists [his term for theistic rationalists]."[33] Ahlstrom suggested, as does this study, that Adams, Franklin, and Jefferson were representative of this movement:

> Each of these men sought to express the new rationalism with complete intellectual integrity. Each of them tried in a serious way, through a long and active career, to deal coherently with the separate but interrelated problems of man, God, nature, and society. Each of them exemplified in a unique way how the Puritan heritage, an emerging pattern of middle-class democracy, and the fresh influences of the Enlightenment were preparing the American colonies for a common and united destiny.[34]

Conventional wisdom in the academic community says that Franklin and Jefferson were deistic anomalies among the Founders, but Ahlstrom concluded that "only an extensive essay could clarify the religious differences of the major Founding Fathers."[35] He was right because the major Founders were theistic rationalists, and the only differences between them were those that resulted from differences in what individuals considered reasonable.

Three of the most respected American religious historians, then, came upon theistic rationalism in their study of the encounter between Enlightenment thought and Christianity in the eighteenth century. Although their own predilections caused them to use different terminology and to emphasize some aspects while missing others, they all recognized the creation and significance of what I have called theistic rationalism.

Finally, political scientist Thomas Pangle saw the same developments but emphasized the political import. Pangle began *The Spirit of Modern Republicanism* by observing that "the American Founding came to be dominated by a small minority of geniuses who seized the initiative not merely by conciliating and reflecting common opinion but also by spearheading new or uncommon opinion."[36] The specific context for this statement was not a discussion of political theology, but his explication of the statement included political theology. Pangle posed some vital questions about the key Founders' relationship to Christianity. His answer to those questions was that eighteenth-century American political thought was "dominated" by a "new conception" of "human nature and politics." That new conception was "antagonistic to traditional political theology, both Protestant and Catholic: the new thinking means to reinterpret the Bible, to found a new tradition of political theology, and to establish a new relationship between church and state."[37] Pangle recognized the advent of a new, non-Christian political theology, but he did not investigate it in detail.

The observations of others could be brought to bear, but it should be clear that a new belief system came into being in eighteenth-century America and that it produced a new political theology. Some scholars and historians have recognized the existence of the belief system that I have called "theistic rationalism," but those who have tried to give it a name have relegated it to the realm of religious history and identified it only with theologians and preachers. No one has applied it to the central political figures. Several terms have been used to identify this hybrid concept, but all are inadequate or misleading. It has been variously referred to as "supernatural rationalism," "theological rationalism," "Christian rationalism," or "rational Christianity."

Conrad Wright, who uses "supernatural rationalism," attributes the term to early twentieth-century works by A. C. McGiffert and John Randall, but he notes that it has been used by other scholars as well. It has, in fact, been employed by a number of religious historians. Though the term is manifestly similar to "theistic rationalism," there is a significant difference that makes the former misleading and inadequate. "Supernatural" merely indicates belief in *something* above or beyond the natural world. That something might be personal or impersonal; it might be multiple gods or a force or some set of mystical creatures, such as angels. The key Founders and patriotic preachers were decidedly and explicitly "theist." They believed in a personal *God* above nature, about whom they had well-formed and well-defined ideas. Not completely comfortable with the term himself, Wright has expressed a "wish that some other term had come into common use."[38] I offer such a term.

Cushing Strout describes the system as "theological rationalism,"[39] which is a more appropriate term. Yet it suffers from the same problem as the other in that it does not indicate belief in a particular God, which is central to the system. For example, one might rightly describe Plato's views on the gods and reincarnation as "theological rationalism." The theism of the Founders and preachers is vital and must be included in a proper description of their belief system.

McMurry Richey calls the system "Christian rationalism," and Sydney Ahlstrom labels adherents "Christian rationalists." Ahlstrom and Henry May refer to the system as "enlightened Christianity" or "reasonable Christianity" or "rationalist Christianity." To Michael Zuckert, it is "rational Christianity."[40] These formulations accord with Jefferson's own description of his belief system as "rational Christianity."[41] The problem with these appellations is that the adherents to this system were not Christians and the system was not a subset of Christianity. Those here identified as theistic rationalists denied every fundamental doctrine of Christianity as it was defined and understood in their day. Jefferson specifically did so item by item in a letter to William Short.[42] If rejecting every fundamental tenet of a religion does not separate one from it, what does? In particular, they denied the person and work of the Christ of *Christ*ianity, without Whom the term itself makes no sense. Mere affiliation with a Christian denomination or sect did not make one a Christian in eighteenth-century America. There was no such thing as Christianity by association. One may have been a Baptist or Presbyterian or Episcopalian by association, but being a Christian required adherence to certain beliefs.

It was meaningless when someone such as Jefferson described his religion as rational Christianity because his description was based on his own personal definition of Christianity, which did not comport with the way every major church defined it. Those theistic rationalists who claimed to be Christians—and not all of them did—appropriated the word *Christianity* and attached it to a belief system that they constructed and found more to their liking than authentic Christianity. It would be interesting to ask those scholars who use such a term whether the ones who did not even claim to be Christians were also rational Christians. Christianity is not an ethnicity; no one is born a Christian. Like all religious faiths, Christianity is chosen. Since it is chosen, it can be not chosen or rejected. The theistic rationalists preferred a belief system of their own creation and rejected Christianity. Consequently, it is improper and misleading to include a form of the word *Christian* in a term for those whom I describe as theistic rationalists.

I think that *theistic rationalism* is a much more accurate and useful term to describe the belief system of a number of intellectual elites, both political and religious, in eighteenth-century America. It is, in my view, certainly more accurate and useful than *Christianity* or a broad, generic, catchall usage of *deism*.

DEISM, CHRISTIANITY, AND RATIONALISM

What, exactly, was this new belief system at the center of the American Founding? Theistic rationalism was a hybrid belief system mixing elements of natural religion, Christianity, and rationalism, with rationalism as the predominant element. Largely because natural religion and rationalism were critical components, theistic rationalism was not a popular system but appealed only to the well-educated elite—specifically, those versed in Enlightenment thought. Adherents of theistic rationalism believed that these three elements would generally complement one another; but when conflict between them could not be resolved or ignored, reason had to play the decisive role. Therefore, *rationalism* is the essence of the hybrid, and *theistic* is the descriptor. Adherents were willing to define God in whatever way their reason indicated and to jettison Christian beliefs that did not conform to reason. Theistic rationalism was not really a religion or denomination per se but rather a religious belief system and an approach to religious belief. Theistic rationalists did not call themselves by that name, meet or act in concert, or develop views as members of a group. They were alienated from the groups and categories that prevailed in their time, and they forged their own trail of belief. Thomas Jefferson famously claimed to be a "sect of one"; for theistic rationalists, that would make sense, as they assembled their own package of views from the most convincing ideas they encountered.

Though the term has a number of applications, *rationalism* in the context of this study refers to the philosophical view that regards reason as the chief source and test of knowledge. Of course, emphasis on reason had been an accepted part of Christianity since the work of Thomas Aquinas. Yet the Thomistic view of reason and its role differed significantly from that of the theistic rationalists. Aquinas taught that the function of reason was to show that revelation was true. He "employed" reason to "support faith" rather than to destroy it and in order to develop "an impregnable rational proof of a divinely ordered world." For Aquinas, the aim was to "reconcile experience with revealed truth." As he saw it, faith was above reason and more certain than reason because it was based on direct revelation from God. Reason had to be faulty if it seemed to contradict revelation. For him, truth was not derived from reason itself but from an authoritative source, with reason providing support.[43]

Aquinas differed from Muslim philosophers who taught that reason was the "sole judge of the truth of Revelation." In this regard, the theistic rationalists shared the Muslim position. For Aquinas, God was the author of both reason and revelation, so there could be no real discrepancy between them. Any apparent discrepancy was "traceable to the imperfection of the human mind." So, for Aquinas, reason bowed to revelation. As Ernest Fortin put it, Aquinas made reason a "handmaid" to Christianity. The theistic rationalists, as we shall see, made reason the ultimate standard and considered revelation a supplement to reason. If there was a discrepancy between reason and revelation, they considered the revelation to be flawed or illegitimate. It is one thing to stress the importance of reason in understanding revelation; it is quite another to suggest that reason ought to determine revelation. Aquinas believed that "it is foolish for man to reject God's revelation on the ground that it seems at some points to contradict man's natural knowledge."[44] That was precisely what the theistic rationalists did. Their rationalism was a significant departure from the rationalism of Aquinas.

Natural religion is a system of thought centered on the belief that reliable information about God and about what He wills is best discovered and understood by examining the evidence of nature and the laws of nature, which He established. Though they were not synonymous, the primary expression of natural religion in the eighteenth century was *deism*. In the latter half of the eighteenth century, deism influenced almost every educated man in England, France, and the United States.[45] Because of that fact and because one of the prevailing views today of the political theology of the Founding era is that most of the Founders were deists, it is important to understand the basics of deism.

Largely because of a false dichotomy promoted by modern observers that recognizes deism and Christianity as the only two categories of eighteenth-century religious belief, both *deism* and *Christianity* have become amorphous and nebulous terms in studies of that period. Many define deism in such general terms and include such a wide range of adherents that it is essentially a meaningless and, therefore, useless concept. A number of individuals have been identified as deists simply in the absence of another option besides Christian, not because they actually adhered to the fundamental beliefs of deism. There is far too much blurring when several Founders, such as John Adams, James Wilson, and George Washington, can alternately be identified by scholars as Christians and as deists.

For this reason, the definitions of deism and Christianity put forward here are bare-bones definitions reflecting essentials that every deist or Christian of whatever stripe would adhere to. These definitions are designed more to identify who was *not* a deist or Christian than to identify who was. Although some deists might add certain beliefs or attitudes to this definition, all would concur that one who disagreed with certain fundamentals was something other than a deist.

Eighteenth-century American deism was, at once, both a belief system on its own and a critique of Christianity. Lord Herbert of Cherbury was the recognized "father of deism." An editor of one of Herbert's works summarized the historical philosophical definition of deism as the belief that God "has withdrawn his active presence" from the universe and "remains completely aloof while it functions in strict accordance with the natural laws with which he originally endowed it." He added that "the withdrawal of God distinguishes deism from theism." This definition highlights a critical element of deism: the effective absence of God. As deism scholar Kerry Walters summarized, "The God of nature . . . assumed the aloof character of an absentee landlord, so far removed from the everyday existence of ordinary people as to be completely indifferent to their petitions and worship."[46]

Another critical element of deism was the denial of any written revelation from God; revelation was credible to the theist but not to the deist. Another scholar argued that deism was the position that "natural religion contains all that is true in revealed religion; where the latter differs, the differences are either morally insignificant or superstitious."[47] For prominent American deist Thomas Paine, the first premise of deism was "that nature, viewed by reason, is the only valid source of God's revelation to man." Deists considered biblical revelation to be tradition or history at best and more often simply hearsay or worse. Paine, for instance, said of the Bible, "It would be more consistent that we called it the word of a demon, than the Word of God," and he added, "For my part, I sincerely detest it."[48]

These two elements, the effective absence of God and the denial of written revelation, clearly divided the deists and the theistic rationalists. Though it appears inconsequential to many today in light of modern sensibilities, that divide was "decisive" in the eighteenth century, according to deism scholar Peter Gay. It made "all the difference" whether one accepted some revelation and a generally Protestant concept of God or rejected both. As Gay put it: "If it is true that the deists took only a single step, it is also true that the step they took was across an unbridgeable abyss." Conrad Wright used a similar metaphor—a "gulf" that was "unbridgeable"—in arguing that the religion of the period cannot be understood without recognition of this difference.[49] The decisive issues were revelation and the presence of God.

Deism was as much a critique of Christianity as a religion of its own, however. Jonathan Edwards, who dealt with deists firsthand, said that they "deny the whole Christian religion" and "deny the whole Scripture." In fact, according to Edwards, deists went a step further: "They deny any revealed religion, or any word of God at all, and say that God has given mankind no other light to walk by but his own reason."[50] Fundamentals of Christianity rejected by the deists included the Incarnation, the Virgin Birth, original sin, miracles, the atonement, the Resurrection, eternal damnation, and the Christian notion of faith. They condemned Christianity for intolerance, persecution, and the "scriptural depiction of the deity as a capricious and wicked celestial tyrant." The supernatural worldview of Christianity was also criticized as illogical and irrational, in violation of both human experience and reason.[51]

In addition, some deists criticized Jesus for being petty, for exalting the weaknesses of humility and meekness to virtues, for having no system to His moralizing, and for not being original in His ethics (they said the Greeks and Romans did it better). Though a few deists shared Paine's view that Jesus was "a virtuous and amiable man," most exhibited "malice" and "an earnest desire to find a flaw in the most perfect character" and sought ways to "fix a stain upon" the character of Jesus.[52] Indeed, the so-called bible of deism, Elihu Palmer's *Principles of Nature*, depicted Jesus as duplicitous and a hypocrite. He was referred to as a "religious imposter," "immoral," "criminal" in conduct, and an "enemy to moral virtue." His moral system was described as "pretended excellence," "inaccurate and incomplete," and "trifling." Palmer even called Jesus "a murderer in principle."[53] Edwards further testified that the deists believed Jesus to be "a mere cheat."[54] Clearly, most deists wanted nothing to do with Christianity or its central figure. Although the theistic rationalists shared some ideas with the deists, they had a much greater regard for Christianity and for Jesus than did most deists.

Surprisingly, deists did believe that God should be worshipped and that a future state of rewards and punishments awaited mankind.[55] In their view, the best way to worship God was to do good to and for one's fellow man. Their view of a future state was a largely impersonal settling of accounts, the teaching of which was necessary to encourage morality.

For the purposes of this study, Christianity as a belief system will be defined by the standards of eighteenth-century America. It refers, then, to a set of beliefs officially espoused by all of the major Christian sects in America in the 1700s. Those who held these beliefs were considered to be Christians, and those who did not were considered to be "infidels." The fundamentals of Christianity were common knowledge to contemporaries of the period, as they are to modern scholars who have written about the period. Those who held these basic beliefs were referred to as "the orthodox" by those who would be classified as "infidels" and by modern scholars.

Disputes over church polity and sacramental issues resulted in a number of sects, yet the period saw remarkable unanimity regarding central doctrines. The Congregational, Baptist, Presbyterian, and Anglican/Episcopalian denominations were the largest in America during that time. All of the individuals identified as theistic rationalists in this study were affiliated with one or more of these denominations, as were forty-seven of the fifty-five members of the Constitutional Convention.[56] According to their creeds, confessions, catechisms, and articles of faith, all of these denominations shared common belief in: the Trinity, the deity of Jesus, a God active in human affairs, original sin, the Virgin Birth, the atoning work of Christ in satisfaction for man's sins, the bodily Resurrection of Christ, eternal punishment for sin, justification by faith, and the authority of the Scriptures. The fact that the Catholic Church, though irreconcilably separated from the Protestant churches, also embraced all of these fundamental doctrines is further evidence of the consensus concerning the basic core content of Christianity. A Calvinist might add doctrines to the definition that an Anglican or Baptist would not, but none of them would subtract any of these. Again, the definition is designed to identify who was *not* a Christian or who would not be considered Christian by any of the denominations.

With the addition of a little explication, the fundamental doctrines become clearer. Regarding God, Christians taught that God was Triune (one God comprehending three persons: Father, Son, and Holy Spirit); that the God of the Old Testament was the same as that of the New Testament; and that, in addition to being loving and benevolent, God was holy, jealous, and just. Furthermore, God the Creator, Who remained active in His creation, could and did intervene in nature and in human affairs. Christians believed that Jesus Christ was God the Son (the second person of the Trinity), was preexistent as God, and became man as well as God incarnate when born into this world of a virgin. He lived a perfect, sinless life and died a sacrificial death to atone for the sins of mankind and to provide satisfaction to a just and holy God for those sins. He was bodily resurrected to prove the acceptance of His sacrifice and to guarantee resurrection to eternal life for all believers in Him and His work.

Christians believed that man was born with a sin nature as a result of Adam's Fall (original sin), that all men sinned, and that all men deserved eternal punishment and separation from God because of their sin. Men could only be saved from that damnation by the grace of God through faith in the atoning work of Christ, not by any works of their own or via any other religious system. The saving work of Christ regenerated man and empowered him to do good works as evidence of his faith. Finally, Christians believed that the whole Bible was divinely inspired, was God's special revelation of Himself, and was the only infallible authority in all matters that it treated. Theistic rationalists shared some beliefs with Christians but only those that passed the test of reasonableness in their eyes.

Table 1.1 Christianity in Eighteenth-Century America

Doctrine	Presbyterian and Congregationalist[a]	Lutheran[b]	Baptist[c]	Anglican and Episcopalian[d]	Catholic[e]
The Trinity	X	X	X	X	X
God active in human affairs	X	X	X	X	X
The deity of Christ	X	X	X	X	X
Original sin	X	X	X	X	X
Virgin Birth	X	X	X	X	X
Atoning work of Christ/satisfaction for sins	X	X	X	X	X
Resurrection	X	X	X	X	X
Eternal punishment for sin	X	X	X	X	X
Justification by faith	X	X	X	X	X*
Inspiration/authority of Scripture	X	X	X	X	X

[a]Westminster Creed (1646) = official creed of Presbyterian and Calvinist churches—Affirmed by Congregationalists in 1680 and again in 1708

[b]Augsburg Confession (1530) = official creed of Lutherans and some Reformed churches

[c]Philadelphia Confession (1689, 1720) = official creed of Baptists and churches that emphasized baptism

[d]Apostles' Creed (215), Nicene Creed (325), Athanasius' Creed (500), and Thirty-nine Articles (1662)—combined to form creed of Anglicans/Episcopalians

[e]Council of Trent (1547) = official creed of Catholic Church

*Although Catholics disagreed with Protestants about the sufficiency of faith for justification, they agreed that justification required faith.

Largest Denominations (number of churches):	1776	1780	1790
Congregational	660–800	700	750
Presbyterian	500+	625	725
Baptist	470+	500	860
Anglican/Episcopalian	400+	150	170

Source: Ronald Hoffman and Peter J. Albert, eds., *Religion in a Revolutionary Age* (Charlottesville: University Press of Virginia, 1994), table 1, p. 190.

Note: Numbers are rounded to the nearest multiple of 5.

Theistic rationalists believed in a powerful, rational, and benevolent creator God who established laws by which the universe functioned. Their God was a unitary personal God who was present and active and who intervened in human affairs. Consequently, they believed that prayers were heard and effectual. They believed that the main factor in serving God was living a good and moral life, that promotion of morality was central to the value of religion, and that the morality engendered by religion was indispensable to society. Because virtually all religions promoted morality, they believed that many—perhaps all—religious traditions or systems were valid and led to the same God.

Though theistic rationalists did not believe that Jesus was God, they considered Him a great moral teacher and held a higher view of Him than did most deists. They believed in a personal afterlife in which the wicked would be temporarily punished and the good would experience happiness forever. Although they thought that God primarily revealed Himself through nature, theistic rationalists believed that some written revelation was legitimate revelation from God. Finally, though they believed that reason and revelation generally agreed with each other, theistic rationalists thought that revelation was designed to complement reason (not vice versa). Reason was the ultimate standard for learning and evaluating truth and for determining legitimate revelation from God.

Throughout this book, theistic rationalism will be contrasted with deism, on the one hand, and with Christianity, on the other. Theistic rationalism was a sort of mean between those two belief systems. Theistic rationalists held some beliefs in common with deists, some beliefs in common with Christians, and some beliefs that were inconsistent with both deism and Christianity. Theistic rationalism was not a popular system. Its import did not stem from the number of Americans who were adherents but rather from the position and intellectual power of its adherents. Theistic rationalism was a belief system for the educated elite. It held little appeal for the average American congregant but was a natural system for an individual raised in Protestantism and educated in Enlightenment rationalism. That was particularly true for ministers who, as will be demonstrated in this study, were trained in Enlightenment thought under the auspices of the seminary.

THE RELIGIOUS DIVIDE BETWEEN ELITES AND THE MASSES

Russell Kirk and others have recognized increased religious controversy leading up to the eighteenth century. As Kirk notes, "Scientific and metaphysical speculation, late in the seventeenth century and throughout the eighteenth, had weakened Christian belief among many of the educated."[57] Those steeped in rationalism could not reconcile the many seemingly irrational elements of Christianity with their belief that all truth had to accord with nature and make sense to the rational mind. As a result, educated gentlemen throughout the colonies shared a belief in some form of rationalism in the years leading up to the Revolution.[58] Just as a generation of college graduates was shaped by the liberalism of the Vietnam era, a generation of Revolutionary era gentlemen was shaped by their immersion in Enlightenment thought.

They had the leisure to read widely and to correspond with peers. As will be demonstrated in subsequent chapters, they generally "confined unorthodox thoughts to their diaries and to their letters to other gentlemen." Indeed, they occasionally instructed recipients of correspondence to keep their views secret and away from public knowledge. It is important to note that, though their ideas resulted from a rejection of Christianity, "the Enlightened gentlemen who had abandoned orthodoxy . . . could still *sound* Protestant when talking politics."[59] That was particularly true as liberal democratic politics and republicanism were insinuated into mainstream Protestant thought. Consequently, positions of political leadership were not threatened by the more conventionally religious masses, and ministers could effectively challenge traditional thought and shape public opinion without setting off alarms among the congregants.

The divide between the religious beliefs of the educated elite and the majority of the people has been recognized by most analysts of the period. May notes that Enlightenment thought "developed among the middle and upper classes . . . and failed to reach the agrarian majority." Wright determines that what is here called theistic rationalism "appealed especially to men of prestige and influence." Stephen Marini concludes that it "burst into full flower" among "the political, economic, military, and literary elites." David Robinson identifies its roots with "the Boston establishment."[60] Mead, Ahlstrom, and Kraynak limit its appeal to "the intellectuals," "the educated classes," and "educated people," respectively.[61] One of Franklin's biographers has said that "evangelism appealed to the generally unsophisticated" and that rationalism "gained the favor of colonial intellectuals." According to Russel Blaine Nye, they found in what I have termed theistic rationalism Franklin's desired "essentials of religion . . . to which all educated men could agree." The social class factor is so important to Gustav Koch that, for him, it was the primary difference between the deists and those I call theistic rationalists.[62] Although I believe that Koch is wrong, his view highlights the social gap.

A final indicator of the social divide can be seen in the uneven reception evangelist George Whitefield received during his trips to the United States. Whitefield was an orthodox Christian and, by many accounts, the most effective of all Christian missionaries of the period. Franklin regularly went to hear him because of his prowess as a speaker, and they eventually became friends. As a general rule, however, Whitefield was "especially disliked by the educated and refined."[63] Most interesting is an observation made by Jonathan Mayhew, a contemporary of Whitefield's and a progenitor of theistic rationalism. Mayhew said: "When [Whitefield] was lately in Boston, many persons attended him, but chiefly of the more illiterate sort, except some who went out of curiosity."[64] Either Mayhew was being exceedingly petty or the educated class was not interested in Whitefield's message.

An understanding of the difference in religious belief between the educated elite and the common people is necessary to properly grapple with a number of otherwise perplexing matters. For example, it helps to explain why men who did not hold Christian beliefs regularly attended Christian churches and used language Christians would find familiar and comfortable. To maintain positions of authority and power, they had to be acceptable to a religious people and communicate effectively to their audience.

Theistic rationalism was an elite understanding of the eighteenth century, shared by the key Founders and by many preachers. A gentle, hopeful, and nondenominational belief system that borrowed from Christianity and from deism, it never became the property of the masses. But it equipped elites to describe the projects of the Revolution and the Founding in terms that did not offend popular religion. If it never conquered the evangelical spirit of popular Christianity nor wholly displaced orthodox and traditional religion, it nevertheless was enormously influential in reshaping religious understandings in a way that made them welcoming of revolution, republicanism, and rights. If America can be both religious and republican today, it is partly because the Founders, in their day, were theistic rationalists.

2

"Divine" Sources of Theistic Rationalism

Moral virtue is . . . the essence and the life of all true religion.

Samuel Clarke

THE KEY FOUNDERS AND PATRIOTIC PREACHERS did not develop their political theology in a vacuum. A number of "divines," as theologians and clergymen were called at the time, significantly impacted their views of God and politics. Yet even though they were heavily influenced by certain divines, the key Founders and preachers, for the most part, borrowed and adapted ideas and patterns of thought rather than adopting systems entirely. In short, they appropriated agreeable ideas in order to construct their own beliefs. The result of this process was a common belief in theistic rationalism. This chapter will demonstrate the importance of several prominent divines to the thought of the key Founders and preachers and will indicate the most central ideas in the development of theistic rationalism.

Due to his nearly ubiquitous influence, John Locke's name will periodically appear in the following discussion. His impact on the political theology of the patriotic preachers is detailed in another chapter, and his importance to the key Founders has been the subject of numerous books. Consequently, this chapter will not treat him directly but will focus upon the less recognized divines whose thought most significantly impacted the political theology of the Founding period.

Of the seven men profiled, four primarily influenced key Founders, two primarily influenced preachers, and one influenced both groups to a significant extent. As noted, the Founders and preachers borrowed and adapted selected ideas from these influences but did not embrace their teaching in totality. Consequently, these sources were not necessarily theistic rationalists themselves, but elements of their thought contributed to the development of theistic rationalism.

SHAFTESBURY (1671–1713)

Anthony Ashley Cooper, Earl of Shaftesbury, will be referred to here by his universal appellation—Shaftesbury. Shaftesbury was Locke's patron (a patronage begun by his grandfather)[1] and student. He was groomed for the political life, but his poor health excluded him from a political career. Therefore, he studied the classics, philosophy, and art, ultimately becoming a highly respected art critic and theoretician. Though not technically a divine, Shaftesbury wrote prominent works of natural religion. His influence was not widespread in America, but it was vital in the development of Benjamin Franklin's thought.[2] Shaftesbury's work had a direct impact on a few particulars in Franklin's theology and affected the general tone of Franklin's thinking. It should be noted that there are different schools of thought concerning Shaftesbury's religious views.[3] What is presented here is simply the view of Shaftesbury that influenced Franklin, and it is not intended as an endorsement of that view.

Shaftesbury rejected "appeal to authority per se as a criterion of truth." He demanded argument from what Franklin called "plain Reasoning . . . unsupported by the Authority of any Books or Men how sacred so-ever."[4] In other words, he emphasized reasoning completely independent of Scripture. It was Shaftesbury's view that one should be skeptical and modest in handling the Bible. He occasionally disparaged the Old Testament, in particular. He asserted "the primacy of reason over revelation." In his opinion, "'True religion' should be based on 'Nature' rather than on Revelation."[5]

His influence on Franklin in this regard can be clearly seen in Franklin's "Articles of Belief and Acts of Religion." Shaftesbury emphasized the teleological argument for the existence of God and argued that contemplation of the universe and its laws was "the only means which could establish the *sound Belief* of a Deity." Further, he stressed nature to such an extent that God and nature appeared, at times, to be one. Though Franklin was always clear to distinguish nature from God, his "Articles" began with contemplation of the universe and conclusions about God drawn from that contemplation. Throughout the "Articles," he emphasized nature while eschewing any mention of Scripture.[6]

From his contemplation of the universe, Franklin drew many of the same conclusions about God as did Shaftesbury. For Shaftesbury, "the concept of Deity must be the product of the highest reach of the imagination." In the "First Principles" section of his "Articles," Franklin explicitly gave free rein to his imagination in order to contemplate God. Shaftesbury concluded that such anthropomorphic terms for God as *friend* and *father* were appropriate, and Franklin repeatedly employed both. Shaftesbury determined that the most important attributes of God were His goodness, omnipotence, and rationality; he insisted that God could have "no malice in His nature." Franklin drew the same three characteristics from the evidence of nature and specified "malice" as being opposed to God's character.[7]

Another of Shaftesbury's applications of nature was his emphasis on the natural morality of men and the importance of morality in religion. He thought it "natural" for man to be moral and believed a man was a "good man" when he did good in society. Franklin, in turn, famously stressed doing good in society and ended his "Articles" with two sections devoted to the cultivation of moral virtue.[8] Finally, Shaftesbury stressed God's creation of laws of nature to promote justice and the common good, and he argued that "the conception of a universe governed by law is the only foundation of true theism." Franklin's "Articles" similarly identified God as the source of the laws of nature, justice, and the common good and detailed his conception of God's rule over the universe.[9]

There is one other crucial way in which Franklin learned from Shaftesbury. Both men were attracted to deism, but both expressly separated themselves from the deists at the point of deism's denial of Providence. According to Shaftesbury scholar Stanley Grean, "Shaftesbury stressed the immanence of God, while the Deists placed greater stress on His transcendence." He said the deists were wrong to conceive of God as removed from contact with His creation. For Shaftesbury, the very concept of God was "dry and barren" if God did not remain involved with His creation. He similarly criticized Hobbes and Descartes for depicting God as an "idle spectator" in the universe.[10] Building upon Shaftesbury's base, Franklin wrote his essay "On the Providence of God in the Government of the World" and specifically criticized the deist position. He used the same concept as Shaftesbury, describing the deist God as a "spectator" in the universe. He also employed another concept close to Shaftesbury's when he suggested that one had to deny God's "infinite Goodness" in order to hold that God was "utterly unconcern'd what becomes of the Beings and Things he has created."[11]

Shaftesbury's thought influenced Franklin in his formation of theistic rationalism. Shaftesbury essentially argued that "we may cultivate a judicious belief in the Supreme Being of the eighteenth century, but we must keep clear of Jupiter or Jehovah."[12] Franklin agreed, with the exception that, for him, one could even believe in those particular images of God if it resulted in moral behavior.

CONYERS MIDDLETON (1683–1750)

Another whose impact was confined to one Founder was Conyers Middleton. Middleton was a controversial Anglican divine who influenced the thought of Thomas Jefferson. Allen Jayne has built an impressive circumstantial case for Bolingbroke's influence on Jefferson's theology, and interested readers should consult his work for that argument. Jefferson himself, however, identified two primary influences on his theology. He testified that he would "rest" on Joseph Priestley's writings "and on Middleton's writings, especially his letters from Rome, and to Waterland, as the basis of my own faith." He went on to say, "I cling to their learning, so much superior to my own." This was a remarkable confession from a man who declared, "I am of a sect by myself, as far as I know."[13] The thoughts of the well-known Priestley will be treated later in this chapter, but what was the teaching of the relatively obscure Middleton that made such an impression on Jefferson?

In *A Letter from Rome*, which Jefferson specifically mentioned, Middleton showed "in scholarly detail" the "residue of pagan rites in Catholic ritual." He wrote to discredit what he considered the false "miracles" of "popery" but not Christianity in general or Protestantism. Middleton said elsewhere that he would "admit no miracles but those of the Scriptures; and . . . all the rest are either justly suspected or certainly forged." *A Letter from Rome* presented pages of examples of the parallels between pagan rituals and those of the Catholic Church and "proofs" of the falsehood of miracles recognized by the Church. In this work, Middleton affirmed the miracles of the Bible as having stood the test of time despite "the perpetual opposition and scrutiny of the ages." For him, this fact "cannot reasonably be ascribed to any other cause, but to the natural force and effect of truth."[14]

His use of the term *reasonably* is important. Despite his profession of the "sufficiency of the Scriptures," Middleton argued that where miracles were concerned, the "credibility of facts lies open to the trial of our reason and senses."[15] The primary lesson learned by Jefferson from his study of *A Letter from Rome* was, no doubt, the practice of submitting the miraculous to the test of reason.

The other Middleton work mentioned by Jefferson as the "basis" of his "faith" was *A Letter to Dr. Waterland*. There, Middleton argued against the biblical account of the Fall of man, circumcision, and the Tower of Babel. These served merely as illustrations of his thesis, which was to expose the "wrong principle" "that *every single passage of the Scriptures, we call Canonical, must needs be received as the very word and as the voice of God himself.*" Once again, Middleton appealed to reason and the senses.

He maintained that this "wrong principle" exposed Christianity to "the contempt and ridicule of all rational men, who can never embrace an *Hypothesis* . . . which they see contrary to fact and the *plain conviction of their senses.*"[16] His conclusion was that the result of such flawed argumentation was the contempt of religion that Jefferson bemoaned among rational men of his day. As will be mentioned in chapter 5, Jefferson attempted to convince the leading deists of his day that religious faith could be reconciled with rationality.

Middleton paved the way for a theistic rationalist with a pair of scissors to determine for himself which portions of the Bible were legitimately from God when he wrote: "If *any narration* can be shewn to be *false;* any *doctrine irrational* or *immoral;* 'tis not all the *external evidence in the world* that can or ought to convince us, that *such a doctrine* comes from *God."* Middleton's ultimate conclusion was that Christian apologists should quit defending the rationally indefensible parts of Scripture and retreat to a moralizing religion. He suggested that good citizens would continue to support Christianity—even if they could not believe the core of its theology—because they recognized its utility for society.[17]

Middleton's *Letter to Dr. Waterland,* then, reaffirmed for Jefferson the method of submitting religious questions to the test of reason and observation. It encouraged him to determine for himself the legitimacy of biblical revelation, and it emphasized the value of religion as a moralizing force in support of social order. Finally, Middleton's other contribution to Jefferson's growing theistic rationalism was the force of his example as one who was somewhere between orthodoxy and deism. Middleton was critical of the deists for their "unhistorical mentality." He also "struck at the root "of the deist position that "simple unspoiled man . . . can grasp religious truths by his own untutored intuition."[18] As was mentioned earlier, Middleton contended for the "sufficiency of the Scriptures"; the only question was *which* Scriptures. Contrary to the deist position, some revelation was necessary. Nature was not enough. Furthermore, real study had to be done to be able to properly determine the validity of revelation. In Middleton, Jefferson could see an individual who was too rational for orthodoxy but not willing to completely jettison all revelation.

JOSEPH PRIESTLEY (1733–1804)

As noted, Jefferson identified two influences on his theology; the primary influence was Joseph Priestley. Priestley was a minister and a scientist. He is renowned in the scientific community as a pathfinder in the study of gases and as the discoverer of oxygen—or at least as the one who first isolated it. Despite his scientific achievements, his primary interest was religion and the promulgation of what he believed to be true Christianity.[19] His political and religious views were so controversial, however, that a mob once burned his home and laboratory. Although he was not a resident of France, he was named a French citizen and even elected to the National Assembly—honors that he declined. He moved to America in 1794 in search of peace and died in Pennsylvania in 1804.

It would be difficult to overstate the importance of Priestley to the development of the political theology of the American Founding. One scholar suggested that "if Jefferson, Franklin, and Madison—comprising a philosophical trio among the Founding Fathers—had been asked to name a contemporary who for depth of intellect, moral imagination, and precision of thought most excited their admiration, it is likely they would have agreed on Joseph Priestley."[20] When one includes in the list another key Founder, John Adams, who was also heavily influenced by him, Priestley's prominence takes on even greater dimension. Jefferson, Franklin, and Adams were the most studious and prolific of the Founders where religion was concerned.

A few pieces of evidence will suffice to demonstrate Priestley's position as the preeminent theological source among the key Founders. Adams, Jefferson, and Franklin showed the influence of Priestley with their frequent references to "the corruptions of Christianity" or to "corrupting changes" or "corruptions" in the doctrines of Jesus. In a letter to John Adams, Jefferson said of Priestley: "I have read his Corruptions of Christianity, and Early opinions of Jesus, over and over again; and I rest on them . . . as the basis of my own faith. These writings have never been answered, nor can be answered, by quoting historical proofs, as they have done. For these facts therefore I cling to their learning, so much superior to my own."[21] In the same letter, Jefferson mentioned that Priestley was one of only two people to whom he had entrusted a copy of his secret *Syllabus* and said that "every thing Priestley wrote" was "executed with learning and candor." The letter was written, in part, to respond to a series of letters from Adams imploring Jefferson to help publish Priestley's works in America. In those letters, Adams recommended other Priestley works, which he had read, to Jefferson.[22]

That Jefferson and Adams considered Priestley *the* authority in religious matters can be seen in Adams's repeatedly expressed desire to have Priestley answer difficult questions. Adams asserted that "no M[an] was more capable" of answering them, and after Priestley's death, he bemoaned the fact that the minister was no longer alive to do so. Similarly, when Jefferson had the idea of producing a definitive work of moral religion, he tried to recruit Priestley to write it, saying, "You are the person who of all others would do it best." Upon learning that Priestley would undertake the project, Jefferson was ecstatic: "I rejoice that you have undertaken the task. . . . You are so much in possession of the whole subject, that you will do it easier & better than any other person living."[23] Adams attributed certain of his own beliefs to Priestley's influence and declared that Priestley had "one of the greatest" souls. Jefferson, in turn, said that only those who "live by mystery and *charlatanerie*" would try to deny Priestley's "well-earnt and well-deserved fame."[24]

Paul Conkin, who has written an insightful essay on Priestley's influence on Jefferson, noted that "[Jefferson] completely embraced Priestley's Unitarian Christianity, and he retained this commitment until his death. Priestley rescued him from earlier ambivalence and for the first time clarified a type of Christianity that Jefferson could wholeheartedly embrace."[25] As Conkin concluded, Priestley's work allowed Jefferson to construct his own theology and "call the product Christianity." According to Conkin, George Washington also "at least expressed an interest in his doctrines."[26] This was highly unusual for Washington, who was famously taciturn about his religious beliefs.

The numerous accounts of Priestley's 1796 and 1797 lecture series in Philadelphia further attest to his influence. Because of his heterodoxy, he was denied all pulpits but that of the Lombard Street Universalist Church. Despite the controversial speaker and platform, a large number of image-conscious politicians risked public disapproval and went to hear the lectures: by all accounts, they were well attended by those in government. Priestley himself recorded that "most of the members of the congress of the United States . . . and of the executive officers of the government" were in the audience. Other accounts reported that "many" members of Congress attended, along with Vice President Adams in 1796 and Vice President Jefferson in 1797.

Joseph Priestley can safely be said to have had the greatest influence of any divine on the key Founders. According to a biographer, he wanted to be the "Apostle of Rational Religion in the New World."[27] And though he may not have reached the general populace, he may well have achieved that goal among the political elite. But what beliefs of Priestley's contributed to the development of theistic rationalism?

The appropriate place to begin an analysis of Priestley's thought is his hermeneutics, that is, his approach to the interpretation and understanding of the Bible. As Gustav Koch noted, Priestley's "first principles were a mixture of rationalism, materialism, and supernaturalism."[28] Like the theistic rationalists who learned from him, he accepted some Scripture as revelation from God—namely, those portions that conformed to his own reason. Reason and revelation were seen to work together, with reason taking priority "if there should be found any difficulty in accommodating the one to the other." He distinguished between stress on "particular texts" and stress on "general considerations, derived from the whole tenor of scripture and the dictates of reason." This distinction allowed him to avoid disagreeable portions of Scripture (particular texts) and to concentrate on "the moral government of God, the nature of things, and the general plan of revelation" (general considerations). Of course, the latter were vague concepts subject to his own rational determination. Priestley was especially uncomfortable with "particular expressions in the apostolical epistles." He had, early in his ministry, become convinced that Paul's epistles were flawed.[29]

To illustrate this point, Priestley discussed the literal interpretation of Romans 5:12 as it related to the Christian doctrine of original sin. His conclusion was that the literal interpretation was "unnatural" and "evidently contrary to sense and reason,"[30] so he rejected that literal conclusion. In Priestley's terminology, the "particular text" was made to give way to "the dictates of reason."

Included in Priestley's list of the "corruptions" of Christianity was "the doctrine of the plenary inspiration of the scriptures," which he described as "as great a cause of infidelity as any other." He denied the infallibility of the Scriptures and largely attributed them to human sources. He viewed the Bible as, primarily, a human history that was partially reliable. He believed Paul to be unreliable and relied instead upon the words of Jesus in the Gospels that seemed consistent with *his* view of Jesus. As Conkin has pointed out, "Priestley used his own conception of Jesus to make these judgments, and thus the circularity of his arguments. He . . . rejected out of hand the . . . clearly mythical stories about Jesus' birth, including the notion of a virgin birth."[31] Here, one can clearly see the inspiration for Jefferson's idea of attacking the New Testament with a pair of scissors and excising the miraculous and supernatural.

To his own way of thinking, Priestley maintained a respect for revelation. Near the end of one of his works, he said, "Nothing, therefore, that I have advanced in this work, can be at all understood to lessen the great value of revelation." He was careful, for example, to note that even though natural religion was adequate to attain to the knowledge of God, "little" of such knowledge was known in nations "which never enjoyed the light of revelation" and did not have "the assistance of revelation."[32] He particularly noted the utility of revelation to quell natural religion's tendency to lead to polytheism.

It is instructive to recognize, however, that in the same *theological* work, Priestley excluded any appeal to revelation from his method of argument. He identified "everything that I shall contend for" as "perfectly consonant to the principles of sound philosophy" and said that he would "use no other *modes of reasoning* than those that are universally adopted."[33] Basil Willey offered a cogent summary of Priestley's method: "Good sense and a 'just view of things' are, to be sure, his real standards, but Scripture, often admittedly in natural harmony with these standards, must be made to corroborate them, if necessary by force."[34] The theistic rationalists adopted the same method: determine what is valid revelation and interpretation by the dictates of reason, and maintain a respect for revelation but only for revelation of one's own choosing.

Despite the fact that Priestley professed respect for revelation, he relegated it to secondary status by essentially reducing it to his own logical construct and by making it supplemental to reason—rather than the reverse, which was the established position of Christianity. In his system, it was *natural* religion that existed on an equal level with reason, not *revealed* religion. According to Priestley, "the works of nature" and history functioned together to reveal to man "the ways of God" and "knowledge of his perfections, and his will."[35] In more than one of his theological works, he made the natural religion case for the existence of God, His attributes, and a future state for man rather than appealing to the Bible. He also relied upon nature rather than Scripture in making decisions on such doctrinal questions as the Trinity and the possibility of miracles.[36]

In his *Institutes of Natural and Revealed Religion,* revealed religion decidedly took a backseat to natural religion. He discussed the collaboration between reason and natural religion and argued that the two of them were sufficient to attain to the knowledge of God without revelation. This knowledge was "attainable" though "never attained." Indeed, nature did "contain and teach those lessons," and men had "the means of learning them" in "the light they had" and "the powers that were given them." Madison and others influenced by Priestley, in contrast to the orthodox, similarly believed that there was a "road from nature up to nature's God."[37]

According to Priestley, nature taught, first, that God existed. For him, the big difference was between atheists and theists rather than between various forms of theism. He argued for the superiority of the theist and went so far as to state that the atheist had a "debased" nature. Once one crossed the chasm even to the level of "*serious deism*," though, Priestley declared, "I shall have little doubt of his soon becoming a serious christian."[38]

Second, Priestly argued that nature taught the nature of God. Like the theistic rationalists who learned from him, he stressed that God was, fundamentally, benevolent: "The source of all the moral perfections of God seems to be his benevolence. . . . Every other truly venerable or amiable attribute can be nothing but a *modification* of this. A perfectly good, or benevolent Being, must be, in every other respect, whatever can be the object of our reverence, or our love."[39] In fact, the view of God as a benevolent deity whose primary concern was the happiness of man has been characterized as "the cornerstone of Priestley's theology." Furthermore, Priestley openly acknowledged what is obvious but was generally unspoken by the men of the eighteenth century: their idea of God was essentially "human perfections magnified."[40] That was a result of the confluence of nature and reason or natural reason. They rejected biblical accounts of God's wrath and vengeance, for instance, as being inconsistent with gentlemanly behavior. Scriptural accounts of seemingly arbitrary acts of God were rejected as unworthy of a perfectly rational Being.

Third, he asserted that nature taught that God was providential and cared about His creatures. As Conkin put it, "Priestley believed completely in God's providence—all that took place in history had some good purpose." To Priestley, natural reason made God's providential care obvious: "For since he made us, it must be evident that we are not beneath his notice and attention; and since all the laws of nature, to which we are subject, are his establishment, nothing that befals [sic] us can be unforeseen, or, consequently, unintended by him."[41]

The fact of God's providential care led to the fourth lesson taught by nature according to Priestley—nature taught man that he should pray to God:

> If reverence, gratitude, obedience and confidence be our duty with respect to God (which we infer from the analogy of those duties to men) it is agreeable to the same analogy, that we *express* these sentiments in words; and this is done in the most natural manner, agreeably to the same analogy, in a direct *address* to the Author of our being, so that the principles of natural religion, properly pursued, will lead us to *prayer*.[42]

Note that duty to God was inferred from duty to men. According to Priestley, man should pray even though God should know our needs and even if all things were predetermined. Prayer to God was a "natural duty."[43]

In addition to these four basic lessons about God, he stated that nature conspired with reason to suggest certain unorthodox positions on key doctrinal issues, as well. Rather than trust the Scriptures where doctrinal matters were concerned, Priestley sought the direction of nature and reason and then selected and conveniently interpreted Scriptures to support his views—ignoring or dismissing as "unreliable" any contradictory "particular texts." He could not completely ignore the biblical record, however, and he felt the need to try to prove that doctrines he rejected were not really taught in the Bible.[44]

Priestley famously labeled those doctrines with which he disagreed as "corruptions" of authentic or "primitive" Christianity. He defined "corruption" as "a departure from the original scheme, or an *innovation*."[45] Anything beyond a call to moral and virtuous living counted as such an innovation, and he identified the source. According to David Robinson, "Priestley traced the corruption to the tendency of Platonic philosophers of the early church to elevate the idea of logos (word) from an '*attribute* of the divine mind itself' into 'an *intelligent principle* or *being*, distinct from God, though an emanation from him.'"[46] This should call to mind Jefferson's explication of the concept of *logos* in the first chapter of the Gospel of John, as well as his repeated criticism of "Platonic Christianity." An extended quote from the "General Conclusion to Part I" of Priestley's *Corruptions* will clarify this point and will introduce Priestley's explanation for the origin of the doctrine of the deity of Christ, which he considered to be the primary "corruption":

> The causes of the corruptions were almost wholly contained in the established opinions of the heathen world, and especially the philosophical part of it; so that when those heathens embraced christianity they mixed their former tenets and prejudices with it. Also, both Jews and heathens were so much scandalized at the idea of being the disciples of a man who had been crucified as a common malefactor, that christians in general were sufficiently disposed to adopt any opinion that would most effectually wipe away this reproach.[47]

Largely because of pride, Platonists had complicated the simple moralizing message of Jesus and concocted myths to make Him what He never claimed to be—God. The first part of Priestley's *Corruptions* was entirely and explicitly devoted to a refutation of the doctrine of the deity of Christ. The second part was specifically devoted to a refutation of the doctrine of Christ's atonement for the sins of man.

There were a number of these corruptions, including "nearly everything considered by the orthodox" to be the "very essence" and "fundamental doctrines" of Christianity.[48] According to Priestley, the "principal of these, besides the doctrines that are peculiar to the Roman Catholics, are those of a trinity of persons in the godhead, original sin, arbitrary predestination, atonement for the sins of men by the death of Christ, and . . . the doctrine of the plenary inspiration of the scriptures." He recognized that his belief system was something other than orthodox and suggested that he was not interested in "the reputation of orthodoxy" when he had "no just title" to it.[49] Interestingly, in his presentation of the simple "truth" about Jesus, Priestley affirmed that Jesus performed miracles and that He rose from the dead. Basil Willey summarized Priestley's position as accepting "the historical miracles, while rejecting the doctrinal mysteries, of Christianity"; he called this an example of the "eclecticism of Priestley's thought" and of Priestley deferring to Scripture "as he understood it." In Willey's words, Priestley took the miracles and the Resurrection as "incontestably scriptural."[50]

As was mentioned, the most important of the doctrinal mysteries and "corruptions" were the deity of Christ and its corollary doctrine, the Trinity. Priestley recognized that this doctrine was related to several others. In arguing for unitarianism, he expressed the centrality of the issue: "You cannot say that this is a matter of no great consequence in Christianity. It affects the most fundamental principles of all religion, the first and the greatest of all the commandments." The orthodox, who adhered to the core doctrines of Christianity, certainly agreed with him in that regard. Priestley was an outspoken and influential unitarian whom Samuel Taylor Coleridge called "the author of modern Unitarianism,"[51] with the term *modern* designed to distinguish him from the ancient founder, Socinus.

One branch of unitarian thought, Arianism, taught that though Jesus was not God, He was a supernatural, divine being between God and man. Socinian unitarianism taught that Jesus was just a man, though created perfect and with special authority from God. Priestley was Socinian. He argued for "the simple humanity of Christ" and taught a "humanitarian theology— that is, his denial of divinity as well as deity to Christ." Priestley maintained that "it cannot be said that anything is ascribed to him that a mere man (aided, as he himself says he was, by the power of God, his Father) was not equal to."[52] It may be that Priestley's materialism and chemical experiments led to his Socinian Christology; he claimed that there was not "any fact in *nature*" that demanded belief in the Trinity. Because he was a materialist, Priestley denied the concept of a separable soul and, consequently, any idea of Incarnation or preexistence by Christ.[53]

Another related doctrine rejected by Priestley was the atonement for the sins of men by the death of Christ. He became convinced that the atonement was false early in his ministry. As he saw it, this doctrine was closely connected to the doctrine of the deity of Christ. His own words best express the connection: "This corruption [atonement] of the genuine doctrine of revelation is connected with the doctrine of the divinity of Christ; because it is said, that sin, as an offence against an *infinite being*, requires an *infinite satisfaction*, which can only be made by an *infinite person*, that is, one who is no less than God himself."[54] Priestley also rejected it because it flew in the face of two other fundamental aspects of his religious system—the benevolence of God and religion's purpose in promoting morality. Priestley's benevolent God was "always ready to forgive any penitent sinner," and consequently,

> the doctrine of the *natural placability of the divine being,* and our ideas of the equity of his government, have been greatly debased by the gradual introduction of the modern doctrine of *atonement*, which represents the divine being as withholding his mercy from the truly penitent, till a full satisfaction be made to his justice; and for that purpose, as substituting his own innocent son in the place of sinful men.[55]

This made no sense to Priestley, whose image of God stressed His benevolence to the exclusion of His holiness or justice. In Priestley's view, the atonement also destroyed the very purpose of religion: "Moreover, as the sins of men have been thus imputed to Christ, his righteousness is, on the other hand, imputed to them: and thus they are accepted of God, not on account of what they have done themselves, but for what Christ had done for them. . . . I conceive this doctrine to be a gross misrepresentation of the character and moral government of God."[56] The first part of this quote shows that Priestley perfectly understood the doctrine of the atonement, but his religion existed primarily to promote morality and virtue in men. If men were saved by the work of Christ irrespective of their own virtue and works, he could see no point to morality and no practical point to religion.

Another central doctrine of Christianity that Priestley opposed was the doctrine of original sin. Even as a young man, he was "refused admittance as a communicant in his congregation because he was unsound on the subject of the sin of Adam." It was noted earlier that he dismissed a literal reading of the clearest biblical passage on the issue as being "unnatural" and "so evidently contrary to sense and reason." He also believed that the nature of God and His rule over man demanded the rejection of original sin: "That it must be naturally in the power of man to do the will of God, must be taken for granted, if we suppose the moral government of God to be at all an equitable one."[57]

One fundamental Christian doctrine that Priestley emphatically embraced was the Resurrection of Jesus. In fact, he listed the doctrine of Resurrection as one of the "great truths of religion," along with the "unity of God" and "the state of future retribution."[58] For Priestley, the Resurrection of Christ, a mere man, was to be an *example* of a general "resurrection to immortal life" and "a type or earnest of that of all men."[59] As a result of his materialist rejection of the concept of a separable soul, Priestley thought that the only avenue to eternal life was that the fully dead had to come back to life. Since this doctrine was not self-evident or provable by reason, one had to accept it on faith. This "faith" was not mystical but simply a belief in the credibility of the many witnesses to Jesus's Resurrection.[60] Without a physical Resurrection, there was no hope for eternal life and, more important for Priestley's system, no future rewards and punishments respecting behavior in this life.

Priestley wrote extensive arguments concerning doctrines, but ultimately, both doctrines and his version of "christianity" were means to an end for him, not ends in themselves:

> Christianity is less to be considered as a system of opinions, than a rule of life. . . . All the doctrines of Christianity have for their object Christian morals, which are no other than the well-known duties of life; and the advantage we derive from this religion is, that the principles of it assist us in maintaining that steady regard to the providence and moral government of God, and to a future state, which facilitates and ensures the practice of those duties; inspiring greater piety towards God, greater benevolence to man, and that heavenly-mindedness which raises the heart and affections above those mean and low pursuits which are the source of almost all vices.[61]

According to Priestley, morals were the object of *all* of the doctrines of Christianity, and the "advantage" Christianity provided its adherents was stimulus to morality and virtue—not a relationship with Christ or forgiveness of sins. He said that "*morals* . . . are the object and end of all religion."[62] For Priestley and the Founders who learned from him, the real value and purpose of religion was to promote morality and virtue.

Of the message of Christianity in particular, he contended that "the universal parent of mankind commissioned Jesus Christ to invite men to the practice of virtue, by the assurance of his mercy to the penitent, and of his purpose to raise to immortal life and happiness all the virtuous and the good, but to inflict an adequate punishment on the wicked." Furthermore, the "great object of the mission and death of Christ [was] to give the fullest proof of a future life of retribution, in order to supply the strongest motives to virtue." For Priestley,

> christian faith implies a belief of all the great historical facts recorded in the Old and New Testament, in which we are informed concerning the creation and government of the world, the history of the discourses, miracles, death, and resurrection of Christ, and his assurance of the resurrection of all the dead to a future life of retribution; and *this is the doctrine that is of the most consequence, to enforce the good conduct of men.* (Emphasis mine.)[63]

For Priestley and the Founders who learned from him, religion was to be believed or practiced not because it was true or revealed by God or the means of salvation but because it had laudable effects.

> Now it is certainly the doctrine of reason, as well as of the Old Testament, that God is merciful to the penitent, and that nothing is requisite to make men, in all situations, the objects of his favour, but such moral conduct as he has made them capable of. *This is a simple and a pleasing view of God and his moral government,* and the consideration of it cannot but *have the best effect* on the temper of our minds and conduct in life. (Emphases mine.)[64]

It mattered not that this was not the doctrine of the New Testament, which Christ claimed was the new covenant between God and man, which Christ claimed was the fulfillment of the Old Testament, and which is the record of the life and teachings of Christ and His disciples.

In addition, for Priestley and the Founders who learned from him, *any* religion would serve the purpose, as all promoted a fundamental level of morality in society. As Priestley put it, "In all the modes of religion, which subsist among mankind, however subversive of virtue they may be in theory, there is some *salvo* for good morals; so that, in fact, they enforce the more essential parts, at least, of that conduct, which the good order of society requires." The good of society actually played a crucial role in determining morality: "Virtue and right conduct consist in those affections and actions which terminate in the public good."[65]

An example of applying this "good of society" standard as a determinant of proper conduct involved the issue of interference in religious liberty. According to Priestley, "If the interference would be for the good of the society upon the whole, it is wise, and right; if it would do more harm than good, it is foolish and wrong." In making such a decision, "*fact* and *experience* seem to be our only safe guides." Pointing to a number of examples of peoples "flourishing and happy" since granting religious liberty, Priestley concluded that "judging from what is past, the consequences of *unbounded liberty, in matters of religion,* promise to be so very favourable to the best interests of mankind."[66] This is, perhaps, the real source of the key Founders' willingness to allow full religious liberty.

Within the "Christian" community, Priestley sought to eliminate all sects, to unite all who claimed to be Christians, and "to leave all particular opinions to every man's conscience." In his vision, differences would be discussed, and "prejudice" and "bigotry" would fall away.[67] The intriguing part of this vision is his claim that all could "meet as brethren, and the disciples of one common master." But who *was* that master? Just a few pages earlier, he had claimed that the trinitarian versus unitarian question was of "great consequence" because it affected the "first and the greatest of all the commandments." In other words, one could not love God and have no other gods before Him if one did not know *who God was.* Was He the Triune God of Christianity or the unitarian God of Priestley? Priestley here reflected a level of naïveté also exhibited by the key Founders—namely, a conviction that everyone should simply be able to set aside their fundamental beliefs about the particular identity and nature of God and accept the unitarian vision of God as a sort of universal supernatural entity who appeared in various forms to those of various traditions. For someone who viewed religion as merely a means to an end and subject to personal determination, it was perhaps difficult to understand the deep-seated beliefs of those who thought they were following the actual Word of God. Priestley, like Jefferson, anticipated eventual universal recognition of the "truth of unitarianism."[68]

One other related element of Priestley's thought must be mentioned. Priestley attested to the difference between the religious views of the elite and those of the common people. He observed, for instance, that Calvinist doctrines were only held by "persons of little learning or education" and that "the belief of them will be kept up among the vulgar." He endeavored, in contrast, to "exhibit a view of Christianity to which a *philosopher* cannot have so much to object." In his *Memoirs,* he reported: "I can truly say that the greatest satisfaction I receive from the success of my philosophical pursuits, arises from the weight it may give to my attempts to defend Christianity, and to free it from those corruptions which prevent its reception with philosophical and thinking persons, whose influence with the vulgar, and the unthinking, is very great."[69] Priestley's religion was for *philosophical and thinking persons,* who might then pass it down to the rest, who were *vulgar* and *unthinking.* His work certainly impacted its primary target in the American Founding era, but it never achieved the universal acceptance among the common people that he hoped for and expected.

JOHN WITHERSPOON (1723–1794)

Undoubtedly, the best known of those who influenced the key Founders is John Witherspoon. His name remains familiar because he was himself a Founder. Witherspoon was a preacher in Scotland who moved to America to preside over Princeton and became heavily involved in Revolutionary politics. John Adams said he was "as high a son of liberty as any man in America." He was a member of the Continental Congress for five years, a member of the Second Continental Congress, a signer of the Declaration of Independence, and he served on a number of committees. However, Witherspoon's ultimate significance may have been the impact he had on his students at Princeton.[70]

Witherspoon is generally remembered as James Madison's mentor, but the list of his students includes: 114 who became ministers; 19 who became college presidents or professors, including 13 college presidents in 8 states; 6 who became members of the Continental Congress; 6 who were members of the Constitutional Convention; 56 who became state legislators; 12 who became governors; 39 who became representatives; 21 who became senators; 30 who became judges, including 3 Supreme Court justices; 10 who became cabinet officers; 1 who became vice president of the United States; and 1 (Madison) who became president.[71]

In addition to his influence on students who would become powerful and prominent members of American society, Witherspoon's impact on American higher education extended beyond his school and his lifetime. Princeton, which shaped much of the educational thinking throughout the colonies and the young country, "dominated philosophical thought in American higher education for many decades." During Witherspoon's presidency, the university shifted "from training ministers to educating men for public affairs"; in other words, it became "less a theological seminary, more a school for statesmen."[72] Though that might seem a strange development under the leadership of a former minister, it really points to a change in Witherspoon that coincided with his arrival in America and that will be discussed in the pages ahead.

All are agreed that Witherspoon was exceedingly influential, but there is some disagreement on the nature and particulars of his influence. The most common argument is that Madison was deeply affected by Wither- spoon's Calvinist teachings on the nature of man and, specifically, human depravity. According to that view, the impact of Witherspoon's Calvinism can be seen in Madison's assertion in Federalist No. 10 that the causes of faction are "sown in the nature of man" and in the principle of separa- tion of powers in the Constitution. For example, James Smylie has made an impressive circumstantial case for Calvinism's widespread effect on Madi- son's political thought and, consequently, on the American political system by linking parts of Madison's thinking with Witherspoon's.[73] Furthermore, according to Ashbel Green, a faculty member at Princeton, Witherspoon himself regarded the Constitution "as embracing principles and carrying into effect measures, which he had long advocated, as essential to the pres- ervation of the liberties, and the promotion of the peace and prosperity of the country."[74]

It may be, however, that Witherspoon's influence on Madison involved more method or approach than content. As one Witherspoon scholar has noted, "Although he did not lack recognition from his contemporaries, any effort to trace Witherspoon's contribution to the thinking of his prominent students is frustrated because so few of them acknowledged the ways in which their Scottish teacher had contributed to their intellectual develop- ment. His most prominent student, James Madison, a prolific political pam- phleteer and correspondent . . . never gave any written acknowledgment of Witherspoon's influence upon his own thinking."[75] The explanation for this may be that students were more impressed by *how* Witherspoon thought than by *what* he thought. It was the "intellectual stimulus" provided by his classes on moral philosophy that left a lasting impression on students. It is generally agreed that Witherspoon's *Lectures on Moral Philosophy* had the "greatest effect on his students"; they were "the main source of the politi- cal philosophy to which Princeton graduates were introduced for a quarter of a century," and, indeed, had a "wide influence" in America as a whole. One scholar claimed that "of all the means by which Witherspoon's influ- ence as an educator spread, none was more pervasive than his *Lectures on Moral Philosophy*. Princeton graduates who taught in colleges often used their copies of Witherspoon's lectures as the texts for teaching moral phi- losophy. Witherspoon's lectures were also employed by many who were not his students."[76] In those lectures, Witherspoon's emphasis was on *method or approach* or *how* to think about religion and politics—and his approach was decidedly rationalistic and naturalistic.

Those who stress Witherspoon's Calvinism typically cite his sermons and explicitly theological lectures and essays. Smylie, for one, cited eight of Witherspoon's theological works in twelve footnotes in his journal article—all in support of significant theological points. By contrast, he cited the *Lectures on Moral Philosophy* only three times, and each was a strictly political reference. Witherspoon's Calvinism may be evident in his theological works, but it is not at all evident in the *Lectures,* which was the text for the one course that he taught and that had such a profound impact on his students. It was not Witherspoon the Calvinist but Witherspoon the rationalist and naturalist who influenced a generation of American political leaders—and Madison in particular.

The change in Witherspoon alluded to earlier was an apparent intellectual "conversion" coinciding with his move to America to assume the presidency of Princeton. In Scotland, Witherspoon had staunchly defended orthodoxy against the Enlightenment thought of such men as David Hume and Francis Hutcheson. He was particularly critical of their claims that construction of moral and political theory did not require Scripture. In preparing his *Lectures,* however, he "turned instinctively to the books of his erstwhile theological opponents, Hume, Hutcheson, and other philosophers of the Scottish Enlightenment." Some have suggested that the Scottish Enlightenment had affected him to a much greater extent than he realized. In Witherspoon, one sees "a background conflict between conservative theology and Enlightenment philosophy which the Princeton professor never synthesized. . . . From the very beginning, he attempted to live in two different, but not unrelated camps: Federal theology and Enlightenment philosophy."[77]

So, one can find an abundance of quotes from the philosophically schizophrenic Witherspoon in support of Calvinism if one avoids the text that was the source of his influence. Even then, Witherspoon's version of Calvinism showed the effects of the intellectual movement of the day. Even Smylie, who wanted to demonstrate a dominant Calvinist influence, admitted that Witherspoon "strained" his Calvinism through Enlightenment thought. If one posits a direct influence by Witherspoon's Calvinism on Madison, one can see this "strained" version in Madison's contributions to *The Federalist Papers.* Madison makes no mention of "sin," and man is not depicted as totally depraved but as having a "degree of depravity" yet "sufficient virtue" to make republican government work.[78]

As a result, Witherspoon can justly be described as "an eclectic Enlightenment thinker whose Calvinism was less than completely orthodox and whose evangelicalism was not easy to detect."[79] Like the theistic rationalists who were influenced by him, Witherspoon mixed elements of Christianity with Enlightenment thought. The difference between Witherspoon and the key Founders was that his appropriation from Enlightenment thought was confined to method, not content, and it was applied only in the realm of politics and morality, not theology. The method or approach that he adopted and taught and meant to be restricted to political use led students such as Madison to theistic rationalism when applied more generally and liberally.

But what was the Enlightenment method or approach that Witherspoon embraced? According to prominent scholars, "His *approach,* though not his *conclusions,* was as humanistic as anything in the eighteenth-century Enlightenment."[80] In the moral and political sphere, Witherspoon employed only rational, empirical, and naturalistic means. He began his *Lectures* by describing moral philosophy as "an inquiry into the nature and grounds of moral obligation by *reason, as distinct from revelation*" (emphasis mine). He said that "there are but two ways in which we come to the knowledge of things, viz. 1st, Sensation, 2nd, Reflection." He regularly appealed to "reason" and "common utility" as the ground of argument. Witherspoon put great confidence in man's reason and its power to understand God. Rather than appealing to Genesis, his argument for the "belief of a Divine Being" was that it was "well supported by the clearest reason."[81]

Concerning the nature of that Divine Being, since reason was the source, the image put forward in Witherspoon's *Lectures* was quite similar to that of other rationalists, such as Priestley. God was depicted as "our Maker, preserver and benefactor" and "governor." The emphasized attributes of God, which were "founded on reason," were His "wisdom and power" and His "goodness." Witherspoon's use of reason even led the Calvinist to flirt with unitarianism: "As to the nature of God, the first thing to be observed is the unity of God. . . . There is a necessity for the existence of one supreme Being, the first cause, but no necessity for more; nay, one supreme independent Being does not admit any more."[82] But Witherspoon, like Priestley and the theistic rationalists, did see a role for revelation in understanding God. Some of God's attributes, such as mercy, could not be discovered by "nature and reason alone."[83] Witherspoon clearly separated his system from deism.

Unlike many Christian authors before him, Witherspoon did not see full employment of man's fallen reason as an inherently flawed path to knowledge or as a threat to revelation. In fact, he was "confident that reason will validate revelation. . . . Throughout the *Lectures* Witherspoon employs reason with a confidence atypical of earlier Calvinism. He reflects a phenomenon of his time: rationalism had entered the house of Calvinism."[84] In support of revelation, he contended that "there is nothing certain or valuable in moral philosophy, but what is perfectly coincident with the scripture." Witherspoon explained his view concerning reason and revelation in the following way: "If the Scripture is true, the discoveries of reason cannot be contrary to it; and therefore, it has nothing to fear from that quarter." He continued: "There may be an illustration and confirmation of the inspired writings, from reason and observation, which will greatly add to their beauty and force."[85] Witherspoon seemed to assume here, as did many in the eighteenth century, that discoveries of reason were infallible. It was his view that "the whole Scripture is perfectly agreeable to sound philosophy; yet certainly it was never intended to teach us everything."[86]

Apparently, since he did not use Scripture for his course, he did not believe that Scripture was intended to teach moral philosophy and politics. According to James McAllister, "The answer to the question regarding the biblical contribution to Witherspoon's teaching about civil law and liberty is: almost nothing." McAllister says that "his theory of society and civil law was based not on revelation but on the moral sense enlightened by reason and common experience."[87] A similar observation has been made by Mark Noll, Nathan Hatch, and George Marsden: "Witherspoon did not derive his politics from the Bible. He did not think the Christian God had a specific role to play in public life, where the rule of nature prevailed. And he did not worry about assuming an Enlightenment perspective on political matters."[88] Witherspoon's political theories were "drawn from over a century of English experience and thought, so he began his *Lectures* not with premises guaranteed by religion or revelation, but from the construction of human nature as learned by observation."[89] This is particularly striking given that others with a lower view of Scripture, such as Jefferson and Franklin, said that the doctrines of Jesus were the best source for morals.

Witherspoon identified moral philosophy as "nothing else but the knowledge of human nature." He introduced that discussion with the following problem:

> It seems a point agreed upon, that the principles of duty and obligation must be drawn from the nature of man. That is to say, *if we can discover how his Maker formed him*, or for what he intended him, that certainly is what it ought to be. The *knowledge of human nature*, however, is either *perplexed and difficult* of itself, or hath been made so, by the manner in which writers in all ages have treated it. (Emphases mine.)[90]

Witherspoon began the *Lectures* by eliminating from consideration the only actual record of how God formed man (Scripture), so knowledge of human nature became understandably perplexed and difficult. He devised a solution consistent with his chosen approach: "The result of the whole is, that we ought to take the rule of duty from conscience enlightened by reason, experience, and every way by which we can be supposed to learn the will of our Maker, and his intention in creating us such as we are."[91] Reason and experience, then, were the keys. Despite appealing to *every* way by which we could be supposed to learn the will of the Maker, he had already ruled out revelation as a necessary or even appropriate way. Instead, as he proceeded through the argument, he equated the light of reason with revelation,[92] so it was given the place that might have been given to revelation. He did mention biblical examples when convenient, but the references were used merely as illustrations of points already made and not as the bases or sources of arguments. Some have even asserted that "Witherspoon's *Lectures* builds on a naturalistic view of human nature that goes even further than Hutcheson in broadening the natural affections to include religious ones. We can only conjecture as to the reasons for this seeming 'conversion' in Witherspoon's attitude toward moral philosophy. . . . In any case there is a question of consistency between his ethical and theological views."[93] As was mentioned previously, there was a significant difference between his theological writings and his moral philosophy, which was the subject taken by his students.

For Witherspoon, moral and political man had to operate using observation, experience, and reason, working in conjunction with an innate moral sense. Henry May noted that Witherspoon's political thought was "frankly naturalistic" and "lack[ed] essential elements of a genuinely Christian approach to public life." In his classic study *The Enlightenment in America*, May observed: "Assuming, but not arguing, the truth of basic Protestant doctrine, Witherspoon recommended to his students a catholic range of moralists. . . . Most of these came from the canon of the moderate Enlightenment," including Hume.[94]

Witherspoon's approach to politics led to a result that was, no doubt, unintended by him—it "opened the door to secularization":

Other than rationalism, an additional factor subverting Calvinism in the eighteenth century was secularization. This process changed the essentially religious orientation of the colonies in the early eighteenth century to a primarily political and hence worldly orientation by the end of the century. . . . The Revolution is seen as the watershed in a significant transformation of America's intellectual focus. And no individual is more representative of this intellectual transition than John Witherspoon.[95]

Secularization refers to the differentiation of thought in which religion becomes one sector or category and other branches of thought and action may proceed independent of it. In other words, "the casing of thought ceases to be theological."[96] "This is exactly the process underway in the Revolutionary period. It describes precisely the ideas which Witherspoon communicated to his students at Princeton. . . . Patriotic thought, even when expressed by Christians like Witherspoon, was proceeding on its own. It was independent from the 'casing' of Christian doctrine or the Bible."[97]

Though Witherspoon's primary influence was in the approach that he taught, the content of his political and moral teachings (since they were based on the same rational and naturalistic presuppositions) largely echoed that of the others in our study. For example, Witherspoon placed great stress on moral living and on the promotion of morality by religion and by the government. In his religious teaching, he "combined orthodoxy with an insistence that religion teach morality."[98] To him, "virtue and piety are inseparably connected . . . to promote true religion is the best and most effectual way of making a virtuous and regular people." Toward that end, he taught that magistrates should "promote and encourage piety and virtue" and that men's duty to each other, which he summed up as "benevolence," should be directed by "a calm good will to all."[99]

At the core of his teaching concerning morality was his belief that all men possess an innate "moral sense" that enables them to act morally. He said that this moral sense is "precisely the same thing with what, in scripture and common language, we call conscience."[100] According to him, man's will is guided by reason and his moral sense to allow him to be a morally responsible being. McAllister has summarized Witherspoon's view: "The purpose of political philosophy is to describe the norms of human society conformable to the moral law known by the conscience or moral sense, which is enlightened by reason and made manifest in the accumulated social experience of man."[101]

The primary difference between Witherspoon, on the one hand, and Priestley and the theistic rationalists, on the other, is that Witherspoon restricted his application of naturalistic principles to politics and morals; thus, he did not believe that living morally was the means by which one made oneself acceptable to God. In his theological writings, he argued, as did Jesus, that one had to be "born again" to "enter into the kingdom of God." Witherspoon held orthodox beliefs concerning salvation and believed in the atonement and imputed righteousness of Christ, beliefs that Priestley scorned.[102] In other words, he was a Christian in the eighteenth-century sense of the term.

Since he was a Founder, one would expect his political views to coincide with those of the Revolution he supported—and they did. It is universally agreed that "he was a Lockean who embraced the whig contractual theory of government."[103] Lecture 12 of his *Lectures,* entitled "Of Civil Society," was essentially a Lockean presentation of the origin and nature of civil society.[104] He presupposed a state of nature and, following Locke, argued that it did not matter whether it existed historically; it was the concept that was important. He gave the same example as Locke had for a state of nature—the relationship between sovereign states. He taught the social contract theory and stressed the importance of the consent of the governed. He posited the existence of "unalienable" and "natural" rights and charged the government with the primary responsibility for protecting those rights. He justified "resistance" to "tyranny" on the same grounds as Locke did and under the same conditions.[105] Witherspoon was a patriot as the term was applied during the American Revolutionary period.

What, ultimately, should one make of John Witherspoon and his contribution to the political theology of the American Founding? He was an evangelical, orthodox Christian who, when it came to political matters, set aside the Scriptures and succumbed to the spirit of the age. One analyst has suggested that the "conflicting elements in Witherspoon's political philosophy and the passion of his real interests make it possible to conclude that in his classroom as in his political activities this recently arrived American was less interested in careful and consistent political philosophizing than in justifying and spurring on the cause of American independence."[106] That he did spur on the cause and that he influenced a critical generation of American leaders is beyond question. He could have used his position of influence to promote a Christian perspective in his students; that is, no doubt, what the trustees expected when they brought him to Princeton. He could have become a shining example of the Christian and biblical roots of America (as the "Christian America" people claim he is), but instead,

> in Witherspoon, the most self-consciously evangelical of the founding fathers, there is little of the effort which marked the work of earlier Christian thinkers to ground politics in specifically Christian propositions. Augustine, Thomas Aquinas, John Calvin, John Knox, and (after Witherspoon's day) Abraham Kuyper in the Netherlands all tried to develop political theory which reflected the truths of Scripture as well as the natural constitution of human beings and society. But Witherspoon and his fellow patriots did not.[107]

SAMUEL CLARKE (1675–1729)

Samuel Clarke is unique among those who influenced the theistic rationalists because his impact was felt both among the key Founders and among the patriotic preachers. Clarke was an Anglican divine who was nearly defrocked for his controversial views. He survived by promising to stop promulgating them. He was also a scientist who specialized in Newtonian physics, a philosopher, and occasionally an official at court.

Among the key Founders, John Adams confessed to having read Clarke, and Benjamin Franklin was reportedly "deeply influenced by Clarke." But of all the Founders, it was James Madison who was most significantly influenced by him. Madison was first introduced to Clarke's writings by John Witherspoon at Princeton. Witherspoon recommended Clarke to his students as a prime example of rational religion. Since Witherspoon was not overly fond of rational *religion,* his was a rather "qualified appreciation" of Clarke's work. But he did include Clarke on the reading list for his influential course in moral philosophy,[108] and whether Witherspoon intended it or not, Clarke's arguments made a lasting impression on Madison.

Two events fifty years after Madison's sojourn at Princeton attest to Clarke's lasting impact on the future president. In 1824, Madison was asked to recommend a list of theological works for the library of the University of Virginia. He included Clarke's books on that list. More important, Madison was asked, in 1825, to comment on a friend's pamphlet about the being and attributes of God. He responded by saying that in order to do justice to the friend's arguments, he would have to "resort to the celebrated work of Dr. Clarke." He went on to say that the "reasoning which could satisfy such a mind as that of Clarke" would have to be included in any discussion of that issue. Apparently, Madison found Clarke's arguments on the subject so persuasive that he still recurred to them after fifty years. As Ralph Ketcham concluded, "There can be little doubt that the kind of rational religion propounded in *The Being and Attributes of God* [Clarke's work] was fundamental to Madison's outlook."[109]

In addition to his influence on key Founders, Clarke had a significant impact on the clergy of the Founding era. Jonathan Mayhew, who will be discussed at length, "was a great admirer of Samuel Clarke." And Clarke is regularly listed among the three or four most "read and quoted" or most "widely read and influential" or most "commonly read" divines in the colonies. In particular, Clarke's *Demonstration of the Being and Attributes of God* was high on the reading lists of those training for the ministry in New

England in the eighteenth century. That work and his *Scripture Doctrine of the Trinity* occupied places on what the orthodox called "Satan's book-shelf" at Harvard.[110]

Those who read Clarke's works encountered an "attempt to formulate a middle way between orthodoxy and deism" that "caused him to be quoted by both sides, and attacked by both as well." That description of his purpose suggests why Clarke was a natural influence on the theistic rationalists, who were attempting to do the same thing. He was more strident and open in opposing the deists, but that is understandable given his position as an Anglican minister. Some have argued, as well, that his emphasis on the necessity of revelation separated him further from the deists than from the orthodox.[111] Clarke argued that revelation was necessary and supplied by God because of the fallen state of man's reason. He said that because of the corrupt state of reason, "there was plainly wanting *a Divine Revelation,* to recover Mankind out of their universally degenerate estate." Specifically, "there was a Necessity of some *particular Divine Revelation,* to make the whole Doctrine of Religion *clear and obvious* to all Capacities." The implication is that revelation was needed to make religion intelligible to the less intelligent masses,[112] but it might be unnecessary for the intellectually gifted. Parenthetically, this remark points, once again, to a religious distinction between the many and the elite. Regardless, revelation was seen to support reason rather than work against it.[113]

It is instructive to note, however, that in Clarke's formulation, the Bible was in service to reason—not vice versa. On this point, Clarke agreed with Locke that revelation was needed to "reinforce reason," as a necessary "supplement to reason in religion." In addition to helping the many grasp religious truth, revelation could supplement reason in other ways. Because of His goodness, God could act on behalf of man in ways that reason could not ascertain. For example, reason might indicate that God had to pardon those who repent, but it could not prove it. Revelation, then, confirmed what reason suspected. But with Locke and Clarke, "the centre of gravity has shifted, and Revelation has become an adjunct, not a first consideration."[114]

For Clarke, revelation and reason worked together so well because "natural and revealed religion were essentially one" and because "Christianity is the religion of reason and nature." He did not see any real conflict between them. As Henry May has noted, "For Clarke, the correctness of such precepts as the Golden Rule was exactly as certain as the conclusions of geometry, and provable in the same way. . . . The doctrines of Jesus, though not all discoverable by the light of nature, proved, when once revealed to be exactly the sort one would expect from a divine being, and clearly conformable to the teachings of sound and unprejudiced reason."[115] Clarke started by insisting upon the clearness, immutability, and universality of the law of nature. In fact, according to him, "that which is truly the *Law of Nature,* or the *Reason of Things,* is in like manner the *Will of God.*"[116] Reason and nature and revelation were so closely intertwined in Clarke's system that they were virtually interchangeable.

Consequently, he was comfortable beginning his discourse on the existence and attributes of God without reference to Scripture, using only arguments of a necessary "first cause" in a "great chain of being" and arguments designed to convince prominent, committed atheists.[117] Yet in the same work, he could, without conflict in his own mind, assert that the Christian revelation was "positively and directly proved, to be actually and immediately sent to us from God; by the many infallible *Signs and Miracles,* which the Author of it worked, . . . by the exact completion both of the *Prophecies . . .* and by the *Testimony of his Followers.*" Because of the range of argument, Clarke felt justified to claim: "They who will not, by the Arguments and Proofs before-mentioned, be convinced of the Truth and Certainty of the Christian Religion . . . would not be convinced . . . by any other Evidence whatsoever."[118]

Clarke's argument for the legitimacy and authenticity of "the Christian religion" invoked all three parts of the nature, reason, and revelation triad. He said:

> The necessary Marks and Proofs of a Religion coming from God, are these. *First,* that the *Duties* it injoyns [*sic*], be all such, as are agreeable to our *Natural* [emphasis mine] notions of God; and perfective of the *Nature* [emphasis mine] and conducive to the happiness and Wellbeing of men. And that the *Doctrines* it teaches, be all such, as . . . may be consistent with, and agreeable to, sound and unprejudiced *Reason* [emphasis mine]. . . . *Secondly,* . . . the *Motives* likewise, by which it is recommended to Mens [*sic*] Belief and Practice . . . must be such as are *suitable* [emphasis mine] to the excellent Wisdom of God, and *fitted* [emphasis mine] to amend the Manners and *perfect the Minds* [emphasis mine] of Men. *Lastly,* it must moreover be *positively and directly proved* to *come from God* [emphasis mine], by such certain *Signs and Matters of Fact,* as may be undeniable evidences of its Author's having actually a *Divine Commission* [emphasis mine].[119]

Clarke was careful, though, to qualify what he meant by "the Christian religion." It was the Christian religion "considered in its primitive simplicity"

for which he contended. He maintained that "all the *Credenda or Doctrines*
which the true, simple, and uncorrupted Christian Religion requires our
particular assent to, or firm belief of, . . . are . . . most *agreeable* to sound
unprejudiced *Reason* . . . and do *together* make up an infinitely more *consistent and rational* Scheme of belief" than any ever invented.[120] Clarke,
like Priestley, was willing to defend only the doctrines of an "uncorrupted"
Christian religion that passed the test of reason.

Although he assented to many more orthodox doctrines than did Priestley, Clarke was prevented from being elevated to the See of Canterbury
because of his heterodoxy. Bishop Edmund Gibson reportedly told Queen
Caroline that Clarke was the "most learned and honest man in her domin-
ions, but with one defect—he was not a Christian."[121] Clarke did have a
firmly orthodox view of God's Providence. He taught that "the same God
who Created all things by the Word of his Power, and upholds and preserves
them by his continual Concourse, does also by his All-wise *Providence* per-
petually govern and direct the issues and events of things." Furthermore, he
argued that "God is substantially present in nature" and that most of what
is ascribed to "the behavior of matter" is really "modalities of operation
of divine power." According to Clarke, the course of nature is really God
continually acting upon matter.[122] These remarks are particularly interesting coming as they did from a renowned Newtonian physicist. Clarke also
believed that the "history" of the Old Testament and the "history of the life
of Christ" in the New Testament were "true relations of matter of fact."
He believed in the Incarnation of the son of God, declaring it "credible"
and "reasonable." He believed it "credible" that God sent His Son, Jesus;
that Jesus gave Himself as "a Sacrifice and Expiation for Sin"; and that he
became "a Mediatour and Intercessour between God and man" and "the
Saviour and Judge of mankind." Finally, he believed in bodily resurrection
and judgment followed by "everlasting" reward or punishment.[123]

One might well wonder what caused Bishop Gibson to determine that
Clarke was not a Christian. What orthodox doctrine or doctrines did he not
believe? The sticking point for Clarke, as for almost all of those treated in
this book, was the Trinity. Clarke did not believe Christ was God, except
in a secondary, inferior sense—something akin to a Greek demigod. Clarke
was an Arian and one of the most influential anti-Trinitarians.[124] Arians believed that Jesus was God's Son and a divine being but that He was created
by God and less than God. The Arian view of Jesus, then, was somewhere
between the Socinian view of Jesus as simply man and the Christian view of
Jesus as God and man. As Levi Paine explained, "Samuel Clarke and others,

took the same essential ground with Firmin, that God is unipersonal, and hence that the Son is a distinct personal being, distinguishing God the Father as the absolute Deity from the Son whom they regarded as God in a relative or secondary sense, being derived from the Father and having his beginning from Him."[125] Clarke said that God "did from Eternity generate of his own Substance a Divine Person or Emanation from Himself; stiled the *Logos*, the *Word*, or *Wisdom*, or *Son* of God" and that the same was true for the Holy Spirit. He determined that the Bible did not teach either the orthodox position or that of the Arians but that reason clearly demanded the Arian position.[126] Bishop Gibson held the orthodox position that one could not be a *Christ*ian while denying the person of the *Christ* at its core. Unitarians and Trinitarians, by definition, worshipped different Gods; hence, Gibson had to classify Clarke as non-Christian.

Clarke's image of God was typical of that held by the leading figures of the eighteenth century. To him, God was the creator, sustainer, and governor of the world, "All-wise," "omnipotent," "reasonable," and "supremely benevolent." The supreme characteristic, again, was the benevolence of God. All that God commanded had to be "conducive to the Happiness and Well-being of Men," and one of two great purposes of revelation was to explain his acts of "goodness," which were over and above what reason could ascertain.[127] Although Clarke's proof of the existence and attributes of God was considered extraordinary and made a lasting impression, he reached the same conclusions concerning the nature of God as many others who later reasoned from a mix of revelation, natural religion, and rationalism.

One final element of Clarke's teaching remains to be addressed. In concert with all of the other persons treated in this book, Clarke gave morality a central role in religion. One of the primary "marks and proofs" of a truly divine revelation, he said, was its "natural *Tendency,* and . . . direct and powerful *Influence,* to *reform* Men's minds and *correct* their manners" or to "amend" those manners. His primary argument for the existence of a "future state" of "rewards and punishments" was that men have "eternal Moral Obligations" that must "certainly and necessarily be attended with *Rewards and Punishments.*" He saw "immortality" as a "required enforcement of virtue." Finally, Clarke's work contains a statement concerning religion and morality that might have been made by almost any person in this study: "*Moral Virtue* is the Foundation and the Summ, the Essence and the Life of all true Religion."[128] His ideas about God, His nature, and His activity in the universe influenced both political and religious leaders in the American Founding era.

CHARLES CHAUNCY (1705–1787)

Charles Chauncy was a Congregationalist minister who pastored the First Church, Boston, for the sixty years spanning the middle of the eighteenth century. He played a significant role in the major events of his time. He was so heavily involved in the patriot cause that his name appeared on a list of the "fifteen most dangerous men in Boston passed among the British troops in the area." And according to Cushing Strout, it was Chauncy's "theological rationalism" that gave him "a firm basis for devotion to the republican revolutionary cause."[129] Chauncy is important not for political or military reasons, however, but for his influence on the Revolutionary era clergy. No less an authority than Douglass Adair called him "the most influential minister of his time in Boston."[130] In addition to his sermons, lectures, and publications, Chauncy was able to influence fellow Bostonian ministers through their weekly meetings and dinner gatherings. Also, these men preached in each other's pulpits and participated in special services in which several clergymen would speak. Consequently, Chauncy had many opportunities and channels by which to exert influence upon the American clergy in general and the Boston clergy in particular.

The theological views and approach to theology that Chauncy represented were "far more sharply defined, prevalent, and significant" in eighteenth-century America "than any of our scholars, whether philosophers or historical theologians or church historians, have ever intimated"; indeed, Chauncy was "perhaps *the* major figure in this tradition."[131] According to Charles Lippy, whose assessment may not be as hyperbolic as it first appears, "Chauncy's contributions to American religious life stand as significant as those of [Jonathan] Edwards. His challenge to evangelicalism enabled a more rationalistic form of religious belief and practice to enter the mainstream of American religion."[132] Arguably, as many churches in twenty-first century America are heirs of Chauncy's tradition as of that of Edwards. And even if there are not *as* many, certainly there are entire denominations and hundreds of churches that fall into that category. Of course, Chauncy was not the only progenitor, but he was deemed the most influential by many. As James Jones observed: "If it can be said to be a mark of modern theology that it concentrates on anthropological rather than strictly theological themes, Chauncy was America's first major modern theologian."[133] Whether or not Lippy or Jones are correct, Chauncy was, without question, very influential in his own time.

Those who study Chauncy's thought recognize that he attempted to find a middle ground between orthodoxy and deism. He saw both as equally flawed and equally obstructive to the redemption of the world. He was more familiar with the orthodox position and became convinced that it "lent itself by its very nature to abuse." For that reason—and in order to stake out his own position—he was generally more critical of the orthodox. He engaged Edwards in a war of printed words and was particularly critical of Edwards's protégé, the orthodox Congregationalist Samuel Hopkins. For instance, Chauncy said: "I had much rather be an episcopalian, or that others shd, than [that] I or they shd be Hopkintonians. . . . Tis as bad, if not worse [than] paganism." The effect of his works was to "undercut the heart of orthodox theology" by mixing Enlightenment rationalism with Calvinist orthodoxy.[134] His has been properly described as a "hybrid position" or "middle position that mixes elements" of several "contradictory tendencies in the culture." Edward Griffin echoed a theme of this book when he observed, "It is actually deceptive to divide the eighteenth century between Edward's [*sic*] evangelicalism and Franklin's Deism. The middle ground that Chauncy defended was a vast and well-populated territory with a long history of its own."[135] The theistic rationalists who founded America composed a significant portion of that population.

Chauncy's middle ground has been called supernatural or theological rationalism because he combined or mixed biblical religion with Enlightenment thought, emphasizing reason and natural religion. Though he affirmed natural religion and its focus on reason as the route to religious truth, Chauncy reserved a special and necessary role for the Bible, as well. He was confident that rationalism and revelation were perfectly compatible. In fact, as he saw it, he gave primacy to Scripture. If Scripture supported orthodoxy, then he would be orthodox; if not, then he would continue to search for the truth. By "Scripture," however, Chauncy meant the Bible approached with "an unprejudiced Mind," or reason, as the test of truth. This approach was necessary because, for Chauncy, "the intent of scripture is not always clearly expressed in the language of scripture," so "an expositor need only look beyond words to the ideas that they truly express." In his view, individuals, guided by reason, could make "private judgments" about religious truth.[136]

He saw this mix of natural theology and Scripture on which he depended as "a reasoned explication of Scripture." For Chauncy, "The usefulness of the Bible is dependent on the rational interpretation of it."[137] Perhaps his greatest criticism of the "New Lights" of the Great Awakening involved their apparent disdain for reason. He said that "in nothing does the *enthusiasm* of these persons discover itself more, than in the disregard they express to the Dictates of *reason*." In the end, Chauncy had to admit that his own application of reason and Scripture led him away from orthodoxy.[138] Furthermore, in *The Mystery Hid from Ages and Generations*, his ultimate deviation from orthodoxy, he spent 400 pages trying to argue that his view was scriptural. He claimed that he was "gradually and insensibly" led to his conclusion by Scripture.[139]

Chauncy's approach to Scripture led him to draw an interesting blend of orthodox and unorthodox conclusions concerning doctrine. To understand his doctrine, one must begin with his view of the nature of God. Although the benevolence of God was a standard and central tenet in the thought of virtually everyone studied in this book, Chauncy raised it to the supreme and overriding—almost sole—attribute of God. His entire theology was based upon it: "Every theological statement must flow from and be judged by its accordance with God's benevolence." Indeed, as one scholar has noted, "the twin pillars of the new theology for the eighteenth century were, according to Chauncy, the benevolence of the deity and the creation of the world for man's own happiness. It was the infinitely benevolent God who created the world not for his own glory but for man's own pleasure."[140] His favorite description for God was "infinitely benevolent." He believed that God's benevolence was the primary lesson of Scripture properly understood and that natural theology demonstrated its primacy through the created order, which "reflected the work of a benevolent God."[141]

His elevation of and focus upon this one attribute led to an upheaval of Christian doctrine. For example, because of it, Chauncy "equat[ed] human happiness with the glory of God. In his scheme God reaped the greatest glory in those expressions of benevolence which promoted creaturely happiness."[142] A commentator has noted the consequences of such a view: "Before the good of man consisted ultimately in glorifying God; now, the glory of God consists in the good of man. Before man lived to worship and to serve God, and now God lives to serve human happiness."[143] The result was a complete inversion of the relationship between God and man and a completely different view of the nature of God. James Jones illustrated the difference by contrasting Chauncy's view with that of Jonathan Edwards:

> For Edwards, God's actions must be consistent with God's own nature and intentions; for Chauncy, God's actions must be consistent with what he calls "the common happiness." For Edwards, God's actions must be consistent only with his own glory. For Chauncy, since God's benevolence is directed not toward God himself but primarily toward creation, God's actions must be consistent with the good of creation. Some things, Chauncy said, clearly are not good for man, "and this

must be known to a perfectly intelligent agent." Having decided that the good of creation was the chief end of God's actions and knowing infallibly what is necessary to bring it about, Chauncy set about redefining God to bring him into agreement with this standard.[144]

The result was a brand of humanism in which even God was man-centered. This anthropocentric theology was the norm among the rationalists of the period.

Jones put his finger on the real issue, which was a fundamental problem in the thought of almost everyone in this study—the attempt to make God whatever the individual preferred Him to be. In Chauncy's case, he denied that God was "essentially different from creation" and "went a long way toward making God over in man's image, or at least in the image of the enlightened, intelligent, moral gentleman of Chauncy's congregation." Essentially, by Chauncy's view, "God must conform to what intelligence, trained at Harvard, infallibly knew was good for the universe."[145] This sarcastic remark by Jones highlighted the arrogance of those who, like Chauncy, approached God's revelation of Himself selectively and formed an image of God based on personal preferences and what seemed "reasonable" to them. Chauncy was quite willing to confine God to limits placed by his own reason. He said:

> Some may be ready to think, that the *will* of the Supreme Being is the only measure of *fitness*, in the communication of good; that what he *wills* is for that reason *fit*, and there is no need of any other to make it so. But this is a great mistake. There is, beyond all doubt, a certain *fitness* and *unfitness* of conduct, in order to the production of good, antecedently to, and independently of, all will whatsoever, not excepting even the will of *God* himself.[146]

The will of God, then, was bound by what Chauncy and people of his ilk determined to be "fit." Although Chauncy's view resembled that of Aquinas, the difference was that Chauncy felt free to simply reject the legitimacy of any Scripture he found to be inconsistent with his own determination of what was fit. Aquinas, conversely, strove to make his own understanding comply with God's Word. Once again, Jones effectively summarized the arrogance of Chauncy's position: "Man's reason independently arrives at judgments as to what is good for creation, and especially for man, and then demands that God comply. It is no dishonor to God that he submits to the dictates of man's reason; rather it reflects his rationality and good sense that he agreed with Chauncy as to what is good for his creation."[147] This tone of infallibility was a common problem for the rationalists, theistic or otherwise, who decided for themselves which parts of God's revelation to man were worthy of their attention and assent.

Chauncy's infatuation with the benevolence of God did not cause him to reject all the doctrines of orthodoxy. He assented to the necessity of Christ's atoning work and sacrifice for mankind's redemption, to justification by faith, and to the operation of God's Providence in the world. He maintained that Christianity was the only true religion and that faith in Jesus Christ was a necessary condition for salvation.[148]

But Chauncy parted company with orthodox Christianity on three fundamental doctrines. First, though he did not stake out specific ground, he did not affirm Christ as God. He saw Jesus as a human guide and as an example of proper conduct leading to happiness. "Chauncy placed great emphasis on the mediatorial and exemplary roles of Christ. Christ served as mediator between humanity and divinity because he did not fall into sin . . . and therefore demonstrated that attainment of ultimate happiness was a real possibility for ordinary human beings. Equally important, Christ served as an example of the life which persons intent on eternal happiness should lead."[149] Since he identified Christ as an example for ordinary human beings, he appears to have been Socinian. Second, although it was not a point of emphasis for him, Chauncy firmly denied and criticized the doctrine of original sin.[150] But it was the third orthodox doctrine rejected by Chauncy that was most critical to him and for which he is primarily remembered. In fact, his position was so controversial that he refrained from publishing it for many years and eventually published it anonymously.[151] Chauncy rejected the concept of eternal punishment and contended for the eventual salvation of all men.

Universal salvation was a logical deduction from his premise of a singularly benevolent God. Such a one-dimensional God, who existed simply to make men happy, had to do what was "most beneficial to men," and that meant providing them with eternal happiness. Chauncy expressed this view in the first sentence of *The Mystery Hid*: "As the First Cause of all things is infinitely benevolent, 'tis not easy to conceive, that he should bring mankind into existence, unless he intended to make them finally happy."[152] To Chauncy, only a shockingly false idea of God could support the orthodox position: "A more shocking idea can scarce be given of the *Deity*, than that which represents him as *arbitrarily dooming the greater part of the race of men to eternal misery*. Was he wholly destitute of goodness, yea, positively *malevolent* in his nature, a worse representation could not be well made of him."[153] According to Chauncy, the only logical expression of the "good-ness" of an "infinitely benevolent" God was universal salvation.

> It does not appear to me, that it would be honourable to the infinitely righteous and benevolent Governor of the world, to make wicked men *everlastingly miserable*. For, in what point of light soever we take a view of sin, it is certainly, in its nature, a *finite evil*. It is the fault of a *finite creature*, and the effect of *finite* principles, passions, and appetites. To say, therefore, that the sinner is doomed to *infinite misery* for the *finite* faults of a *finite* life looks like a reflection on the *infinite justice,* as well as goodness, of God.[154]

Chauncy believed that God's reputation among rational and "honourable" men was at stake in the issue of universal salvation.

Interestingly, he did not reject the concept of hell; in fact, he made it an integral part of his system. He was quick to separate his view of universal salvation from that of the "heretic" John Murray. Murray taught that all men went straight to heaven upon their death. Chauncy, by contrast, taught that those who had faith in Christ went directly and immediately to heaven at death but that the wicked went to hell for a period of rehabilitation and purification. The amount of time needed in hell depended on their level of wickedness. He described, essentially, the Catholic concept of purgatory: "Though I affirm, that all men will be finally happy, yet I deny not but that many of them will be miserable in the next state of existence, and to a great degree, and for a long time, in proportion to the moral depravity they have contracted in this."[155] While the wicked were in hell, Christ would work to redeem them, and they eventually would develop the faith in Christ needed for salvation. "The process continues until all people finally reach heaven."[156] For Chauncy, then, hell became a function of God's goodness, and any concept or trace of God's judgment was entirely removed.

Chauncy thought Murray's view irresponsible because it eliminated any motivation for morality in this life. As Jones noted, "Chauncy's universal-ism preserved hell as a stimulus to moral endeavor. Men were still exhorted to repent and reform or face torment in the next life."[157] Chauncy empha-sized morality and made it a necessary element of salvation. According to him, God had appointed "means of grace"—including the sacraments, the preaching of the Word, the work of the clergy, and private reading of Scrip-ture—to lead people to salvation. For Chauncy, there were three compo-nents integral to salvation: "divine grace, human effort, and the 'means of grace' which enabled human effort to appropriate divine grace and thus achieve both salvation and justification." Justification was "essentially a process of growth in moral living."[158]

To Chauncy, the whole plan was simple and clear: "The plain truth is, God, man, and means are all concerned in the formation of that character, without which we cannot inherit eternal life."[159] Thanks to the infinitely benevolent God, who obviously had to give divine grace to all, man could save himself from any punishment by his moral works and the development of his character. Essentially, God became "simply a servant and support for the morality man arrived at on his own." Chauncy went so far as to suggest that men "may attain to a moral likeness to God."[160] Man had to work for his own salvation, but he could achieve it through the development of his own potential. So, along with his own version of purgatory, Chauncy essentially reintroduced into Protestantism the Catholic idea of works contributing to salvation. And like the others studied in this book, he also suggested that "real religion" should be judged by its moral results.[161]

One other element of Chauncy's thought must be briefly discussed. Chauncy was involved in the patriot movement and promoted republican and revolutionary views concerning government. Though his political views were not unique in Revolutionary America, one should note that, for him, they were the logical extension of his fixation on the benevolence of God. Cushing Strout said his "theological rationalism" gave Chauncy a "firm basis for devotion to the republican revolutionary cause."[162]

Chauncy echoed many other Americans of the period in arguing that the end of civil government was "the general good of mankind; . . . to guard men's lives; to secure their rights; to defend their properties and liberties; to make their way to justice easy; . . . and, in general, to promote public welfare." Government, then, was another means by which the infinitely benevolent God extended His goodness to man. In the abstract, government was ordained by God, but the particular form of government that was appropriate for a given group of people was up to them to determine according to their assessment of the public good. Rulers were entrusted with power in order to promote that public good, and that was the extent of their authority from God. Chauncy drew the same conclusion concerning abuse of that power that many Americans of his day did. He stated that for rulers who "abuse their power; applying it to the purposes of tyranny and oppression, rather than to serve the good ends of government, it ought to be taken out of their hands."[163] His revolutionary rhetoric provided theological justification for "the cause," which was a logical outgrowth of his belief in God's benevolence and influenced the many ministers who shared that belief.

JONATHAN MAYHEW (1720–1766)

Jonathan Mayhew was the pastor of Boston's West Church from 1747 to his death in 1766. Although he died young, he made an enormous impact on the clergy of New England and, indeed, throughout America. One scholar said of Mayhew: "His influence was soon powerfully felt in the town, and his name came to stand for liberty in politics as well as in religion. His sermons were rapidly printed and distributed widely. They were read in every part of New England with great eagerness; they were reprinted in England."[164] Mayhew's particular distinction was having the courage to unabashedly speak or print the radical and unorthodox views that were quietly held by many. Historians maintain that "Mayhew was not so much the intellectual innovator as the pulpit herald of the changing political and theological views." He was "the first open antagonist of Calvinism in New England," "the first openly avowed Arminian to ascend a New England pulpit," and "the first outspoken Unitarian in New England."[165]

Mayhew's attributes extended beyond mere brazenness, however. His sermon entitled *A Discourse Concerning Unlimited Submission and Non-resistance to the Higher Powers* was so influential that it has been described as the "MORNING GUN OF THE REVOLUTION."[166] John Adams said, "If the orators on the 4th of July really wish to investigate the principles and feelings which produced the Revolution, they ought to study . . . Dr. Mayhew's sermon on passive obedience and non-resistance." He further remarked that the sermon was "read by everybody."[167] In perhaps the best-known collection of Revolutionary era sermons, it is Mayhew's likeness that is placed opposite the title page.[168]

Mayhew contributed to the Revolutionary cause in other ways, as well. Among other things, he gave James Otis the idea of establishing committees of correspondence.[169] And his pamphlets in opposition to efforts by the Anglican Church to expand its power in America were widely quoted. Adams reported that the controversy "soon interested all men" when Mayhew's pamphlets appeared. In fact, "all denominations in America became interested in it." Robert Treat Paine, a member of the Continental Congress and a signer of the Declaration of Independence, called Mayhew "The Father of Civil and Religious Liberty in Massachusetts and America." Adams described him as "a whig of the first magnitude," as a "writer of great abilities" and "transcendent genius" who "seemed to be raised up to revive all their animosities against tyranny," and as a divine who "had raised a great reputation both in Europe and America."[170]

The reputation of which Adams spoke was based on Mayhew's theology in general as well as his political theology. For example, Adams reported in his diary that a visiting minister "supposed" that Adams "took" his views concerning the deity and satisfaction of Christ "from Dr. Mayhew."[171] Clearly, certain unorthodox views were identified with Mayhew. He broadly influenced American clergymen but most particularly through his sermon countering the biblical prohibition of revolution.

The defining feature of Mayhew's religion was rationalism. In George Willis Cooke's assessment, "He unhesitantly applied the rational method to all theological problems, and to him reason was the final court of appeal for everything connected with religion."[172] That is not surprising given that he was influenced by Locke and Clarke. Indeed, he was "a great admirer of Samuel Clarke." Like the others in this study, Mayhew was impressed by "moderate English rationalism" rather than by the "more radical deistic rationalism of Tindal, Toland, and Voltaire" or the atheism of the French Enlightenment. He also acknowledged an intellectual debt to Plato, Demosthenes, Cicero, Algernon Sidney, John Milton, and Benjamin Hoadly, saying simply, "I liked them; they seemed rational." For Mayhew, that was the key—reason was the test of truth.[173]

McMurry Richey has labeled Mayhew's system as "Christian rationalism." Yet this label, similar to others discussed earlier—and the inverse of Jefferson's "rational Christianity"—is inadequate because it is inaccurate. As will be demonstrated, Mayhew was not a Christian; rather, like almost all of the men in this study, he sacrificed Christianity on the altar of rationalism. To be sure, he considered himself a Christian and continued to use language familiar to Christians, but he had abandoned the fundamental beliefs that comprised Christian faith.[174]

Mayhew traveled that middle course between deism and orthodoxy charted by others in this book, and like them, he "found reason generally adequate but revelation also necessary." His regular practice was to "establish his point by reason, then confirm it by revelation." He believed that natural religion had to be supplemented by revelation in a way that did not allow for contradiction. On the contrary, Mayhew insisted that reason and revelation "do not contradict, but mutually confirm and illustrate each other."[175] That mutual relationship depended, however, on reason being the ultimate criterion and judge of what counted as revelation and of how it should be interpreted. For Mayhew,

It necessarily follows from the supposition of our rational faculties being *limited*, that there is *room* for our being instructed by revelation. . . . However upon supposition of such a revelation, we must be supposed to be able to see the evidence of its being such. It is the proper office of reason to determine whether what is proposed to us under the notion of a revelation from God, be attended with suitable attestations and credentials, or not. So that even in this case, we may *of ourselves judge what is right.*[176]

Once true revelation was authenticated by reason, proper interpretation of it became a second office of reason. Richey has noted that, in agreement "with the rationalists in general, Mayhew made reason the final test even of revelation, which requires both authentication and explanation by reason."[177]

Mayhew was confident that, with the aid of revelation, the reason of fallen men was adequate to the task of discovering truth. Richey has summarized Mayhew's principles for making such a determination: "Four things are involved: suspended judgment, unbiased effort to examine evidence rationally; exertion of reason in active inquiry and weighing arguments . . . ; embracing the truth when it is found, whether we like it or not, without 'superstitious veneration for great names'; and finally, assent proportional to evidence."[178] Mayhew taught his flock to judge matters of religion for themselves. The individuals in his congregation had to accept or reject doctrine on the same basis as he would, as a minister—rationality. Was any doctrine or article of faith above such evaluation? No. Mayhew warned that "neither Papists nor Protestants should . . . think that nonsense and contradictions can ever be too *sacred* to be *ridiculous.*" In fact, he believed that the power of God Himself was limited by "the everlasting *tables* of right reason."[179] To function within the realm of reason, then, was no more and no less than God required. According to Mayhew, this right of all to judge for themselves in religious matters was "given them by God and nature, and by the gospel of Christ":

Did I say, we have a *right* to judge and act for ourselves? I now add—it is our *indispensible* [sic] *duty* to do it. This is a right we cannot relinquish or neglect to exercise if we would . . . for it is absolutely unalienable in its own nature. . . . God and nature and the gospel of Christ injoin [sic] upon us a duty to maintain the right of private judgment, and to worship God according to our consciences.[180]

The logical extension of such a right, if it truly came from God, would be that any religion was acceptable to God—as long as it was sincerely held.

That was what the key Founders believed, as well. As James Jones has said, "God was made over in the image of man's reason to make him comprehensible to man."[181]

What did Mayhew's reason tell him about God? Given Clarke's and Chauncy's conclusions about the nature of God, there are no surprises in Mayhew's view. He decided that God was "perfect in all those moral qualities and excellencies which we esteem amiable in mankind."[182] God's moral perfection could be summed up as *goodness*. Like Chauncy's elevation of benevolence, all of the attributes of Mayhew's God were subsidiary to goodness. The natural outgrowth of such an emphasis was his replacement of theocentric orthodoxy with an anthropocentric system of his own construction. Although orthodoxy said that man's chief end was to glorify God and enjoy him forever, Mayhew saw God and nature working together for the happiness of man—which *was* the glory of God.[183] He asserted, "As the natural and moral world are under one and the same common direction or government; so God's end in all things . . . is really one and uniform . . . all tend to the same point at last; the moral perfection and happiness of the creatures capable of it, or the glory of God; which, in any good and intelligent sense, seems to amount to the same thing."[184] He viewed *all* of God's actions as designed for the purpose of making men happy, even punishment from God and suffering. Mayhew argued that "mankind, in the present state, actually need trials and afflictions, as a means of promoting their moral good, and future happiness."[185]

Mayhew explicitly tried to remove the awe, terror, and fear of the Lord that, according to portions of the Bible he did not favor, were the beginning of wisdom and central to Christianity. Such concepts were obsolete in light of Mayhew's enlightened understanding of the "humane and benevolent" God.[186] Speaking of God's justice and sovereignty, he said that "being considered as inseparably connected with goodness, which is equally essential to the divine nature, and exercised towards all the works of God; those otherwise formidable attributes, are, in great degree, stripped of their terror."[187] To remove the terror of God, Mayhew argued that God did punish people and send suffering but only as a means of rehabilitation for their good—never as penalty or for retribution or because justice demanded satisfaction.[188]

Reason taught Mayhew two other things about God. The first was that He was not Triune. Mayhew, as was mentioned, was "the first outspoken Unitarian in New England." He openly taught unitarianism from the pulpit and in a published book of sermons. In his rejection of the Trinity, he took the Arian view of Christ.[189] The second thing reason taught Mayhew about God was that He was providential. He expressed a "firm belief" in God's "universal providence" and often spoke of God's governance over the world and the universe.[190]

Although he tried to minimize their ultimate importance, Mayhew was outspoken about numerous doctrines. He "specifically attacked as unChristian and unscriptural the orthodox . . . doctrines of imputation, justification by faith, total depravity, and the need of irresistable grace." He was "openly critical" of the Virgin Birth and held unorthodox views concerning regeneration, grace, the satisfaction of Christ, and original sin.[191] Regarding original sin and total depravity, Mayhew held that "the doctrine of a total ignorance, and incapacity to judge of moral and religious truths, brought upon mankind by the apostasy of our *First Parents,* is without foundation." Regarding the satisfaction of Christ, Mayhew held a *governmental,* or *Grotian,* view of the atonement. In other words, Christ's death served merely as an example to men of the consequences of sin; it did not provide any "satisfaction" of God's justice.[192] Consistent with his Arian views, Mayhew saw Christ as a "mediator" between God and men "who should do and suffer what might have a tendency, and be sufficient to vindicate the honor of his laws, by exciting and preserving in all, a just veneration for his government, at the same time that guilty creatures were made partakers of his lenity and grace." Put another way, Jesus came "to give mankind the most perfect and engaging example of obedience to the will of God."[193] The rationalists were correct in seeing a relationship between the doctrines of the Trinity and the atonement. Mayhew's view of the atonement gave the greatest importance a unitarian could give to Christ's death.

Despite taking doctrinal positions, Mayhew argued that one's beliefs were not particularly important when it came to salvation. In his view: "It is infinitely dishonourable to the all good and perfect Governor of the world, to imagine that he has suspended the eternal salvation of men upon any *niceties of speculation*: Or that any one who honestly aims at finding the truth, and at doing the will of his maker, shall be finally discarded because he fell into *some erroneous opinions*" (emphases mine).[194] He continued: "Nor, indeed, is there any *speculative error,* however great, which can exclude a good and upright man, who obeys the laws of Christianity, from the kingdom of heaven" (emphasis mine).[195] Mayhew so discounted the significance of doctrines that he described them as "niceties of speculation" and wrong beliefs merely as "erroneous opinions" or "speculative error." He even contended that "how much soever any man may be mistaken in opinion concerning the terms of salvation; yet if he is practically in the right, there is no doubt but he will be accepted of God."[196] In Mayhew's view, one did not even have to believe what is right concerning salvation in order to be saved. This is further evidence of his belief that many, or perhaps any, religions led to God. Other implications of this will be addressed in a later section.

If doctrinal beliefs were not important—even beliefs about the terms of salvation—what *was* important for Mayhew? Clues can be seen in his statements de-emphasizing doctrine, as cited previously. He contended that God would not suspend salvation for any one who "honestly aims at finding the truth, and at doing the will of his maker." Further, he said that "a good and upright man, who obeys the laws of Christianity" would not be excluded. A man would be accepted of God if he was "practically in the right." These hints point toward the fact that for Mayhew, like the other rationalists, Christianity was not belief in a set of doctrines but "a practical science; the art of living piously and virtuously." His religion was essentially a universal system of ethics and morality.[197] As he defined it, the purpose of Christianity was to bring men to "that moral purity of heart and life, which is comprised in the love of God and of our neighbor." According to him, "The whole tenor of our Lord's preaching was *moral*: he seldom inculcated any thing upon his hearers besides piety towards God, and righteousness and charity towards man."[198]

The emphasis on morality colored Mayhew's perspective on several doctrines, as well. He developed his own doctrine of justification by grace, in which justification became a "standard to attain" rather than an "act of God in pardoning individuals" and God accepted the efforts of man to be moral despite not being required to do so. According to Mayhew, there were certain rules to be followed "so that those who comply therewith, are justified of course, upon such compliance."[199] The doctrine of imputed righteousness also ran afoul of Mayhew's stress on morality. He called it a "grand, capital error" and "grand mistake" to say "that the merits of Christ's obedience and sufferings, may be so applied or imputed to sinners, as to be available to their justification and salvation, altho' they are destitute of all personal inherent goodness." In a clear repudiation of this central doctrine of Christianity, Mayhew expressed disagreement with those "who place the whole of religion in faith, and dependance [*sic*] upon the righteousness of Christ."[200]

Because of the central role of morality, salvation became a matter of works and grace for Mayhew, with "grace" given his own peculiar definition. By his definitions, salvation by merit would require perfect obedience; salvation by grace meant that God accepted imperfect obedience, even though he was not required to do so. Either way, salvation was a matter of works. Mayhew answered orthodox critics of this concept with the following admission: "If it should be objected, that this doctrine leads men to *trust to their own righteousness*; I answer it is very reasonable that they should do so." For him, conversion was a matter of character development and self-improvement.[201]

Mayhew's emphasis on morality joined with his emphasis on the goodness of God to produce one other unorthodox doctrine. Though he did, in contrast to Chauncy, see hell as eternal punishment, he believed it was for those who were not good rather than for those who did not have Christian faith. Hell provided a motive for moral exertion rather than for conversion. Mayhew explained God's establishment of hell in this way: "Neither does he inflict any punishments, but what he considers as needful for the support of his government;—if not for the particular good of those that suffer, as in capital cases, yet for the good of his people in general, by way of example and terror, that good order may be preserved."[202] So, hell was for man's good, for the good of society as a whole. Although, as was mentioned earlier, Mayhew tried to remove the terror of the Lord that he found to be inconsistent with the notion of a benevolent God, the terror of punishment served to promote morality that, in turn, preserved "good order."

There was one final result of Mayhew's stress on religion for the sake of morality. It contributed to the theistic rationalist belief that all religions followed the "light of nature" in promoting morality and, consequently, that virtually any religion was satisfactory. A longer quote from Mayhew summarized his view in this regard:

Upon the whole, then, the case seems to stand thus—Although the christian revelation brings us acquainted with many truths besides those which the light of nature suggests, or Judaism plainly taught; although it injoins [*sic*] us to do several things which would not have been obligatory without an explicit command; although it furnishes us with a great variety of new and excellent motives to excite us to the practice of our duty in all its branches; and although christianity cannot, for these reasons, with any sense or propriety be said to be the same with natural religion, or only a re-publication of the law of nature; yet the principal, the most important and fundamental duties required by christianity are, nevertheless, the same which were injoined [*sic*] as such under the legal dispensation; and the same which are dictated by the light of nature. They are natural moral duties, inforced [*sic*] with revealed and supernatural motives; and to be performed from principles peculiar to the gospel. And indeed, it is plain beyond dispute, that the substance of true religion must necessarily be the same, not only under the jewish and christian dispensations, but also, in all countries, to all rational creatures, in all parts of the universe, in all periods of time.[203]

According to Mayhew, Christianity and Judaism were unique only in that they had their own special means and motives for performing the same "natural moral duties" as every other religion. But any religion would do because the "substance of true religion" was the same everywhere, for everyone, at all times. As McMurry Richey put it: "This amounts to a sort of negative or permissive justification of the Christian revelation: it is essentially ethical, and it is at one with universal religion."[204]

Although Mayhew's theology and his approach to theology had a significant impact on the ministers of the Founding era, he is best remembered for his momentous sermon justifying revolution. That sermon, *A Discourse Concerning Unlimited Submission and Non-resistance to the Higher Powers,* provided many patriotic preachers with a religious and ostensibly biblical basis for promoting rebellion. It is not within the scope of this chapter to examine the sermon in detail or to critique it, but its thrust and main arguments must be treated.

To properly understand the sermon, one must recognize that Mayhew was, as he acknowledged, significantly influenced by Locke's social contract theory. From the positing of a state of nature to the surrender of certain rights in order to enter civil society, Mayhew's premises were Lockean. He stressed that "civil liberty also supposeth, that those laws, by which a nation is governed, are made by common consent and choice."[205] He further stressed that certain rights, such as the rights to life, liberty, and property, were inalienable and were carried into civil society. Included among those rights was the right of the people to determine for themselves when their ruler had overstepped his bounds. As Mayhew put it, the people kept "to themselves a right to judge, whether he discharges his trust well or ill, to discard him, and appoint another in his stead."[206] He applied his admittedly Lockean presuppositions to the classic biblical text enjoining submission to political authorities (Romans 13), and the result was a justification of rebellion in place of a prohibition of rebellion.

Mayhew summed up the "apostle's doctrine, in the passage thus explained" in several "observations." The first observation was that the purpose of government was to secure the good of civil society. The second was that all civil rulers, "*as such,*" were ordained by God and were ministers of God. The strategically placed and italicized *as such* indicated that only those rulers who pursued the good of civil society counted as "civil rulers" who were "ministers of God" in his accounting. The third observation was that the term *civil rulers* applied "to inferior officers no less than to the supreme." The fourth was that disobedience to civil rulers "in the due exercise of their authority" was both a *"political sin"* and "a heinous *offence against God* and *religion.*" Significantly, Mayhew's qualifying phrase suggested that rulers' authority was restricted and that it was not necessarily a sin or offense to disobey when rulers stepped outside certain bounds. The fifth observation was that "the true ground and reason of our obligation to be subject to the *higher powers*" was "the usefulness of magistracy (when properly exercised) to human society, and its subserviency to the general welfare." The sixth was that obedience was "required under all forms of government, which answer the sole end of all government, the good of society." Mayhew's final observation was that subjection was due to those who were *"actually* vested with authority."[207]

In a crucial footnote to this seventh point, Mayhew said: "Who these persons were, whether *Nero,* &c., or not, the apostle does not say; but leaves it to be determined by those to whom he writes."[208] The note is critical because it was Mayhew's way of sidestepping the fact that Nero was actually the ruler over the people to whom Paul was writing. Mayhew's entire interpretation makes no sense if one recognizes that Paul was instructing Christians to be subject to an actual unelected tyrant who had never sought their consent. It is very interesting that this vital point was only addressed by Mayhew in a footnote of the printed version of the sermon, not in the text or in the version heard by his congregation.

From these "observations," Mayhew developed a line of argument that resulted in a climactic pair of revolutionary conclusions. The first was that Paul was arguing for submission "only, to those who *actually* perform the duty of rulers, by exercising a reasonable and just authority, for the good of human society"—not to "all who bear the *title* of rulers." In connection with that, he famously stated, "Rulers have no authority from God to do mischief." The second great conclusion was that "if it be our duty . . . to obey our king, merely for this reason, that he rules for the public welfare, (which is the only argument the apostle makes use of) it follows, by a parity of reason, that when he turns tyrant . . . we are bound to throw off our allegiance to him, and to resist."[209] According to Mayhew's creative interpretation, Paul in Romans 13 was making the case for rebellion rather than prohibiting it. From this point on, patriotic ministers could cite this Scripture in support of the Lockean idea that "those in authority may abuse their *trust* and power *to such a degree* . . . that they should be totally *discarded*; and the authority which they were before vested with, transferred to others."[210] Since this passage was a great obstacle in the minds of the faithful and was regularly quoted by English and loyalist Anglican divines, Mayhew's service to the Revolutionary cause was immeasurable.

In this chapter, I have sought to explicate the relevant religious beliefs of those divines most influential in the development of theistic rationalism in the key Founders and patriotic preachers. No claim is made here that the individuals discussed in this chapter were themselves theistic rationalists. It is clear, for example, that John Witherspoon was a Christian. It is equally clear, however, that by the latter third of the eighteenth century, elements of the theology and methodology of these divines had been incorporated into the hybrid belief system that I have labeled theistic rationalism. Many of those following in their footsteps stood in America's pulpits on Sundays and spread the good news of liberal democracy and, ultimately, of political revolution. The next chapter investigates the substance and effect of patriotic preaching before, during, and after the American Revolution and shows how religious beliefs paved the way for revolution and the resultant republican government of America.

3

Theistic Rationalism in the Revolutionary Pulpit

Explaining [the Scriptures] in a manner friendly to the cause of freedom.
Charles Turner

UNTIL THE MIDDLE OF THE EIGHTEENTH CENTURY, none of the political theologies of the religious groups in America were particularly friendly to liberal democratic thought or republican government. The Anglican and Catholic churches, with much invested in monarchs and their own hierarchies, resisted democratic influences and remained committed to monarchy until after the Revolution. In the nonconformist churches (those that did not conform to the established Church of England), theology militated against democratic thought until the mid-1700s, when the Enlightenment-based education of the clergy began to be exhibited in the expounding of liberal democratic and republican principles from the pulpit. By the 1770s in these denominations, democratic theory based on natural religion had either replaced the Bible as the primary source or had inspired revised interpretations of biblical texts to fit its "self-evident" truths. Although the ministers and their preaching had little impact on political leaders, they provided a critical link between the people and those political leaders. The dominant political theology of the Founding era pulpit was theistic rationalism, which was expressed in liberal democratic theory and republicanism.

Parenthetically, it must be noted that in the battle between natural religion and revealed religion, early salvos were fired in England on behalf of natural religion by John Locke in *The Reasonableness of Christianity* (1695) and by John Toland in *Christianity Not Mysterious* (1696). In America, Elisha Williams's *Essential Rights and Liberties of Protestants* (1744) sounded the clarion call for clergymen emphasizing reason and political theory over the confines of revelation. This current study, however, will be limited to an analysis of the Founding era sermons.

In the eighteenth century, the main theological obstacle to an acceptance of democratic theory in American churches was Calvinism. Calvinism had

69

been the prevailing theology of the previous century, and it remained the official theology of a majority of American churches. Calvinist teaching stressed authority, and the so-called five points of Calvinism emphasized the sovereignty of God and de-emphasized the power of individual men. For example, "'unconditional election' seemed to deny that men were fully capable of determining the course of their own lives. The antidemocratic tendency of the doctrine of election emerged even more clearly in the idea of a 'limited atonement,' that Christ's death was somehow restricted to those whom God elected to salvation."[1] Freewill Baptist minister William Smyth Babcock found Calvinism "antithetical to democratic common sense" and said, "Its doctrine is denied in the Practice of every converted soul in the first exercises of the mind after receiving liberty."[2]

As suggested by Babcock, the Calvinist view of liberty also contradicted that of the Whigs. Calvinism saw liberty as freedom *for* fulfillment and hope, which was found only in being a *servant* of God; the Whigs, by contrast, saw liberty as freedom *from* tyranny, oppression, and the arbitrary exercise of power. Presbyterian minister Nathaniel Niles argued that "no man can be a Christian and not a friend to civil liberty, in the strictest sense." Ultimately, "Calvinism was being dropped not in response to theological arguments but because it violated the spirit of Revolutionary liberty. During the early history of the United States self-evident principles of democracy persuaded any number of former Calvinists to strike out for a new faith."[3] For many of the educated elite, that new faith was theistic rationalism, a hybrid combining what could be rationally salvaged of Calvinism with the democratic theory of the Whigs. Since the Puritan theory of church government was based on the concept of "covenant" and included the election of aristocratic magistrates by the "visible elect," the theoretical marriage was fairly natural for educated clergy. As Cushing Strout has noted, "Whigs and pietist Calvinists spoke overlapping but different languages that enabled them to cooperate, but it was the clergy who had learned most from the collaboration by politicizing the gospel to suit the revolutionary case."[4]

Not surprisingly, given the momentum afforded by victory in the Revolution, the politicization of the American pulpit continued throughout the remainder of the Founding period. With Calvinist theology marginalized or co-opted, Enlightenment rationalism that reinterpreted or rejected biblical teaching could be openly espoused in churches swept up in the emotion of political events and led by ministers trained in that rationalism.

THE EDUCATION OF MINISTERS

As was mentioned in chapter 1, theistic rationalism was a belief system of the educated class that grew out of their exposure to Enlightenment thought. The New England clergy were "for the most part a 'learned clergy,' graduates of Harvard or Yale." According to Charles Chauncy's estimation, there were at least 550 ministers in New England in 1767 and all had been educated at a college.[5] An actual survey of 800 ministers ordained between 1740 and 1810 showed that fewer than 20 "were not definitely known to have a college degree."[6] But what were the seminary students learning?

It was the published treatises of "the principal controversialists . . . which constituted a principal part of the reading done by . . . better trained clergy-men in preparation for the pulpit."[7] John Locke and Samuel Clarke were widely read and influential in the seminaries, along with other rationalists such as John Tillotson and William Wollaston. Clarke's *Demonstration of the Being and Attributes of God* "was throughout the eighteenth century and into the nineteenth to occupy a position of prominence on the reading lists of New England's preparing clergymen." Seminary students were taught to rely upon "natural law and human reason," which "tended to arouse skepticism both as to the necessity and the credibility of supernatural revelation." Doubts began to surface concerning other fundamental doctrines, as well. For instance, a "complete reliance upon reason and evidence . . . was leading many toward an anti-Trinitarian belief."[8]

As early as the 1740s, famed evangelist George Whitefield stated: "As for the Universities, I believe it may be said, their Light is become Darkness, Darkness that may be felt, and is complained of by the most godly Ministers." In particular, Whitefield "complained of the low state of religion at Harvard, and made a similar criticism of the clergy at Yale." In fact, while visiting Harvard, he "criticised [*sic*] the teaching there on the ground that it was not sufficiently devout and earnest, and that the pupils were not examined as to their religious experiences." During his visit, Whitefield "preached on the text, 'We are not as many who corrupt the Word of God,' and in the Conclusion he 'made a close Application to Tutors and Students.'"[9] Since Harvard and Yale were the preeminent seminaries, some discussion of the educational experience at those institutions should suffice to demonstrate that eighteenth-century preachers received an education that prepared them for theistic rationalism.

Some have traced the movement away from Christianity at Harvard to the new Massachusetts charter that came from William and Mary in 1691: "From that time a new life entered into the college, that put it uncompromisingly on the liberal side a century later." Originally, only church members—and the "visible elect" at that—were allowed to participate actively in the colony. Changes that culminated in the new charter opened the doors of participation to virtually all inhabitants. Those who had not been allowed to vote or to participate in running the college, the church, and the state began to have an influence.[10]

The influence of those who were not church members as well as dissenters combined with intellectual pressure to study the works of Enlightenment writers and caused a rapid theological shift. Harvard "came more and more to disregard fine points of theology"; in fact, the belief that Harvard had "already forsaken some of the fundamentals of the faith" played a large role in the founding of Yale in 1701. Enlightenment works had been "standard fare" since the beginning of the eighteenth century, and by 1723, Harvard had a "Satan's bookshelf" of rationalist authors whose works "began to form an essential part of the Harvard intellectual milieu."[11]

By the middle of the century, Harvard "in particular" was "condemned for its rationalism." In 1755, the Dudleian lectures were established "to prove, explain or shew [sic] the proper use and improvement of the principles of Natural Religion." Held once every four years, these lectures had by the end of the century taught forty years' worth of Harvard students that reason and natural religion were the core of religion and that they needed revelation only to speed up the progress of moral science. The transformation of Harvard during this period was so complete that the last Dudleian lecture of the century (in 1799) was a defense of religion against atheism spawned by rationalism.[12] The fact that Charles Chauncy and Jonathan Mayhew were members of the Board of Overseers at Harvard is illustrative of the prevailing religious sentiment.

Ministerial candidates from Harvard "sometimes found themselves at a disadvantage because of the reputation of their alma mater." The reason was that "in increasing numbers, Harvard was graduating ministers who preached a humanistic moralism that bore little resemblance to the old orthodoxy,"[13] and many churches remained orthodox. By the latter part of the century, according to Josiah Quincy's *History of Harvard University,* the "most eminent" of the clergymen who "openly avowed . . . Arminianism, Arianism, Pelagianism, Socinianism, and Deism" were alumni from Harvard. Quincy asserted that "the influences of the institution were not unfavorable to the extension of such doctrines." Graduates testified that "the tendency of all classes was to skepticism," and they spoke of "the infidel and irreligious spirit, which prevailed at that period among the students at Cambridge."[14] In fact, "the theological professorship was vacant for a time, skepticism prevailed, and the Sabbath was desecrated." By the end of the century, students considered atheism more attractive or possible than Calvinism, and Harvard "came to be regarded as suitable only to prepare for Unitarian pulpits."[15]

The history of Yale shows a similar growth of rationalism and natural religion through the eighteenth century. Samuel Johnson, who graduated in 1714, later attributed his rejection of orthodoxy to "the influence of the library" at Yale. Yale professors "quite freely used as texts the treatises of rationalist philosophers" and those that "rested almost wholly upon principles of natural religion" from the middle to the end of the century. After his graduation, Lyman Beecher recalled that near the close of the century at Yale, "most of the students were skeptical" and "the college church was almost extinct."[16] When Timothy Dwight, who was orthodox, became president of Yale in 1795, "conditions [of orthodoxy] were regarded as deplorable. European rationalistic philosophers were popular and students considered it smart to be called by the name of some 'infidel.' Traditional religious teachings were openly questioned, and membership in the college church dwindled."[17] As will become evident, by the Revolutionary period and continuing through the Founding era, the universities certainly made their presence felt in the pulpits.

According to Edmund Morgan, "Ministers who had spent their lives in the study of theology and who had perhaps been touched by the Enlightenment . . . were already several steps down the road that led to Arminianism, Universalism, Unitarianism, and deism." The first three of these terms were theological names for elements of theistic rationalism. Conrad Wright has identified Arminians as "supernatural rationalists" (akin to theistic rationalists) who "believed in the soundness of natural religion, but . . . also admitted the claims of revealed religion."[18] One can see the three constituent elements of theistic rationalism in that description.

Basil Willey has noted that "Priestley in his development from Calvinism to Unitarianism merely illustrates in epitome what was going on widely amongst the dissenting congregations in the eighteenth century."[19] A few numerical estimates help to illustrate the situation in America. It has been estimated that from 1730 to 1750, a total of thirty-three ministers "had adopted more or less distinctly some form of Arminianism or Arianism" and stopped teaching Calvinism. Wright lists sixty ministers who were known to be Arminians and concludes that there were "doubtless as many more whose Arminianism cannot now be proved, since they published little." In contrast, he finds only twenty-one who remained orthodox among the most prominent ministers.[20]

The orthodox—those who remained true to the doctrines that composed Christianity in eighteenth-century America—saw all of the rational religions as centers of "infidelity." For example, Timothy Dwight, who was Jonathan Edwards's grandson and "the leader of conservative theology in New England," equated "infidelity" with "deism, Unitarianism, or religious liberalism of any kind" and "modern liberality" with "mere indifference to truth and error." Modern scholars have also concluded that "to orthodox Presbyterians and Episcopalians and to evangelical Methodists and Baptists alike, the distinctions between atheism, deism, and Unitarianism were only a quibble."[21] All of the rationalist ministers were unitarian, so they were colleagues with atheists and deists as far as the orthodox were concerned.

One need not dig too deeply to find the attitude of the orthodox toward the rationalist ministers. Whitefield reported in his journal: "The Lord gave me to open my Mouth boldly, against unconverted Ministers. . . . *For I am verily persuaded, the Generality of Preachers talk of an unknown, unfelt Christ.*"[22] Similarly, Gilbert Tennent "was often heard to declare that the greatest part of the ministers of New England were carnal, unconverted men."[23] James Davenport reportedly prayed: "Good LORD, . . . I will not mince the Matter any longer with thee, for thou knowest that I know, that the most of the Ministers of the Town of *BOSTON* and the *COUNTRY* are unconverted, and are leading their People blindfold to Hell."[24] The Reverend James Madison, cousin of the Madison in this study, was the first bishop of the Episcopal Church in Virginia but was alternately called an atheist and a deist.[25]

Dwight sermonized on "The Present Dangers of Infidelity" and delineated those dangers as he saw them. Quoting John 3:19–20, he argued that one cause of the infidelity of the rationalists was *"the opposition of a heart which loves sin, and dreads the punishment of it, to that truth which, with infinite authority, and under an immense penalty, demands of all men a holy life."* According to Dwight, the other primary cause was *"philosophists; the authors of vain and deceitful philosophy; of science falsely so called; . . . alluring others, . . . promising them liberty, as their reward, and yet being themselves, and making their disciples, the lowest and most wretched of all slaves, the slaves of corruption"* (italics in the original).[26] He further argued: "Infidelity has been assumed because it was loved, and not because it was *supported by evidence;* and has been maintained and defended, *to quiet the mind in sin,* and *to indulge the pride of talents and speculation.* . . . It has, in three things at least, preserved a general consistency: *opposition to Christianity, devotion to sin and lust,* and *a pompous profession of love to Liberty"* (italics in the original).[27] He charged that the work of the rationalists had been presented "under the form of new systems of philosophy; which, if believed, are utterly subversive of Christianity, but in which no direct attack is made on Christianity." To Dwight, then, their methods were deceptive and all the more despicable. He criticized their use of "wholly abstract" terms (God-words) and "phraseology so mysterious" that the reader was "lost in a mist of doubtful expressions and unsettled sentiments." He said that "while they 'cursed their God, and looked upward,' they announced themselves worshippers of the *Supreme Being.*" He saved his greatest scorn for the "graver ones" who "through an affected tenderness for the votaries of Christianity, adopted a more decent manner of despising it"—in other words, the ministers.[28]

By the eighteenth century, religious authorities no longer held political power, and the options for sanctioning heretical ministers were few. Peer pressure and shame were about the only means available. To cite one example, Jonathan Mayhew's ordination had to be rescheduled because an insufficient number of ministers attended. That simply delayed the ordination, however, for enough like-minded ministers eventually got together to ordain him. "Now and then a man of more pronounced convictions and utterance was shunned by his ministerial neighbors, but this rarely occurred and had little practical effect. So long as a preacher gave satisfaction to his own congregation, and had behind him the voters and the tax-list of his town, his heresies were passed by with only comment and gossip."[29] With seminarians being trained in theistic rationalism, those holding true to orthodox Christianity rapidly became the minority, and even those means of punishment were removed.

Doctrinal deviation began with attacks on the controversial doctrines of Calvinism—election, foreordination, and total depravity. These were doctrines that separated denominations, but they were not considered central to Christianity itself. Men could disagree on these issues and still be Christians by the standards of the day. Attacks on these doctrines were only the beginning, however. Eventually, the theistic rationalists assaulted nearly every fundamental doctrine of Christianity. Henry May explained: "The religion of the New England Arminians, as it had been worked out by 1750, was the moderate English rationalism adapted to a Calvinist audience. . . . Thirty years later, their rationalism was to lead them farther afield, to a denial of Hell and a tacit disbelief in the Trinity."[30] Actually, it did not take thirty years for many of them. According to Mayhew's early biographer, there were at least thirty-three preachers in his day who "openly opposed or quietly refrained from teaching and advocating" the "Trinitarian theology."[31]

Englishman Thomas Emlyn's defense of unitarianism was republished in Boston in 1756. Samuel Webster published a pamphlet openly and vehemently attacking original sin in 1757. A Congregationalist minister named John Rogers was dismissed from his pulpit for "not believing the Divinity of Christ" in 1758. In 1759, Joseph Bellamy said of those here called theistic rationalists that "too many" ministers had "fallen in with them" and that the doctrine of the Trinity had been "publicly treated" in a manner "not only heretical, but highly blasphemous." A year later, Bellamy complained that "this party" wanted to change the catechism "to alter, or entirely leave out, the doctrine of the Trinity, of the decrees of our first parents being created holy, of original sin, Christ satisfying divine justice, effectual calling, justification," and other doctrines. A group of New Hampshire churches did, in fact, publish a revision of the Shorter Catechism that omitted the doctrine of the Trinity.[32]

In the decades leading up to and including the Founding era, the theistic rationalist ministers were more open and less apologetic in their renunciation of Christian doctrine. Indeed, the denial of Christian doctrine by outspoken and influential ministers became an open secret. Alden Bradford identified by name fifty such ministers at the time of Jonathan Mayhew's ordination in 1747, including a number of those mentioned in this study: Mayhew, Ebenezer Gay, Charles Chauncy, Samuel Cooke, Samuel Webster, John Tucker, Gad Hitchcock, Samuel Cooper, Simeon Howard, and Samuel West. Samuel Hopkins told a Boston congregation that disbelief in and/or neglect of the deity of Christ was rampant among Boston ministers. The prestigious *Sprague's Annals* included Gay, Chauncy, Mayhew, Hitchcock, Howard, and West among those who openly rejected the Trinity. An early history of Boston's West Church recorded that Simeon Howard was both an Arminian and an Arian and that he was "a believer neither in the Trinity" nor the doctrines of Calvinism nor that of "necessary ruin to any human soul."[33]

Arianism was the most common variety of anti-Trinitarianism in the eighteenth century. Arianism taught that Christ was a created being who was inferior to God but superior to man. The Arian heresy spread rapidly through America. The other option for anti-Trinitarians was Socinianism, which taught that Christ was just a man. It was best exemplified in Joseph Priestley. Some referred to Christ as "the Son of God" in order "to emphasize his subordination to the Father." Another method of emphasizing the mere humanity of Jesus was to refer to Him as "Jesus of Nazareth," which put the stress on His earthly origin and existence. For Christians, the Trinity doctrine was not merely a debate topic. As Henry May observed, "The most central doctrines of their faith depended on the full divinity and sonship of Christ and the continuing inspiration of the Holy Spirit."[34]

Once the deity of Christ was cast aside, the theistic rationalists were free to assign to him whatever role their reason demanded. Given the nature of God and of man that they considered reasonable, their rationalism led them to develop an anti-Christian notion of "salvation" and, particularly, of the atonement. "If man was essentially good, as the Unitarians believed, no such drastic measure as the crucifixion of Christ was required for atonement. The orthodox doctrine of atonement, the Unitarians thought, was not only based on a false idea of man's character, but also implied cruelty on the part of God, who, according to the conception they had become accustomed to, was infinitely benevolent."[35] In their view, "Christ's death serves as an example to sinners, warning them of the horrible nature and consequences of sin." They rejected the Christian doctrine that Christ's death was a necessary satisfaction of God's justice and that men are justified by the imputation of Christ's righteousness on behalf of those who believe. The theistic rationalists' view "enabled them to reject the imputation of the righteousness of Christ and to emphasize the benevolence of God, without making Christ superfluous." For the theistic rationalists, "Christ finally became simply the source of revelation from God, who inspires men by his example"[36] or simply an exemplary moral teacher.

Given their presuppositions about the benevolence of God and the moralizing purpose of religion, the theistic rationalists had to develop their own concepts of salvation. Their rationalism eventually caused them to repudiate the Christian concepts of hell and eternal punishment, as well.

> God's goodness is shown most clearly in the salvation of human souls. Should any man be condemned to eternal punishment, God would have to be regarded as less than infinitely benevolent. . . . The Arminians disputed the notion that God punishes men vengefully because his justice must be satisfied. Punishment is for discipline; and if moral progress can be achieved without exacting the last measure of retribution, God will remit the penalty which men deserve on the score of strict justice.[37]

The rational conclusion was that asserted by Chauncy: all men will eventually be saved and enter eternal bliss. Though the theistic rationalists believed in punishment after death, they did not believe it would be—or could be—eternal.

Before grafting political principles to their belief system, the theistic rationalists pruned away all of the elements of Christianity that would not thrive in the light of rationalism. The end result was a distinctly different plant, a hybrid whose main stalk was formed of political principles.

POLITICAL PULPITS

In 1747, Jonathan Edwards called for concerted prayer to reverse moral decay. Forty years later, a group of ministers made a similar call for the same purpose, but "in addition to the necessity of renewed piety, these ministers called for incessant prayer that 'the spirit of true republican government may universally pervade the citizens of the United States.' For the same moral cancer which Edwards had diagnosed, they prayed that God would send the healing of 'true political virtue.'"[38] This anecdote illustrates the extent to which liberal democratic and republican political principles pervaded the thinking of the Founding era ministers. As Nathan Hatch has observed, "Few New England clergymen throughout the eighteenth century avoided the charge that they made politics, rather than divinity, their study." According to Patricia Bonomi, "A few preachers apologized for the excessive political content of their sermons, but most simply pointed to the widely accepted belief that human liberty was of divine origin."[39]

Bonomi has demonstrated that clergymen influenced public opinion by discussing political issues from pulpits outside New England, as well. She has determined that the "sermon literature of the 1770s—north and south . . . shows a striking uniformity of language and belief. Nearly every sermon addressed the political crisis, and did so in the idiom of the radical whigs." According to Bonomi, "Clergymen throughout the colonies" preached opposition to passive obedience to political authority.[40]

> Preachers in colonies outside New England . . . also used their pulpits as drums for politics. John Adams was delighted to discover in 1775 that the Philadelphia ministers "thunder and lighten every sabbath" against British oppression. When the House of Burgesses appointed a day of fasting and prayer in 1774 to rouse Virginians against the closing of Boston's port, Thomas Jefferson recorded that the pulpit oratory ran "like a shock of electricity" through the whole colony.[41]

Bonomi has also noted that many middle colony preachers sat on committees of correspondence and that three-fourths of the Anglican clergy in South Carolina supported the Revolution, along with a "similar proportion" of the Anglican clergy of Virginia.[42]

Accounts from the period support Bonomi's claims. In 1775, John Adams reported from Philadelphia: "The clergy of all denominations here preached upon politics and war in a manner that I never heard in New England. They are a flame of fire." In 1776, according to the rector of a New York church, "the Presbyterian ministers, at a Synod where most of them in the middle colonies were collected, passed a resolve to support the Continental Congress in all their measures." A Tory recorded a complaint about the Presbyterian ministers: "The few who pretend to preach are mere retailers of politics, sowers of sedition and rebellion, serve to blow the cole [sic] of discord and excite the people to arms." His assessment was supported by a 1783 pastoral letter of the Presbyterian Synod of New York and Philadelphia, which included this commendation: "We cannot help congratulating you on the general and almost universal attachment of the Presbyterian body to the cause of liberty and the rights of mankind."[43]

For many during the middle of the eighteenth century, the cause of liberty became as sacred as their religious beliefs. Ministers used political metaphors to explain religion, and ultimate priority was given to civil liberty. By the time of the Revolution, "the real center of New England's intellectual universe had become the ideals of liberty defined by the eighteenth-century Real Whig tradition."[44] Using Nathaniel Niles's example as indicative of the patriotic preachers, Cushing Strout explained that Niles "had infused the gospel with a political commitment not intrinsic to it but to his own loyalties to American patriots." Strout further explained that the Whigs and the ministers "spoke overlapping but different languages that enabled them to cooperate, but it was the clergy who had learned the most from the collaboration by politicizing the gospel to suit the revolutionary cause."[45]

In her classic work entitled *The New England Clergy and the American Revolution*, Alice Baldwin argued that the clergy "preserved, extended, and popularized the essential doctrines" of liberal democratic theory and reinterpreted the Bible "in the light of new philosophy." They taught not only that their congregants had rights but also that those rights were "sacred" and that "to preserve them they had a legal right of resistance." The patriotic preachers, then, gave "religious sanction" to the liberal democratic theories.[46] Daniel Leonard made the same point during the period in his pamphlet *Massachusettensis:* "What effect must it have had upon the audience to hear the same sentiments and principles, which they had before read in a newspaper, delivered on Sundays from the sacred desk, with a religious awe, and the most solemn appeals to heaven, from lips which they had been taught, from their cradles, to believe could utter nothing but eternal truths?"[47] Leonard put his finger on the reason that the pulpit was such an effective tool for the Revolutionaries.

And it was an effective tool of persuasion and motivation for the Revolutionary cause. According to Baldwin, the preachers were "able and zealous propagandists" who gave "warmth and color to the cause." More important, "With a vocabulary enriched by the Bible they made resistance and at last independence and war a holy cause."[48] As Bonomi explained, "Patriotic clergymen told their congregations that failure to oppose British tyranny would be an offense in the sight of Heaven. . . . By turning colonial resistance into a righteous cause, and by crying the message to all ranks in all parts of the colonies, ministers did the work of secular radicalism and did it better; they resolved doubts, overcame inertia, fired the heart, and exalted the soul."[49] Preachers were particularly valuable heralds of the cause on the frontier, "carrying the whig gospel to hamlets and homesteads beyond the reach of newspapers and committees of correspondence." The Continental Congress even sponsored a trip to the frontier by ministers to "woo settlers to the patriot side."[50]

After the Revolution, the pulpits remained prominent sources of political socialization for the young republic. The Founders saw religion as the ultimate source for the moral training necessary for a republican form of government. Specifically, "political leaders saw churches as schools in which the faithful could be educated to overcome their arrogance and selfishness, to develop concern for others, and to be ready to accept public responsibility. Civic virtue, which republican theorists would so heavily emphasize, more readily sprang from sectarian religious training than from any other source."[51] Whether exciting the people to revolt or encouraging stability through the teaching of civic virtue, the pulpit was a critical element in the American Founding era and a most effective platform for the transmission of theistic rationalism.

One might well ask how the ministers could have such a profound influence if theistic rationalism was an elite belief system and did not appeal to the masses. The answer is that the ministers were savvy enough not to teach and preach full-fledged theistic rationalism right away. They introduced it gradually, beginning with elements that were more popularly acceptable. This has happened in thousands of churches across America down through the years. Churches and entire denominations have gradually become less orthodox. One need only think of the recent controversy over homosexual bishops in the Episcopal Church or changes in various denominations regarding the role of women. The eighteenth-century ministers packaged their theistic rationalist message in digestable bites. The key aspect of this for our purposes is that the people largely *wanted* to affirm the theistic rationalists' *political* message. They therefore tended to be willing to overlook the changes in method and to enthusiastically embrace creative interpretations of Scripture that gave them permission to do what they really wanted to do anyway.

HERMENEUTICS

The fusion of liberal democratic theory with theistic rationalism on the part of the patriotic preachers is evident in an analysis of their sermons. Before beginning to analyze sermons, however, one should attempt to discern the hermeneutics employed by the authors. The hermeneutic used by the Founding era preachers was best expressed by Charles Turner in 1773: "The Scriptures cannot be rightfully expounded without explaining them in a manner friendly to the cause of freedom."[52] Actually, although *spiritual* freedom from sin is a very important biblical concept, the cause of political freedom (which is what Turner referred to) is of little consequence in the Bible.

In fact, the Bible *never* discusses political freedom. Tory minister Jonathan Boucher correctly noted, "The word *liberty*, as meaning civil liberty, does not, I believe, occur in all the Scriptures."[53] The Founding era preachers appealed to the Exodus of Israelites from Egypt and to selected New Testament verses. An attentive reading of the text reveals that God's desire that Israel have political freedom was never given as a reason for the Exodus. God's purposes were to free his people to worship him (see, for example, Exodus 4:23, 5:1 and 3, 7:16) and to force Egypt to recognize him as the true God (Exodus 5:2, 7:5 and 17, 10:2). Similarly, the verses quoted by the Founding era preachers in support of political liberty actually extol *spiritual* liberty—freedom from *sin* (2 Corinthians 3:17, Galatians 5:1 and 13, and John 8:32). Phillips Payson and other ministers recognized the difference but proceeded to make the political application anyway.[54] The principles of liberal democracy had so replaced those of the Gospel that they became a prism through which Scripture was read.

When reading these sermons carefully, one is struck by the frequency with which passages of Scripture are interpreted in a manner convenient to the argument being made but unrelated or opposed to their clear sense. Whether expounding upon a historical example or a statement of doctrine, the ministers were little concerned with standard rules of interpretation, such as adherence to context, comparison with similar passages, and fidelity to the plain meaning of a passage when the terms were not ambiguous.

For instance, Samuel West was forced into several pages of contradictory statements concerning the necessity of obeying rulers because he began by stating the clear sense of Titus 3:1 and Romans 13 but then, to make democratic arguments, had to conclude that the apostle Paul meant the opposite of what he said.[55] West was following in the footsteps of Jonathan Mayhew, whose classic 1750 sermon *A Discourse Concerning Unlimited Submission to the Higher Powers* purports to be an exposition of Romans 13 but actually "interprets" Paul to mean exactly the opposite of what the text unambiguously says. Even scholars who find Christianity in support of liberal democratic theory, such as Harry Jaffa, admit that "for more than a millennium and a half of the history of the Christian West, the prevailing opinion was that political authority descended from the top down, from God to kings and rulers, and that the obligation of the ruled was simply to obey." Jaffa attributed that opinion directly to centuries of reading of Romans 13 and 1 Peter 2 literally.[56]

Jaffa explained that, according to Paul, all who possess power have the right to rule and there is no distinction between just and unjust governments. As subjects, "we have no more choice of our rulers than of our parents." Paul and Peter accepted the imperial regime of Rome "apparently without qualification," and they "do not envisage the least participation in government by the governed." Furthermore, the "responsibility of the ruled to the rulers is unconditional. The rulers are responsible to God alone."[57]

Other scholars have similarly asserted that the ministers "invoked St. Paul's doctrine against itself." In fact, Steven Dworetz suggests:

> Basing a revolutionary teaching on the scriptural authority of chapter 13 of St. Paul's Epistle to the Romans must rank as one of the greatest ironies in the history of political thought. This passage . . . served as the touchstone for passive obedience and unconditional submission from Augustine and Gregory to Luther and Calvin. . . . The medieval church fathers as well as the reformers and counter-reformers of the sixteenth century all invoked this doctrine in denouncing disobedience and resistance to civil authorities.[58]

Ministers who remained loyal to Great Britain argued from the "very simply constructed text" of 1 Peter 2 and the accepted, literal reading of Romans 13. For example, Samuel Seabury admonished his audience: "Our duty to obey our Rulers and Governors arises from our Duty to obey God. He has commanded us to obey Magistrates; to honor all Men according to their Degree in Authority. If we fear God we shall obey his Command from a Principle of Duty to him.—Civil Government is the Institution and Ordinance of God:—He hath ordained the Powers that are."[59] Seabury also reminded his listeners that Peter and Paul "commanded Honor and Respect," "Duty and Submission" to heathen emperors—"even to Nero and Caligula." Jonathan Boucher got to the heart of the issue and Paul's primary point: "When Christians are disobedient to human ordinances, they are also disobedient to God."[60]

Although it was rarely, if ever, done at the time, scholars today have invoked a "lesser magistrate exception" as a justification for rebellion in support of lower-level magistrates. It is based on the misapplication of a remark by John Calvin. In his *Institutes of the Christian Religion*, Calvin taught the opposite of revolutionary theory and made it abundantly clear that rebellion was never justified. He declared that "whatever they are and however they govern," magistrates derive their authority "from him [God] alone." He added, "If we keep firmly in mind that even the very worst kings are appointed by this same decree which establishes the authority of kings [in general], then we will never permit ourselves the seditious idea that a king is to be treated according to his deserts, or that we need not obey a king who does not conduct himself towards us like a king."[61] Calvin also said that "we are to be subject not only to the authority of those princes who do their duty towards us as they should, and uprightly, but to all of them, however they came by their office, even if the very last thing they do is act like [true] princes." "We must honour [even] the worst tyrant in the office in which the Lord has seen fit to set him," he contended, and "if you go on to infer that only just governments are to be repaid by obedience, your reasoning is stupid." Calvin, like Boucher, warned: "Make no mistake: it is impossible to resist the magistrate without also resisting God."[62] Finally, Calvin said:

> As for us . . . let us take the greatest possible care never to hold in contempt, or trespass upon, that plenitude of authority of magistrates whose majesty it is for us to venerate and which God has confirmed by the most weighty pronouncements, *even when it is exercised by individuals who are wholly unworthy of it* and who do their best to defile it by their wickedness. And even if the punishment of unbridled tyranny is the Lord's vengeance [on tyrants], *we are not to imagine that it is we ourselves who have been called upon to inflict it. All that has been assigned to us is to obey and suffer.* (Emphasis mine.)[63]

So what is the basis for the so-called lesser magistrate exception? The passage immediately following the extended quote has been misapplied. Calvin explained that *if,* within the system of government, there were "magistrates established to defend the people" and "to restrain the licentiousness of kings," then they should act "in accordance with their duty" to restrain "the licentiousness and frenzy of kings."[64] So that he would not be misinterpreted, he gave historical examples of officials who were part of their respective governmental systems and were expressly given the authority to restrain rulers. He never used any form of the words *rebel* or *revolt,* however. Their actions were legal and a recognized part of the system of government—akin to the power of the Congress to impeach and remove the American president. One cannot legitimately employ Calvin to justify rebellion, which is why the patriotic preachers argued in the terms of "Mr. Locke's doctrine"[65] rather than Calvin's.

The other interpretive element that must be discussed is the preachers' emphasis on reason and nature. Their sermons relegated revelation to a secondary status, as it was not considered reliable or applicable unless it comported with reason and/or nature. Indeed, references to Scripture or revelation were almost invariably made in the context of agreement with reason or nature or both. I am not suggesting that arguments based on reason are invalid; rather, contrary to what one would expect, these arguments were made by *preachers* in *sermons* and far outnumber and outweigh appeals to Scripture.

Samuel Cooke appealed to "reason and experience" to determine the best form of government, and he argued that men "can be subjected to no human restrictions which are not founded in reason." His equating of "the voice of nature" with "the voice of God" reveals the depth of his reliance upon nature.[66] In his discussion of Romans 13, Samuel West put revelation in its place—second to reason: "The doctrine of non-resistance and unlimited passive obedience to the worst of tyrants could never have found credit among mankind had the voice of reason been hearkened to for a guide, because such a doctrine would immediately have been discerned to be contrary to natural law."[67] Whereas Cooke equated the voice of nature with the voice of God, West equated reason with the voice of God and said that "whatever right reason requires as necessary to be done is as much the will and law of God as though it were enjoined us by an immediate revelation from heaven, or commanded in the sacred Scriptures." Biblical revelation could not be superior to reason, according to West, who repeatedly emphasized the preeminence of "reason and common sense" as the proper standard for action. Finally, concerning political matters, West taught that the clergy had to "thoroughly study the law of nature" in order to perform "the right and faithful discharge of this part of our ministry."[68] Clearly, biblical revelation was not sufficient.

Revelation was not sufficient for other preachers, either. Discussing the ultimate argument in support of a position, Simeon Howard stated, "There is, I apprehend, nothing in this supposition inconsistent with the principles of rational theology and natural religion." John Tucker, like Cooke and West, equated nature and reason with God: "It is the dictate of nature:—It is the voice of reason, which may be said to be the voice of God."[69] Taking another route to the same destination, Gad Hitchcock effectively denuded part of Scripture by removing its supernaturally revealed status when he referred to Romans 13 as Paul's "rational point of view."[70] Samuel Cooper went one logical step further and made conformity to reason the test of the validity of Scripture: "These are the plain dictates of that reason and common sense with which the common parent of men has informed the human bosom. It is, however, a satisfaction to observe such everlasting maxims of equity confirmed, and impressed upon the consciences of men, by the instructions, precepts, and examples given us in the sacred oracles; one internal mark of their divine original, and that they come from him."[71] We have already established that, for the theistic rationalists, reason was the standard for determining legitimate revelation. In the pre-1750 pulpit, the converse was true: conformity to Scripture was considered the test of reason. Cooper maintained that his were "the principles . . . which reason and scripture will forever sanctify"; but his references were to Sidney, Locke, and even the atheist Voltaire—not to Moses, Paul, and Jesus.[72]

LOCKE AND LIBERAL DEMOCRATIC THEORY

Steven Dworetz has said that "the clergy's indispensable contribution to the Revolution . . . cannot be fully understood without reference to Locke and, indeed, to the Locke of theistic liberalism."[73] The debt owed by the Founding era clergy to Locke has been recognized by virtually every student of the sermons of the period.[74] Observers have been surprised by the frequency with which his "very phrases" or "exact words" were used.[75] As Michael Zuckert has noted, "The best and most thorough surveys of clerical writing and sermonizing of the second two quarters of the eighteenth century show . . . both that the preachers spoke out regularly and vociferously on politics, and that they . . . spoke the language of Locke and the natural rights philosophy." Furthermore, "when the divines of the eighteenth

century endorsed the Lockean doctrine of the harmonious relationship between reason and revelation, the self-sufficiency of reason in the political
sphere, and the primacy of a rational hermeneutic, they were enacting a
substantial break with the reigning political theology of the previous century."[76] Zuckert correctly identifies the emphasis on reason and the rational
hermeneutic as the major difference between the political theology of the
theistic rationalist ministers and that of the previous century.

Although many suggest a Puritan origin for Lockean liberalism, Zuckert astutely observes that "Lockean principles are no mere continuation
of Protestant principles, either in their Lutheran or their Calvinist vari-
ant." Given the theoretical distance between them, it has been suggested
that it was "no small interpretive feat to refashion the Puritans in Lockean
garb."[77] A significant dose of Enlightenment thought had to be absorbed
by the eighteenth-century descendants of the Puritans to accomplish the
transformation.

In his account of the dominance of Lockean thought, Dworetz recognizes
that Locke and the eighteenth-century clergy had "similar 'religious preoccupations'" and shared a "general philosophical perspective." He argues
that the clergy used Locke not simply because his views were useful but also
because they had an "informed appreciation for the theistic framework of
'religious preoccupations' and 'theological commitments' within which that
argument was essentially embedded." The relationship between reason and
revelation was the key. As a result of their natural connection, "the ministers conveyed the Lockean message, regularly and with great moral authority, to their congregations, by whom they were taken very seriously indeed."
Consequently, most Americans knew Lockean political theory without having read Locke.[78]

Zuckert agrees that Locke was dominant, but he argues for "a Lockean
conquest, or at least assimilation, of Puritan political thought." His fundamental reasoning is simple but persuasive: "Before Locke, the Puritans
said one sort of thing about politics; after Locke, they said quite different
sorts of things, which turn out to be the same things Locke said, in more or
less the language of Locke."[79] Though he recognizes elements of Christian
influence in the ministers' presentation of Locke, his observations leave no
doubt as to the weightier influence:

Dependent as the ministers are on Locke, their political sermons do
often add elements to Locke of a loosely Christian character. . . . What
is most remarkable, however, about the clerical modifications is how
shallow they are, how little they really change or add. It would not be

correct to say they are merely rhetorical, but it would be incorrect to say that Lockean doctrine is substantially Christianized by their patronage of it.[80]

Zuckert's summary of the differences between the ministers and Locke reflects their theistic rationalism. First, they appealed to Scripture to a greater extent than did Locke. Second, they emphasized divine Providence to a greater extent. Third, they emphasized religion's potential contribution to society and its role as a necessary support of society to a much greater extent than did Locke.[81] In fact, at the end of his summary, Zuckert questions whether "Puritan" thinkers could still be "rightly called" Puritans after the later years of the seventeenth century because of their emphasis on natural religion "as a supplement, if not a replacement, for the older scriptural theology." He calls the result "a 'rational Christianity' related to the Bible, yet deploying reason all along the way."[82] Since it bears little resemblance to Christianity, I call it theistic rationalism.

The writings of Locke and the social contract theorists were a critical, almost ubiquitous, influence on the occupants of the pulpits in the Founding era. Many of them clearly owed more to Locke than to the Holy Spirit when it came to political exhortation. To begin with, Locke's vision of the *state of nature* constituted—or at least heavily informed—their concept of the origin of society.

State of Nature

In his 1770 election sermon, Samuel Cooke presupposed a state of nature and gave a very Lockean description of it. Simeon Howard also posited the existence of a state of nature and described life in the state of nature in a manner that borrowed from Locke and Hobbes. John Tucker, Gad Hitchcock,[83] and Moses Mather[84] based arguments on the assumption of a state of nature, and Zabdiel Adams, like Hobbes, equated the state of nature with a state of war.[85]

Likewise, Samuel West recognized the state of nature and appeared to equate it with Eden before the Fall. Rather than relying on the biblical account, however, he identified "Mr. Locke" as the best source for its description. West's account illustrates the contradictory nature of the hybrid religion of the period, as he struggled to blend the Enlightenment version of the law of nature with the ethics of faith: "The law of nature gives men no right to do anything that is immoral, or contrary to the will of God, and injurious to their fellow-creatures; for a state of nature is properly a state of law and government, even a government founded upon the unchange-able nature of the Deity, and a law resulting from the eternal fitness of things."[86] Of course, he would not want to call attention to the biblical ac-count because, as Walter Berns has noted, "the idea of the state of nature is incompatible with Christian doctrine."[87] The biblical account of Eden, the Fall, and the origin of human society bears little resemblance to a world of free agents restrained only by natural law forming society on the basis of voluntary consent. As will be discussed, the liberal democratic emphasis on self-preservation also runs contrary to the core beliefs of Christianity.

Equality

The Founding era preachers not only borrowed Locke's concept of a state of nature, they also drew the same conclusions from it. The foremost of such conclusions was the essential *equality* of man. They reminded listeners that the state of nature is "a state in which all are equal" and that "a soci-ety emerging from a state of nature, in respect to authority, are all upon a level."[88] Some tried to make a theological argument that would support the claims of equality. Concerning a faithful ruler, Cooke said, "He will not for-get that he ruleth over men,—men who are of the same species with himself, and by nature equal,—men who are the offspring of God, and alike formed after his glorious image,—men of like passions and feelings with himself, and, as men, in the sight of their common Creator of equal importance."[89] In a similar vein, he stressed that rulers must "stand before the dread tribu-nal of Heaven" and "lie down in the dust" "without distinction." For their part, Howard and Tucker emphasized Locke's contention that all in the state of nature have an equal right or claim to liberty. And Cooper emphasized that the principle of equality was not gleaned from Scripture: "We want not . . . a special revelation from heaven to teach us that men are born equal and free. . . . These are the plain dictates of that reason and common sense with which the common parent of men has informed the human bosom."[90]

Consent

The Founding era preachers also stressed the Lockean concept of *consent.* Some emphasized individual consent with regard to rights of property and taxation. Samuel West declared, "Reason and equity require that no one be obliged to pay a tax that he has never consented to, either by himself or by his representative." John Tucker made an identical argument. Moses Mather called the rights of property "sacred" and affirmed that only one's consent or the consent of one's representative could divest one of private property by any means, including taxation.[91]

In addition to individual consent, the preachers highlighted the importance of the common or general consent of the community. For most of them, the central idea was that consent conferred legitimacy upon rulers and ruling bodies. For example, Samuel Cooke said that "no individual can justly challenge a right to make or execute the laws . . . but only by the choice or general consent of the community." Moses Mather put it succinctly: "The right of dominion over the persons and properties of others, is not natural, but derived; and there are but two sources from whence it can be derived; from the almighty, who is the absolute proprietor of all, and from our own free consent."[92] For Samuel West, this was the answer to one of the classic questions of political philosophy: Why obey?[93]

Related to the legitimacy issue was the role of common consent in establishing boundaries for civil rulers. John Tucker put it this way: "Rulers, receiving their authority originally and solely from the people, can be rightfully possessed of no more, than these have consented to, and conveyed to them." He maintained that the "fundamental laws" to which the people consent "fix the chief lines and boundaries between the authority of Rulers, and the liberties and privileges of the people."[94] Ezra Stiles, Gad Hitchcock, and Zabdiel Adams went so far as to suggest that God Himself voluntarily observed limits circumscribed by the consent of the governed. Stiles argued that God could have "dictated" a law of "invincible force and obligation without any reference to the consent of the governed" but instead "condescended to a mutual covenant" and "thereupon" "took them for a peculiar people to himself." Hitchcock said that to suggest that God would require obedience to those who rule without consent "is representing him [God] under the horrid character of a tyrant." Adams said of God's relationship with the Israelites that "he would not rule them in a manner contrary to their own inclination." He summed up the application of the principle to civil rulers: "It concerns rulers . . . to keep within the boundaries established by common consent." On a more positive note, Adams pointed out that, in addition to its role in reining in rulers, consent gives "energy and power" to government through the support it provides.[95]

Law of Self-Preservation

Another concept that the preachers borrowed from Locke and the social contract theorists was the idea that there is a "principle" or "law" of self-preservation that motivates and, occasionally, justifies men's actions. They suggested that it was "unreasonable" to suppose that people would agree to live under a nonrepresentative system without reserving the right to withdraw from it, pointing out that if they did, "the bargain would be void, as counteracting the will of heaven, and the powerful law of self-preservation." They alternately referred to it as the "principle" and the "law" of self-preservation when urging parishioners to disobey tyrants and to oppose tyranny. West clearly indicated the source of this principle when he said that the fact that some ignore it was "a plain proof how easily men may be led to pervert the very first and plainest principles of reason and common sense" and when he identified it as "the first law of nature."[96]

Since the Gospel is centered not on self-preservation but on self-*sacrifice*, as exhibited by Jesus Christ's death for mankind and His command that His followers deny self, it is clear that liberal democracy won this battle of dogmas, as well. The first and greatest commandment in Christianity is to love God, and the second is to love one's neighbor as one's self. In the state of nature, however, a man has no obligation to love anyone and is urged "*to preserve the rest of Mankind*" only "when his own Preservation comes not in competition."[97]

Popular Sovereignty

The Founding era preachers also chose Locke's concept of popular sovereignty over the orthodox Christian teaching that God is the source of governmental authority. Some merely proceeded with popular sovereignty as a given; others tried to find popular sovereignty in biblical texts and, thereby, "harmonize" liberal democratic theory with Scripture. The result of that effort is an example of the hybrid religion that emerged from this period.

Phillips Payson did not try to "prove" the truth of popular sovereignty from the Bible. He simply asserted that "a free and righteous government originates from the people, and is under their direction and control." He referred to governmental power as a "delegation" from the people, and in addressing members of the Massachusetts legislature who were in his audience, he reminded them that the people had delegated "their [the people's] powers" to them. After a discussion of history, not Scripture, Ezra Stiles declared, "With the people . . . resides the aggregate of original power." Samuel Langdon reiterated the principle, stating, "The power in all our republics is acknowledged to originate in the people."[98]

Some affirmed popular sovereignty but also attributed a role to God in delegating authority. According to Simeon Howard, "The magistrate is properly the trustee of the people. He can have no just power but what he receives from them." When reminding officeholders in his audience that their powers were "delegated to them by the people," however, he identified God as "the origin of all power." Zabdiel Adams made the same point: "Under God, the original source of all power, mankind enjoy, or ought to do so, the liberty of governing themselves. The powers of government are vested in the body of the people."[99] Moses Mather echoed Howard and Adams, claiming, "Government originates (under God) from the people; as from its native source."[100] Though recognizing that God had some unspecified role in delegating authority, these preachers did not explain how God and the people could both be simultaneously sovereign and the source of governmental power.

Other preachers of the hybrid religion did attempt to make Locke "square" with revelation. To do so, they had to reinterpret the two New Testament passages that were most commonly—and historically—interpreted in a manner that precluded popular sovereignty: 1 Peter 2:13–14 and Romans 13:1–2. John Tucker showed the way by interspersing a rather convenient interpretation with extensive quotes from Locke.

In his exposition of 1 Peter 2, Tucker defined the terms of the passage in such a way as to make the idea of popular sovereignty plausible:

> The first thing offered to our consideration is, the ORIGIN of civil government, from whence all authority in the state must take its rise. And this is said to be from man. *Submit yourselves to every ordinance of man,* etc. More intelligibly, perhaps, it might be rendered, "to every human institution or appointment." And this may be justly understood, as having respect to every kind of civil government, under whatever form it is administered:—It is the ordinance,—the institution or appointment of man.[101]

The idea that Tucker simply assumed in his definition was that every "human institution" arises from the *majority* of men, as opposed to one man or a small group of men creating a human institution through force for their own purposes. He later stated, "All right therefore in any to rule over others, must originate from those they rule over, and be granted by them. . . . Whatever authority therefore the supreme power has . . . being an authority derived from the community, and granted by them, can be justly exercised, only within certain limits, and to a certain extent, according to agreement."[102] That is, of course, true only if the "human institution" was created by the *community.* Tucker either naively or cleverly equated "the people" with "man": "Now, all Rulers in a state, and all power and authority with which they are vested;—the very being, and form of government, with all its constitutional laws, being thus from the people, hence civil government, is called, and with great propriety, the *ordinance of man,*—an human institution."[103]

Before this statement in Tucker's sermon was an extended quote from Locke; after it was reference to the Magna Carta. If Tucker really wanted to accurately interpret this material, he might instead have grappled with some of the numerous biblical passages that support subjection to nondemocratic authorities and indicate that "every human institution" includes those that were not established by "the people." For example, it would be interesting to see Tucker's explanation of Jesus's affirmation of Pilate's authority in John 19:11. Like Howard, Adams, and Mathers, Tucker affirmed that God had a role in delegating authority. But unlike them, he gave scriptural support for that idea. He quoted the first two verses of Romans 13, but his explanation of them removed any real significance from the idea that authority is "from God": "But civil government may be said to be from God . . . especially and chiefly, as civil government is founded in the very nature of man, as a social being, and in the nature and constitution of things."[104] So, God can be said to be the source of authority to about the same extent as the person who invented musical script is the source of a Beethoven symphony. For Tucker, the real source of authority was the people.

Like Tucker, Gad Hitchcock maintained that "rulers have their distinct powers assigned to them by the people, who are the only source of civil authority on earth." Following Tucker's logic, if not his entire argument, Hitchcock responded to the challenge of Romans 13 by deciding that God's role was limited to His fashioning of "the human constitution, and the circumstances men are placed in." As for government itself, he said: "But it is from man, as for the same end . . . they have, in conformity to their make and circumstances, and the dictates of reason, voluntarily instituted it. And thus the government is the ordinance both of God and man."[105] For Hitchcock as for Tucker, the people were the immediate source of authority in government, and in this regard, God resembled the watchmaker of the deists. This view misses Paul's point in Romans 13:1 and eviscerates the admonition in 13:2 against resisting the government. That is, of course, precisely what one must do to justify participation in revolution.

By the time of Samuel West's "1776 Election Sermon," these interpretations of Romans 13 and 1 Peter 2 were probably commonplace. West also assumed "human institution" to be a community creation: "Here we see that the apostle asserts that magistracy is of human creation and appointment; that is, that magistrates have no power or authority but what they derive from the people."[106] West's understanding of Romans 13 provided another portrait of the watchmaker God painted by Tucker and Hitchcock. Given their God, "civil rulers and magistrates are properly of human creation; they are set up by the people to be the guardians of their rights," and "magistrates have no authority but what they derive from the people."[107] Like those who had gone before, West made an attempt to reconcile the conflicting views of liberal democracy and Scripture regarding the source of authority: "Though magistrates are to consider themselves as the servants of the people, seeing from them it is that they derive their power and authority, yet they may also be considered as the ministers of God ordained by him for the good of mankind."[108] For the preachers of the hybrid religion of the American Founding, liberal democratic theory was their doctrine, and inconvenient revelation was either made to conform or explained away.

Of course, the literal, traditional view of Romans 13 is not a fundamental Christian doctrine, and one need not hold that view in order to be a Christian. Interpretation of that passage was critical, however, to the Christian's perspective on the legitimacy of rebellion.

Self-Determination

Closely related to the concept of popular sovereignty in liberal democratic theory is the principle of self-determination. The sovereign people have a *right* to determine which form of government to institute and to whom they will delegate power and authority. Not surprisingly, the Founding era preachers proclaimed such a right.

According to Samuel Cooke, "The Supreme Ruler . . . has directed to no particular mode of civil government . . . the particular form is left to the choice and determination of mankind." Furthermore, in his discussion of governing authority, Cooke declared, "The people, the collective body only, have a right, under God, to determine who shall exercise this trust for the common interest, and to fix the bounds of their authority."[109] Samuel Langdon recognized the same right. In addition, he expounded its source: "Thanks be to God that he has given us, as men, natural rights. . . . By the law of nature, any body of people, destitute of order and government, may form themselves into a civil society, according to their best prudence, and so provide for their common safety and advantage."[110] His effort to credit God and nature for providing this right reflects, once again, theistic rationalism.

Others, by contrast, suggested not that God was the source of the right of self-determination but that He was its guarantor: "We are reminded of the gratitude which we owe to God that he has not permitted the natural and important right which every society has of electing its own rulers to be wrested out of our hands."[111] But why is such a right important? What is its significance? Zabdiel Adams explained the importance of the right of self-determination and the consequences of its denial: "To be deprived of the power of chusing [*sic*] our rulers, is to be deprived of self dominion. If *they* are appointed over us, by those over whom we have no controul, we are in a state of slavery. . . . Indeed, it is generally allowed at the present day, by men of the first character, that the choice of the people is the only source of power."[112] Many preachers, including Ezra Stiles, Gad Hitchcock, and Moses Mather, made similar arguments. None, however, captured all the facets of the principle as succinctly as Samuel Cooper did in asserting that men "have a right freely to determine by whom and in what manner their own affairs shall be administered."[113] This was not a right that was gleaned from a careful expository study of the Bible; it was a doctrine of the liberal democratic theory that dominated the Founding era pulpit.

Social Contract

Locke's school of that liberal democratic theory is most commonly identified with the concept of the social contract. That concept was easily adaptable to Bible believers of the Founding era because it seemed to comport well with the biblical concept of *covenant*. Indeed, the Puritans had long before associated the biblical concept with church and civil polity. It is interesting to note, however, that, with few exceptions, the preachers of the Founding era spoke the language of social contract theory instead of the biblical language of the covenant. Simeon Howard, to cite one case, sounded like Locke in discussing the reservation of certain rights "which no man is supposed to give up, or may lawfully give up, when he enters into society." In his discussion of the contract, Gad Hitchcock identified one of those rights as the right to resist, in a Lockean sense, a tyrant: "It is altogether unreasonable to suppose a number of persons by a free and voluntary contract, should give up themselves, their families and estates so absolutely into the hands of any rulers, as not to make a reserve of the right of saving themselves from ruin."[114] Preachers from the Revolutionary period emphasized the contract between rulers and subjects in order to be able to claim that the king had violated the contract and to justify resistance in Lockean terms. In this context, they said of the king that "he is bound to protect and they to obey" and of the principle that "protection mutually entitles to subjection, and subjection to protection." The ministers also suggested that the compact made disobedience a "breach of faith." John Tucker summed up the preachers' view of the compact: "Hence, all government, consistent with that natural freedom, to which all have an equal claim, is founded in compact, or agreement between the parties;—between Rulers and their Subjects, and can be no otherwise."[115] The thinking of the Founding era preachers was shaped by the liberal democratic idea of the social contract. Even those who spoke of covenants, such as Samuel Cooper and Ezra Stiles,[116] emphasized the social contract elements of consent and mutual obligation. For them, the biblical examples of covenants put a revelatory stamp of approval on the social contract theory.

Rulers Accountable to People

Another idea that the preachers clearly borrowed from liberal democratic theory rather than the Bible was the notion that rulers are accountable to their people. The distinction is a function of the difference between popular sovereignty and the sovereignty of God. Biblically, rulers are accountable to God because they receive their authority and legitimacy from Him. In contrast, the preachers adhered to the liberal democratic principle that rulers receive their authority and legitimacy from the people; consequently, it follows that they should be accountable to the people. As Samuel Cooke put it, "Those in authority, in the whole of their public conduct, are accountable to the society which gave them their political existence." Similarly, Simeon Howard described the magistrate as "the trustee of the people" who received his power from them; so, "to them he ought to be accountable for the use he makes of this power." Samuel Langdon also drew the logical conclusion that, since "every magistrate and officer" received his power from the people, "to the people all in authority are accountable."[117]

Phillips Payson, like Howard, called rulers "trustees" and charged legislators with "the most sacred obligation to fidelity." According to Langdon, if leaders "betray their trust . . . reason and justice require that they should be discarded, and others appointed in their room." Cooke summed up the principle in this statement:

Rulers are appointed for this very end—to be ministers of God for good. The people have a right to expect this from them, and to require it . . . as their unquestionable due. It is the express or implicit condition upon which they were chosen and continued in public office, that they attend continually upon this very thing. Their time, their abilities, their authority—by their acceptance of the public trust—are consecrated to the community . . . they are obliged to seek the welfare of the people, and exert all their powers to promote the common interest.[118]

In the previous century, a minister would have contended that God, not the people, expected and required rulers to act for good and that rulers were "consecrated" to God, not the community. Although a form of democracy coexisted with orthodox Christianity in seventeenth-century Puritan New England, the understanding before the infusion of Lockean principles was that rulers were ultimately accountable to God rather than to the people.

The Purpose of Government

The end of the quote from Cooke introduces yet another central element of liberal democracy that contrasts with Scripture but was taught by the Founding era preachers—the idea that the end or purpose of government is to secure the common good or common interest. From Genesis 9 through Romans 13 and 1 Peter 2, the Bible teaches that the purpose of government is to restrain man's evil tendencies and propensity toward violence. There is an element of that in the liberal democratic idea that men form government for self-protection. Liberal democracy goes much further, however, in positing that government exists to secure certain rights of men and that "the people" determine for themselves what is in their interest and just what the public good is and that government exists to pursue that goal. Every sermon analyzed for this study addressed the end or purpose of government, and every one promoted the liberal democratic view.

Consistent with the aforementioned quote, Cooke declared the end of government to be "the public benefit, the good of the people; that they may be protected in their persons, and secured in the enjoyment of all their rights"—in short, "the benefit of the community." For him, every office was "constituted for the common interest," and God required pursuit of the "public good" by all rulers at all levels. Langdon recognized the right of nations to create a government "which to them may appear most conducive to their common welfare," and he asserted that when "a government is in its prime, the public good engages the attention of the whole."[119] West's discussion of the end of government is peppered with references to the "public good," the "general good," the "good of the community," the "welfare of the state," the "welfare of the public," and protection "in the enjoyment of liberty" of "just rights."[120]

According to Phillips Payson, "The voice of reason and the voice of God both teach us that the great object or end of government is the public good."

John Tucker said that the institution of civil government was "manifestly for the good of society" and that its end was "the good of the community." In a statement on this issue that would make Locke proud, Tucker said, "Nor can any other end be imagined, worthy of reasonable beings, why men should put themselves out of a state of natural freedom, and subject themselves to the authority and rule of others, but for their greater good."[121] In Cooper's emphasis, that greater good was "common security and happiness." Zabdiel Adams echoed Cooper's stress upon common happiness, asserting that "government was instituted for the happiness of the community at large." According to Moses Mather, the good of the people was the "ultimate object" of government. Finally, in a concise summation of liberal democratic theory itself, Mather proclaimed that "civil government is constituted for the good of the people, and not the people for government."[122]

Natural Rights

Intimately related to the idea of contract and to the purpose or end of government in liberal democratic theory is the guarantee of rights and freedom. Having been schooled in liberal democratic theory, the preachers of the hybrid religion placed great emphasis on rights and freedom, as well. They stressed that some rights were God given and natural to all men. Langdon expressed thanks to God for giving men, "as men, natural rights"; Samuel West spoke of "the inalienable rights that the God of nature has given us as men and rational beings." Tucker said, "All men are naturally in a state of freedom, and have an equal claim to liberty." Others referred to "the unalienable rights of men and christians" and to "natural rights and civil privileges."[123]

They also spoke in Lockean terms of the voluntary relinquishment of some rights upon entering civil society and the necessary retention of others. Listeners and readers were reminded that, according to Locke, all men in the state of nature are in "a state of perfect freedom." Men must give up their right to "perfect" freedom, but "there are certain rights of men, which are unalienable even by themselves; and others which they do not mean to alienate, when they enter into civil society." But what are these rights? According to Simeon Howard:

> The people should invest them with power to do this, so far as is consistent with the sacred and inalienable rights of conscience, which no man is supposed to give up, or may lawfully give up, when he enters into society. But, reserving these, the people may and ought to give up

every right and power to the magistrate which will enable him more efficiently to promote the common good, without putting it in his power essentially to injure it.[124]

Zabdiel Adams's suggestion was slightly different: "*Reason* and *Freedom* are our own, and given to continue so. We are to use, but cannot resign them, without rebelling against him who gave them."[125] For Adams, then, obedience to God, not just our good, required their retention. The Bible never speaks of men having rights—whether from God or any other source.

Liberty

Freedom, or liberty, was extolled in most of the sermons of the period. Protection of liberty was identified as a key motivation in the formation of civil society; civil liberty was proclaimed "the greatest of all human blessings"; and love of liberty was credited as "the cement of the political body." Individual freedoms, such as "the sacred rights of conscience" and "a decent freedom of speech," were claimed as rights "inherent in the people."[126]

Attempts to relate concepts of liberty to Christianity produced two different results. Payson suggested that "a people formed upon the morals and principles of the gospel are capacitated to enjoy the highest degree of civil liberty." Tucker, by contrast, sought to limit God by liberal democracy's demand for liberty. He said of Christ's kingdom that "none of its injunctions can be inconsistent with that love of liberty he himself has implanted in us, nor interfere with the laws and government of human societies, whose constitution is consistent with the rights of men."[127] Once again, the principles of liberal democracy became the standard by which God's kingdom was to be judged or anticipated. The fact that the Bible does not declare any rights for man or emphasize or guarantee his political liberty was not a significant problem for these ministers. Their faith in reason and democratic theory trumped the biblical record and was, to their minds, sufficient.

Confidence in the Majority

The Founding era ministers also shared Locke's confidence in the majority. Consistent with social contract theory, they said that "it is the major part of a community that have the sole right of establishing a constitution and authorizing magistrates" and that the "collective body, not a few individuals, ought to constitute the supreme authority of the state." Some went so far as to suggest that "the public is always willing to be rightly informed, and when it has proper matter of conviction laid before it its judgment is always right." "And even if the people should sometimes err, yet each assembly of the states, and the body of the people, always embosom wisdom sufficient to correct themselves; so that a political mischief cannot be durable."[128] The preachers were "sold" on this aspect of liberal democratic theory as well and even expressed perhaps greater confidence in the majority than did Locke. Previous generations of ministers did not believe such a confidence fit with the emphasis on the depravity of man in the biblical record and Calvinist theology.

Republican Government

Having accepted the presuppositions of liberal democratic theory, it was only natural for the Founding era preachers to draw the same conclusions concerning appropriate forms of government. Consequently, for large communities, they argued in favor of republican government and against any form of "arbitrary" government. Zabdiel Adams expressed the idea this way: "The ruling power of every state or kingdom should be elected by the body of the people. As no man is born a ruler, so there is no possible way for him to get regularly into office, but by the election of his fellow-citizens."[129] Samuel West's discussion of the same topic took the argument from first principles of the state of nature to the Revolutionary case against taxation without representation:

All men being by nature equal, all the members of a community have a natural right to assemble themselves together, and act and vote for such regulations as they judge are necessary for the good of the whole. But when a community is become very numerous, it is very difficult, and in many cases impossible, for all to meet together to regulate the affairs of the state; hence comes the necessity of appointing delegates to represent the people in a general assembly. And this ought to be looked upon as a sacred and inalienable right, of which no human authority can in equity ever take from them, viz., that no one be obliged to submit to any law except such as are made either by himself or by his representative.[130]

Moses Mather said it was "absurd" that a man should be subject to a government "without having any part or voice in its administration." West went on to suggest that it "becomes" him not to say which form of government is best but then immediately declared that absolute monarchy and "aristocracy not subject to the control of the people" were two of the most "exceptionable" forms. Some of the sermons discussed "democratical, aristocratical, or monarchical" types of republics and suggested that they ranged "from absolute government up to perfect liberty."[131] According to them, it was principally the hereditary nature of monarchy and aristocracy that resulted in the loss of liberty.

Republican government was seen as offering a number of advantages over other forms. It promoted science and knowledge; it made it possible for "wise men, patriots, and heroes" to rule; it paved the way for "moral" and "virtuous" men to be developed and rise to positions of authority; it promoted the "general or universal interest"; it attracted men of "public and conspicuous merit"; and it was a safeguard against and remedy for corruption. Republican government was also "judged the most friendly to the rights and liberties of the people, and the most conducive to the public welfare."[132]

Running parallel to the discussion of republican government was a concern for the separation of powers. In line with contemporary secular thought, the preachers taught that "various branches of power . . . are a mutual check to each other in their several departments, and jointly secure the common interest." There was no appeal to Scripture for this idea; generally, an appeal was made to the example of Great Britain. The ministers extolled the original British ideal and complained about its deterioration. That ideal was "an exact counterbalance of power between the sovereign, the nobles and the commons, so that the three branches shall be an effectual check upon each other, and the united wisdom of the whole shall conspire to promote the national felicity." In the American sermons of the Founding era, belief in the British ideal was restored. The preachers believed that a "form of government may be so constructed as to have useful checks in the legislature, and yet capable of acting with union, vigor, and despatch [*sic*], with a representation equally proportioned, preserving the legislative and executive branches distinct, and the great essentials of liberty be preserved and secured."[133] This was not a biblical concept but another idea borrowed from liberal democratic theory.

The Founding era preachers were so concerned to make the case for republican government and against "arbitrary rule" that a number of them engaged in rather creative interpretations of the Old Testament record and created a revisionist history of ancient Israel that declared it to be "a perfect republic." In 1788, for example, Samuel Langdon preached a sermon entitled "The Republic of the Israelites an Example to the American States." In the preachers' mythic accounts of this republic, God made the laws, but judges, administrators, officers, and generals were chosen by the people.[134]

Typically, the Israelites were depicted as "wholly unskilled in legislation" and unable to form an original constitution but trustworthy in everyday matters. The sermons seem to depict God's role as something similar to Rousseau's legislator. He disinterestedly established the foundational law for the benefit of society but did not live under it. In their version and consistent with democratic theory, God established it all "for their happiness" rather than to achieve the fulfillment of a sovereignly determined plan. By their account, God submitted the laws to the people for their approval and acceptance (as per Rousseau's legislator). As Samuel Cooper contended:

> Even the law of Moses, though framed by God himself, was not imposed upon that people against their will; it was laid open before the whole congregation of Israel; they freely adopted it, and it became their law, not only by divine appointment, but by their own voluntary and express consent. . . . The memorable act of the day depended intirely [*sic*] on the consent of the people . . . the Supreme Ruler himself had not established their polity without their own free concurrence, and . . . the Hebrew nation, lately redeemed from tyranny, had now a civil and religious constitution of their own choice, and were governed by laws to which they had given their solemn consent.[135]

The basic argument was that men had no right to impose rule or laws on others without their consent if God Himself would not do so. In this creative version of Old Testament history, the government of God's chosen people was "a free republic" and "the sovereignty resided in the people."[136]

Some of the ministers who identified the Mosaic commonwealth as a republic nonetheless acknowledged that it was a "theocrasy [*sic*], God himself being eminently their king." That school argued that Israelites lost their republican form of government when they demanded an earthly king. For them, Israel's downfall was the failure to replace the officers chosen by the previous generations, which led to "despotic" rule by kings. Others saw the people's choice extending to the choice of the kings. Simeon Howard said that "the Jews always exercised this right of choosing their own rulers; even Saul and David, and all their successors in the throne, were made kings by the voice of the people [1 Samuel 11:15, 2 Samuel 2:4–5 and 8]. This natural and important right God never deprived them of."[137] Howard insisted that the Israelites "elected" their kings, and he dismissed God's immediate choice and the anointing by Samuel with the casual concession that "in some few instances God did expressly point out to them the person whom they ought to choose."[138]

The biblical record does not speak of elections with regard to the kings or any other officers, but the preachers proceeded under the assumption of such elections. Consequently, they couched their statements with phrases such as "it is *generally supposed* that they were chosen by the people"; "these officers were *without doubt* elected by the people"; and "as to the choice of this senate, *doubtless* the people were consulted" (emphases mine).[139] Although the discussion of Israel was supported by numerous citations of Scripture, the interpretations and applications of the cited passages were very convenient and self-serving.

Resistance to Tyranny

There remains one element of liberal democratic theory that was espoused by the Founding era preachers and that demonstrates their preference for democratic theory over Scripture in political matters—the question of tyranny and what should be done about it. In their zeal to universalize opposition to rule without consent, the ministers even argued that God's rule was subject to human approval. In his discussion of the Jews' request for a king, Zabdiel Adams said, "The request, as being to their own disadvantage, was displeasing to the God of heaven. But, as he would not rule them in a manner contrary to their own inclination, he consented to their petition."[140] One should note that, according to Adams, God only opposed the idea because it was not for their good—not because it was a rejection of his rule over them, which is the reason God explicitly gave (1 Samuel 8:7, 10:19, 12:12). In a similar vein, John Tucker said, "Even the supreme Ruler of the world, is not a despotic, arbitrary Monarch, nor does he require obedience by meer [*sic*] authority. His sacred laws,—all framed agreeable to the perfect rectitude of his nature, and resulting from his infinite goodness, and righteousness, are wisely adapted to the human system, and calculated for its good."[141] It is clear that they drew their understanding is this area from rational argument and Whig thought, not from revelation. The Bible mentions rebellion 131 times, and every reference is condemnatory and negative. The American Founding era preachers desperately wanted, however, to justify a rebellion. They found support for their cause in John Locke and other democratic theorists and deftly ignored or reinterpreted problem passages in Scripture.

Two such passages, Romans 13 and 1 Peter 2, were discussed earlier in connection with the issue of popular sovereignty. Romans 13:2, for example, specifically and clearly states that to resist authority is to oppose the ordinance of God. It was so understood by previous generations of American preachers—and by many of the Founding era. Those who wished to justify revolution (and who did not simply ignore the passage) emasculated or reversed the meaning of the passage by adopting convenient definitions of terms or by reading absent words into the passage.

The most common example concerns the definition of the term *ruler* or *magistrate*. Despite the fact that Romans 13:1 says there is no authority except from God and those that exist are established by God, ministers such as Samuel West simply declared that "tyrants are no magistrates" and that "no tyrant can be a ruler." West decided that "when they act contrary to the end and design of their creation [the idea of which he also imported from democratic theory] they cease being magistrates." The Bible nowhere—certainly not in the passage at hand—suggests such an idea. West tried to win the argument by defining away the opposing position. He did not stop there, however; he went on to say that rulers who do not seek the general good become "ministers of the powers of darkness" or "ministers of Satan." The apostle Paul does not even hint at such an idea in the passage, but on the basis of that idea, West concluded that "Paul, instead of being a friend to tyranny and arbitrary government, turns out to be a strong advocate for the just rights of mankind." Having placed authorities of which he did not approve in an infernal category, he could announce that "it becomes our indispensable duty to resist and oppose them"[142]—despite Paul's clear instruction in Romans 13:2 that to resist *any* authority that exists is to oppose the ordinance of God.

Examples of reading into the passage what one wishes it said include this idea that Paul advocates a "duty to resist and oppose." Paul says nothing remotely close to that in Romans 13 or any other epistle. Another egregious example of reading into the text is the insistence that governments *can* or *should* be ministers of God—that they must somehow qualify for that status by their actions. According to the text, all governments *are* ministers of God. Paul never says or implies that magistrates must meet some standard of the people's choice in order to be considered ministers of God. He simply states that all magistrates *are* such ministers.

Whatever credit should be given to West for not dodging the passage (as most did), it is clear that his "take" on it was formed by his political perspective. Zuckert thus refers to West's sermon as "the Lockeanized version of Romans 13."[143] West's understanding of the text fell victim to his secular presuppositions. He could not come to a biblical understanding because his presuppositions were natural, not biblical. For instance, he said that "the law of self-preservation will always justify opposing a cruel and tyrannical imposition," but Scripture does not posit or recognize such a law. Whereas Paul identifies God as the source of all governmental authority and that fact leads to particular conclusions, West identified the people as the source of governmental authority and added:

> Consequently, the authority of a tyrant is of itself null and void; for as no man can have a right to act contrary to the law of nature, it is impossible that any individual, or even the greatest number of men, can confer a right upon another of which they themselves are not possessed; *i.e.*, no body of men can justly and lawfully authorize any person to tyrannize over and enslave his fellow-creatures. . . . As magistrates have no authority but what they derive from the people, whenever they act contrary to the public good, and pursue measures destructive of the peace and safety of the community, they forfeit their right to govern the people.[144]

Of course, Paul's point in verses 1 and 2 is that bodies of men do not endow rulers with authority—God does. West, then, read the principles of liberal democratic theory into the biblical text in order to appropriate revelation in support of that theory. Therefore, his conclusion from the passage was that "the community is under the strongest obligation of duty, both to God and to its own members, to resist and oppose them, which will be so far from resisting the ordinance of God that it will be strictly obeying his commands"[145]—the exact opposite of what Paul said.

Most of the preachers did not bother to address problem passages but simply made their arguments out of the whole cloth of democratic theory. Borrowing once again from Locke, they claimed for the people a right of resistance and the right to take back authority from the government and to bestow it on another. According to the sermons, "That the people have a right to resist, is undeniable," and when abused by civil authority, the people "are equally bound in duty to resume it, and transfer it to others." If the government becomes absolute, "they must resort to their native rights, and be justified in making insurrection." Concerning rulers, the sermons held that "the people which gave them their authority have the right to take it from them again"; "they being only of human appointment, the authority which the people gave them the public have a right to take from them, and to confer it upon those who are more worthy." The people were, essentially, employers and therefore had "a right to dismiss from their service such persons as counteract their plans and designs." The colonies, according to the argument, had

> an undoubted right to throw off the yoke, and to assert their liberty . . . they have not only an undoubted right, but it is their indis-

pensable duty, if they cannot be redressed any other way, to renounce all submission to the government that has oppressed them, and set up an independent state of their own . . . no rational man . . . can have any doubt in his own mind whether such a people have a right to form themselves into a body politic.[146]

As did Locke, the ministers stressed that it was up to the majority to determine if and when to "put an end" to one form of government and set up another and that "it is only the major part of the community that can claim the right of altering the constitution, and displacing the magistrates." That is a curious way of stating the point, since we were told that those who would be displaced were not, in fact, magistrates at all. West addressed the question directly:

If it be asked, Who are the proper judges to determine when rulers are guilty of tyranny and oppression? I answer, the public. Not a few disaffected individuals, but the collective body of the state, must decide this question; for, as it is the collective body that invests rulers with their power and authority, so it is the collective body that has the sole right of judging whether rulers act up to the end of their institution or not.[147]

Ezra Stiles made the same point in a slightly different fashion: "We can only say that there still remains in the body of the people at large—the body of mankind, of any and every generation—a power, with which they are invested by the Author of their being, to wrest government out of the hands of reigning tyrants, and originate new policies, adapted to the conservation of liberty, and promoting the public welfare."[148] Locke argued in *The Second Treatise* that the right of resistance would not "on slight occasions, *disturb the Government*" but only when "the Body of the People" or "the Majority of the People" feel threatened.[149] The Founding era preachers, then, used the same argument as Locke to defend against the charge that recognition of a right to overthrow a tyrant could lead to perpetual revolution. Given Locke's influence on the American pulpit of the period, one ought not be surprised.

This chapter has focused on sermons from the nonconformist churches of the American Founding era. Since a Christian sermon might be expected to be based on the Bible, an observer might be struck by the paucity of Scripture or by the many instances in which *anti*biblical positions were taken. But the ministers of those churches received an education similar to that of the political leaders of the period—that is, they were schooled in Enlightenment rationalist thought. As Mark Noll astutely put it: "In 1700 religion had been an 'exporter' of ideas and behavior patterns to American society; by 1800 it was an 'importer.'"[150] Given the preachers' training, rationalist thought and natural religion came to dominate and push out the elements of orthodox Christianity that could not be reconciled with reason. The Old Testament viewed simply as history fit best, as it made few theological demands. A hybrid religion mixing the so-called rational elements of Christianity with natural religion and enlightened social thought was the result—theistic rationalism.

The pulpits of the theistic rationalist churches became a boon to the Revolutionary cause and to the new federal republic. Although the ministers and their preaching had little impact on political leaders, they provided a critical link between the people and those leaders. Hearing the tenets of liberal democratic theory proclaimed from the pulpit as a divine message solidly reinforced those principles in the minds of the people and plowed the mental ground into which leaders sowed political seeds. Once the preachers removed theological obstacles, the people were free to embrace the spirit of the age and to wed the cause of America with the cause of Christ. The ultimate result was an American civil religion that remains to this day and that many identify with Christianity.

But what of the political leaders at the head of the Revolution and the new republic? What did they believe? And how did it affect their political lives and the nation they created? The following chapters dig beneath the surface of conventional wisdom and denominational affiliation for an in-depth look into the religious beliefs of the key Founders. I will begin by considering the expressed beliefs of a supposed orthodox Christian and in the process reveal perhaps the clearest representative of theistic rationalism.

4

The Theistic Rationalism of John Adams

Ye will say I am no Christian.   John Adams

THIS BOOK REGULARLY SPEAKS of the *key Founders*, referring specifically to John Adams, Thomas Jefferson, Benjamin Franklin, George Washington, James Madison, Alexander Hamilton, Gouverneur Morris, and James Wilson. These eight were selected for study because of their profound influence on the critical Founding documents, the Declaration of Independence and the Constitution, and their critical role in putting the Constitution into effect. It is a happy coincidence that they include the first four presidents of the United States. Adams, Jefferson, and Franklin were the most prominent members of the committee entrusted with writing the Declaration, and the other five were arguably the most influential members of the Constitutional Convention and/or were instrumental in its ratification and initial implementation.[1]

The prevailing wisdom among secularists is that the Founders were rational secularists or deists. By contrast, the Christian America camp goes to great lengths to demonstrate that the Founders were orthodox Christians. The purpose of this and the succeeding chapters is to show that the key Founders were neither deists nor Christians but theistic rationalists and to settle the argument for the honest reader by disclosing what they, in fact, said they believed. In the next several chapters, the Founders' own words will serve as the basis for analysis. The men will, for the most part, speak for themselves concerning their beliefs.

Of the key Founders, those who contributed to the Declaration—the document that contains the basic philosophy at the root of the American experiment—investigated religious thought to the greatest degree and wrote the most about it. It would be difficult to find laymen of that era who read more about religion and religions than did Adams and Jefferson or one who wrote more about religion than did Franklin. There is virtual consensus among secularists and Christian America advocates alike that Jefferson and

Franklin were deists and that Adams was a more or less orthodox Christian. The evidence, however, will show that all three shared the same basic beliefs and that all were theistic rationalists.

John Adams was raised in a religious and relatively orthodox home.[2] But by the time he reached college age, he had begun to think for himself regarding religious matters. From that point on, his religious thinking remained remarkably constant. Adams broke from the Calvinism that defined his ancestors and his upbringing, hammering out a set of religious understandings that were more liberal, less Calvinist, less Christian, and based on reason.

Adams shared with both deists and Christians the belief that God created the world and that God ought to be worshipped. He routinely referred to "the Creator" and also spoke of "the mechanician of the universe," "the Author of the Universe," "the Maker of the Universe, the cause of all things," and the "great and Almighty author of nature."[3] His view of *how* the Creation was effected comported with that of deism, not Christianity. While musing on "the amazing harmony of our solar system" in his diary, Adams observed that "the Stupendous Plan of operation was projected by him who rules the universe, and a part assigned to every particle of matter, to act in this great and complicated Drama. The Creator looked into the remotest Futurity, and saw his great Designs accomplished by this inextricable, this mysterious Complication of Causes."[4] This passage provides an early glimpse of the dual emphasis on God and nature in the thought of Adams and the other Founders. Adams's affinity with the deist conception of Creation is reflected in his use of the classic deist metaphor of a watchmaker: "The watchmaker has in his head an idea of the system of a watch before he makes it. The mechanician of the universe had a compleat [*sic*] idea of the universe before he made it: and this idea, this logos, was almighty or at least powerful enough to produce the world, but it must be made of matter which was eternal. For creation out of nothing was impossible."[5] One should notice the reference to matter being eternal, which also separates the supposedly orthodox Adams's view from that of Christianity. Occasionally, his references to the creator God were less than personal. For example, after making the case that what some call fate is God, he asked, "Why, then, should we abhor the word God, and fall in love with the word fate? We know there exists energy and intellect enough to produce such a world as this." In a discussion of the afterlife, Adams said, "The Maker of the Universe, the cause of all things, whether we call *it* [emphasis mine] *fate,* or *chance,* or GOD, has inspired this hope."[6]

Although he shared with Christians a belief that God ought to be worshipped, he often advocated the deist mode of worship. The deity was to be worshipped by "implicitly and piously" obeying his commands, by "the love of God and his creation," and by "allegiance to the Creator . . . and benevolence to all his creatures." According to Adams, "He who loves the workman and his work, and does what he can to preserve and improve it, shall be accepted of him." Adams, however, reserved a place for traditional worship as well because he continued and encouraged regular church attendance to the end of his life.[7]

He shared many perspectives with the deists, but Adams clearly was not one of them. Deism rejected any and all supernatural activity and intervention by God; consequently, deists did not believe in miracles or in particular Providence. Deism also rejected any special revelation from God, including the Bible. Nature was God's only revelation and the only one necessary in order for man to live rightly and well. But Adams did believe in miracles, Providence, and to a certain extent the Bible as revelation.

He made it quite clear in his diary that he believed in miracles in general and those of Jesus in particular: "The great and Almighty author of nature, who at first established those rules which regulate the World, can as easily Suspend those Laws whenever his providence sees sufficient reason for such suspension. This can be no objection, then, to the miracles of J[esus] C[hrist]." Adams here made a rational case for miracles without appeal to revelation. One should also note the reference to God's active Providence. Adams went on to explain that God "commisioned [*sic*]" agents and then used miracles to validate them and to more easily turn men toward truth.[8] Nearly fifty years later, he expressed belief in the ultimate miracle—the Resurrection of Jesus: "The Christian religion was intended to give peace of mind to its disciples in all cases whatsoever but not to send civil or political peace upon earth but a sword, and a sword it has sent; and peace of mind, too, to millions *by conquering death and taking away his sting*" (emphasis mine).[9] The last phrase is unquestionably a reference to Christ's Resurrection (1 Corinthians 15:54–55), which was vehemently denied by the deists. It will be demonstrated later in the chapter that Adams, like the deists, did not believe in the deity of Jesus, but one need not believe in the deity of Jesus in order to believe that he was resurrected. At another point, Adams expressed belief in God's interference with nature via the Flood.[10]

Adams also believed in God's Providence, or intervention in human affairs, although he conceded that the "designs of Providence are inscrutable." An example of this belief can be found in his discussion of prominent families and "plebeians," in which he suggested that Providence worked with nature to establish both in their respective positions. Later, as president, Adams declared that Americans have "reason to rejoice in the local destination assigned us by Providence." He told Benjamin Rush that "God throws empires and kingdoms, as he does rains, plagues, earthquakes, storms, sunshine, good and evil, in a manner that we cannot comprehend," but added that "we have reasons enough to establish a rational belief that all these things are disposed by unerring wisdom, justice, and benevolence."[11] God's Providence, then, applies to the forces of nature and to men's political affairs. But we know this, according to Adams, via *rational* processes, not through the authority of divinely inspired revelation.

Although Adams's views concerning the Bible and revelation were not orthodox, he did believe in some revelation and in the importance of the Bible. When questioned about the views of prominent writers, he criticized Marquis D'Argens for trying to "destroy the credibility of the *whole* Bible" (emphasis mine), although Adams himself rejected the credibility of some of it. He further told F. A. Van der Kemp: "I cannot say with Dupuis that a revelation is impossible or improbable. Christianity, you will say, was a fresh revelation. I will not deny this. As I understand the Christian religion, it was, and is, a revelation." Discussing Christianity in an earlier letter to Benjamin Rush, he suggested that "neither savage nor civilized man, without a revelation, could ever have discovered or invented it." According to Adams, the Puritan form of government "was founded in revelation and in reason too." He once opined that if a nation would "take the Bible for their only law-book, and every member should regulate his conduct by the precepts there exhibited . . . what a Utopia; what a Paradise would this region be!"[12] Adams concluded that "the Bible contains the most profound philosophy, the most perfect morality, and the most refined policy, that ever was conceived upon earth"; more simply, he stated that "the Bible is the best book in the world." In one work, he referred to the Bible as "the Word of God."[13] His letters indicate that he studied the Bible, was familiar with its teachings, and was concerned with questions regarding the veracity of Scripture.[14] One diary entry even suggested a connection between miracles, the apostles, and revelation: "The reasoning of Phylosophers [*sic*], having nothing surprizing [*sic*] in them, could not overcome the force of Prejudice, Custom, Passion, and Bigotry. But when wise and virtuous men commisioned [*sic*] from heaven, by miracles awakened mens [*sic*] attention to their Reasonings, the force of Truth made its way, with ease to their minds."[15] Thus, Adams supported views of the supernatural and revelation that distanced him from deism but were perfectly consonant with theistic rationalism. One should note, to cite one instance, that the statements concerning miracles emphasized reason and made a rational case for the miraculous.

Adams could believe in God, some miracles, and some special revelation because he thought those beliefs to be rational.

He also held some beliefs that neither deists nor Christians espoused. His theistic rationalism, like that of the other key Founders, was a sort of middle ground between protestantism and deism. For example, his complaint that "millions of fables, tales, legends, have been blended with both Jewish and Christian revelation" to make "the most bloody religion that ever existed" would not please either camp.[16] Deists could not countenance the recognition of legitimate revelation, and Christians would not appreciate either the characterization of parts of Scripture as "fables, tales, legends" or the use of the "most bloody religion" label.

Adams had a higher view of Jesus than did most deists, but he put Him in a lower position than did Christians. As was mentioned earlier, he believed that Jesus did perform or might have performed miracles. He quoted Jesus as an authority on the "future state"; he believed that "Jesus is benevolence personified, an example for all men"; and he said that to achieve the best in religion, "we must come to the principles of Jesus."[17] However, like the deists, Adams did not believe in the deity of Jesus or in His satisfaction for the sins of man on the cross. Thus, Adams recorded the following in his diary: "Major Greene this Evening fell into some conversation with me about the Divinity and Satisfaction of Jesus Christ. All the argument he advanced was, 'that a mere creature, or finite Being, could not make Satisfaction to infinite Justice, for any Crimes,' and that 'these things are very misterious [sic].' Thus mystery is made a convenient Cover for absurdity."[18] Adams disputed those issues with acquaintances and ministers more than once. As Henry May put it, he spoke with "hostility . . . of the most central doctrines of orthodox Christianity, including both the Trinity and the Incarnation."[19] In a satirical diary entry in which he mused on information from astronomers that many planets are inhabited, Adams said, "If so, I ask a Calvinist, whether he will subscribe to this Alternitive [sic], 'either God almighty must assume the respective shapes of all these different Species, and suffer the Penalties of their Crimes in their Stead, or else all these Being[s] must be consigned to everlasting Perdition?'"[20] For Adams and the other theistic rationalists, Jesus was an exemplary man who left an example to follow and who deserved to be imitated, but He was not God and did not pay the price for men's sins. Rather, Adams simply saw Jesus as the first example of the resurrection of all men by God.

Despite his lack of belief in the person and work of the *Christ* of *Christianity*, Adams was much more concerned about and attentive to the nature

of Christianity than any deist would have been. He gave a description of it
to Benjamin Rush that borders on the rhapsodic: "The Christian religion, as
I understand it, is the brightness of the glory and the express portrait of the
character of the eternal, self-existent, independent, benevolent, all powerful
and all merciful creator, preserver, and father of the universe, the first good,
first perfect, and first fair. It will last as long as the world."[21] Although,
as will be demonstrated, he believed that virtually all religions were valid
roads to heaven, he implied here that Christianity—as he understood it—
was the best of the many options.

During the Revolutionary period, Adams, like the patriotic preachers, essentially equated Christianity with the Revolutionary cause:

> If a clergyman, of whatever character, preaches against *the principles of
> the revolution,* and tells people that, upon pain of damnation, they must
> submit to an established government, the tories cry him up as an excel-
> lent man and a wonderful preacher. . . . But if a clergyman preaches
> *Christianity,* and tells the magistrates that they were not distinguished
> from their brethren for their private emolument, but for the good of the
> people; that the people are bound in conscience to obey a good govern-
> ment, but are not bound to submit to one that aims at destroying all the
> ends of government,—oh sedition! treason! (Emphases mine.)[22]

In the same essay, he said the clergy took their sermons from the Bible "unless it be a few, who preach passive obedience."[23] Forty years later, Adams
shared memories with Jefferson of the "forefathers" who brought about
independence. In describing those "who composed that army of fine young
fellows," he said that among them were:

> Roman Catholicks [*sic*], English Episcopalians, Scotch and American
> Presbyterians, Methodists, Moravians, Anababtists [*sic*], German Lu-
> therans, German Calvinists Universalists, Arians, Priestleyans, Socin-
> ians, Independents, Congregationalists, Horse Protestants and House
> Protestants, *Deists* and *Atheists* [emphases mine], and 'Protestans qui
> ne croyent rien' ['Protestants *who believe nothing*' (emphasis mine)].
> Very few however of several of these species. Never the less *all educated
> in the general principles of Christianity* [emphasis mine, though "gen-
> eral principles" is italicized in the original]: and the general principles of
> English and American liberty. . . . The *general principles,* on which the
> fathers atchieved [*sic*] independence, were the only principles in which
> that beautiful assembly of young men could unite. . . . And what were
> these *general principles?* I answer, *the general principles of Christianity,*

in which all those sects were united [emphasis mine]: and the *general principles* of English and American liberty.[24]

So, for Adams, the general principles of Christianity were something to which deists, atheists, and those "who believe nothing" all subscribed. He went on to claim that he "could fill sheets of quotations" in favor of these principles with statements from a number of well-known sources, including two very notorious atheists: Hume and Voltaire.[25] This was not the Christianity of the orthodox, who did not believe that deists, atheists, and those who believed nothing were united with true Christians on any principles of Christianity.

Adams and other theistic rationalists who were influenced by Joseph Priestley contended for a "pure and simple" Christianity and complained that it had been "corrupted" by changes introduced by the apostle Paul and by clergymen down through the ages. Adams told Jefferson: "The substance and essence of Christianity as I understand it is eternal and unchangeable and will bear examination forever but it has been mixed with extraneous ingredients, which I think will not bear examination and they ought to be separated." He suggested that "Luther and his associates and followers, went less than half way in detecting the corruptions of Christianity." After bemoaning the burning of "carloads of Hebrew books" in the thirteenth century, Adams asked, "How many proofs of the corruptions of Christianity might we find in the passages burnt?"[26] In discussing the new national Bible Society dedicated to distributing the King James Version to the nations, he asked, "Would it not be better to apply these pious subscriptions to purify Christendom from the corruptions of Christianity than to propagate those corruptions in Europe, in Asia, Africa, and America?" Nonetheless, he was quick to add: "Conclude not from all this, that I have renounced the Christian religion. . . . Far from it. I see in every page, something to recommend Christianity in its purity, and something to discredit its corruptions." Unlike Jefferson, Adams did not identify exactly what he considered such corruptions to be. Given that he was influenced by Joseph Priestley, that he expressed accord with Jefferson, and that he used the term *corruptions* routinely and without clarification in correspondence with Jefferson, one may safely assume that he meant what they did by the use of the term—that is, most of the fundamental doctrines of orthodox Christianity. Although he did not specifically identify them as corruptions, Adams did deny the deity and atonement of Christ, which were the central corruptions according to Priestley and Jefferson. He also said that "placing all religion in grace, and its offspring, faith" was "Antichristianity."[27]

It should be stressed that, unlike a deist, Adams chose to identify with Christianity. To be sure, it was *his* version of Christianity, shorn of what he considered various corruptions. But he did not identify at all with deism. Of course, to the orthodox, those so-called corruptions are the essence of true Christianity, and Adams's denial of the person (deity) and work (atonement) of Christ excludes him from the Christian camp.

Both deism and Christianity taught the reality of an afterlife of rewards and punishments, but Adams's views in this regard did not align him with either school. Deists believed in a "future state," as they regularly put it, but Adams put much greater emphasis upon the concept and its importance. He once asked Jefferson, "What is there in life to attach us, to it; but the hope of a future and a better?" He told another friend that he would advise everyone to take opium if it were ever proved that there is no afterlife. He explained such drastic advice by suggesting that "every hope will fail us, if the last hope, that of a future state, is extinguished."[28] He reiterated the importance of the afterlife in another letter to Jefferson: "In fine, without the supposition of a future state, mankind and this globe appear to me the most sublime and beautifull [*sic*] bubble and bauble that imagination can conceive. Let us then wish for immortality at all hazards."[29] Adams also expressed confidence that he and those who believed as he did would enjoy the next life together. In the same discussion with Jefferson on this subject, he said: "Upon this principle I prophecy that you and I shall soon meet and be better friends than ever."[30] And nine years after Priestley's death, he told Jefferson, "I will ask Priestley, when I see him." This confidence was best expressed in a statement to Samuel Miller: "That you and I shall meet in a better world, I have no more doubt than I have that we now exist on the same globe."[31]

Although Adams's use of Jesus as an authority regarding the next life and his enthusiasm for the afterlife would seem to align him with Christianity, other of his views on the subject distance him once again. In particular, he differed with Christian teaching concerning the extent of punishment in the hereafter and concerning what is required for entry into heaven. Regarding the first matter, Adams said, "I believe, too, in a future state of rewards and punishment, but not eternal."[32] He was, in other words, a universalist who did not accept the Christian teaching that those who do not accept Christ as their savior will suffer for eternity. Universalists believe that all men will eventually make it to heaven, though some may have to suffer temporarily for their injustices in this world.

Regarding the second matter, Adams believed that all "good men" who are "sincere and conscientious" in their efforts to "implicitly and piously" obey God's commands and follow the Golden Rule would have "the sure prospect of a happy immortality." In his discussion of the Hindu Shastra, he spoke approvingly of the teachings of Hindus and Greek philosophers and concluded that "all ended in Heaven, if they became virtuous." Reflecting an eclecticism typical of theistic rationalists, Adams credited his "natural reason" and the teachings of Cicero and Jesus for his views concerning the afterlife.[33] In a letter to Jefferson, he revealed some of his logical reasoning on this subject: "Suppose, the cause of the universe, should reveal to all mankind, at once a certainty that they must all die within a century, and that death is an eternal extinction of all living powers, of all sensation and reflection. . . . What would men say to their Maker? would they thank him? No they would reproach him; they would curse him to his face."[34] As was common among theistic rationalists, Adams developed his own concept—in this case, of an afterlife—by subjecting the orthodox protestant training of his youth to the test of rationalism.

There was one other issue in which Adams held a view divergent from both deism and his understanding of Protestantism: the perfectibility of man. It is a commonplace that Enlightenment thought taught the inevitable progress and ultimate perfectibility of man. Christian thought teaches that one should strive for perfection in this life and that believers in Jesus Christ will be made perfect in the next life. Adams, however, did not believe either source in this regard. The fundamental concern for him and children of the Enlightenment was the mind:

> The Christian religion has adopted and sanctioned this theory in stronger terms than any modern philosophers have employed. Be ye perfect, even as your Father in heaven is perfect. The eternal, omniscient, omnipotent, and all-benevolent model of perfection is placed before men for their perpetual meditation and imitation. By this, however, it is not intended that every man can ever become eternal, almighty, and all-wise. It is an idea of the Christian religion, and ever has been of all believers in the immortality of the soul, that the intellectual part of man is capable of progressive improvement for ever.[35]

He told Jefferson, "I never could understand the doctrine of the perfectability [sic] of the human mind,"[36] and for theistic rationalists, what could not be understood could not be believed. He later expressed his significant doubt more openly, observing, "I leave those profound phylosophers [sic] whose sagacity perceives the perfectibility of human nature, and those illuminated theologians who expect the apocalyptic reign, to enjoy their transporting hopes; provided always that they will not engage us in crusades and French Revolutions, nor burn us for doubting."[37] Although his view was closer to that of Christianity, Adams did not have a deist or Christian view of the perfectibility of man.

Despite the fact that, as has been shown, a number of his religious beliefs were inconsistent with or opposed to deism, many of them reflected the influence of natural religion and rationalism and in fact closely resembled those of the deists. Adams joined other rationalists in heavily—sometimes brutally—attacking the teachings of Calvinism. His attacks were significant because Calvinism was the prevailing theology of the previous century in America and remained the official theology of roughly two-thirds of American churches in the Founding era (see Table 1.1). Calvinism was also the brand of Christianity by which Adams was raised and the official theology of his denomination. He is routinely identified as a Christian largely because of this denominational affiliation. He certainly understood the issues involved, as he sat in on "Ecclesiastical Councils" "concerning the five points" of Calvinism throughout his collegiate years.[38] Although raised by Calvinist parents in an originally Calvinist church, he confessed:

> I must be a very unnatural son to entertain any prejudices against the Calvinists, or Calvinism . . . for my father and mother, my uncles and aunts, and all my predecessors, from our common ancestor, who landed in this country two hundred years ago, wanting five months, were of that persuasion. Indeed, I have never known any better people than the Calvinists. Nevertheless, I must acknowledge that I cannot class myself under that denomination.[39]

On more than one occasion, Adams made that last point blatantly obvious. Upon suggesting that vanity caused writers to say that genius is a gift given to few, he drew the following parallel:

> The same vanity which gave rise to that strange religious Dogma, that God elected a precious few . . . to Life eternal without regard to any foreseen Virtue, and reprobated all the Rest, without regard to any foreseen Vice—A doctrine which, with serious gravity, represents the world, as under the government of Humour and Caprice. . . . If the orthodox doctrine of Genius is not so detestable as that of unconditional Election, it is not much less invidious, nor much less hurtful. One represents eternal life, as an unattainable Thing without the special favor of the Father—and even with that attainable by very few . . . and so tends to discourage the practice of virtue. . . . You and I shall never be persuaded

or frightened . . . to believe that the world of nature, learning and grace is governed by such arbitrary Will or inflexible fatality. We have much higher Notions of the efficacy of human endeavours in all Cases.[40]

Interestingly, even though he contended that Calvinism discouraged the practice of virtue, he nonetheless testified that he had "never known any better people than the Calvinists."

Adams attacked, directly or indirectly, all five points of the Calvinists. He very directly decried the doctrine of total depravity, claiming, "So far from believing in the total and universal depravity of human nature; I believe there is no individual totally depraved. The most abandoned scoundrel that ever existed, never yet wholly extinguished his conscience, and while conscience remains there is some religion."[41] He also argued that the "fatalism" of Calvinism appeared to him to "render all prayer futile and absurd."[42] But like many other theistic rationalists, Adams saved his most savage assaults for the Calvinist concepts of election and predestination:

God has infinite wisdom, goodness and power. He created the universe. . . . He created this speck of dirt and the human species for his glory: and with the deliberate design of making nine tenths of our species miserable forever, for his glory. This is the doctrine of Christian theologians in general, ten to one. Now, my friend, can prophecies, or miracles convince you, or me, that infinite benevolence, wisdom and power, created and preserves, for a time, innumerable millions to make them miserable, forever; for his own glory? Wretch! What is his glory? Is he ambitious? does he want promotion? Is he vain? tickled with adulation? Exulting and tryumphing [*sic*] in his power and the sweetness of his vengeance? Pardon me, my Maker, for these aweful [*sic*] questions. My answer to them is always ready: I believe no such things. My adoration of the Author of the Universe is too profound and too sincere. . . . Howl, snarl, bite, ye Calvinistick [*sic*]! Ye Athanasian divines, if you will. Ye will say, I am no Christian: I say ye are no Christians: and there the account is ballanced [*sic*].[43]

Adams so rejected Calvinism that he emphasized that he was not even a Calvinist in a single point. Commenting on Jefferson's restored health, he said, "May it continue till you shall become as perfect a calvinist as I am in one particular."[44]

Calvinists pointed to the Bible as authoritative evidence for their doctrines. Adams and the other theistic rationalists could not accept what seemed to them to be irrational and illogical simply because it was taught by a Bible that they believed was only partially inspired.[45] The standard was always the same—reason. They would only believe what was taught in the parts of the Bible they considered legitimate revelation, and the portions of Scripture they would accept as revelation were determined by their reason. Unlike the deists, they did accept some revelation as legitimate but only insofar as it comported with reason.

Adams did not believe that men were saved by God's grace. He called such a notion "Antichristianity." He did not believe in instantaneous conversion of any sort.[46] On what basis, then, were men to be made acceptable to the creator God? For Adams and the theistic rationalists, the substance, purpose, and end of religion were the same—morality or good works. Shortly after college, Adams, partly in response to Calvinism, wrote what may be the best statement of a central belief of theistic rationalism: "The design of Christianity was not to make men good Riddle Solvers, or good mystery mongers, but good men, good majestrates [*sic*], and good Subjects, good Husbands and good Wives, good Parents and good Children, good masters and good servants."[47] Nearly sixty years later, he delineated the responsibility of an individual regarding the creator:

> I have searched after truth by every means and by every opportunity in my power, and with a sincerity and impartiality, for which I can appeal to God, my adored Maker. My religion is founded on the love of God and my neighbor; on the hope of pardon for my offences; upon contrition; upon the duty as well as necessity of supporting with patience the inevitable evils of life; in the duty of doing no wrong, but all the good I can, to the creation, of which I am but an infinitesimal part.[48]

Because of his emphasis on morals and ethics, Adams could claim, "The Ten Commandments and the Sermon on the Mount contain my religion." Because of this emphasis, he could tell Jefferson: "Now, I see not, but you are as good a Christian as Priestley and Lindsey. Piety and morality were the end and object of the Christian system according to them, and according to you."[49] Because of this emphasis, Adams and other theistic rationalists could admire and exalt Jesus as a moral teacher. Thus, Adams wrote: "Jesus is benevolence personified, an example for all men. Dupuis has made no alteration in my opinion of the Christian religion, in its primitive purity and simplicity, which I have entertained for more than sixty years. It is the religion of reason, equity, and love; it is the religion of the head and of the heart."[50] Note that "reason" heads his list. Adams's testimony here also refutes those who would claim that his views concerning Christianity changed in his later years. Because of this emphasis on morals and ethics, theistic rationalists could afford to be indifferent toward specific denominations, creeds, and modes of worship. As long as a sect promoted good morals, they could feel a sense of common cause and support it.

This observation leads to another important element of theistic rationalism that is inconsistent with Christianity—that there are many roads to God. Adams, who may have read more books about religion and religions than anyone of his day, concluded, "I have endeavored to obtain as much information as I could of all the religions which have ever existed in the world. . . . The great result of all my researches has been a most diffusive and comprehensive charity. I believe with Justin Martyr, that all good men are Christians, and I believe there have been, and are, good men in all nations, sincere and conscientious."[51] In the theistic rationalism that Adams identified as Christianity, the central factor is a sincere and conscientious goodness. Since that goodness can be found in the representatives and creeds of many religions, there are many paths to God.

Since orthodox Christianity taught that there is only one way to God, Adams and the others saw in its adherents "a spirit of dogmatism and bigotry." In fact, Adams said he decided not to become a clergyman because "I perceived very clearly, as I thought, that the Study of Theology, and the pursuit of it as a Profession would involve me in endless Altercations . . . without any prospect of doing any good to my fellow Men." He expressed relief in knowing that "I shall have Liberty to think for myself without molesting others or being molested myself."[52] The theological disputes Adams sought to avoid professionally, however, became his lifelong hobby, or "the marbles and nine-pins of old age": "For more than sixty years I have been attentive to this great subject. Controversies, between Calvinists and Arminians, Trinitarians and Uniterians [*sic*], Deists and Christians, Atheists and both, have attracted my attention. . . . I think, I can now say I have read away bigotry, if not enthusiasm."[53] In the eighteenth century, "bigotry" in religion meant commitment to specific doctrines. He testified to having "read away" such commitment. Adams studied all religions and religious controversies for the purpose of finding commonalities upon which to build moral societies, not to try and discern truth:

Bigotry, superstition, and enthusiasm on religious subjects I have long since set at defiance. I have attended public worship in all countries and with all sects and believe them all much better than no religion, though I have not thought myself obliged to believe all I heard. Religion I hold to be essential to morals. I never read of an irreligious character in Greek or Roman history, nor in any other history, nor have I known one in life, who was not a rascal.[54]

As he saw it, Christianity was one of many useful belief systems. Adams emphasized that the same "moral liberty resides in Hindoos and Mahometans, as well as in Christians,"[55] and he asked, "Where is to be found theology more orthodox or phylosophy [sic] more profound than in the introduction to the [Hindu] Shast[r]a?"[56]

Adams's attribution of the label *Christian* to any belief system with which he agreed is evident in his claim that the "Preamble to the Laws of Zaleucus . . . is as orthodox Christian Theology as Priestleys [sic]."[57] If a set of laws supposedly handed down from Athena 600 years before the birth of Christ can be categorized as *Christian,* does the term retain any real meaning? His unwillingness to discriminate between belief systems is reflected in the list of works he said he would prefer to those of atheists: "I should even prefer the Shast[r]a of Indostan, or the Chaldean Egyptian, Indian, Greek, Christian Mahometan Tubonic or Celtic theology."[58] At times, then, Christianity had no special place or preference in his thought; it was simply one of many interesting options or alternatives.

For one who considered virtually all sects and creeds as equally legitimate, a distinction between Christian groups or churches would certainly not be made. Indeed, Adams insisted, "Ask me not, then, whether I am a Catholic or Protestant, Calvinist or Arminian. As far as they are Christians, I wish to be a fellow-disciple with them all."[59] The following is his favorite story to illustrate this point:

> I know of no philosopher, or theologian, or moralist ancient or modern more profound, more infallible than Whitefield, if the anecdote that I heard be true. He began; "Father Abraham! . . . who have you there with you?" ["]have you Catholicks [sic]?" No. "Have you Protestants." No. "Have you Churchmen." No. "Have you Dissenters." No. "Have you Presbyterians?" No. "Quakers?" No. ["]Anabaptists?" No. "Who have you then?" "Are you alone?" No. "My brethren,! You have the answer to all these questions in the words of my text, 'He who feareth God and worketh righteousness, shall be accepted of him.'"[60]

To Adams and the other theistic rationalists, the issues that divided various religious groups had no ultimate importance. God, as they pictured Him, was concerned only with man's behavior. Consequently, they were unconcerned with doctrine or with which sect held sway in a given region.

Like the deists, Adams was anti-Trinitarian. According to him, "The Pythagorean as well as the Platonic phylosophers [*sic*] probably concurred in the fabrication of the Christian Trinity."[61] One historian has noted that Jefferson was envious of the fact that Adams was a member of a Unitarian congregation. He was buried in its churchyard at Quincy. United First Parish Church, of which Adams was a lifelong member, officially became Unitarian in 1750.[62] Whatever scorn he did not heap upon predestination, Adams saved for the doctrine of the Trinity.

In an attempt to prove that Adams believed in the Trinity, Christian America advocate David Barton is fond of publicly reading a portion of a letter from Adams to Benjamin Rush that includes this statement: "There is no Authority civil or religious: there can be no legitimate Government but what is administered by this Holy Ghost." Barton stops reading just before the context illuminates Adams's real point, however. After talking about the Holy Ghost for several rapturous sentences, Adams said: "All this is all Artifice and Cunning in the secret original of the heart, yet they all believe it so sincerely that they would lay down their Lives under the Ax [*sic*] or the fiery Fagot for it. Alas the poor weak ignorant Dupe human Nature." The whole section extolling the Holy Ghost was written with dripping sarcasm. Adams concluded by asking, "Do you wonder that Voltaire and Paine [notorious infidels] have made Proselytes?" Keenly aware of its controversial nature, Adams asked Rush to burn the letter.[63]

One other rather extended quote is necessary and sufficient to demonstrate how zealously and completely Adams denied the doctrine of the Trinity:

> The bill in parliament for the relief of Antitrinitarians is a great event; and will form an epoch in ecclesiastical history. . . . The human understanding is a revelation from its Maker which can never be disputed or doubted. . . . This revelation has made it certain that two and one make three; and that one is not three; nor can three be one. We can never be so certain of any prophecy, or the fullfillment [*sic*] of any prophecy; or of any miracle, or the design of any miracle as we are, from the revelation of nature i.e. natures [*sic*] God that two and two are equal to four. . . . Had you and I been forty days with Moses on Mount Sinai and admitted to behold, the divine Shekinah, and there told that one was three and three, one: we might not have had courage to deny it, but we could not have believed it. The thunders and lightenings [*sic*] and earthq[ua]kes and the transcendant splendors and glories, might have overwhelmed us with terror and amazement: but we could not have believed the doctrine. We should be more likely to say in our hearts,

whatever we might say with our lips, this is chance. There is no God! No truth. This is all delusion, fiction and a lie: or it is all chance.[64]

The significance of being with Moses on Mount Sinai, of course, is that that is where God gave direct revelation. Adams was so opposed to the doctrine of the Trinity that he said he would not believe it if directly told of it by God Himself. Because it appeared to them to be irrational, Adams and the theistic rationalists could not believe in the Trinity. Adams thought his reason more reliable than direct revelation from God.

This leads to Adams's view of the Bible, which was not quite that of either deists or Christians. As was noted earlier, Adams did accept parts of the Bible as inspired revelation, but he had serious doubts about the rest. For example, he agreed with Priestley that the Fall of man in Genesis "is either an allegory, or founded on uncertain tradition: that it is an hypothesis to account for the origin of evil, adopted by Moses, which by no means accounts for the facts." Those, like Adams and Priestley, who rejected the doctrine of original sin had to hold that or a similar view. In a discussion of an alternative set of the Ten Commandments, Adams suggested that the biblical record was unreliable—that "authentic copies" of the original were lost. In expressing his opposition to a law that required belief in the divine inspiration of the entire Bible, he said that such measures were "great obstructions to the improvement of the human mind" and that "books that cannot bear examination certainly ought not to be established as divine inspiration by penal laws."[65] According to Adams, the entire Bible could not bear examination when it came to divine inspiration.

In a telling comment to Jefferson, he expressed his ambivalence regarding revelation and his (and Jefferson's) preference for rational arguments:

> Hundreds of millions of Christians expect and hope for a millennium in which Jesus is to reign for a thousand years over the whole world before it is burnt up. . . . All these hopes are founded on real or pretended revelation. . . . You and I hope for splendid improvements in human society and vast ameliorations in the condition of mankind. Our faith may be supported by more rational arguments than any of the former.[66]

For Adams, then, the revelatory status of individual parts of Scripture could have been real or "pretended," but rational argument carried the day when revelation and reason collided. For many Christians, among them Thomas Aquinas, reason is an important—indeed, a crucial—supplement to revelation, but revelation stands in the first position. For Adams, however, reason held the primary position, and revelation was an occasionally unnecessary supplement. This was even true if the revelation in question had been confirmed as divine by miracles: "Phylosophy [*sic*] which is the result of reason, is the first, the original revelation of the Creator to his creature, man. When this revelation is clear and certain, by intuition or necessary induction, no subsequent revelation supported by prophecies or miracles can supercede [*sic*] it." One should note the confidence, bordering on arrogance, in the assertion that man's intuition and inductive abilities are preferred and more reliable than special revelation from the God who created him. Recall that in the anecdote about Mount Sinai, Adams said that his reason would not allow him to believe in the Trinity even if God Himself told him it was true. His statement reflects the theistic rationalist perspective. In a letter to F. A. Van der Kemp, he said that "the question before mankind is . . . whether authority is from nature and reason, or from miraculous revelation" and that man is responsible to God for "an impartial verdict and judgment."[67] His subsequent comments made it clear that he sided with reason. Reason and revelation were both important and usually complemented each other, but reason trumped revelation when the two conflicted.

Another of Adams's remarks concerning Scripture leads to a final emphasis in the religious thought of Adams and theistic rationalists. Speaking of the Bible, he said: "It is the most republican book in the world, and therefore I will still revere it."[68] Adams and the other Founders stressed the importance of religiously based morality as a support for republican government in particular, society in general, and civilization as a whole. He told his cousin Zabdiel: "Statesmen, my dear Sir, may plan and speculate for liberty, but it is religion and morality alone, which can establish the principles upon which freedom can securely stand. The only foundation of a free constitution is pure virtue."[69] According to Adams, "Without virtue, there can be no political liberty" and "religion and virtue are the only foundations, not only of republicanism and of all free government, but of social felicity under all governments and in all the combinations of human society." Furthermore, "the doctrine of a supreme, intelligent, wise, almighty sovereign of the universe" was "the great essential principle of all morality, and consequently of all civilization."[70] In specific reference to the American situation, Adams famously said: "We have no government armed with power capable of contending with human passions unbridled by morality and religion. . . . Our Constitution was made only for a moral and religious people. It is wholly inadequate to the government of any other."[71] This is one of the statements by Adams that is most frequently quoted by adherents to the Christian America position. But Adams did not specify *Christianity* as being necessary—only a "moral and religious" citizenry. As was demonstrated earlier, he and the theistic rationalists believed that almost any religion was sufficient for that purpose.

Three months before he was elected president of the United States, John Adams recorded in his diary fundamentals of theistic rationalism under the label of "the Christian religion":

> One great Advantage of the Christian Religion is that it brings the great Principle of the Law of Nature and Nations, Love your Neighbor as yourself, and do unto others as you would that others should do to you, to the Knowledge, Belief and Veneration of the whole People. Children, Servants, Women, and Men are all Professors in the science of public and private Morality. No other Institution for Education, no kind of political Discipline, could diffuse this kind of necessary Information, so universally among all Ranks and Descriptions of Citizens. The Duties and Rights of The Man and the Citizen are thus taught, from early Infancy to every Creature. The Sanctions of a future Life are thus added to the Observance of civil and political as well as domestic and private Duties. Prudence, Justice, Temperance and Fortitude are thus taught to be the means and Conditions of future as well as present Happiness.[72]

The law of nature concurred with a biblical principle that was important for public and private morality. Religion existed to spread this morality to all members of society and was the most effective means for that purpose. In addition, what was critical for the good of society in this life was, conveniently, also what was required in order to qualify for happiness in the next life. Although John Adams is regularly identified as a Christian, his writings present perhaps the clearest expression of theistic rationalism.

Men from various backgrounds and religious associations came to theistic rationalist conclusions. From one routinely labeled a Christian, the study now turns to two theistic rationalists universally tagged as deists. As in the case of the supposed Christian Adams, the evidence from the words of Thomas Jefferson and Benjamin Franklin does not support their conventional religious categorization.

5

The Theistic Rationalism of Thomas Jefferson and Benjamin Franklin

Your own reason is the only oracle given you by heaven.

Thomas Jefferson

"UNFAIR!" THAT IS THE IMMEDIATE RESPONSE from the Christian America camp if one begins to quote Thomas Jefferson or Benjamin Franklin in order to make any kind of general arguments about the religion of the Founders. They claim that those two were unusually radical and that it is invalid to draw any broad conclusions from such outlier sources. Interestingly, however, Christian America advocates regularly cite the religious language that Jefferson wrote in the Declaration, and they are fond of recounting the story of Franklin calling for prayer at the Constitutional Convention. The secular camp agrees that the two men were unusually radical, and its accepted view is that both were deists. So, the prevailing consensus today is that Thomas Jefferson and Benjamin Franklin were deists whose religious views were radical and far afield from those of the rest of the American Founders.

Comprehensive study of their expressed beliefs reveals, however, that they were neither deists nor religious radicals in comparison with other Founders. One scholar aptly concludes that they "epitomized the sort of religious liberalism that swept through America's cultural elite during the late eighteenth century."[1] An illustration of my point is the fact that John Adams, generally considered one of the more orthodox Christians, several times affirmed that he and Jefferson were in fundamental agreement on religious matters. He further said that the son he raised, John Quincy Adams, also agreed with Jefferson on "most of the essential points" of religion.[2] Due to their extensive and frank correspondence on religious questions, Adams probably knew more about Jefferson's beliefs than anyone else, and he summed up his solidarity with them in the following way:

I agree with you, as far as you go. Most cordially and I think solidly. How much farther I go, how much more I believe than you, I may explain in a future letter. Thus much I will say at present, I have found so many difficulties, that I am not astonished at your stopping where you are. And so far from sentencing you to perdition, I hope soon to meet you in another country.[3]

Jefferson, in turn, said, "I very much suspect that if thinking men would have the courage to think for themselves, and to speak what they think, it would be found they do not differ in religious opinions, as much as is supposed."[4] A comparison of Jefferson's expressed beliefs with those of Adams shows that the differences between them were matters of detail and degree, not of essence.

It is interesting that scholars writing about deism regularly note areas in which Jefferson and Franklin were exceptions but caution against "overstating" the level of their "ambivalence."[5] I would argue that on the contrary, one should be cautious not to overstate the extent of their agreement with deism. One such expert admits that Franklin "never quite reconciled his deistic conviction that physical reality was explicable in terms of immutable and absolute mechanistic laws with his Calvinist-inspired suspicion that providential or miraculous interventions in the cosmic machinery's functions were both logical and actual possibilities."[6] I contend that Franklin and Jefferson appear to be exceptions for an honest reason: they were not deists. This chapter will focus on the evidence that the two Founders most firmly held to be deists were, in fact, not. Instead, like the supposedly orthodox Christian Adams, they were theistic rationalists.

Jefferson and Franklin shared the belief in a creator God with Christians and deists alike, but some of Jefferson's reasoning sets him apart from the deist camp. He regularly referred to "the Creator" or "wise creator" and discussed the subject at length in a letter to Adams. There, he began with an argument from reason, contending that "it is impossible for the human mind not to perceive and feel a conviction of design, consummate skill, and indefinite power in every atom" of the universe. He then argued from history that the evidence is so "irrestistible" that men throughout time have believed in a creator "in the proportion of a million at least to unit." Jefferson's concluding argument, however, was a biblical one that would not be made by someone who did not believe in written revelation. He expounded his own translation of the first three verses of John, which, according to Jefferson, "explains rationally the eternal pre-existence of God, and his creation of the world." Significantly, he emphasized that the passage explains creation "rationally," which would be a critical factor for a theistic rationalist. On the basis of his translation of the passage, he further proclaimed it "the doctrine of Jesus that the world was created by the supreme, intelligent being."[7] The Christian teaching, based on John 1:3 and other passages,[8] was that Jesus, as the Word of God and second person of the Godhead, created the universe. Though Jefferson's interpretation differed from that of Christians, the fact that he appealed seriously to the Bible as an authoritative source and that he considered "the doctrine of Jesus" to be a valuable contribution to the argument distinguishes him from the typical deist.

Franklin's reasoning in support of a creator God was based entirely on natural revelation and could have been argued by a deist. In his *Autobiography*, Franklin confessed that he "never doubted . . . the existence of a Deity" or "that he made the world."[9] He began his *Articles of Belief and Acts of Religion* with a quote from Cato proclaiming the existence of God: "If there is a Pow'r above us, (And that there is, all Nature cries aloud, Thro' all her Works)." In the "Adoration" section, he contended that God is the source of the laws of nature and that evidence of His power, wisdom, and goodness can be seen in nature: "By thy Power hast thou made the glorious Sun, with his attending Worlds; from the Energy of thy mighty Will, they first received [their prodigious] Motion, and by thy Wisdom hast thou prescribed the wondrous Laws by which they move. . . . Thy Wisdom, thy Power, and thy Goodness are every where clearly seen; in the Air and in the Water, in the Heavens and on the Earth."[10] When stating his own creed, he always began by expressing a belief in one God who "made all things" or was "creator of the universe." In letters, he extolled the wisdom of God in creation.[11] In his essay "On the Providence of God," Franklin said that he skipped proving the existence of God and His being the creator in order to avoid offending his readers by suggesting that they were "ignorant of what all Mankind in all Ages have agreed in." He then used the facts of God's actions in creation to prove His goodness and power.[12] In the "First Principles" section of his *Articles of Belief and Acts of Religion*, Franklin said: "It is that particular wise and good God, who is the Author and Owner of our System, that I propose for the Object of my Praise and Adoration." In the "Adoration" section, he addressed God as creator; called for the reading of "part of some such Book as Ray's *Wisdom of God in the Creation*, or *Blacmore on the Creation*, or the Archbishop of Cambray's *Demonstration of the Being of a God*; &c."; and included the singing of Milton's *Hymn to the Creator.*[13] Years after composing these devotions, Franklin reassured his sister: "I am so far from thinking that God is not to be worshipped, that I have compos'd and wrote a whole Book of Devotions for my own Use." Elsewhere, Franklin said that the "worship of God is a Duty," and he always included in his creed the affirmation that God "ought to be worshipped."[14]

His reasoning in support of a belief in a creator God mirrored that of a deist, but as will be discussed, elements of his plan for worship reflected his rejection of deism.

Franklin joined Jefferson in rejecting one of the defining beliefs of deism, for both believed in an active, present God who intervened in human affairs. Jefferson, for example, expressed belief in God's intervention in "calamities and misfortunes" and contended in such events for "a perfect resignation to the Divine will, to consider that whatever does happen, must happen." Jefferson believed in a God who was active in sustaining the universe. A watchmaker God or an absent God who merely established laws by which the universe functioned did not exert or display "will" concerning particular events. Jefferson saw "evident proofs of the necessity of a superintending power to maintain the universe in it's [*sic*] course and order." He also expressed belief in God's intervention in human affairs on a large scale when he said that independence was achieved "under the favor of heaven" and that "Providence ever pleases to direct the issue of our contest in favor of that side where justice was."[15] Providence here is not simply an expression of general, natural processes but rather "pleases" to "direct" events, which reflects will and active participation.

Without question, his best-known affirmation of God's active interest in human affairs is the following statement regarding slavery, which appeared in his *Notes on the State of Virginia:*

> Can the liberties of a nation be thought secure when we have removed their only firm basis, a conviction in the minds of the people that these liberties are of the gift of God? That they are not to be violated but with his wrath? Indeed, *I tremble for my country when I reflect that God is just; that his justice cannot sleep forever*; that considering numbers, nature and natural means only, a revolution of the wheel of fortune, an exchange of situation is among possible events; that *it may become probable by supernatural interference!* The Almighty has no attribute which can take side with us in such a contest. (Emphases mine.)[16]

Jefferson not only recognized the possibility of "supernatural interference" but also called it "probable." This thinking runs precisely counter to one of the defining elements of deism, which categorically rejects the possibility of supernatural interference. In his subsequent discussion of improvement in the slave situation, he expressed a hope that Providence would aid in his desired solution to the problem of slavery, "the way I hope preparing under the auspices of heaven, for a total emancipation."[17] Jefferson also expressed belief in God's personal involvement in the lives of individuals. He confessed an effort "to trust for the future to him who has been so good for the past" and said that "a consciousness that you are acting under his eye, and that he approves you" is "a vast additional incitement" to virtue.[18]

Jefferson's prayers also reflected a belief in divine intervention in both large-scale and personal human affairs. He prayed for the "future welfare" of the Baltimore Baptists and for "that of our beloved country." He prayed that God would "bless" and "support" John Adams on the death of his wife. Referring to heaven, Jefferson even prayed that he and Miles King "may there meet and embrace."[19] Jefferson's expressed belief in divine intervention and activity separates him from deism, but it is consistent with theistic rationalism.

It is important to note that although Jefferson claimed to be a Christian more than once, he never claimed to be a deist. Further, as will be seen, he spoke of deists in the third person. Franklin is unique in that he is the only one of the key Founders who claimed to have embraced deism at some point in his life. Those who class Franklin among deists are fond of quoting the following:

> But I was scarce fifteen, when, after doubting by turns of several points, as I found them disputed in the different books I read, I began to doubt of the Revelation itself. Some books against Deism fell into my hands. . . . It happened, that they wrought an effect on me quite contrary to what was intended by them. For the arguments of the Deists, which were quoted to be refuted, appeared to me much stronger than the refutations; in short, I soon became a thorough Deist.[20]

Scholars often end their investigation there, with Franklin at fifteen years of age, and neglect what he wrote (voluminously) over the succeeding seventy years of his life! In fact, one need not go far to find a disclaimer, for Franklin wrote in the same *Autobiography:* "I began to suspect that this doctrine, though it might be true, was not very useful." Indeed, he decided that several arguments "appeared now not so clever a performance as I once thought it."[21] As we shall see, he would later completely and adamantly oppose crucial deist doctrines.

Franklin's rejection of deism is most clear and evident in his strong belief in the particular Providence of God. Each time he delineated his creed, he acknowledged that God "governs the world by his providence." Looking back on his "dangerous youth" when he was in his seventies, he acknowledged that "the kind hand of Providence" had protected him.[22] Like the other theistic rationalists, Franklin believed in a God who was active and intervened in cosmic matters and in personal human affairs. His "updating" of the Lord's Prayer reflected both perspectives.[23] On one hand, Franklin affirmed that God is able to give motion to the earth, sun, planets, and stars "and yet so to govern them in their greatest Velocity as that they shall not flie [*sic*] off out of their appointed Bounds." On the other hand, he said that God "is not above caring for us." He proposed that divinity students study natural history in order to "strengthen [their sermons] by new Proofs of Divine Providence." After clarifying that Providence is separate from "the natural and universal Chain of Causes," Franklin argued that natural events "are sometimes set aside or postpon'd for wise and good Reasons by the *immediate particular* Dispositions of Providence" (emphasis mine).[24] On a more personal note, he reported receiving "the blessing of God" and said, "What reverses may attend the remainder [of his years] is in the hand of Providence." Regarding his opportunities to spend time with his grandchildren, he stated, "I . . . enjoy among them the present hour, and leave the future to Providence." One of his *Poor Richard* proverbs was: "Ni ffyddra llaw dyn, er gwneithr da idd ei hun" (Man's hand alone, without God's help, cannot do himself good).[25]

His thinking concerning God's intervention in personal human affairs brought him to the conclusion that "without the Belief of a Providence that takes Cognizance of, guards and guides and may favour particular Persons, there is no Motive to Worship a Deity, to fear its Displeasure, or to pray for its Protection."[26] One should recall the "Adoration" section of his *Articles of Belief and Acts of Religion*. It makes no sense to offer praise and adoration to a being who is impersonal, not present, or not paying attention. How could a deist address an absent or impersonal God? The deist notion of worship was simply being moral and doing good, not offering praise or adoration. Franklin, however, said that God was "pleas'd with our praise, and offended when we slight Him." He evinced belief in a personal God when he addressed God as "my Friend" and again as "my Friend, my Father, and my Benefactor." His God was not only present and paying attention; Franklin also claimed that God was "delighted to see me happy" and that "he delights to see me Virtuous, because he is pleas'd when he sees me Happy." Further, in his address to God, he said, "Thou art *pleas'd with the pleasure* of thy Children." As he neared the end of his life, he connected the activity of Providence in his life with his confidence in the afterlife. He acknowledged a curiosity about "some other" world and said he could "cheerfully, with filial confidence, resign my spirit to the conduct of that great and good Parent of mankind, who created it, and who has so

graciously protected and prospered me from my birth to the present hour."
A month before he died, he said that "having experienced the goodness of
that Being in conducting me prosperously through a long life, I have no
doubt of its continuance in the next."[27]

Franklin also believed that the hand of Providence was active in the life
of the nation. Regarding victory in the Revolution, he confessed that "if it
had not been for the justice of our cause, and the consequent interposition
of Providence, in which we had faith, we must have been ruined. If I had
ever before been an atheist, I should now have been convinced of the being
and government of a Deity!"[28] He was equally clear about God's role in the
Constitutional Convention:

> I beg I may not be understood to infer, that our General Convention
> was divinely inspired . . . yet I must own I have so much faith in the
> general government of the world by Providence, that I can hardly con-
> ceive a transaction of such momentous importance to the welfare of
> millions . . . should be suffered to pass without being in some degree
> influenced, guided, and governed by that omnipotent, omnipresent, and
> beneficent Ruler, in whom all inferior spirits live, and move, and have
> their being.[29]

He, like Jefferson, warned that slavery put the nation at risk from an actively just God and would bring "the displeasure of the great and impartial
Ruler of the Universe upon our country."[30]

Clearly the best known of Franklin's many statements on the Providence
of God, however, is his speech during the great impasse over representation
in the Constitutional Convention. He acknowledged "the Father of lights"
for His "divine protection" in "the Contest with G. Britain" and continued:

> All of us who were engaged in the struggle must have observed frequent
> instances of a Superintending providence in our favor. To that kind
> providence we owe this happy opportunity of consulting in peace on
> the means of establishing our future national felicity. And have we now
> forgotten that powerful friend? or do we imagine that we no longer
> need his assistance? I have lived, Sir, a long time, and the longer I live,
> the more convincing proofs I see of this truth—*that God governs in the*
> *affairs of men.*[31]

He then alluded to three biblical metaphors illustrative of God's intervention in human affairs and declared: "I firmly believe this." Referring to this

event, Herbert Storing has suggested that "Franklin sought to restore proportion by turning the delegates' minds to the fallibility of human reason, to the War of Independence, and to Divine Providence."[32]

Long before the convention, Franklin was so concerned with God's activity and intervention that he wrote an essay entitled "On the Providence of God in the Government of the World." In that essay, he outlined four possible positions regarding God's Providence. He evinced disdain for the idea that God "unchangeably decreed and appointed every Thing that comes to pass; and left nothing to the Course of Nature, nor . . . free agency," which was the position of Calvinism as he saw it. He expressed equal disdain for the idea that "without decreeing any thing, he left all to general Nature and the Events of Free Agency in his Creatures, which he never alters or interrupts." This was the position of deism. Franklin found them both to be "inconsistent with the common Light of Reason."[33] And for him, as a theistic rationalist, there was no greater condemnation.

According to Franklin, the Calvinist position made God no longer God, and He had "divested himself of all further Power." He was now no more powerful than an idol, and there was no reason to worship Him or pray to Him. Furthermore, "he has decreed some things contrary to the very Notion of a wise and good Being" (such as that people injure each other and pray to Him even though he has already determined their fate). In contrast, Franklin argued, if the deist position was correct, then God must either have abandoned the universe or simply become a spectator rooting for the good guys and hoping chance would punish the bad. According to Franklin, "There can be no Reason to imagine he would make so glorious a Universe meerly [*sic*] to abandon it." He asked: "How is it possible to believe a wise and an infinitely Good Being can be delighted in this Circumstance; and be utterly unconcern'd what becomes of the Beings and Things he has created?"[34] Unlike the deists, Franklin did not believe that was the case.

As he saw it, the third option was that God "decreed some Things unchangeably, and left others to general Nature and the Events of Free agency, which also he never alters or interrupts." Such a position was unacceptable to him because, if true, "you unGod him . . . he has nothing to do; he can cause us neither Good nor Harm; he is no more to be regarded than a lifeless Image." Franklin described this position as "an Absurdity."[35]

According to his thinking, since the other options did not stand up to the test of reason, people were "necessarily driven" to accept his supposition "that the Deity sometimes interferes by his *particular* Providence, and sets aside the Events which would otherwise have been produc'd in the Course of Nature, or by the Free Agency of Men" (emphasis mine).[36] To illustrate,

Franklin posited a situation in which the righteous were oppressed and cried out to God for deliverance: "If you say he cannot, you deny his infinite Power, which [you] at first acknowledg'd; if you say he will not, you must directly deny his infinite Goodness. You are then of necessity oblig'd to allow, that 'tis highly reasonable to believe a Providence because tis highly absurd to believe otherwise."[37] For Franklin, it was irrational to disbelieve in God's Providence, and beyond that, he believed Providence was the basis of religion:

> Now if tis unreasonable to suppose it out of the Power of the Deity to help and favour us particularly or that we are out of his Hearing or Notice or that Good Actions do not procure more of his Favour than ill Ones. Then I conclude, that believing a Providence we have the Foundation of all true Religion; for we should love and revere that Deity for his Goodness and thank him for his Benefits; we should adore him for his Wisdom, fear him for his Power, and pray to him for his Favour and Protection; and this Religion will be a Powerful Regulater [*sic*] of our Actions, give us Peace and Tranquility within our own Minds, and render us Benevolent, Useful and Beneficial to others.[38]

For Franklin, rational argument proved Providence, and most of the other core beliefs of theistic rationalism followed from the belief in Providence.

Related to the belief in Providence is another of Franklin's beliefs that distance him from deism: belief in the efficacy of prayer. He included prayer in his creed, modernized the Lord's Prayer to make it more accessible, and composed a daily prayer for his own use. According to his autobiography, his daily routine began: "Rise, wash and address *Powerful Goodness!*" which was the term he used for God in his devotions. In his *Articles of Belief and Acts of Religion*, Franklin included two periods of prayer in his personal liturgy. In the "Adoration" section, he affirmed God's attributes and asked for a continuance of favor. He also had an entire "Petition" section, in which he asked for help in being more virtuous,[39] something that could not be done by an absent God.

The best-known example of his interest in, and perhaps commitment to, prayer is his suggestion that the sessions of the Constitutional Convention should begin with prayer. In his famous speech, Franklin reminded the delegates that their prayers during the Revolution "were heard, and they were graciously answered." He ended his speech with a motion: "I therefore beg leave to move—that henceforth prayers imploring the assistance of Heaven, and its blessings on our deliberations, be held in this Assembly

Table 5.1 **Four Views of God's Providence** (according to Benjamin Franklin)

Views	Does God decree what happens?	Does the course of nature determine what happens?	Does the free agency of God's creatures determine what happens?	Does God alter or interrupt decrees, course of nature, and/or free agency?
Calvinism[a]	All	No	No	No*
Deism[b]	No	Some	Some	No*
No one[c]	Some	Some	Some	No*
Franklin and many Christians[d]	No	Some	Some	Yes

"If God does not sometimes interfere by his Providence tis either because he cannot, or because he will not, which of these Positions will you chuse?"

[a]He is no longer God—he was powerful but has "divested himself of all further power"; now, he is no more powerful than an idol; "he has decreed some things contrary to the very Notion of a wise and good Being"

[b]He must either have abandoned the universe or simply be a spectator; "there can be no Reason to imagine he would make so glorious a Universe merely to abandon it"; "How is it possible to believe a wise and an infinitely Good Being can be . . . utterly unconcern'd what becomes of the Beings and Things he has created?"

[c]"You unGod him . . . he has nothing to do; he can cause us neither Good nor Harm"

[d]"We are then necessarily driven into the fourth Supposition" by reason

* = There is no reason to pray

Source: Benjamin Franklin, "On the Providence of God in the Government of the World" [1730], in *Benjamin Franklin, Writings*, ed. J. A. Leo Lemay (New York: Library of America, 1987), 163–168.

every morning before we proceed to business, and that one or more of the Clergy of this City be requested to officiate in that service."[40] It is likely that Franklin's suggestion was calculated to allow cooler heads to prevail and "to restore the sense of proportion and of the obligations of statesmanship which the Convention seemed in danger of losing."[41] Nonetheless, it was consistent with his belief in prayer and in God's providential interest in the future of America.

A vast mythology has grown up around this event, largely based on an apocryphal account that was published in the *National Intelligencer* in 1826. The story is regularly repeated by Christian America advocates and is recounted in a number of their publications. According to this account, Washington and others were "delighted" at Franklin's suggestion, and only Alexander Hamilton opposed it. The motion was carried unanimously (or with Hamilton's "solitary negative"), and the delegates adjourned for three days to seek God in prayer. The author of the account said it was accurate "as far as my memory serves me," but he admitted it was secondhand information based on "a recollection of ten years" by the original source.[42] James Madison, whose convention notes are the most complete and considered most reliable, specifically denied the apocryphal account on three occasions.[43] The convention notes of Madison, Robert Yates, Rufus King, and William Paterson all indicate that there was no three-day recess. The record is clear that the convention took no action on Franklin's motion. Even Franklin himself commented that "the convention, except for three or four persons, thought prayers unnecessary."[44] But in either version of this event, his interest in public prayer is evident.

Jefferson also showed much more interest and belief in written revelation than deism would allow. An anonymous pamphlet writer in 1800 offered as "proof of his regard for the word of God" the fact that Jefferson bought "the most expensive and handsome edition of the word of God ever published in these states" (the "Hot-Press Bible published at Philadelphia").[45] One may not find that evidence particularly convincing, but there are other indications that Jefferson held a higher view of revelation than did the deists. One of the cardinal beliefs of deism was a rejection of any and all written revelation; deists believed only in natural revelation. When deists looked at the Bible at all, they did so for the sole purpose of refuting or mocking it. Kerry Walters has observed that Jefferson's "analysis of Scripture was based upon an exegetical methodology which was both thoughtful and systematic." Deists tended to use a "shotgun approach in their criticisms of Scripture," but Jefferson "carefully sifted through scriptural accounts in order to salvage the reasonable wheat from the unreasonable chaff." Unlike deists, he did not automatically dismiss biblical testimony; he tested it.[46] In response to a correspondent who claimed to have received a revelation from God, Jefferson expressed doubt but did not deny the possibility that the revelation was real.[47] In fact, he indicated that real written revelation did exist when he wrote that "revelation has, for reasons unknown to us, chosen to leave us in the dark" regarding transmigration of souls and again with the comment that "if revealed language has not been able to guard itself against misinterpretations, I could not expect it."[48]

Referring to the books of the Old Testament, Jefferson argued that only "parts of them are genuine"—but that means he believed that parts of them *are genuine.* For example, he sang the praises of the Psalms.[49] In a discussion of "sublime ideas" in the Gospels, he argued: "These could not be inventions of the grovelling authors who relate them. They are far beyond the powers of their feeble minds."[50] This was backhanded praise, to be sure, but affirmation of revelation from God nonetheless. Jefferson's use of biblical metaphors and biblical phrases such as "prove all things, hold fast that which is good," and "well done, good and faithful servants" demonstrated a familiarity and respect for Scripture not normal for deists. He even quoted entire verses or passages of Scripture to make a point, explain a concept, or support an argument.[51] His argument against the deity of Jesus included a study of John 1:1–3 in the original Greek; a deist would have dismissed John's account as irrelevant or ridiculed it. His well-known construction of *The Philosophy of Jesus* and *The Life and Morals of Jesus* using scissor-clipped extracts from the Gospels was at once an indictment of the parts of the Bible left on the cutting room floor and a greater affirmation of a significant portion of the New Testament than any deist would espouse. In fact, Jefferson claimed that "it is a document in proof that *I* am a *real Christian.*"[52]

Though Jefferson had greater respect for the Bible and the concept of revelation than did the deists, he did share some of their perspectives and doubts. For instance, he believed that nature provided sufficient proof of the existence of God as to make revelation unnecessary for that purpose. As he put it, "I think that every Christian sect gives a great handle to atheism by their general dogma that, without a revelation, there would not be sufficient proof of the being of a god."[53] For Christians, of course, recognition of the existence of *a god* was not at all sufficient and hardly made revelation unnecessary.

Another example of his affinity with deists is his questioning of the veracity and authenticity of significant portions of the Bible. Regarding the Old Testament, Jefferson said that "the whole history of these books is so defective and doubtful that it seems vain to attempt minute enquiry into it."[54] He was more charitable toward the New Testament, but still, he was interested only in the history and teachings of Jesus as recorded in the Gospels.

> We must reduce our volume to the simple evangelists, select, even from them, the very words only of Jesus, paring off the amphibologisms into which they have been led by forgetting often, or not understanding, what had fallen from him, by giving their own misconceptions as his dicta, and expressing unintelligibly for others what they had not understood themselves. There will be found remaining the most sublime and benevolent code of morals which has ever been offered to man. I have performed this operation for my own use, by cutting verse by verse out of the printed book, and arranging, the matter which is evidently his, and which is as easily distinguishable as diamonds in a dunghill.[55]

Jefferson's favorite way to describe the "genuine" words of Jesus was by referring to them as "diamonds" in the "dunghills" of the rest of the New

Testament.[56] Another repeated metaphor he used for the same process was "winnowing the grain from the chaff."[57] He claimed that it was "easy" to make such determinations because "there is internal evidence that parts of it [the New Testament] have proceeded from an extraordinary man; and that other parts are of the fabric of very inferior minds." He abstracted "from the Evangelists" "whatever has the stamp of the eloquence and fine imagination of Jesus." He relied on the "style and spirit" of the writings to determine what was "genuine, and [Jesus's] own." When he found "passages of fine imagination, correct morality, and of the most lovely benevolence," he judged them to be legitimate words of Jesus.[58] Similarly, Jefferson declared passages to be true descriptions of Jesus when they contained "sublime ideas of the Supreme Being, aphorisms, and precepts of the purest morality and benevolence, sanctioned by a life of humility, innocence and simplicity of manners, neglect of riches, absence of worldly ambition and honors, with an eloquence and persuasiveness which have not been surpassed."[59] In short, using his own reason, he determined for himself what were legitimately the words of Jesus.

In the "dunghills" of the rest of the New Testament, Jefferson found "a groundwork of vulgar ignorance, of things impossible, of superstitions, fanaticisms, and fabrications." He found "so much ignorance, so much absurdity, so much untruth, charlatanism and imposture, as to pronounce it impossible that such contradictions should have proceeded from the same being." He ascribed "trivialities and imbecilities" to the authors of the parts of the New Testament of which he did not approve, and he called the non-Gospel authors "Pseudo-evangelists" who "pretended to inspiration."[60] Jefferson was singularly critical of the apostle Paul, who was the only biblical writer mentioned by name in his diatribes: "I separate, therefore, the gold from the dross; restore to him the former, and leave the latter to the stupidity of some, and roguery of others of his disciples. Of this band of dupes and impostors, Paul was the great Coryphaeus, and first corruptor of the doctrines of Jesus."[61]

Nevertheless, as was mentioned earlier, Jefferson did not agree with all of what he determined to be the words of Jesus. Speaking of Jesus's doctrines, he said: "I read them as I do those of other ancient and modern moralists, with a mixture of approbation and dissent."[62] For some reason, however, he felt the need to make excuses for the flaws in Jesus's teachings. He explained one excuse to Priestley: "To do him justice, it would be necessary to remark the disadvantages his doctrines had to encounter, not having been committed to writing by himself, but by the most unlettered of men, by memory, long after they had heard them from him; when much was forgotten, much misunderstood, & presented in every paradoxical shapes."[63] After similar remarks in his *Syllabus,* Jefferson explained, "Hence, the doctrines which he really delivered were defective as a whole, and fragments only of what he did deliver have come to us mutilated, misstated, and often unintelligible." A second excuse was that Jesus might have believed Himself inspired and, therefore, taken Himself too seriously.[64] The final excuse advanced by Jefferson was related to Jesus's mission to reform Judaism and "the circumstances under which he acted":

> Jesus had to walk on the perilous confines of reason and religion; and a step to right or left might place him within the grasp of the priests of the superstition, a blood-thirsty race, as cruel and remorseless as the being whom they represented as the family God of Abraham, of Isaac and of Jacob, and the local God of Israel. They were constantly laying snares, too, to entangle him in the web of the law. He was justifiable, therefore, in avoiding these by evasions, by sophisms, by misconstructions and misapplications of scraps of the prophets, and in defending himself with these their own weapons, as sufficient, *ad homines,* at least.[65]

The biblical record of Jesus was not infallible, nor were Jesus and His teachings perfect. "Notwithstanding these disadvantages, a system of morals is presented to us, which, if filled up in the true style and spirit of the rich fragments he left us, would be the most perfect and sublime that has ever been taught by man."[66]

Since morality was the ultimate standard in their system and doctrines were viewed as divisive, Jefferson could also join Adams in elevating philosophical works to the level of Scripture. As he saw it, "Epictetus and Epicurus give laws for governing ourselves, Jesus a *supplement* of the duties and charities we owe to others" (emphasis mine).[67] He wanted to "subjoin" "the genuine doctrines of Epicurus from the Syntagma of Gassendi" to an "abstract from the Evangelists" of the words of Jesus that Jefferson felt were genuine.[68] He eventually did produce such a work, which he entitled *Syllabus of an Estimate of the Merit of the Doctrines of Jesus, Compared with Those of Others.* It constituted, as he put it, "my view of the Christian system." It contained, first, "a general view of the moral doctrines of the most remarkable of the antient [sic] philosophers"; then, "a view of the deism and ethics of the Jews" and their degradation; and finally, "a view of the life, character, & doctrines of Jesus."[69] It should be stressed that Jefferson, like Adams, included obviously non-Christian material in *his* view of Christianity. When he and the others used the term *Christianity,* they meant their own system, which was actually theistic rationalism.

The fundamental question regarding revelation that remained to be answered by Jefferson was how one should approach the biblical text. Jefferson clearly expressed the foundational rule of theistic rationalists—that is, that reason was the standard and guide to the interpretation and evaluation of revelation. According to him, "Man, once surrendering his reason, has no remaining guard against absurdities the most monstrous," and "gullability [*sic*], which they call faith, takes the helm from the hand of reason, and the mind becomes a wreck." Jefferson nearly described the process he advocated as theistic rationalism when he said, "No one sees with greater pleasure than myself the progress of reason in its advances towards *rational Christianity*" (emphasis mine).[70] He explained the proper approach to Miles King, who claimed to have had a revelation from God:

> Whether the particular revelation which you suppose to have been made to yourself were real or imaginary, your reason alone is the competent judge. For dispute as long as we will on religious tenets, our reason at last must ultimately decide, as it is the only oracle which God has given us to determine between what really comes from him and the phantasms of a disordered or deluded imagination.[71]

Notice that Jefferson told King "*your* reason *alone* [emphases mine]" is competent to judge the *reality* of whether or not he had received a revelation—not a council of wise men or a panel of philosophers. He clearly had as much confidence in any individual's reason as did Adams. Perhaps most important, though, is that Jefferson here affirmed that there *is* revelation from God when he referred to "what really comes from him [God]." To his young nephew Peter Carr, he gave specific advice concerning the handling of Scripture, which, as it outlines the theistic rationalist hermeneutic, is worth quoting at length:

> Read the bible then, as you would read Livy or Tacitus. The facts which are within the ordinary course of nature you will believe on the authority of the writer, as you do those of the same kind in Livy and Tacitus. The testimony of the writer weighs in their favor in one scale, and their not being against the laws of nature does not weigh against them. But those facts in the bible which contradict the laws of nature, must be examined with more care, and under a variety of faces. Here you must recur to the pretensions of the writer to inspiration from god. Examine upon what evidence his pretensions are founded, and whether that evidence is so strong, as that it's [*sic*] falshood [*sic*] would be more improb-

able than a change of the laws of nature in the case he relates. . . . The pretension is entitled to your enquiry, because millions believe it.[72]

He went on to admonish Carr to "fix reason firmly in her seat, and call to her tribunal every fact, every opinion." Carr was told, "Keep your reason firmly on the watch in reading," and he was advised, "*You* are to judge" the "pretensions" of biblical writers "by *your own* reason" (emphases mine]. Then, in a statement similar to the one he made to Miles King, Jefferson told Carr: "*Your own* reason is the only oracle given you by heaven, and you are answerable not for the rightness but uprightness of the decision" (emphasis mine).[73] Apparently, an individual's reason might err, but errors in religious thought were excusable as long as the individual was sincere. According to Jefferson, it was the thought that counted.

He argued that when other historians tell tall tales, we dismiss them as that and not as history: "In like manner, when an historian, speaking of a character well known and established on satisfactory testimony, imputes to it things incompatible with that character, we reject them without hesitation, and assent to that only of which we have better evidence." According to the theistic rationalists, when approaching Scripture, "it is surely time for men to think for themselves, and to throw off the authority of names so artificially magnified."[74]

Franklin's view of the Bible was also higher than that of the deists but lower than that of Christians. In his autobiography, he reported that "Revelation had indeed no weight with me" when he was "a thorough Deist" as a youth. In writing his autobiography at age seventy-five, he reflected on this youthful view of revelation and saw it as inadequate. He then credited Providence "or some guardian angel" with preserving him "through this dangerous time of youth . . . free from any *wilful* [sic] gross immorality or injustice, that might have been expected from my want of religion."[75] Throughout the rest of his life, Franklin frequently based arguments on scriptural passages and principles, and he regularly quoted or listed biblical passages to illustrate the points he made. He also instructed his daughter on how to live in such a way as to receive "the favour of God" according to "a promise in the Commandment."[76]

Although he did find Scripture useful and although he did appeal to it at times, Franklin certainly did not consider use of Scripture necessary or all of the Bible to be divinely inspired revelation. He included the reading of other books, but he did not include any Scripture in his own, self-composed liturgy.[77] He intentionally did not appeal to Scripture when writing an essay on as theological a subject as the Providence of God, explaining, "I intend to offer you nothing but plain Reasoning . . . unsupported by the Authority of any Books or Men how sacred soever; because I know that no Authority is more convincing to Men of Reason than the Authority of Reason itself."[78] In true theistic rationalist fashion, the emphasis was on reason.

He was occasionally irreverent concerning the Bible. One of his favorite "party tricks" was to open a Bible, quote the apocryphal *Parable against Persecution* while pretending to read the (nonexistent) fifty-first chapter of Genesis, and then observe the reactions of listeners who purported to know the Bible well. He did this so often that some historians have reported he wrote the parable himself, but copies of it have been found in much earlier writings in other languages. Nevertheless, Franklin is still credited with giving it "biblical style" as well as its last four verses, which include the "moral," and also its popularity.[79]

At times, Franklin was overtly critical of Scripture. On his own judgment, he cut a part of the Book of Common Prayer that was drawn from Scripture, deciding it was "best omitted." He suggested that the wording of part of the Lord's Prayer was based on what "the compilers thought an inconvenient idea," that another part was "presumptuous," another part "improper," and another "unworthy of God." Since his own reason was the standard that he applied, he really meant that it was unworthy of *him*. In a letter to Priestley, Franklin agreed with the minister that "there are several things in the Old Testament, impossible to be given by *divine* inspiration." After giving a specific example from Judges 4, Franklin added, "If the rest of the Book were like that, I should rather suppose it given by Inspiration from another Quarter, and renounce the whole."[80] In other words, his inclination was to consider portions of the Bible that did not conform to his reason to be satanic in origin. Franklin held a mixed view of the Bible and written revelation, one that was consistent with the theistic rationalist position.

Jefferson also expressed much greater concern for and interest in Christianity than would a deist. In fact, on more than one occasion, he claimed to *be* a Christian,[81] and he said his views of "the Christian religion" were "the result of a life of inquiry & reflection." He stated that he was conversant with and an adherent to the "doctrines" of "the *unlettered* Apostles, the Apostolic fathers, and the Christians of the 1st century."[82] In concert with Adams and the other theistic rationalists influenced by Joseph Priestley, Jefferson opposed what he saw as "the corruptions" of Christianity and embraced his own version, which consisted of "the doctrines of Jesus" and "the genuine precepts of Jesus" as he interpreted them. He claimed to "have a view of the subject which ought to displease neither the rational

Christian or Deist; & would reconcile many [deists] to a character [Jesus] they have too hastily rejected."[83] He complained about the "artificial systems, invented by ultra-Christian sects" that had disfigured the religion of Jesus beyond recognition. Jefferson's partial list of these artificial systems included: "the immaculate conception of Jesus, his deification, the creation of the world by him, his miraculous powers, his resurrection and visible ascension . . . the Trinity, original sin, atonement, regeneration, election . . . &c."[84] As was noted with regard to Adams, these so-called corruptions and artificial systems constitute the core of orthodox Christianity. Like Adams and the other theistic rationalists, Jefferson denied the defining elements of Christianity—the person and work of Christ. Nonetheless, he was much more interested in an understanding of and identification with Christianity than any deist would have been. Like other theistic rationalists, he fashioned his own preferred version of Christianity.

Franklin had his own understanding of Christianity, too, but he was more concerned with what constituted Christianity and with maintaining a connection to it than any deist. On one hand, Franklin extolled the "Excellency of the CHRISTIAN RELIGION above all others antient [*sic*] or modern" and concerned himself with what comprised "the true Spirit of Christianity." He did not publicly criticize religious enthusiasm, and he was sensitive to the ideas of "Christians in these times."[85] On the other hand, Franklin reported that the evangelist George Whitefield used "to pray for my conversion, but never had the satisfaction of believing that his prayers were heard." Jared Sparks said of Franklin, "It is deeply to be regretted, that he did not bestow more attention than he seems to have done on the evidences of Christianity." As was noted previously, Franklin shared the theistic rationalist view that Christianity had undergone "various corrupting changes" from the pure system of morals taught by Jesus.[86]

It is clear from the views expressed in his defense of a heterodox young minister that Franklin's version of Christianity bore little resemblance to the orthodoxy of the day. Speaking of the Westminster Confession, which defined Presbyterian orthodoxy, Franklin stated that "it cannot be reasonable to silence one of our own Preachers, for preaching a Doctrine exactly agreeable to Christianity, only because he does not perhaps zealously propagate all the Doctrines of an old Confession."[87] Here, he tacitly admitted that *his* Christianity was at least not that of orthodox Presbyterianism. Nonetheless, in contrast to deists, he identified with Christianity and was concerned about its nature.

But what was Franklin's version of Christianity—and what were the corrupting changes that had marred the doctrines of Jesus? As one would expect from a theistic rationalist, the key to Franklin's religion involved morality and good works. For him, the goal in life was to be "a good Parent, a good Child, a good Husband, or Wife, a good Neighbour or Friend, a good Subject or Citizen, that is, in short, a good Christian." The crux of Christianity, according to Franklin, was goodness. Each time he laid out his creed, he declared that "the most acceptable service of God is doing good to man" and that one's soul "will be treated with justice in another life respecting its conduct in this"; similarly, he stated that God "loves such of his Creatures as love and do good to others" and makes them "more happy or miserable after this Life according to their Actions." In his personal liturgy, the continuing theme was God's "delight" in virtue and the happiness that results from virtuous living. He addressed God in the "Adoration" section as one who abhorred every "hurtful Vice" and loved "every Virtue."[88]

As a theistic rationalist, Franklin saw morality as central to both private and public religious life. As Sparks explained, Franklin's writings "inculcate virtue and piety, which he regarded not more as duties of great moment in the present life, than as an essential preparation for the well-being of every individual in a future state of existence."[89] In the private sphere, according to Franklin, morality was the means of "salvation" for the individual, but religion was indispensable for the production of that morality. His views in this regard were made clear in his defense of a young heterodox preacher named Samuel Hemphill. Franklin reported that Hemphill delivered "most excellent discourses," and he stated, "I became one of his constant hearers, his sermons pleasing me, as they had little of the dogmatical kind, but inculcated strongly the practice of virtue, or what in the religious style are called *good works*."[90] The Presbyterian Synod was not equally impressed with Hemphill, however, and charged him with heterodoxy. Franklin came to his defense and denied the right of the synod to question a preacher who was "cultivating morality." Among the charges that Franklin admitted were accurate were that Hemphill taught (1) that people born in Christian families who led moral lives did not need not be converted, and (2) that man was "ultimately saved by his virtue." According to one Franklin scholar, he was willing to admit these points because they were "sound doctrine to both Franklin and Hemphill."[91]

Franklin's primary weapon in defense of Hemphill was the pen or, more precisely, the printing press. He wrote *Dialogue between Two Presbyterians* in Hemphill's defense. In that revealing work, Franklin argued that "morality made the principal Part" of the preaching of Christ and the apostles and that Christ warned His audience in the Sermon on the Mount to depend on works, rather than faith, for salvation. Regarding salvation by faith,

Franklin maintained that "Faith is recommended as a Means of producing Morality. . . . Thus Faith would be a Means of producing Morality, and Morality of Salvation. But that from such Faith alone Salvation may be expected, appears to me to be neither a Christian Doctrine nor a reasonable one."[92] Note that Franklin required doctrines to be "reasonable." In these matters, he and Hemphill took a position closer to that of the Catholic Church than that of their Presbyterian Church. Franklin clarified his substitution of morality for salvation by faith in another argument in the *Dialogue*: "Morality or Virtue is the End, Faith only a Means to obtain that End: And if the End be obtained, it is no matter by what Means. . . . Faith in Christ, however, may be and is of great Use to produce a good Life, but . . . it can conduce nothing towards Salvation where it does not conduce to Virtue."[93] His blatant opposition to orthodoxy reached a crescendo in his summary argument in defense of Hemphill. There, he stated that "Peace, Unity and Virtue in any Church are more to be regarded than Orthodoxy" and that a "virtuous Heretick [sic] shall be saved before a wicked Christian."[94]

Franklin made similar arguments in personal correspondence: "I think vital Religion has always suffer'd, when Orthodoxy is more regarded than Virtue. And Scripture assures me, that at the last Day, we shall not be examin'd what we *thought*, but what we *did*; and our Recommendation will not be that we said *Lord, Lord*, but that we did GOOD to our Fellow Creatures."[95] One other extensive passage from his personal correspondence will serve to solidify Franklin's argument and to crystallize his distance from orthodox Christianity:

The Faith you mention has doubtless its use in the World; I do not desire to see it diminished, nor would I endeavour to lessen it in any Man. But I wish it were more productive of Good Works than I have generally seen it: I mean real good Works, Works of Kindness, Charity, Mercy, and Publick [sic] Spirit. . . . The Worship of God is a Duty, the hearing and reading of Sermons may be useful; but if Men rest in Hearing and Praying, as too many do, it is as if a Tree should value itself on being water'd and putting forth Leaves, tho' it never produc'd any Fruit. Your great Master tho't much less of these outward Appearances and Professions than many of his modern Disciples. He prefer'd the Doers of the Word to the meer [sic] Hearers . . . and those who gave Food to the hungry, Drink to the Thirsty, Raiment to the Naked, Entertainment to the Stranger, and Relief to the Sick, &c. *tho' they never heard of his Name*, he declares shall in the last Day be accepted, when those who cry Lord, Lord; who value themselves on their Faith tho' great enough to perform Miracles but have neglected good Works shall be rejected. (Emphasis mine.)[96]

Franklin could hardly have made clearer his reliance upon works or his rejection of a "faith" based on the claim that there is salvation only by that name and that Jesus is the only way to salvation.[97]

As a good theistic rationalist, Franklin had another reason for emphasizing morality. Religious morality made good citizens and promoted public morality, which, subsequently, benefited society. In his argument for the teaching of history, he pointed out that "*History* will also afford frequent Opportunities of showing the Necessity of a *Publick Religion,* from its Usefulness to the Publick" to "the Advantage of a Religious Character among private persons" and other advantages. Franklin argued that most people need religion in order to be virtuous until it becomes habitual. As he put it: "If Men are so wicked as we now see them *with Religion* what would they be if *without it?*"[98]

As Franklin saw it, the primary role of a minister was to inculcate morality in order to produce good citizens. At one point, he blamed his spotty church attendance on the preaching of the local Presbyterian minister. He complained that "his discourses were chiefly either polemic arguments, or explications of the peculiar doctrines of our sect, and were all to me very dry, uninteresting, and unedifying; since not a single moral principle was inculcated or enforced; their aim seeming to be rather to make us *Presbyterians* than *good citizens.*" Such an emphasis on doctrine rather than morality was unforgivable for one with the public's ear. Renowned evangelist George Whitefield must have included a sufficient plea for morality in his sermons because Franklin frequented them and commented, "It was wonderful to see the change soon made in the manners of our inhabitants."[99]

For his own part, Franklin made plans to start a new sect called "THE SOCIETY OF THE FREE AND EASY" based on his creed and the pursuit of virtue. Although the organization never got off the ground, he concluded that it would have been "very useful, by forming a great number of good citizens."[100] For a theistic rationalist, there was no higher praise for a sect. For Franklin and his fellows, that was "Christianity."

In the absence of his own sect, Franklin identified himself with a local church, was very supportive of Philadelphia churches, and encouraged church attendance. This was not the norm for a deist. One of his expressed goals in producing an abridgement of the Book of Common Prayer was "to occasion a more frequent attendance on the worship of God." He urged his daughter not to leave "*our* church" (emphasis mine) and instructed her: "Go constantly to church, whoever preaches." He told her that the act of devotion, participating in prayer, and learning from the sermons made church attendance valuable. His own attendance was infrequent at best. He noted that he once went "for five Sundays successively" and "might have continued" if the preacher had been more to his liking. Though his own church attendance was sporadic, he "still had an opinion of its propriety, and of its utility when rightly conducted," and he "regularly paid" an "annual subscription for the support of the only Presbyterian minister or meeting we had in Philadelphia." In fact, after his dispute with leaders of the denomination, Franklin "quitted the congregation" but "continued many years" his subscription for the support of its ministers nonetheless.[101] Alfred Owen Aldridge, who wrote the best-known work on Franklin's religion, reported that Franklin "was nominally an Anglican" after separating from the local Presbyterian church. "Although intellectually rejecting practically the entire body of Anglican theology," he participated in many Anglican rituals. Aldridge summarized Franklin's public worship: "He sought method in all he did—and, for him, the Anglican approach to God was expedient and methodical. . . . For him, the Anglican was the most compatible system of public worship. But it was the ritual, not the theology, that counted."[102] Although Franklin's own attendance was inconsistent, he remained attached to churches throughout his life, supported them financially, and encouraged attendance in others.

Like Adams, Jefferson and Franklin held a higher view of Jesus than did most deists and a lower view than did Christians. Jefferson referred to Jesus as the "first of human sages," a "benevolent moralist," a "master workman," and "the most innocent, the most benevolent, the most eloquent and sublime character that ever has been exhibited to man."[103] According to Jefferson, Jesus performed two functions: he was a moralist or ethicist, and he was a reformer. A few examples will suffice to demonstrate his opinion of Jesus as a moralist. Jefferson said: "Of all the systems of morality, ancient or modern, which have come under my observation, none appear to me so pure as that of Jesus"; "I hold the precepts of Jesus, as delivered by himself, to be the most pure, benevolent, and sublime which have ever been preached to man"; and "his part composed the most beautiful morsel of morality which has been given to us by man."[104] In a discussion about applying the morality of Jesus to society, Jefferson claimed, "We all agree in the obligation of the moral precepts of Jesus, and nowhere will they be found delivered in greater purity than in his discourses." According to Jefferson, the doctrines of Jesus were "more pure, correct, and sublime than those of the ancient philosophers" because the latter dealt with "the government of our passions" and "our own tranquility," whereas Jesus dealt with duties to others and with our thoughts.[105]

Regarding the function of reformer, Jefferson hailed Jesus as "the great reformer of the Jewish religion," "the great reformer of the vicious ethics and deism of the Jews," "the greatest of all the reformers of the depraved religion of his own country," "a great reformer of the Hebrew code of religion," and "the benevolent and sublime reformer" of Judaism.[106] Incidentally, he explained that his reference to the "deism" of the Jews simply meant their belief in only one God.[107] Concerning the Jews, Jefferson said that Jesus strove "to reform their moral doctrines to the standard of reason, justice & philanthropy." Note that the first standard was "reason." Ultimately, Jefferson placed Jesus "among the greatest reformers of morals, and scourges of priest-craft that have ever existed."[108]

Although he asserted that Jesus was a great moral teacher, Jefferson included some disclaimers. Even as he sought "to place the character of Jesus in its true and high light," he stated that "it is not to be understood that I am with him in all his doctrines."[109] Furthermore, according to Jefferson, Jesus was killed before His reason "attained the *maximum* of its energy" and before His preaching "presented occasions for developing a complete system of morals. Hence, the doctrines which he really delivered were defective as a whole, and fragments only of what he did deliver have come to us mutilated, misstated, & often unintelligible." Nonetheless, Jefferson maintained that "such are the fragments remaining as to show . . . that his system of morality was the most benevolent & sublime probably that has been ever taught."[110] For him, Jesus was not infallible or perfect, but His teachings were the best one could expect from a mere man. One can only wonder how Jefferson knew that Jesus's teachings had been mutilated and misstated—perhaps this was because he considered some of them to be irrational.

Jefferson quoted Jesus as an authority on the nature of God and claimed to subscribe to "his theology" on that subject,[111] yet he did not believe that Jesus was God or that He ever claimed deity.[112] He wrote at length on this subject to William Short:

That Jesus did not mean to impose himself on mankind as the son of God, physically speaking, I have been convinced by the writings of men more learned than myself in that lore. But that he might conscientiously believe himself inspired from above, is very possible. . . . Elevated by the enthusiasm of a warm and pure heart, conscious of the high strains of an eloquence which had not been taught him, he might readily mistake the coruscations of his own fine genius for inspirations of an higher order. This belief carried, therefore, no more personal imputation, than the belief of Socrates, that himself was under the care and admonitions of a guardian Daemon.[113]

As was noted, Jefferson listed the deity of Christ among the "artificial systems invented by ultra-Christian sects" that were "unauthorized by a single word ever uttered by him."[114] It is important to mention that in his versions of *The Philosophy of Jesus* and *The Life and Morals of Jesus* (which were constructed by cutting and pasting New Testament verses), Jefferson omitted the passages in which Jesus so clearly claimed His own deity that the Jews tried to stone Him.[115] In his *Syllabus* on the doctrines of Jesus, Jefferson evaded the issue: "The question of his being a member of the Godhead, or in direct communication with it, claimed for him by some of his followers, and denied by others is foreign to the present view, which is merely an estimate of the intrinsic merit of his doctrines."[116] Such a stance assumed, rather than proved, that Jesus's deity was *not* one of His doctrines, which is made easier when one excises the passages in which Jesus clearly claimed to be God.

As Jefferson saw it, Jesus Himself never claimed to be God; rather, His followers claimed that status for Him. Jefferson's self-appointed quest was to "justify the character of Jesus" to the deists "against the fictions of his pseudo-followers, which have exposed him to the inference of being an impostor."[117] Because they could not accept His claim to be God, deists often referred to Jesus as an impostor. Jefferson was conscious of the deist position when he said that "the incidents of his life require little research. They are all at hand, and need only to be put into human dress; noticing such only as are within the physical laws of nature, and offending none by a denial or even a mention of what is not."[118] He reached out to the deists by acknowledging that they would be correct if Jesus believed what the Gospel writers and generations of Christians said of Him: "For if we could believe that he really countenanced the follies, the falsehoods, and the charlatanisms which his biographers father on him, and admit the misconstructions, interpolations, and theorizations of the fathers of the early, and fanatics of the later ages, the conclusion would be irresistible by every sound mind, that he was an impostor."[119] According to Jefferson, however, we need not think that Jesus believed such things.

In his view, "pseudo-priests" had "perverted" the doctrines of Jesus, as had those "calling themselves the expositors" of Jesus's doctrines. Those

doctrines had been "disfigured" by "schismatising followers" who had succeeded in "sophisticating and perverting" them. Furthermore, "those who
pretend[ed] to be his special disciples" had "disfigured and sophisticated
his actions & precepts." As a result, "they have caused good men to reject
the whole in disgust and to view Jesus himself as an impostor."[120] Those
"good men" were deists whose reason would not allow them to accept the
Incarnation. Jefferson understood how the deists could arrive at their low
opinion of Jesus: "The religion-builders have so distorted and deformed
the doctrines of Jesus, so muffled them in mysticisms, fancies and falsehoods, have caricatured them into forms so monstrous and inconceivable,
as to shock reasonable thinkers, to revolt them against the whole, and drive
them rashly to pronounce its founder an impostor."[121] Jefferson wanted to
assure them that all of what they found "incomprehensible" was "without
any foundation in his genuine words"[122]—at least His "genuine" words as
determined by a Jefferson who was wielding scissors. Of course, he made
all of these determinations on the basis of his own reason. In all of this,
Jefferson's view of Jesus was that of a theistic rationalist and not that of a
Christian or deist.

Franklin shared with Jefferson and the deists the denial of the deity of
Jesus and of His satisfaction for sins. He confessed that his mother "grieves"
over his denial of the Trinity.[123] In a letter to Congregationalist minister
Ezra Stiles, Franklin referred to "Jesus of *Nazareth*," which was a common
method used to emphasize His mere humanity (emphasis mine). More important, in speaking of Jesus, Franklin confessed to having

> some doubts as to his Divinity; though it is a question I do not dogma-
> tize upon, having never studied it, and think it needless to busy myself
> with it now, when I expect soon an opportunity of knowing the truth
> with less trouble. I see no harm, however, in its being believed, if that
> belief has the good consequence, as probably it has, of making his doc-
> trines more respected and more observed.[124]

Expressing "some doubts" to someone who believed was the polite
eighteenth-century way of saying that one did not share the belief. As for
the rest of the statement, such a cavalier attitude from an eighty-four-year-
old who was by his own admission "very infirm" and soon to confront
death confirms that he had more than "some doubts" that Jesus was the
God to whom he would soon be accountable. In his defense of Hemphill,
Franklin attacked the orthodox image of God as a righteous judge who
must be satisfied as, in the words of one scholar, "repugnant both to reason

and to God." One would expect him to oppose the doctrine that followed from that presupposition—that is, that Christ came to offer an acceptable sacrifice. Indeed, Franklin tried to defend Hemphill against the charge that he denied "the true and proper satisfaction of Christ" by diminishing its significance and by changing the subject.[125]

However, like Jefferson, Franklin held a higher view of Jesus than did deists. In the preface to his abridgement of the Book of Common Prayer, Franklin claimed to hold "in the highest veneration the doctrines of Jesus Christ." He said that Jesus's life "should be the constant Object of our Imitation," and under "humility" in his own plan for being moral, he simply wrote, "Imitate Jesus and Socrates." In his defense of the preacher accused of heterodoxy, Franklin approvingly defended preaching Jesus as "a rational teacher and giver of moral laws."[126] His most succinct remarks are found in the aforementioned letter to Ezra Stiles: "As to Jesus of Nazareth, my opinion of whom you particularly desire, I think his system of morals and his religion, as he left them to us, the best the world ever saw or is like to see; but I apprehend it has received various corrupting changes, and I have, with most of the present Dissenters in England, some doubts as to his Divinity."[127] Like fellow theistic rationalists Adams and Jefferson, Franklin saw Jesus as a great moral teacher and supported His doctrines as he, Franklin, defined them. That definition did not include fundamental doctrines of Christianity, such as Jesus's deity, that Franklin viewed as "corrupting changes" in Jesus's "system of morals and his religion." As was discussed earlier, Franklin's definition of Jesus's doctrines focused on morality and good works. If belief in His deity encouraged people to follow His teaching, then Franklin would allow the false but beneficial belief.

Neither Jefferson's nor Franklin's view of the afterlife was quite that of deists, either. At times, Jefferson emphasized the rather cold and distant judicial view of the "future state" that was the hallmark of deism. For example, he wrote of "the prospects of a future state of retribution for the evil as well as the good done while here." He also expressed an inclusive, deistic conception of who was likely to be found in heaven.[128] The deistic view posited a largely mechanical and impersonal heaven, in which one essentially deposited the currency of good works into a machine at the gate in order to gain earned entrance and one's individuality was more or less absorbed into an amorphous concept of happiness or bliss. Jefferson sometimes presented a more personal view, however. On more than one occasion when discussing entrance to heaven, he spoke of a need to "trust" in God.[129] He joined with Adams in awaiting God's "time and will" regarding a future life and anticipated reunion with "our antient [*sic*] colleagues." In a poignant letter to Adams on the death of his wife, Jefferson said that "it is of some comfort to us both that the term is not very distant at which we are to deposit, in the same cerement, our sorrows and suffering bodies, and to ascend in essence to an ecstatic meeting with the friends we have loved and lost and whom we shall still love and never lose again."[130] Though this letter must be considered carefully as an attempt to console a friend, it is worth pointing out that deists did not speak of "ecstatic" meetings or of eternal love in the future state. These remarks reflected the influence of protestantism's more personal view of the afterlife—of a heaven. Jefferson's theistic rationalist concepts concerning the afterlife were borrowed from both deism and protestantism, and, therefore, they did not allow him to align with either.

In contrast to the deists, Franklin apparently believed in *bodily* resurrection. He composed an epitaph for himself that indicated such a belief: "The Body of Benjamin Franklin, Printer, (Like the cover of an old book, Its contents torn out, And stript of its lettering and gilding,) Lies here, food for worms. But the work shall not be lost, For it will, as he believed, appear once more, In a new and more elegant edition, Revised and corrected By The Author."[131] This epitaph was not, in fact, used for Franklin's grave, but the fact that he composed it reveals a belief in bodily resurrection. Some have argued that its composition was a joke, but the context does not suggest that; moreover, Franklin also expressed belief in bodily resurrection in another place. In a letter to a friend, he commented on the "great Frugality" of God's works. In doing so, he gave as an example "the natural Reduction of compound Substances to their original Elements, capable of being employ'd in new Compositions" and related that to God's conservation of souls. His conclusion was that since he existed, he would always exist "in some Shape or other," and he said he looked forward to "a new Edition of mine; hoping, however, that the *Errata* of the last may be corrected."[132] Although deists believed in a future state of rewards and punishments for the soul that one would enter in *essence,* they did not believe in bodily resurrection. Franklin also held a personal and profound belief in the afterlife. He wrote that the soul enters "real life" when the body dies and referred to the "happy society" beyond the grave. Referring to a friend who had died, he wrote: "Our friend and we are invited abroad on a party of pleasure—that is to last forever. His chair was first ready and he is gone before us. We could not all conveniently start together, and why should you and I be grieved at this, since we are soon to follow, and we know where to find him."[133] Again, one must be careful with letters of consolation, but given his belief in resurrection and his belief in a benevolent God, there is no reason to doubt that he believed the sentiment expressed here.

Concerning access to heaven, Franklin explicitly denied the deist belief that one could merit heaven by one's good works. He told his sister that he was not "so weake [*sic*] as to imagine, that the little Good we can do here, can *merit* so vast a Reward hereafter."[134] He expanded upon this point to another correspondent ten years later:

> You will see in this my Notion of Good Works, that I am far from expecting . . . that I shall merit Heaven by them. By Heaven we understand, a State of Happiness, infinite in Degree, and eternal in Duration: I can do nothing to deserve such Reward. . . . Even the mix'd imperfect Pleasures we enjoy in this World are rather from God's Goodness than our Merit; how much more such Happiness of Heaven. For my own part, I have not the Vanity to think I deserve it, the Folly to expect it, nor the Ambition to desire it; but content myself in submitting to the Will and Disposal of that God who made me, who has hitherto preserv'd and bless'd me, and in whose fatherly Goodness I may well confide, that he will never make me miserable, and that even the Afflictions I may at any time suffer shall tend to my Benefit.[135]

Once again, Franklin emphasized God's activity and intervention in his life and in his future. A deist would have cringed at the suggestion that one might be reliant upon "the Will and Disposal" of another—even God—for one's position in the afterlife. On another occasion, Franklin confessed *"trust in God"* for a better life after death.[136] Just a month before his death, he spoke of the hope of heaven but denied having "the smallest conceit of meriting such goodness."[137] Though Franklin certainly emphasized morality and believed that good works were necessary to put one in the best possible relationship with God, he did not hold the deist belief that good works *obligated* God to "save" a man. For Franklin, doing good works was a necessary but not sufficient condition for "salvation." Part of the problem for him was his conclusion that one could not live completely virtuously on his or her own accord—that reason could not prevent "slipping":

> It was about this time I conceived the bold and arduous project of arriving at *moral perfection*. I wished to live without committing any fault at any time, and to conquer all that either natural inclination, custom, or company, might lead me into. As I knew, or thought I knew,

what was right and wrong, I did not see why I might not *always* do the one and avoid the other. But I soon found I had undertaken a task of more difficulty than I had imagined. While my attention was taken up, and care employed in guarding against one fault, I was often surprised by another; habit took the advantage of inattention; inclination was sometimes too strong for reason. I concluded at length, that the mere speculative conviction, that it was our interest to be completely virtuous, was not sufficient to prevent our slipping.[138]

Deist thought taught that reason alone was sufficient to allow one to live completely virtuously and that man could achieve perfection. If one were to substitute the word *sin* for *fault* or *slip* in his remarks, the resultant statement would be a fair representation of the Christian concept of the sin nature. Either way, his remarks clearly ran contrary to deist notions.

In addition to his belief in bodily resurrection, Franklin acknowledged another element of supernaturalism. He recognized, though without enthusiasm, at least one biblical miracle—Jesus turning water into wine at Cana. He asserted that rain regularly entered roots of grapevines to be changed to wine and that "the miracle in question was only performed to hasten the operation."[139] He did, nonetheless, affirm that the hastening was a miracle. Deists denied the very concept of a miracle and did not recognize the legitimacy of any supernatural interference in the world. It is also worth noting that Franklin apparently took seriously the passage of Scripture recounting this event.

As theistic rationalists, Jefferson and Franklin disdained particular, exclusivist doctrines and recognized multiple roads to heaven. Since the defining element of any religion was, for them, morality, they could tolerate—and even support—virtually any religion. Advising his young nephew as to how to begin his study of religion, Jefferson said: "In the first place divest yourself of all bias in favour of novelty and singularity of opinion." He declared that he had "no adherence to any particular mode of Christianity" and believed that "bigotry is the disease of ignorance, of morbid minds."[140] He expressed his opinion of doctrinal creeds to a Unitarian clergyman: "I have never permitted myself to meditate a specified creed. These formulas have been the bane and ruin of the Christian church, its own fatal invention, which, through so many ages, made of Christendom a slaughter-house, and at this day divides it into casts of inextinguishable hatred to one another."[141] In another complaint about creeds and confessions of faith, Jefferson concluded: "How much wiser are the Quakers, who, agreeing in the fundamental doctrines of the gospel, schismatize about no mysteries, and, keeping within the pale of common sense, suffer no speculative differences of opinion, any more than of feature, to impair the love of their brethren."[142] In the same spirit, he told a Congregationalist minister that "if we could all . . . leave the subject [God] as undefinable, we should all be of one sect, doers of good, and eschewers of evil."[143] But if one does not define God, how does one know that He is not evil? Such was the ultimate dream and goal of the theistic rationalist—a God largely of each man's own definition honored by good deeds to fellow men. Jefferson tried to do his part to achieve this goal at the University of Virginia, declaring, "We suggest the expediency of encouraging the different religious sects to establish, each for itself, a professorship of their own tenets, on the confines of the university. . . . And by bringing the sects together, and mixing them with the mass of other students, we shall soften their asperities, liberalize and neutralize their prejudices, and make the general religion a religion of peace, reason, and morality."[144] He could see no greater goal than to create a "general religion" of "peace, reason, and morality," and he had learned some time before that "the way to silence religious disputes, is to take no notice of them."[145] Such a strategy was optimal for a theistic rationalist who was committed to no specific creed.

The familiar explanation for Jefferson's support of religious freedom is summarized in this statement in his *Notes on the State of Virginia:* "The legitimate powers of government extend to such acts only as are injurious to others. But it does me no injury for my neighbour to say there are twenty gods, or no god. It neither picks my pocket nor breaks my leg."[146] There were, according to Jefferson, at least two other reasons to tolerate various religious persuasions, one of which essentially allowing for the other. First, for Jefferson and the theistic rationalists, all religious roads led to God, so there was no real need to discriminate between them from the start. Jefferson stated this idea very clearly: "Let us not be uneasy then about the different roads we may pursue, as believing them the shortest, to that our last abode; but, following the guidance of a good conscience, let us be happy in the hope that by these different paths we shall all meet in the end."[147] In his view, the doctrinal disputes between denominations of so-called Christians were nonsensical and meaningless: "We have heard it said that there is not a Quaker or a Baptist, a Presbyterian or an Episcopalian, a Catholic or a Protestant in heaven; that on entering that gate, we leave those badges of schism behind, and find ourselves united in those principles only in which God has united us all."[148]

Not only were doctrinal differences ultimately unimportant in heaven, but they did not need to divide people on earth. All of the followers of the "doctrines of Jesus" should, in particular, be united. "No doctrines of his lead to schism. It is the speculations of crazy theologists which have made a Babel of a religion the most moral and sublime ever preached to man, and calculated to heal, and not to create differences."[149] Jefferson bragged about the liberality of his district in Virginia: "Here, Episcopalian and Presbyterian, Methodist and Baptist, meet together, join in hymning their Maker, listen with attention and devotion to each others' preachers, and all mix in society with perfect harmony. It is not so in the districts where Presbyterianism prevails undividedly. Their ambition and tyranny would tolerate no rival if they had power."[150] This statement is interesting on two grounds. First, it provides insight into one of Jefferson's motivations for supporting the separation of church and state. Second, it is clear that he, like Franklin, did not fathom the idea that people could have firm, uncompromising beliefs that were exclusive of other beliefs and could not "join" or "mix" in "harmony" with those diametrically opposed to them. Doctrinal disagreements between Christians were to be considered insignificant, and furthermore, the "gates of heaven" were open to pagans who were moral, as well:

> I believe . . . that he who steadily observes those moral precepts in which all religions concur, will never be questioned at the gates of heaven, as to the dogmas in which they all differ. That on entering there, all these are left behind us, and the *Aristides* and *Catos,* the Penns and Tillotsons, Presbyterians and Baptists, will find themselves united in all principles which are in concert with the reason of the supreme mind. (Emphases mine.)[151]

Note that the unifying principles shared in heaven were, according to Jefferson, based on *reason*.

This leads to the second reason that Jefferson and the theistic rationalists believed that all religions should be tolerated: they all promoted the morality on which society depended. For instance, regarding Unitarianism and Trinitarianism, he said: "Both religions, I find, make honest men, and that is the only point society has any right to look to." For Jefferson, it was clear that "the interests of society require the observation of those moral precepts only in which all religions agree . . . and that we should not intermeddle with the particular dogmas in which all religions differ, and which are totally unconnected with morality."[152] According to him, the "moral branch of religion" "instructs us how to live well and worthily in society," whereas "dogmas" exist only for the benefit of "the teachers who inculcate them."[153]

It is interesting that Jefferson—the patron saint of separation between church and state—promoted *his own* religious beliefs as normative for the nation. He said, "My religious reading has long been confined to the moral branch of religion, which is the same in all religions,"[154] and his belief that morality was the key to God's acceptance has already been demonstrated in his own words, quoted earlier. One further statement by Jefferson clarifies the point:

> If, by *religion,* we are to understand *sectarian dogmas,* in which no two of them agree, then your exclamation on that hypothesis is just, "that this would be the best of all possible worlds, if there were no religion in it." But if the moral precepts, innate in man, and made a part of his physical constitution, as necessary for a social being, if the sublime doctrines of philanthropism, and deism taught us by Jesus of Nazareth in which all agree, constitute true religion, then, without it, this would be, as you again say, "something not fit to be named, even indeed a hell."[155]

So, for Jefferson, "true religion" was adherence to morality; further, the "interests of society require[d]" such adherence, and society had a "right to look to" that adherence. Because every religion with which he was acquainted taught and promoted morality, he supported a freedom of religion that he thought would benefit his "sect." He was confident, indeed, that "if a sect arises, whose tenets would subvert morals, good sense has fair play, and reasons and laughs it out of doors." According to Jefferson, "If the freedom of religion, guaranteed to us by law *in theory,* can ever rise *in practice* under the overbearing inquisition of public opinion, truth will prevail over fanaticism, and the genuine doctrines of Jesus [Jefferson's religion], so long perverted by his pseudo-priests, will again be restored to their original purity." Furthermore, "a strong proof of the solidity of the primitive faith [Jefferson's religion], is its restoration, as soon as a nation arises which vindicates to itself the freedom of religious opinion, and its external divorce from the civil authority."[156] The theistic rationalists fully expected their religion to prevail in a society shorn of establishment.

Franklin likewise saw a universality in religions on the basis of the promotion of morality. Regarding "the fundamental principles of all sound religion," he said, "I regard them . . . in whatever sect I meet with them." He identified what he considered "the essentials of every religion." According to Franklin, these essentials

> being . . . found in all the religions we had in our country, I respected them all, though with different degrees of respect, as I found them more

or less mixed with other articles, which, without any tendency to inspire, promote, or confirm morality, served principally to divide us, and make us unfriendly to one another. This respect to all, with an opinion that the worst had some good effects, induced me to avoid all discourse that might tend to lessen the good opinion another might have of his own religion; and as our province increased with people, and new places of worship were continually wanted, and generally erected by voluntary contribution, my mite for such purpose, whatever might be the sect, was never refused.[157]

For Franklin, any and all religions that promoted morality were worthy of his support, although he did not respect "articles" that "served principally to divide"—that is, exclusivist doctrines. One way in which he supported various religions was by refraining from dissuading or discouraging their followers. Thus, in a comment to his sister on her doctrinal beliefs, Franklin explained: "I do not agree with, but I do not therefore condemn them, or desire to shake your Belief or Practice of them. . . . I would only have you make me the same Allowances, and have a better Opinion both of Morality and your Brother." Morality was the key. As he told Stiles: "I have ever let others enjoy their religious sentiments, without reflecting on them for those that appeared to me unsupportable or even absurd."[158]

Franklin also gave churches monetary support. As already mentioned, he continued to support his local church after withdrawing from the congregation, and his "mite" for places of worship was never refused. A cynic might see a sort of hedging of bets in Franklin's self-confessed attitude: "All sects here, and we have a great variety, have experienced my good will in assisting them with subscriptions for the building their new places of worship; and, as I have never opposed any of their doctrines, I hope to go out of the world in peace with them all." For the theistic rationalist, however, "no Point of Faith is so plain, as that *Morality* is our Duty, for all Sides agree in that."[159] And as long as "all sides" benefited society by promoting morality, Franklin would support them. In fact, at his urging, a meeting house was built "expressly for the use of *any preacher of any religious persuasion,* who might desire to say something to the people at Philadelphia; the design in building being not to accommodate any particular sect . . . so that even if the Mufti of Constantinople were to send a missionary to preach Mahometanism to us, he would find a pulpit at his service."[160]

Doctrinal differences were of no importance to the theistic rationalist. According to Franklin, "Many a long dispute among Divines may be thus abridg'd, It is so: It is not so. It is so; It is not so." He maintained that "'tis an Uncertainty till we get to Heaven what true Orthodoxy in all points is," so "it little becomes poor fallible Man to be positive and dogmatical in his Opinions." For his own part, he boasted that "perhaps for the last fifty years no one has ever heard a dogmatical expression escape me." Franklin clarified his position on religious opinion by saying, "I think Opinions should be judg'd of by their Influences and Effects; and if a Man holds none that tend to make him less Virtuous or more vicious, it may be concluded he holds none that are dangerous."[161] Again, morality was the standard, and truth or adherence to authority was unimportant. He submitted his abridgement of the Book of Common Prayer, which left out doctrinal points, to "the prudent and dispassionate, and not to enthusiasts and bigots, being convinced in our own breasts, that this shortened method . . . would further religion, remove animosity, and occasion a more frequent attendance on the worship of God."[162] What doctrines were excised did not matter to him; religion and attendance on worship were of ultimate importance—not the content of the religion or worship. Melvin Buxbaum has observed that Franklin "pretends to be unaware that a religious denomination, unlike a club for personal and civic improvement, might believe ardently in a particular theological interpretation as well as in secular virtue."[163]

Franklin contended for religious toleration and diversity on both a wide and a narrow scope. From his observations of America, he concluded that "the Divine Being seems to have manifested his approbation of the mutual forbearance and kindness with which the different sects treat each other, by the remarkable prosperity with which He has been pleased to favor the whole country." According to Franklin's version of *A Parable against Persecution*, the children of Israel were held in Egyptian bondage for centuries because of an intolerant act by Abraham, not because of their disobedience or rejection of God.[164] In an expression of his belief that salvation doctrine would not ultimately matter in the afterlife, Franklin said that "with regard to future bliss, I cannot help imagining, that multitudes of the zealously orthodox of different sects, who at the last day may flock together in hopes of seeing each other damned, will be disappointed, and obliged to rest content with their own salvation."[165] On a more personal level, he tried to keep his own creed "free of every thing that might shock the professors of any religion." Furthermore, in order to make his personal liturgy useful for all, he included in it "no mark of any of the distinguishing tenets of any particular sect." He reported that he "purposely avoided them."[166]

Franklin and a few other theistic rationalists found a fraternal home in Freemasonry. Given his theistic rationalist perspective, Franklin felt comfortable in the Masons, "a group that taught its members morality rather than theology, and stressed fellowship and toleration. Moreover, it expressed belief in one God, who was discovered through reason, and preached that natural religion was universal. That these doctrines appealed to Franklin is attested to by his very regular attendance at Masonic meetings and his subsequent rise in the organization."[167] Regarding that rise, Franklin held offices at least four times, among them "Provincial Grand Master of Pennsylvania." As Freemasonry was supposed to be a secret organization, he did not reveal much about it. He did affirm, however, that Masons had "no principles or Practices that are inconsistent with Religion or good Manners."[168] And they believed in a God discovered through reason.

For Franklin, living according to nature and reason was also consistent with religion. As was mentioned, he emphasized "the Authority of Reason itself" as the most important guide to religious knowledge. In addition, he argued that the study of natural history by a young man "will at the same Time take Care to form his Heart, and lead him by Nature to Religion."[169] He agreed with Hemphill that Christianity was largely a "new edition of nature's laws" and argued that this belief was consistent with the Gospel. Buxbaum has termed the religion advanced by Franklin and Hemphill "rationalistic Christianity."[170] The problem with that designation is that there is precious little Christianity in their system. A better term would be "theistic rationalism."

Another observation by Buxbaum echoes a claim of this study: "If evangelism appealed to the generally unsophisticated and emotionally demonstrative, rationalism . . . gained the favor of colonial intellectuals."[171] It was argued in chapter 1 of this volume that the educated elite of the Founding era were the ones who became theistic rationalists and that most members of the public remained more closely attached to traditional religion. Franklin recognized that his religious views were unorthodox and unlikely to be shared by the public. Even at age eighty-four, just a month before his death, he was concerned for his reputation. Consequently, near the end of his revealing letter to Ezra Stiles, he wrote, "I confide, that you will not expose me to criticisms and censures by publishing any part of this communication to you."[172]

In that light, it should be stressed that Jefferson frequently expressed a desire to keep his religious views from the public. He told Benjamin Rush that he was "averse to the communication of my religious tenets to the public," and he advised James Smith that he did not wish his religious views to be brought "before the public." In another letter containing his religious thoughts, he informed his correspondent: "I am obliged to caution my friends against admitting the possibility of my letters getting into the public papers, or a copy of them to be taken under *any degree of confidence*" (emphasis mine). When his *Syllabus* was copied and published in an obscure magazine in London, Jefferson told William Short, "Happily that repository is scarcely known in this country, and the syllabus, therefore, is still a secret, and in your hands I am sure it will continue so."[173] Jefferson attached a note with the *Syllabus* to "three or four particular friends" in which he instructed them that it was for "their personal satisfaction" and that "when read, the return of the paper with this cover is asked." He wrote to one friend that he was "perfectly free to retain the copy of the syllabus & to make any use of it his discretion would approve, confident as Th: J. is that his discretion would not permit him to let it be copied lest it should get into print." And "Th: J. would thank Mr. L. not to put his name on the paper in filing it away, lest in case of accident to Mr. L. it should get out." He had more than a casual interest in keeping his views a secret. Jefferson's report to Adams concerning his efforts to retrieve and to keep secret copies of his *Syllabus* is revealing. He reported that Rush and Priestley were

> the only depositories of my secret. The fate of my letter to Priestley, after his death, was a warning to me on that of Dr. Rush; and at my request his family was so kind as to quiet me by returning my original letter and Syllabus. . . . Yet I enclose it *to you* with entire confidence, free to be perused by yourself and Mrs. Adams, but by no one else; and to be returned to me.[174]

Jefferson's palpable anxiety about retrieving copies and keeping his views a secret seems to reflect more than simple humility (of which he had very little in religious matters) or normal concern for privacy.

Concerning the publication of his *Philosophy of Jesus,* in which he jettisoned the bulk of the New Testament and surgically removed any reference to the miraculous, Jefferson said, "I ask only one condition, that no possibility shall be admitted of my name being even intimated with the publication."[175] These appear to be the sentiments of a public figure whose views were at variance with those of the public and who wanted desperately to avoid the loss of public esteem and reputation that would likely result from public knowledge of those views. Jefferson's response to a biographer's inquiry into his religious beliefs reflected his concern about public knowledge and provided a cogent summary of that which a theistic rationalist thought most important where religion was concerned: "My answer was 'say nothing of my religion. It is known to my god and myself alone. It's [*sic*] evidence before the world is to be sought in my life. If that has been *honest and dutiful to society*, the religion which has regulated it cannot be a bad one.'"[176] Jefferson expanded upon that personal sentiment in offering the following advice to a young relative: "Adore God. Reverence and cherish your parents. Love your neighbor as yourself, and your country more than yourself. Be just. Be true. Murmur not at the ways of Providence. So shall the life into which you have entered, be the portal to one of eternal and ineffable bliss."[177] This statement is a cogent summary of much of the essence of theistic rationalism—that is, adore God (whatever concept of Him makes the most sense to you), be good, and accept the results of God's intervention in your life; the end result will be acceptance by God and an eternal effort by Him to make you happy.

Finally, Jefferson attributed to Jesus his own process in search of an understanding and explanation of God: "Jesus, taking for his type the best qualities of the human head and heart, wisdom, justice, goodness, and adding to them power, ascribed all of these, but in infinite perfection, to the Supreme Being, and *formed him* really worthy of their adoration" (emphasis mine).[178] According to Jefferson, then, Jesus essentially created God from human qualities—or at least the image of God that he wanted the Jews to hold. This is an apt description of Jefferson's work. He attempted to create God or an image of God that he was comfortable with and that he thought would best benefit society. Reason, of course, was the guideline. As Daniel Boorstin put it, "The Jeffersonian had found in his God what he most admired in men."[179]

Although Jefferson and Franklin are routinely identified as deists, investigation into what they actually said that they believed reveals that they did not hold to the most fundamental beliefs of deism. They did not believe in an aloof, uninvolved, absentee God but in a present God who was active in human affairs on both a large scale and an individual scale. Franklin daily offered praise and adoration to God, which, as he contended, would be a pointless exercise if God were not present or attentive. He and Jefferson did not believe that nature was the only valid revelation from God, and they did not categorically reject any and all written revelation and supernatural intervention but instead considered some Scripture to be authoritative and revealed. Although Jefferson rejected all miracles and Franklin did not, the positions both men held were based on whether they thought it rational for a present, interested God to interrupt or overrule the natural laws he had established. Jefferson never claimed to be a deist (though he did claim to be a Christian), and Franklin recanted his youthful embrace of deism and explicitly repudiated fundamental deist beliefs as irrational. Though deism was itself a critique and rejection of Christianity, Jefferson and Franklin both identified with Christianity by name, albeit their own conceptions of it. As for the central figure of Christianity, Jefferson and Franklin had a higher view of Jesus than was common among deists. Finally, their views of the afterlife were not those of deists, and Franklin specifically rejected the deist idea that one could merit heaven by one's good works.

Although Jefferson and Franklin were not deists, they clearly were not Christians either. Since there is nearly universal agreement on this point— and the evidence is widely available—I will not rehash that argument here. Suffice it to say that they rejected fundamental core doctrines of Christianity as irrational, as well. In particular, they rejected the deity of Jesus and the Trinity, Jesus's atoning work in satisfaction for men's sins, eternal punishment for sin, and justification by faith—in short, the central defining doctrines of Christianity. In the place of either Christianity or deism, they substituted a theology of their own making based on what they considered to be reasonable. Jefferson and Franklin shared some beliefs with deists, but then, almost everyone did and still does. Ultimately, they have been categorized as deists because of a false dichotomy. They clearly were not Christians, and the only other option that has been recognized by scholars has been deism. "Deist" has been a catchall designation for anyone at that time who was not a Christian or atheist, so Jefferson and Franklin have been put in that category.

The vast majority of those who have presented the religious beliefs of Adams, Jefferson, and Franklin in the past have done so selectively to advance an agenda or have simply accepted the labels traditionally applied to them. Chapters 4 and 5 of this study have presented an in-depth, balanced look into the religious beliefs of a supposed Christian and two supposed deists and demonstrated that all three were theistic rationalists. Of the key Founders, these three were the most prolific in expressing their religious beliefs. They appear to have been the most philosophical about religious matters, and all three spent considerable time and effort researching and contemplating religious matters. They earnestly applied their own reason as the determining element in their quest. In the end, they came to believe in a rather generic God who created the world and remained active and interested in it. Though He primarily revealed Himself through nature and reason, He also sponsored some special complementary revelation. This God could be approached in many ways under many names, and He simply asked that His followers live morally and treat others well. This theology may best be termed theistic rationalism. Theistic rationalism, not deism or Christianity, was the political theology that influenced the three primary contributors to the Declaration of Independence.

The authors of the Declaration did not, as some would claim, hold significantly different religious views from the primary framers of the Constitution. As the examination turns to the religious beliefs of those key framers, the excavation of expressed beliefs becomes more difficult and challenging. The potential reward is enticing, however—a deeper, clearer understanding of some rather enigmatic American heroes.

6

The Theistic Rationalism of the Key Framers

The Scriptures . . . do not supersede the operations of reason.

James Wilson

THE CONSTITUTION WAS LARGELY FRAMED by three men—the one-legged lecher in whose hand it was written, an original Supreme Court justice, and the "father of the Constitution." It was sold to the public and put into practice by that "father" and by the man whose face is on the $10 bill. These individuals were all theistic rationalists as well, but they were less philosophical about religious matters and less forthcoming about their religious views than the authors of the Declaration. Consequently, there is far less evidence in their own writings regarding their religious beliefs. Yet there is sufficient evidence to demonstrate that they believed in the main tenets of theistic rationalism or that their beliefs were not inconsistent with theistic rationalism. Each had had conventional religious training as a young man, but as adults, they all reflected a profound indifference toward religious doctrines, which was likely born of theistic rationalist beliefs and which allowed them to promote freedom of religion in America. This chapter will investigate the religious beliefs of Gouverneur Morris, James Wilson, James Madison, and Alexander Hamilton.

Gouverneur Morris spoke more often than anyone at the Constitutional Convention and was an influential member of the critically important Committee of Style. In fact, Morris wrote the Preamble to the Constitution, which "provides, as does the Declaration, a set of dynamic principles by which citizens could measure the actions of their government."[1] According to James Madison, known as the "father of the Constitution," Morris's contribution to the writing of that document did not end with the Preamble:

> The *finish* given to the style and arrangement of the Constitution fairly belongs to the pen of Mr. Morris. . . . A better choice could not have been made, as the performance of the task proved. . . . There was sufficient room for the talents and taste stamped by the author on the face

of it. The alterations made by the Committee are not recollected. They were not such, as to impair the merit of the composition.[2]

In an 1814 letter, Morris himself said of the Constitution, "That instrument was written by the fingers, which write this letter."[3] I will leave it to others to explain why someone with Gouverneur Morris's credentials and accomplishments is unknown to the average American of the twenty-first century. I suspect, however, that things might have been quite different in his case if he had not "declined" when "warmly pressed by Hamilton to assist in writing the Federalist."[4]

One analyst of James Wilson's political and legal philosophy concluded: "James Wilson is perhaps the most underrated founder. One of only six men to sign both the Declaration of Independence and the Constitution, his influence on the latter was second only to that of James Madison." Founding scholar Max Farrand came to a similar conclusion, noting that "second to Madison and almost on a par with him was James Wilson." Another scholar described Wilson as "arguably the most influential framer with regard to Article 2." Wilson was perhaps the period's "foremost advocate of a strong and democratic national government that clearly protects individual rights. . . . Today, the American constitutional system is closer to his vision than to that of any other founder."[5]

Presumably, no case needs to be made for the importance of James Madison, the author of the most commonly studied and quoted essays of *The Federalist Papers*. The plan that Madison took to the Constitutional Convention served as a base model for the delegates' deliberation and as a basic blueprint for the new Constitution.

In 1786, Alexander Hamilton drafted the resolution calling for what would become known as the Constitutional Convention.[6] After service as a delegate to the convention, he led the fight for ratification of the new Constitution in New York. Toward that end, he proposed writing a series of essays designed to explain and support the Constitution, which became known as *The Federalist Papers*. He enlisted James Madison and John Jay to help him, but Hamilton himself wrote about fifty-five of the eighty-five essays. He was appointed the first secretary of the Treasury in the new government. As such, he saw himself as President Washington's prime minister, and he became the primary initiator of the administration's program.

Although Gouverneur Morris is, of course, better known in the scholarly community than elsewhere, his religious beliefs remain for most a mystery. One reason for this is that though Morris was not at all hesitant to speak out on political or social issues, he did not often speak about his religious beliefs, whether in public or in private. John Adams, Thomas Jefferson, and Benjamin Franklin wrote extensively, even systematically at times, about their religious beliefs, but Morris left only scattered clues and isolated comments.

The various efforts to categorize James Wilson's religion epitomize the need for the label *theistic rationalist*. Wilson was raised a Presbyterian in Scotland, but he is often described as a rationalist. He became an Episcopalian in America but was also claimed by the deists as one of their own. In fact, M. E. Bradford listed Wilson as "Episcopalian/Deist" in his accounting of the religious affiliations of the framers. One biographer discussed Wilson's struggle between Calvinism and Enlightenment thought and suggested that he was even "more influenced by the Enlightenment than the Deists."[7]

James Madison was perhaps the most enigmatic of the key Founders where religious belief is concerned. Like John Adams, he considered entering the ministry as a young man, but like George Washington, he studiously avoided any explicit declarations of faith or belief through most of his adult life. As Norman Cousins put it, "Madison referred only rarely to his personal religious beliefs. It was an article of faith with him that a man's relation to the Creator was in itself a sacred matter." It is possible, however, to glean enough from Madison's sparse statements to draw some conclusions about his religious beliefs and to demonstrate that he fell within the theistic rationalist camp. Those who believe in the Christian America view look for hints that indicate an affinity for Christianity, and secularists quote him selectively to "prove" the opposite. Those with less of an agenda rightfully include him among the adherents of some form of "rational religion."[8]

The study of Alexander Hamilton's religion presents a daunting but interesting challenge to the historian. Most biographers discuss the early religious influences on him and his apparent piety during his youth, then mention his religion briefly or not at all until the final years of his life. Hamilton is generally considered to have been a religious enigma during the prime of his life, when he had a significant impact upon the American political scene. One reason for this difficulty is that, as Douglass Adair astutely observed, Hamilton appears to have gone through different religious stages. Adair identified four stages in his religious life: (1) a conventionally religious youth, (2) religious indifference while in power, (3) opportunistic religiosity while in political opposition, and (4) Christian faith in retirement.[9]

All four of these key framers offer an additional and common problem for scholars attempting to label or categorize them in terms of religion: their religious beliefs and practices during the Founding period do not square with either of the traditional categories of deism and Christianity. That choice is actually a false dichotomy, so these real men do not fit neatly into the generally accepted "slots." The dilemma is magnified for those who try to reconcile their denominational affiliations with their expressed beliefs. Since these men were influenced by natural religion, Christianity, and rationalism, those who want to do so can see each of them exclusively as a member of any one of those camps. They may appear to move between camps if one looks from a neutral but traditional perspective, expecting to place them within traditional boundaries. The real solution to the problem is to study what they said that they believed, irrespective of their denominational tags and without imposing an artificial, dichotomous limitation on categories. The result is the recognition that these four key framers represent a third category of religious belief—theistic rationalism.

Because Hamilton converted to Christianity at the end of his life, he provides an interesting opportunity for comparison. We can observe in one individual the difference in word, thought, priority, and action between a theistic rationalist and a Christian.

THE BEING AND ATTRIBUTES OF GOD

As theistic rationalists, the key framers borrowed religious beliefs from Christianity and from natural religion, beginning with their view of God. They believed, of course, in a creator God; nearly everyone in eighteenth-century America did. But what was the nature of that God?

When the key framers thought of God, they saw a being who was present and active in the world and in the lives of men. James Wilson drew upon his Calvinist background in arguing that God "works not without an eternal decree."[10] The primary focus of Wilson's writings was law, and in addition to human and natural law, Wilson believed in "divine" law, the "law eternal," and the "law celestial." His discussions of these concepts are reminiscent of those of Aquinas. Though a firm believer in the laws of nature, Wilson did not assume with the deists that the universe simply functioned on its own according to those laws. Rather, he believed God was the "Preserver" of "all things" and of "the universe." Such a role implied presence and action. According to him, God was not only the "Ruler of all things" and the "Governor of the universe" but also "our" ruler. Wilson's God was not simply an absentee God who put general laws and principles in motion at some time past. Instead, through "the intention of Providence," God appointed "varieties of taste and character" in *individuals*, not simply general laws governing the workings of the universe.[11] Wilson described God's superintendence of man in this way:

> His infinite power enforces his laws, and carries them into full and effectual execution. His infinite wisdom knows and chooses the fittest means for accomplishing the ends which he proposes. His infinite goodness proposes such ends only as promote our felicity. . . . Being infinitely and eternally happy in himself, his goodness alone could move him to create us, and give us the means of happiness. The same principle, that moved his creating, moves his governing power. The rule of his government we shall find to be reduced to this one paternal command—Let man pursue his own perfection and happiness. What an enrapturing view of the moral government of the universe! Over all, goodness infinite reigns, guided by unerring wisdom, and supported by almighty power.[12]

These statements are somewhat ambiguous and could be taken to refer to general providence, but the use of the present tense and active verbs in the context of the rest of Wilson's comments seems to justify a particular reading.

Gouverneur Morris also expressed belief in a God who was active and interested in the affairs of men, and his statements are less ambiguous. Looking at human affairs on a large scale, he said: "My trust is not in a President, Senate, and House of Representatives, but in Him who governs empires, the world, the universe." His belief in God's superintending role was not limited to the outworking of general laws. He declared to the New York Assembly that "Providence has kindly interfered so far for our preservation." Upon observing the behavior of Europeans, he suggested that "the Almighty had prepared a scourge for the abominations, which prevailed among the people" of Europe. He acknowledged the "wisdom," "hand," and "mercy" of God on behalf of refugees.[13] Speaking of the War of 1812, Morris said, "I firmly believe the Almighty will punish those, who voluntarily participate in its prosecution." So, he maintained that God had *interfered* on America's behalf, *responded* to evil acts in Europe, *extended* His "hand" and "mercy" to refugees, and was *paying attention* to who participated in a particular war. Clearly, he believed that God involved Himself in human affairs on a national scale and on an individual scale concerning national issues. His belief in God's superintendence also had personal political significance. He spoke of his "reliance on the Almighty" as "an active principle of political conduct." Although he thought the ways of Providence "inscrutable by man," Morris was confident that the "Almighty will work out his wise ends by the means of human folly."[14]

Morris also believed in God's intervention in individual human lives. In expressing his opposition to the establishment of religion, he argued that "God is sufficiently powerful to do His own Business" and favored leaving it "to the Supreme Being to influence the Thoughts [of men] as He may think proper." An inactive God could not promote His church; an absentee God could not influence men's thoughts. He wrote his mother that he was "confident" that God would "provide for the happiness of his creatures." In a letter to console his sister on the death of her child, Morris confessed a human inability to see the future, and consequently, he encouraged his sister to "submit with something more than patience to the high hand of heaven." He went on to say that God's will could not be resisted but that "His bounty is as unbounded as His power!" He then discussed God's activity in giving and taking away and concluded with, "O God! thy will be done." Similarly, in another letter to a grieving mother, Morris stated that God could "mitigate" her anguish. Going one step further, he said that God's "divine providence acts only according to the designs of his paternal love."[15] Morris, then, expressed belief in an active and intervening God who *loved* His children. Though one must be careful in drawing conclusions from letters to grieving mothers, such an expression was completely foreign to deist thinking.

At times, Morris's statements reflected a level of ambiguity concerning the personality of God's Providence. His references often indicated the personal nature of Providence, as when he spoke of the Almighty or used personal pronouns for Providence such as "him" or "his" or "whose."[16] At other times, however, Morris suggested that Providence was not a personal being. He once said that "fortune" was "but another name for Providence"; on another occasion, he equated "fortune" with "Heaven." He wrote to one correspondent that "Providence has reserved to *it*self the knowledge of what we call events" (emphasis mine). To another correspondent, he wrote, "Circumstances, or to speak more properly, Providence may produce changes both of men and things, which reason can neither direct nor foresee." One author suggested that "Morris seems not to have bestowed enough thought on religion to have worked out a consistent position" on Providence.[17] He may not have worked out all of the details, but the frequency of personal references to God's actions indicates that he did believe in the personal and particular intervention of God in human affairs.

James Madison also expressed belief in a present, active, and intervening God. He spoke of the "care of Providence" and of "the goodness of a superintending Providence,"[18] but most of his references to the intervention and superintendence of God were on a large scale. He was concerned that the Virginia Assembly would be guided by God "into every measure which may be worthy of his blessing." He declared it "impossible for the man of pious reflection not to perceive" in the work of the Constitutional Convention "a finger of that Almighty hand which has been so frequently and signally extended to our relief in the critical stages of the revolution." He acknowledged "the guardianship and guidance of that Almighty Being whose power regulates the destiny of nations, whose blessings have been so conspicuously dispensed to this rising Republic."[19] Upon entering a state of war, Madison committed the justness of the cause to "the hands of the Almighty Disposer of Events," and in the midst of war, he expressed confidence that the justice of the war "invites the smiles of Heaven." So, Madison desired that the assembly be *guided* by God; he recognized God's hand being *involved* in the work of the convention and in *guarding* and *guiding* the nation; and he referred to God as the *disposer of events*—not merely the creator of general laws. Madison must also have thought that God was paying attention, since he expected Him to smile in response to the conduct of the war. His God was present and active, and He dealt in particulars. Although most of his references to Providence concerned national issues, Madison also recognized God's interest in individual matters. He argued that, although "spiritual" matters were "not limited or proportioned always to human means," "the best human means should be ever employed" nonetheless in order to avoid "a lazy presumptious dependance [*sic*] on Providence."[20]

Alexander Hamilton believed in an active and intervening God, as well, but mostly on a large scale. He expressed belief in a "superintending" God "who rules the world" and in a God who actively controlled the elements of nature. He also suggested that the nation could and should "trust in Heaven."[21] In the latter portion of his life when he became more concerned with religious matters, he admonished a friend:

> Arraign not the dispensations of Providence, they must be founded in wisdom and goodness; and when they do not suit us, it must be because there is some fault in ourselves which deserves chastisement; or because there is a kind intent, to correct in us some vice or failing, of which, perhaps, we may not be conscious; or because the general plan requires that we should suffer partial ill. In this situation it is our duty to cultivate resignation, and even humility.[22]

Thus, Hamilton spoke of a God who *actively controlled* the elements of nature, *chastised* in the here and now, and *exercised kind intent* on our behalf. These attributes are indicative of an active, present God. Hamilton always believed in Providence, but his expressions of belief in God's intervention in individual lives were confined to the latter part of his life.

Given their belief in an intervening God, the key framers might be expected to have believed in miracles. Morris and Madison apparently did
so to some extent at least, but Wilson apparently did not. Morris straddled
the fence, so to speak, concerning miracles. He seemed to indicate that he
thought miracles to be possible and certainly within God's power but that
he did not expect to see any: "The strong arm of Omnipotence can indeed
upheave and overturn the foundations of empires, but we cannot prudently
expect miraculous interference."[23] Though Madison rarely addressed the
issue of miracles, he did affirm that Christianity had enjoyed a "period of
miraculous aid" during its infancy before being "left to its own evidence."[24]
The latter remark indicates that Madison saw the miracles of Jesus or the
apostles in the first century as externally provided evidence for the validity
of Christianity. Wilson, like the deists, apparently did not believe in miracles. Reason taught him that the "law of nature is immutable." God could
not or would not violate His own laws. As Wilson stated it: "This immutability of nature's laws has nothing in it repugnant to the supreme power
of an all-perfect Being. Since he himself is the author of our constitution;
he cannot but command or forbid such things as are necessarily agreeable
or disagreeable to this very constitution. He is under the glorious necessity
of not contradicting himself."[25] In Wilson's view, a perfect being would lay
down perfect laws for the governance of the universe, and it would be irrational for him to violate those perfect laws that he established. A miracle
required God to contradict Himself by overruling or suspending the laws
of nature and was, therefore, not possible. The theistic rationalists did not
have a fixed dogma concerning miracles. Some believed them possible; others did not. They did, however, have a consistent position concerning them:
reason (not revelation) was the standard by which to determine whether
miracles were possible. Some theistic rationalists, such as Adams, believed
the possibility of miracles to be rational; others, like Wilson, did not.

Though the key framers shared Christianity's belief in an active, present,
intervening God, other elements of their view of God had more in common
with deism. One such element was their choice of which attributes of God
to emphasize. Projecting a combination of what they conceived a god to be
and what they most admired in men, deists imagined and posited a powerful
being of unmatched wisdom and benevolence. James Wilson likewise emphasized God's "infinite power—infinite wisdom—infinite goodness"; God
was an "all-wise and all-beneficent Creator."[26] He stressed the fact that the
creator was "infinitely wise and good" and endowed humans with various
faculties "for wise and benevolent purposes." In fact, where the entire universe was concerned, he observed that "over all, goodness infinite reigns,
guided by unerring wisdom, and supported by almighty power"—and all in

one being. In his description of "the wisdom which cometh from above," for example, Wilson declared that "the ways of that wisdom are the ways of pleasantness, and all her paths are peace."[27] Attributes of God that would not appeal to reason or humanity, such as His holiness or jealousy, were ignored by deists and by the key framers. One might expect a jurist such as Wilson to focus attention on God's justice rather than His benevolence or a libertine such as Gouverneur Morris to exult in God's grace and forgiveness and mercy.

But when Morris spoke of God's attributes, he emphasized the same deist triad of wisdom, goodness, and power.[28] Madison also stressed that familiar set of attributes and wrote of "belief in a God All Powerful wise & good."[29] Alexander Hamilton's vision of God centered on power, wisdom, and goodness, as well. He alternately referred to God as "Omnipotence," "the Almighty," "supreme intelligence," "rational," and "benefactor." He held that, regardless of appearances, whatever God did "must be founded in wisdom and goodness." Hamilton's God was "beneficent" and the personification of "Infinite Wisdom."[30] Christians certainly also believed that God was powerful, wise, and benevolent, but they did not dwell on these traits to the exclusion of other qualities.

The key framers emphasized and personified nature in a manner reminiscent of deist thought. Nature was given credit for "the faculty of imagination"; for the "moral sense"; for certain precepts; for all "first principles"; for "a principle, which gives him [man] force and superiority" in comparison to animals; and even for making man.[31] In addition, according to Wilson, "nature has implanted in man the desire of his own happiness; she has inspired him with many tender affections towards others . . . she has endowed him with intellectual and with active powers; she has furnished him with a natural impulse to exercise his powers for his own happiness, and the happiness of those, for whom he entertains such tender affections."[32] For Wilson, then, Mother Nature was the source of man's intellect and emotions. Occasionally, he gave credit to "nature's God" or to "the laws of God and nature" or to "the laws of nature and of Nature's God." Mixing and matching God and nature only served to blur the line between the two, however. In one discussion, Wilson caught himself and said, "Nature, or, to speak more properly, the Author of nature."[33] Such a fusion of God and nature reflected a significant influence of natural religion in Wilson's thinking.

Madison similarly emphasized the connection between God and nature. In his discussion of rights and religious rights in particular, he referred to God and nature more or less interchangeably. In fact, he alternately said that the free exercise of religion and "all our other rights" were the "gift of nature" and "divine." Madison expressed belief that there was a "road from nature up to nature's God" that did not require written revelation.[34] As one analyst has observed, with this statement, Madison "was at variance with all the orthodox theologians of his time." In this regard, he was influenced by Samuel Clarke and his seminal work of natural religion, *The Being and Attributes of God,* in which Clarke intentionally avoided employing Scripture in proving the existence and nature of God.[35]

Hamilton also stressed the connection between God and nature. As a young man, he wrote a newspaper report on a hurricane. In it, he hinted that God and nature were one: "That which, in a calm unruffled temper, we call a natural cause, seemed then like the correction of the Deity." The suggestion was that either God or nature could be viewed as the cause: emotion pointed to God whereas reason pointed to nature. In a polemical pamphlet, Hamilton criticized an opponent by noting his similarity to Thomas Hobbes. As an example of the contrast between his own view and that of Hobbes, he posited God's role as the author of natural law.[36] According to John Miller, Hamilton believed that "God and Nature" had established political orders, the sacredness of property, and the economic foundations of the United States.[37] Hamilton also believed that God shaped human nature. In perhaps his best-known statement, he said: "The sacred rights of mankind are not to be rummaged for among old parchments or musty records. They are written, as with a sunbeam, in the whole volume of human nature, by the hand of the Divinity itself, and can never be erased or obscured by mortal power."[38] Finally, after he was out of power, Hamilton spent time contemplating the God of nature. His son reported that "his religious feelings grew with his growing intimacy with the marvellous works of nature, all pointing in their processes and their results to a great pervading, ever active Cause." During that same time, Hamilton studied "Paley's Evidences,"[39] a well-known attempt to prove the existence and attributes of God by, primarily, the evidence of nature. Christians also, of course, saw a connection between God and nature, but for them, God was the creator and sustainer of nature and, most important, was not confused with nature.

The key framers used only generic terms for God, not specifically Christian—or even biblical—terms. As was noted earlier, Wilson often mentioned the "Author" and "Creator." He also variously referred to God as "the Deity," "the Divinity," "incomprehensible Archetype," "divine Architect," "Governor of the universe," and "divine hand."[40] These framers did not use "Jesus," "Christ," "Holy Spirit," or any terms that a Christian would have employed other than "Almighty" and "creator," a usage that was shared with deists. Ron Chernow, author of a recent biography of Hamilton, notes that Hamilton "never talked about Christ and took refuge in vague references to 'providence' or 'heaven.'"[41] One should keep that observation in mind during the discussion that follows of Hamilton's late conversion to Christianity. It is clear that his language changed considerably to reflect his newfound specific faith. In addition to his very generic references to God, Madison insinuated that all religious traditions worshipped the same God when he referred to everyone uniting in worship of "the God of all." As Daniel Boorstin puts it, his was "not the God of anybody's dogma." As he expressed in a discussion of oaths of office, Madison felt that generic affirmation of a "supreme Being" was sufficient. In comparing his thanksgiving proclamations with those of Washington, he emphasized that he had used "general terms" for God, as had Washington, and that those terms "embraced all who believed in a supreme ruler of the Universe."[42]

The key framers were influenced by both Christianity and natural religion in developing their view of God. They referred to God using largely deistic terminology, and they emphasized and personified nature in a manner consonant with natural religion. They separated themselves from deism and exhibited Christian influence, however, with their belief in a present, active God who intervened in the affairs of men. Some of them also believed in the possibility of miracles, a belief that emphatically placed them outside of the deist camp.

DOCTRINES AND TOLERATION

Theistic rationalists disdained sectarian doctrines or "dogmas" as divisive and, ultimately, unimportant. In their view, doctrines only caused conflict. For them, the various roads to God were paved with good deeds and acts of public morality, not adherence to certain beliefs. Since they had no heartfelt attachment to any particular sect—no dog in the race, so to speak—the key framers could *afford* to grant religious liberty and to advocate religious toleration. Toleration was born of a disinterested neutrality where doctrine was concerned and of a belief that there were multiple roads to God.

Gouverneur Morris, for one, advocated reason as a means of understanding God and our obligations to Him, rather than the teachings of sects.[43] He argued for tolerance and complained about its lack: "Each preacher holds fast to his sect, and nine out of ten, even if they can be prevailed upon to leave with Omnipotence the fate of his creatures, will insinuate, if not insist, that unless he deliver over to Satan all but their own adherents, it will require his omniscience to show that he has not broken his word."[44] Like other theistic rationalists, Morris detested Calvinism, partly because of its claim to exclusivity.[45] In private, he often employed his keen sardonic wit to ridicule Catholics and Catholicism,[46] but publicly, he was adamant about ensuring Catholics' religious freedom. Morris disagreed with pacifist sects and tried to convert them to the Revolutionary cause, but he held the Pennsylvania government in contempt for harassing them. His approach was consistent: he did not subscribe to any set of doctrines, and he did not allow his personal views to interfere with what he saw as the proper public position, which was to grant religious freedom.

James Madison advocated the essential equality of all religious systems. In fact, Ralph Ketcham has noted that "one of the most striking features of Madison's life was the warm feelings of mutual respect which generally existed between him and a wide variety of religious groups."[47] That relationship was no doubt primarily based on Madison's extensive work toward securing religious liberty in America. His monumental efforts in this area are well documented. The purpose here is not to analyze the appropriate role of government or to recount Madison's leadership regarding religious freedom but to uncover the beliefs that undergirded that effort.

Madison believed that religious "bigotry," or intolerant devotion to one sect or set of beliefs, was "antiquated." In the same vein, he opposed "sectarian illiberality." When Jefferson asked him to suggest theological books for the library of the University of Virginia,

[Madison's] list for the university included a substantial number of the Fathers of the Church; the lights of the Dominican and Franciscan orders, Thomas Aquinas and Duns Scotus; Catholic and Protestant authors of the Reformation such as Erasmus, Calvin, Socinius; later controversialists, among them the Jesuit Robert Bellarmine and the Protestant champion William Chillingsworth and the Jansenist Catholic Blaise Pascal; and the "celebrated work" of Samuel Clark[e], a theologian warmly recommended at Princeton by the Reverend Witherspoon and still reverently remembered by Mr. Madison.[48]

Madison's list was clearly eclectic and intended to be representative of a wide range of religious opinion rather than to reflect a particular, favored perspective. He opposed efforts to substitute the word *Christian* for *Religious* in a bill to incorporate the Episcopal Church and to insert the name

Jesus Christ into the preamble of a bill for religious liberty. In addition, Madison's support for a "multiplicity of sects" and a "variety of sects" is also well documented.[49] All of this can be explained by his belief that no particular sect or religious system was exclusively correct.

Among the reasons Madison gave in support of "equal laws protecting equal rights" of religious belief and expression was that they were "most favorable to the advancement of truth."[50] He made this argument in a letter to a Jew in a discussion of the place and role of Jewish congregations. Clearly, specific Christian notions of "truth" are diametrically opposed to specific Jewish notions of "truth," so Madison must have meant that religious truth was not specific but generic and disconnected from specific religious systems. In another instance, he referred to the legal equality of sects as a "truly Xn [Christian] principle."[51] For that to be true, Christianity must be seen either as a benevolent mind-set that values "fair play" over eternal truth or a generic, nonsectarian religious system. Both of these options were consistent with Madison's expressed beliefs. Either way, those who did not advocate equality of sects, such as the first Christians in the apostolic age or the Puritan founders of New England, were clearly representative of a different Christianity than Madison's conception.

Madison gave a deeper, more fundamental argument in favor of the equality of sects, focused on the inalienable right to freedom of conscience. With the passage of the Act for Establishing Religious Freedom, he "flatter[ed]" himself that he had "extinguished for ever the ambitious hope of making laws for the human mind," as he believed that "religious bondage shackles and debilitates the mind." In one sense, this was an issue of fair play for him: "Whilst we assert for ourselves a freedom to embrace, to profess and to observe the Religion which we believe to be of divine origin, we cannot deny an equal freedom to those whose minds have not yet yielded to the evidence which has convinced us."[52] In another sense, it was a matter of the nature of religious belief. According to Madison:

> The Religion then of every man must be left to the conviction and conscience of every man; and it is the right of every man to exercise it as these may dictate. This right is in its nature an unalienable right. It is unalienable; because the opinions of men, depending only on the evidence contemplated by their own minds, cannot follow the dictates of other men. It is unalienable also; because what is here a right towards men, is a duty towards the Creator. It is the duty of every man to render to the Creator such homage, and such only, as he believes to be acceptable to him.[53]

Madison elsewhere called this one of the "natural and equal rights of all men" and labeled it "the divine right of conscience." He also argued that "conscience is the most sacred of all property . . . the exercise of that, being a natural and unalienable right." One's own religion could only be determined by one's own "reason and conviction."[54] According to Madison, then, God had given each man an unalienable right to determine for himself what type of worship was acceptable to God. This was not simply a reference to prohibiting state interference; Madison was making the claim that *God* granted this right to every man. The logical extension of this viewpoint was the belief that all religious systems led to the same God. If God had given each man the right to determine what was appropriate worship and different men devised different religious systems; then God was obligated to accept any and all religious systems.

Hamilton also opposed particularist religion and supported toleration. In fact, he trumpeted the equality of religions. He was never formally affiliated with a particular church or denomination. His wife, the former Betsy Schuyler, was "a staunch member of the Dutch Reformed Church" and "was assiduous in the practices of piety." It is interesting that Hamilton did not follow the standard practice for unaffiliated husbands and join her church after their marriage. Before being married, he told a friend, "As to religion a moderate stock will satisfy me. She must believe in god and hate a saint." Hamilton sought an appropriate match—someone who was "moderate" where religion was concerned. He wanted a wife who, like himself, believed in God but was not too enthusiastic about it. Ironically, Betsy's nickname was "the Saint." A nephew reported that Hamilton had a "simple faith, quite unemotional in this respect."[55] Like his fellow theistic rationalists, he felt that belief in God was important and beneficial but that one should not be too specific or enthusiastic regarding religion.

Thus, Hamilton did not identify with a particular denomination, and beyond that, he believed that bigotry, or exclusive devotion to a particular sect, was dangerous. He warned that Europe had lost thousands due to religious bigotry. "There is a bigotry in politics, as well as in religions," he argued, "equally pernicious in both." Bigotry in religion was also unwise policy according to Hamilton: "While some kingdoms were impoverishing and depopulating themselves . . . their wiser neighbors were reaping the fruits of their folly, and augmenting their own numbers, industry and wealth, by receiving with open arms the persecuted fugitives."[56] Like Jefferson and Franklin, he ignored the fact that people could be completely devoted to a particular sect because they believed its specific doctrines to be true. This was typical of theistic rationalists. Hamilton also referred to specific doctrines as mere "speculative notions of religion," a phrase commonly employed by theistic rationalists. He stressed the idea that religion was a matter of individual conscience. Of the typical Protestant Englishman, for example, he said, "The privilege of worshipping the deity in the manner his conscience dictates . . . is one of the dearest he enjoys." Similarly, of Roman Catholics, Hamilton said, "Why should we wound the tender conscience of any and why present oaths to those who are known to be good citizens?"[57] The primary goal and purpose of religion for Hamilton and the theistic rationalists was to produce good citizens, so toleration was to be extended in pursuit of that goal. That was why barriers to the practice of religion were not to be erected and were to be removed when they were discovered.

Promotion of freedom of religion came naturally for the theistic rationalists, as they had no commitment to any particular sect or set of doctrines. Those who were committed to specific doctrines and a specific road to heaven, such as the Puritans in seventeenth-century New England, found it difficult to allow "false" religion within their jurisdiction. The theistic rationalists, however, held to no particular creed but the "essentials" to which "all good men" could agree. They could, in a sense, *afford* to grant religious liberty in a way that those with exclusive beliefs could not. In his "Remarks on the Quebec Bill," Hamilton gave a detailed explanation of the difference between religious establishment and religious toleration and warned of dangers in establishment. Like his fellow theistic rationalists, he recognized an intrinsic connection between civil and religious liberty. As Hamilton put it, "Civil and religious liberty always go together, if the foundation of the one be sapped, the other will fall of course." Consequently, he argued for "what is far more precious than mere religious toleration—a perfect equality of religious privileges."[58]

The theistic rationalism of the key founders may go a long way toward explaining America's exaltation of religious liberty. As long as religion promoted morality—and all of the religions with which they were familiar *did*—there was no reason to restrict religious practice and every reason to promote it. It is hard to see any Christian influence in the key framers' views concerning doctrine and paths to God. Christianity was based on certain core doctrines, so the theistic rationalists' disdain for doctrines, along with their belief in multiple roads to God, clearly separated them from the Christian camp. Although Christians might argue and have argued for religious toleration for various reasons, they would not do so based on the idea that doctrine does not matter or that all religious claims are equally valid or that God must recognize whatever form of worship a man chooses to devise.

MORALITY AND VIRTUE

For the theistic rationalists, morality was central to religion and what God primarily asked of man. Therefore, promotion of morality was the ultimate purpose of religion and its primary—and indispensable—contribution to civil society. Morality was needed to get men to live in civil fashion without coercion in a free society; and religion was the best source of morality. Wilson shared this tenet of theistic rationalism. A biographer has said of Wilson that because of his "insistence on the moral basis of society and of government—he added 'character' to the Lockean trinity of life, liberty, and property." As was his bent, Wilson primarily addressed the issue in terms of law: "That our Creator has a supreme right to prescribe a law for our conduct, and that we are under the most perfect obligation to obey that law, are truths established on the clearest and most solid principles." As he saw it, God placed a "moral sense" in the conscience of each man, and it "govern[ed] our passions as well as our actions." This moral sense was "the voice of God within us" and worked with reason to discern and act upon the "first principles of morals." God "intended us to be social beings" and equipped man toward that end. The will of God and his primary command was that man pursue "his happiness and perfection"; in turn, that happiness and perfection depended on a morality that allowed man to express his natural sociability. For Wilson, religion was an indispensable piece of the societal puzzle, and "Christianity [was] part of the common law" in America.[59]

As will be noted, Gouverneur Morris was something of a rake and a womanizer; but notwithstanding the hypocrisy of his own immoral behavior, he similarly maintained that religion was all about personal and collective morality. At the personal level, he said that "the object of religion is to regulate our conduct," and good men "consider themselves as moral agents accountable to God." At the national level, "destruction of religion" loosened the "bonds of duty, and those of allegiance must ever be weak, where there is a defect both of piety and morality."[60] Morris even had the nerve to tell Swedish ambassador to France Baron Eric Magnus de Stael-Holstein that it was the "prostration of morals which unfits [the French] for good government." In concert with his fellow theistic rationalists, Morris stated, "I believe that religion is the only solid basis of morals, and that morals are the only possible support of free governments."[61] He did have the integrity to admit, however, that he did not trust his own judgment in this regard. Though definitely not consistent with Christianity, Morris's morals might have been, in a sense, consistent with theistic rationalism. For the theistic rationalist, it was public morality, or morality that impacted society, that mattered most. Morris may have seen his escapades as a personal matter with no societal effects—particularly in decadent France.

Madison also emphasized morality and virtue as the core of religion. For example, he congratulated a minister for the "pure benevolence . . . untinctured with sectarian illiberality" that was exhibited in his sermon. He jotted down notes on some biblical passages, but the emphasis was on ethics, morality, and virtue rather than spirituality or theology. Madison qualified one of his statements about the right of each to choose his or her own religion and manner of worship by arguing that, regardless of one's choice of religion, "it is the mutual duty of all to practice Christian forbearance, love, and charity, towards each other." In a discussion of oaths, he also suggested that recognition of belief in a supreme being would positively influence behavior and prevent perjury.[62] Personal morality was, for Madison, a crucial part and benefit of religion.

Like his fellow theistic rationalists, however, Madison was primarily concerned about the effect of religion in promoting morality in society and producing good citizens. When a congressman ridiculed Catholicism during a congressional debate, Madison replied that he "did not approve the ridicule attempted to be thrown out on Roman Catholics. In their religion there was nothing inconsistent with the purest Republicanism. . . . Americans had no right to ridicule Catholics. They had, many of them, proved good citizens during the Revolution."[63] Similarly, he commended Jewish congregations for producing "good citizenship" in their members, and he argued that religious liberty was "the best guarantee of loyalty and love of country" and "necessary to social harmony." To another correspondent, Madison contended that an important advantage of religious liberty was that "rival sects, with equal rights, exercise[d] mutual censorships in favor of good morals."[64] The fact that all of these rival sects promoted differing and conflicting beliefs was unimportant to Madison as long as they promoted morality. He made it clear that he considered religion crucial to the establishment of morality and happiness in society: "And the belief in a God All Powerful wise & good, is so essential to the moral order of the World & to the happiness of man, that arguments which enforce it cannot be drawn from too many sources nor adapted with too much solicitude to the different characters & capacities to be impressed with it."[65] Although Madison favored a policy of noncognizance on the part of the government toward religion,[66] he recognized the critical value of religion in establishing and maintaining the morality that was needed in America. His promotion of noncognizance ought not to be interpreted as a testament of nonimportance.

Hamilton also stressed the centrality of morals to religion and religion's benign influence on the morality of society. Like many of the theistic rationalists, he rarely mentioned religion without mentioning morality.[67] For them, the two concepts went hand in hand. In his suggested draft of a farewell address that he sent to Washington, Hamilton said that "Religion and Morality are essential props" of "political happiness" and "great pillars of human happiness," and he connected "moral and religious obligation" in judicial oaths before adding, "Nor ought we to flatter ourselves that morality can be separated from religion." He then asked: "Can we in prudence suppose that national morality can be maintained in exclusion of religious principles? Does it not require the aid of a generally received and divinely authoritative Religion?" He concluded the religious section by asking: "Can it be that Providence has not connected the permanent felicity of a nation with its virtue?"[68]

In other writings, Hamilton displayed particular concern about the influence of French atheism, arguing that "the moral decay of the United States" would follow "the loss of religious principle" and abandonment of "the simple faith of the early patriots."[69] Among other evils, he believed that irreligion was "subversive of social order."[70] Hamilton vehemently opposed the idea that "religious opinion of any sort is unnecessary to society," and he identified religion as one of the "venerable pillars that support the edifice of civilized society." He further argued that morality could not be separated from religion and that those who loved liberty knew that "morality must fall with religion." Though several of these statements were generated in criticism of the French and used for political purposes, there is no reason to believe that they did not represent Hamilton's sincere perspective, and they were consistent with what he said in other circumstances. Religion *was* under attack in France, and it was the appropriate time for observers to comment on the relationship between "religion, morality, and society,"[71] which were, for theistic rationalists, certainly connected. On at least one occasion, the death of Washington, Hamilton indicated a belief that a life of morality and virtue would secure a place in heaven. Speaking of Washington, he said, "If virtue can secure happiness in another world, he is happy. In this the seal is now put upon *his* glory."[72] Theistic rationalists believed that a man's duty to God was to be a good man and a good citizen and that God would reward the good man in this life and in the next. In this belief, theistic rationalism borrowed more from deism than from Christianity, which exhorted men to be good but taught that justification before God came by faith in the work of Christ.

CHURCH AND THE RELATIONSHIP
TO CHRISTIANITY

The key framers were also a mixed group when it came to their views of Christianity and practices associated with it. James Wilson was raised a Presbyterian and rented a pew in a Presbyterian church until his death in 1798. He had also begun renting a pew in an Episcopalian church four years earlier.[73] Others who clearly were not Christians, such as Benjamin Franklin, also rented pews, so one cannot make any reliable inferences from that information. There is no record of Wilson claiming to be a Christian or of him commenting on Christianity, other than his selective approval of "the mild and tolerating doctrines of Christianity."[74] A deist would not promote anything under the name of Christianity, and an orthodox Christian would not affirm only the "mild" and "tolerating" doctrines of Christianity. Gouverneur Morris's church attendance was regular when he was in America, though quite irregular in Europe. To be fair, it would have been difficult for a non-Catholic to attend church in eighteenth-century France.[75] Morris did not claim to be a Christian, and he did not comment on Christianity per se. The only evidence we have concerning his opinion of Christianity is secondhand testimony from Thomas Jefferson: "I know that Gouverneur Morris, who pretended to be in his secrets & believed himself to be so, has often told me that Genl. Washington believed no more of that system than he himself did."[76]

Madison showed and expressed greater concern for Christianity than a deist would have done. He was raised "in the undemanding Anglicanism of the Virginia establishment," and although he never became a member, he regularly attended an Episcopal church for the rest of his life. He also invited ministers to his house and called Divinity "the most sublime of all Sciences." In addition, due to his schooling at Princeton, he was influenced by "Witherspoon's didactic blend" of Presbyterian and Enlightenment thought.[77] In one of several letters to William Bradford in which he discussed religion, Madison said: "I have sometimes thought there could not be a stronger testimony in favor of Religion . . . than for men who occupy the most honorable and gainful departments and are rising in reputation and wealth, publicly to declare their unsatisfactoriness by becoming fervent Advocates in the cause of Christ."[78] It is significant that Madison did not do so himself, but the fact that he entertained such a thought is instructive. Incidentally, this is the only instance in which he referred to "Christ."

In another such letter to Bradford, Madison expressed concern about "encourage[r]s of free enquiry even such as destroys the most essential Truths, Enemies to serious religion." This remark indicates that he believed there were essential truths in serious religion. On another occasion, writing to a Christian correspondent, Madison affirmed "the Xn religion" as "the best & purest religion." One of his arguments against a piece of legislation was that "the policy of the bill is adverse to the diffusion of the light of Christianity." In that same argument, he referred to Christianity as a "precious gift." One analyst has concluded that Madison had "a deep personal attachment to some general aspects of Christian belief and morality," and another has stated that for Madison, "the best religion is a Christianity ecumenically left undefined."[79] Though we should note the qualifiers *some*, *general*, and *undefined* that were used in describing Madison's relationship to Christianity, it is clear that he was more concerned about it than would be a deist.

Some academics have taken up the claim of the Christian America folk that Madison was heavily influenced by Witherspoon's Calvinism and that Calvinist doctrine concerning depravity, in particular, found its way into the Constitution as a result.[80] The standard "proof texts" for Calvinist influence are Madison's reference to "depravity in mankind" in Federalist No. 55 and his discussion of darker elements of "the nature of man" in Federalist No. 10. The actual influence of Witherspoon was addressed in chapter 2, but two points should be mentioned at this juncture. First, the fact that Madison studied under Witherspoon is no proof that he learned or accepted all that the professor believed. In truth, Madison never credited Witherspoon (or Calvin) for his political views in these or any other cases. As the evidence in chapter 2 demonstrated, it is quite possible that Witherspoon did not even teach his Calvinism to his students. There is little or no evidence that he did so, but we do know that he taught them moral philosophy from rationalist presuppositions.

Second, the two essays in question have to be handled conveniently and quoted inaccurately in order to appear to be Calvinistic. For instance, in order to find Calvinist thought in Madison's reference to "depravity in mankind," one must emphasize the first half of the sentence and ignore the second half,[81] which justifies "a certain portion of esteem and confidence" in human nature. It is certainly no expression of the Calvinist notion of *total* depravity. The original depravity remark in Federalist No. 55 is couched with the qualification "a *degree* of depravity in mankind which requires a *certain degree* of circumspection and distrust" (emphases mine). In fact, the next sentence says that the good qualities are present "in a higher degree" than the bad; otherwise, republican government would not work. Madison's view of human nature was typical of that of the educated elite of the period, holding that man's nature was "an alloy of virtue and vice";[82] in other words, man was capable of great good and great evil. They arrived at that conclusion on the basis of experience and history, not the Bible. In dealing with Federalist No. 10, those who wish to find Calvinism in this essay insert the word *sinful* into the discussion where Madison did not. Using this essay and other examples, some have determined that "Madison's Calvinist convictions, with their emphasis on human sin and weakness, underlie his application of other political philosophies."[83] But Madison never used the word *sin* in Federalist No. 10 or in any of the other examples to which they point. Calvinism was not about *weakness*—it was about *sin*. They are reading into Madison's work what they want or expect to see.

As was noted, Hamilton was never affiliated with any church or denomination. Though he was "conventionally religious" in the early part of his life, "there is little evidence," according to Douglass Adair, "to show [that he had] any great depth or intensity of religious feeling." Nonetheless, at that time, he was sponsored by men who would not have "backed a youth who showed signs of religious heterodoxy." The testimony of his college roommate would suggest that Hamilton was a sincere Christian.[84] There is reason to question Robert Troup's assessment, however, because the next fifteen years of Hamilton's life, as Adair aptly characterizes them, constituted a period of "religious indifference." Adair observes that "there is nothing in Hamilton's published letters during this era of fantastic personal success to indicate that he was emotionally or intellectually concerned with God, the Church, or any religious problems whatsoever."[85] While in the military, Hamilton wrote to a general to recommend a particular minister as a military chaplain. In the letter, he remarked, "He is just what I should like for a military parson, except that he does not whore or drink." He said approvingly of the minister that "he will not insist upon your going to heaven whether you will or not." It was also during this period that Hamilton was accused of making two "wisecracks" about God. The first concerned Franklin's prayer motion and was discussed earlier. The second was Hamilton's reputed remark when asked by old friend Dr. John Rodgers why God was not recognized in the Constitution. Hamilton supposedly replied cavalierly: "Indeed, Doctor, we forgot it." Finally, during this period, Hamilton carried on an adulterous affair with Maria Reynolds, a married woman, "for a considerable time," and he wrote a less than humble public confession of it.[86]

MISCELLANEOUS BELIEFS AND ACTIONS

In various areas of belief, the theistic rationalist framers alternately leaned toward Christianity and toward deism, though never fully embracing either. None of these key framers discussed every point of belief, but each revealed enough to allow an observer to see that they were neither Christians nor deists but theistic rationalists.

The key framers said little about the central figure of Christianity: Jesus Christ. Gouverneur Morris never mentioned Jesus, though he did refer to "our Saviour" in one letter. Given the correspondent, the fact that this letter was the only instance in which he made such a reference, and other evidence that Morris rejected Christianity, nothing more should be read into the remark than an attempt at vague protestant affinity. Hamilton did not mention Jesus until his conversion to Christianity at the end of his life. With the singular exception of a statement about "Christ" in one letter, Madison never specifically referred to Jesus in his voluminous writings. Given the lasting influence that Samuel Clarke had on him, it is likely that Madison shared Clarke's Arian views (that Jesus was more than a man but not God). Madison still referred to Clarke's work more than fifty years after he had read it. Douglass Adair concluded that Madison was a unitarian "like Priestley, in strong revolt against the orthodox doctrines." Though he did not mention "Jesus," Madison did refer to the "Author" of Christianity, to "the Saviour," and to "that holy name."[87] In context, however, each of these designations carried the detached tone of a narrator rather than the warmth of a disciple. Madison was reporting the actions of Christians and appealing to their point of view in trying to persuade them; he was not identifying with them.

One very interesting statement by James Wilson on this subject may distinguish him from other adherents of theistic rationalism. As a rule, theistic rationalists denied the deity of Christ and the Trinity. Though Wilson never mentioned Jesus by name, in his discussion of the importance of sensory evidence, he referred unmistakably to Jesus as "him, by whom our nature was both made and assumed."[88] An Arian might possibly refer to Jesus "assuming" the nature of a man, but if Jesus "made" us, then He was, presumably, the creator—and God. This would appear to be an affirmation of the deity of Jesus and of belief in at least two-thirds of the Trinity. This somewhat cryptic remark is intriguing given that Wilson did not make any reference to Jesus by name or make any claim to be a Christian. If he did believe in the deity of Jesus, then he differed from theistic rationalists in general on that point. It is most interesting that even as deists such as Thomas Paine and Elihu Palmer and purported deists such as Thomas Jefferson talked extensively about Jesus, these four key framers never mentioned his name.

In addition to avoiding the subject of Jesus, Morris and Hamilton did not cite the Bible or discuss the matter of revelation, either. Madison expressed belief in revelation, but it clearly was not a centerpiece of his religion. He acknowledged "written revelation" in a discussion of God's existence and attributes, and he opposed a bill partially because it "discourages those who are strangers to the light of [revelation] from coming into the Region of it" (bracketed word in the original).[89] He only rarely quoted Scripture, however, and then not complete verses or concepts but only isolated phrases for purposes of illustration.[90] Bishop William Meade reported that a conversation with Madison "took such a turn . . . as to call forth some expressions and arguments which left the impression on my mind that his creed was not strictly regulated by the Bible." Madison did jot down notes on some Scripture passages, but they were largely academic and moralizing in nature, rather than theological or even devotional. The emphasis was on morality, ethics, and virtue, although there were a few references to spiritual issues.[91] Madison clearly had a higher view of revelation than the deists, but there is no indication that it played a prominent role in his life.

For his part, Wilson recognized some written revelation from God and gave a significant place to the Bible. He asked: "How shall we, in particular instances, learn the dictates of our duty, and make, with accuracy, the proper distinction between right and wrong; in other words, how shall we, in particular cases, discover the will of God?" His answer comported with the teachings of Christianity but could not have been given by a deist: "We discover it by our conscience, by our reason, and by the Holy Scriptures." In true theistic rationalist fashion, he indicated that reason and revelation were both important. Scripture was important for other purposes, as well. For instance, in his discussion of eternal, celestial, and divine law, Wilson said that they were disclosed by revelation. He even referred to Moses as "the *inspired* legislator of the Jews" (emphasis mine).[92] Wilson also quoted Scripture or alluded to biblical passages to illustrate points,[93] wrote of "the sacred history of the resurrection," and referred to "the sacred oracles" as the "divine monitors without us." It is also worth noting that Wilson occasionally, without qualifiers, referred to the Bible as "the Holy Scriptures" or as "holy writ."[94]

Wilson's discussion of Scripture and its place reflects the quintessential position of theistic rationalism concerning revelation—that some written revelation was legitimate and that the laws of nature, reason, and revelation all came from God, all were limited, and all were meant to complement each other. At the beginning of his lecture on the history of property, Wilson first supported a claim by quoting two passages in Genesis, then added, "The information which is expressly revealed is congenial to those inferences, which may be drawn by sound and legitimate reasoning."[95] Having affirmed that Genesis was "expressly revealed," he felt the need to confirm that the substance of that revelation did not contradict reason. While they generally agreed with one another, when they did not, any conflicts between reason and revelation had to be resolved in support of reason. Regarding natural law and revelation, Wilson stated, "The law of nature and the law of revelation are both divine: they flow, though in different channels, from the same adorable source. It is, indeed, preposterous to separate them from each other. The object of both is—to discover the will of God—and both are necessary for the accomplishment of that end."[96] So, revelation was not sufficient to discover the will of God but had to work with natural knowledge. In that same vein, Wilson introduced a discussion of Scripture and its role by saying, "Reason and conscience can do much; but still they stand in need of support and assistance." It is important to note that Scripture was called upon by Wilson to *support* and *assist* reason—not the reverse. For him, "the Scriptures support, confirm, and corroborate, but do not supersede the operations of reason and the moral sense." That is the theistic rationalist position. Elaborating on revelation's support and assistance of reason and conscience, Wilson explained: "Their weakness is strengthened, their darkness is illuminated, their influence is enlarged by that heaven-descended science, which has brought life and immortality to light. In compassion to the imperfection of our internal powers, our all-gracious Creator, Preserver, and Ruler has been pleased to discover and enforce his laws, by a revelation given to us immediately and directly from himself. This revelation is contained in the Holy Scriptures."[97] Consistent with the theistic rationalist view, Wilson represented God's revelation as *contained in* the Holy Scriptures but not the Scriptures in their entirety. Put another way, some of the Bible was God's revelation, and some was not. As Wilson continued, "On some important subjects, those in particular, which relate to the Deity, to Providence, and to a future state, our natural knowledge is greatly improved, refined, and exalted by that which is revealed."[98] Unlike orthodox Christianity, this perspective held that only *some* of Scripture was God's revelation; unlike deism, it held that there *was* some legitimate revelation from God. Unlike orthodox Christianity, revelation was in service of natural knowledge; unlike deism, natural knowledge was not all there was. Overall, the paucity of references to Scripture by these public men is stark given the public's familiarity with and acceptance of the Bible.

Gouverneur Morris advocated reason as a means of understanding God and our obligations to Him, but he also wrote a sarcastic criticism of deism: "I have lived to see a new religion arise. It consists in a denial of all religion, and its votaries have the superstition of not being superstitious."[99] Madison also shared the deists' views concerning the importance of reason in religion. According to Ralph Ketcham, "Two sources stand out as preeminent in the intellectual background of Madison's religious views. First, the overall rationalism that saturated the theology of the eighteenth century and second, the rather rough-hewn Scottish 'Common Sense' philosophy of the Rev. John Witherspoon, which was in one sense a reaction against rational theology and in another was a natural synthesis for the Enlightenment."[100] Ketcham also noted the influence of Samuel Clarke's rationalism upon Madison. Fifty years after first encountering Clarke's work, Madison was still impressed by "reasoning which could satisfy such a mind as that of Clarke," who, in proving the existence of God, "explicitly denied the support of the Scriptures but rested his case solely on the kind of facts and reasonings which were sure to convince such atheists as Hobbes and Spinoza." Ketcham concluded: "Clarke was an authority whom Witherspoon recommended to his students at Princeton as 'one of the greatest champions of rational religion.' There can be little doubt that the kind of rational religion propounded in *The Being and Attributes of God* was fundamental to Madison's outlook."[101] Clarke's influence can be seen most clearly in a letter from Madison to Frederick Beasley in which he argued for the existence of God on the sole basis of reason. Madison regularly linked reason and religion. He advocated the personal regulation of private affairs "according to the precepts of Wisdom and Religion." He also argued that "reason and the principles of the Xn religion" ought to guide attempts at collective acts of religion. Finally, he said that "religion, or the duty which we owe to our CREATOR, and the manner of discharging it, can be directed only by reason and conviction."[102] Note the use of the word *only*. The Bible and church doctrine were left out of the equation. Scripture and church teaching presumably played a role in helping to form "conviction," but apparently, they were not individually comparable to reason in Madison's view.

Madison appears to have believed in prayer. Bishop Meade reported that Madison led family prayers, and Madison himself reported praying "earnestly" for wisdom for the Virginia Assembly and engaging in "fervent" prayer for the future of the United States.[103] But those reports are both contained in public documents and may have been calculated for effect. As was mentioned, belief in prayer was a logical extension of a belief in a present and active God. It seems clear that Hamilton believed in the efficacy of prayer. As a young man, he not only reported praying but also said that God heard his prayer. Robert Troup, his college roommate, described Hamilton's "habit of praying upon his knees both night and morning."[104] The next recorded evidence of Hamilton's involvement with prayer was the wisecrack he allegedly made in response to Franklin's suggestion that the sessions of the Constitutional Convention be opened with prayer. According to the same source that spawned the apocryphal version of the event, Hamilton supposedly said that they were competent to conduct their business and had no need to call in "foreign aid." Given the unreliable source and Madison's report that Franklin's "proposition was received & treated with the respect due to it,"[105] it is likely that this story was merely one of a number of attempts to besmirch Hamilton's character. In the latter stage of his life, his son reported that Hamilton "now" engaged in "the habit of daily prayer,"[106] so it is likely that his prayer life was minimal during his years in power. The fact that he thought he could get by without divine help during the height of his personal power does not change the fact that he believed in prayer and that he believed that God was there if he felt he needed Him. As will be seen, he returned to active prayer when he, in fact, did feel he needed God's help.

Hamilton's view of the afterlife was consonant with both Christianity and deism. Most of his references reflected Christian terminology. He indicated belief in "the immortality of the soul" and referred to "endless bliss," going to "a peacefull [sic] Shore," "eternal bliss," and to "lay[ing] up a treasure in Heaven."[107] On at least one occasion, he used terminology that was common to deists but was not inconsistent with Christian beliefs, referring to "a future state of rewards and punishments." In connection with the idea of rewards and punishments, he stressed that God "will be the final judge of the universe,"[108]—a belief held by both Christians and deists. More poignant were Hamilton's references to the afterlife when he was facing the immediate prospect of death. In a letter to his wife the day before his final duel, he expressed hope in "a happy immortality" and "the sweet hope of meeting you in a better world." In his will, written the previous day, Hamilton wrote of God's possible "call . . . to the eternal wor[l]d."[109]

He had always believed in an eternal afterlife. Madison, who rarely mentioned the afterlife in his writings, used language common both to the deist conception and to the Christian conception. Like the deists, he wrote of "a future state"; like Christians, he wrote of having his name "enrolled in the annals of Heaven."[110] In another somewhat cryptic reference, Wilson appears to have expressed belief in the Resurrection of Jesus. In his discussion of sensory evidence, he used Jesus's post-Resurrection appearance to His disciples (Luke 24:39–40; John 20:27) to illustrate varying kinds of sensory evidence. The discussion was very matter-of-fact, and there is no reason to believe that he doubted the truth of the passage of Scripture about the Resurrection. He referred to it as "a beautiful and emphatical reference." Indeed, if he did not believe it, he certainly could have come up with some other, more realistic illustration.[111]

If character is related to religious belief, then Gouverneur Morris's conduct was often inconsistent with devotion to either Christianity or deism. Both religious systems emphasized moral living, and Morris strayed a little too frequently to be solidly associated with either. When Morris was nominated to be minister to France, Roger Sherman said, "With regard to moral character I consider him an irreligious and profane man." James Monroe reported, "Upon the grounds of character he was twice refused as a member of the Treasury Board." Though George Washington publicly defended Morris after appointing him, he wrote to him about his "imprudence of conversation and conduct" and asked him to display "more caution and prudence" and "more circumspection." A few years later, Monroe referred to Morris as "a man without morality."[112] This reputation was well earned. Morris once threatened to kill a man if he spoke disrespectfully of him, and he frequently got "very drunk" while in France.[113] His most conspicuous moral problems concerned women, however.

Morris had numerous illicit affairs with married and unmarried women and, by his own admission, was constantly trying to initiate new ones. One of his earliest dalliances resulted in the loss of one of his legs. A cover story was invented that attributed the loss to a cart accident, but the evidence indicates that he lost the leg as a consequence of the affair. John Jay made an admonishing joke about it in a letter of consolation to Morris; apparently, Morris told the whole story to Lord Palmerston at breakfast a decade later. Palmerston wrote in his diary that Morris lost his leg jumping from a window to escape a jealous husband. Circumstantial evidence indicates that the woman involved was probably Eliza Plater, the wife of Col. George Plater. Still, that unfortunate event did not dissuade Morris from pursuing similar activities in the future. In fact, he used the curiosity afforded by his one-legged status to try to seduce other women.[114]

His diary entries during his time in France are filled with sexual escapades. He had an affair with Madame Adelaide de Flahaut for more than three years. She and Morris were eventually so "wanton and flagrant" that they engaged in intercourse "in the passage . . . at the harpsichord . . . downstairs . . . the doors are all open" and in a coach with the coachman staring straight ahead. They became so shameless that they engaged in intercourse inside a convent and even tried to conceive a child while she denied her husband conjugal rights. Morris's diary contains eighteen references to their sexual liaisons, but he claimed that they had made love "several hundred" times.[115] In addition to Madame de Flahaut, he reported having affairs with Madame Simon, an unnamed "damsel," Madame de Lita, Madame de Crayen, Miss Matthiesen and her "young sister," Miss Gehrt, and Mrs. Perez Morton. According to diary entries, he tried to seduce— or at least thought of seducing—Madame de Flahaut's niece, Lady Webster, the "daughter of a Frenchman," Madame Foucault, the daughter of his landlord, Madame de Nadaillac, Madame de Fontana, and even Dolley Madison![116] Thomas Jefferson claimed that Morris confessed to him that he did not believe in Christianity,[117] and Morris's actions certainly gave no reason to believe otherwise. Everyone (except Jesus) sins, of course, but the extent, duration, and brazenness of Morris's immoral conduct must at least call into serious question the idea that he was a Christian. As Jesus said, a tree is known by its fruit (Matthew 12:33). Yet as was suggested earlier, it might have been possible for a theistic rationalist to excuse such behavior as merely a matter of personal morality without societal effects—especially in an already decadent France. Hamilton's somewhat unrepentant confession of an adulterous relationship may be a parallel example.

One other element of Hamilton's life provides some insight into theistic rationalism. For theistic rationalists, religion was primarily valuable for its public utility. The utility they usually had in mind was promotion of morality, which produced good citizens. But Hamilton found other public uses for religion. During the "third stage" of his life, when he was out of power but still actively involved in politics, he used religion to advance his own political causes.[118] When a biographer said that "Hamilton . . . toward the end, confused Federalism with Christianity," he meant that Hamilton did so intentionally and for his own purposes. Adair said it more clearly when he stated that Hamilton "attempted to enlist God in the Federalist party to buttress that party's temporal power."[119] In a letter to William Smith, Hamilton suggested mobilizing "the religious ideas" of Americans against France and called them a "valuable resource." He asserted, "This is an advantage which we shall be very unskilled if we do not use to the utmost," and he added that "a day of humiliation and prayer, beside being very proper, would be extremely useful."[120] Hamilton later wrote a number of articles to arouse the American people against the French and tapped into the "valuable resource" of religious ideas to link Jefferson with the atheism of France.[121]

Hamilton unfairly employed religious arguments in opposition to Jefferson's presidential bid in 1800. In what Adair has called "an ironic commentary on how little the religious issue really meant to Hamilton," one of his contemporaries, Timothy Dwight, found that Hamilton's preferred candidate had essentially the same religious views as Jefferson.[122] Actually, the real irony was that Hamilton himself shared the same basic views as Jefferson. The Christian America camp has praised Hamilton's proposed establishment of a "Christian Constitutional Society," but Adair has correctly described it as a "familiar" effort to use religion to strengthen the Federalists at the expense of the "devilish Jeffersonians." In proposing the society, Hamilton said it was designed "to promote the election of *fit* men"—who all happened to be Federalists, of course—and to promote charitable institutions "in the management of Federalists." The whole proposal was intended to gain credit and "popular favor" for the Federalists. There was nothing "Christian" in Hamilton's description of it, other than an opening statement that one of its purposes would be "the support of the Christian Religion."[123] It is hard to imagine deists or Christians approving of such a cynical use of religion.

As noted at the outset of this chapter, these key framers of the Constitution were not as open or prolific in recording their religious beliefs as were the authors of the Declaration. They did not study religion to the same extent, nor did they feel the need to express their views as openly or frequently as those other Founders. Nonetheless, the attentive reader can glean enough from what they did reveal to see their adherence to theistic rationalism. Stephen Marini wrote about a mixture of Enlightenment thought, marginal protestantism, and Lockean political theory with an insistence on "the power of human reason to understand God and on a God whose actions are rational, not arbitrary." He concluded: "By 1787 this sort of political theology had spread to Presbyterian Federalists like James Wilson."[124] As a result of his study of Madison and religion, Ralph Ketcham came to the following conclusions: "[Madison] was interested in theological and metaphysical speculations, yet was not devoted to any particular dogma. He accepted for the most part the eighteenth century assumption of harmony between the facts of nature and the rational ways of 'Nature's God.' . . . He understood the importance of religion to the psychological health of human beings and to the moral order of society."[125] Madison, in common with his fellow theistic rationalists, believed in God and felt that a belief in God was important. He did not believe in Christianity, however. Franklin Steiner summed up the apparent enigma of Madison's religious position in the following way:

> That a man, who, as a youth, had an ambition to preach religion and save souls, should, in his later years, refuse to discuss it at all, is an enigma, unless policy was consulted, which is scarcely in accord with the supposition that he was religious himself. As we read the four large volumes of Madison's *Writings*, we find, that like Jefferson, he discusses all the great questions of his day. Why should he omit and refuse to discuss religion, which was held to be one of the most vital issues of his time? There are a score of reasons why a man who ceased to be religious should decline to talk, but we can see none for silence on the part of one who is convinced of the truth of Christianity.[126]

Steiner's point is well taken, except that the fact that Madison was not a Christian does not imply that he was not "religious." Like his fellow key Founders, he took a religious journey that ended in theistic rationalism rather than Christianity.

There is one further point to be made concerning Madison and religion. Jasper Adams sent him a copy of his pamphlet, *The Relations of Christianity to Civil Government in the United States*, and asked Madison for comment. In the pamphlet, Adams argued that "the people of the United States have retained the Christian religion as the foundation of their civil, legal, and political institutions." Significantly, in his response letter, Madison did *not* affirm Adams's thesis that Christianity was the foundation of American institutions.[127] This was a golden opportunity for a key Founder to endorse the thesis of the Christian America camp, but Madison did not do so.

THEISTIC RATIONALISM VERSUS CHRISTIANITY: A CASE STUDY (OF SORTS)

The close of Hamilton's life, the fourth of Adair's "stages," illuminated the difference between adhering to theistic rationalism and being devoted to orthodox Christianity. Hamilton's basis of confidence and his entire attitude and language were transformed by his conversion to Christianity at the end of his life.

His religious awakening began with his fall from political power. His son reported that in 1801, "withdrawn for a time from politics, [Hamilton] sought and found relief . . . in the duties of religion." He began to study the Bible and other theological works and to engage in daily prayer. His fall from political power started his religious quest, but it was personal tragedy that "crystallized the change."[128] Hamilton's eldest son, Philip, was killed in a duel, and his eldest daughter lost her sanity in grief over the death. Hamilton turned to a more personal, less generic God for solace and comfort.

With his change of perspective, Hamilton's attitude showed signs of change as well. Despite his career-long bitter rivalry with Jefferson, he used his influence to try to keep Federalist newspapers from printing information on the Jefferson-Hemings scandal as exposed by James Callender.[129] He gained an appreciation for and began "to cultivate resignation, and even humility"[130] before God and men—in stark contrast to the arrogance for which he was known in public life and that he clearly exhibited in his response to the Maria Reynolds affair. Finally, the formerly ambitious and ruthless politician determined "to expose my own life to any extent rather than subject my self to the guilt of taking the life of another"—that is, rather than firing at Aaron Burr in the duel they were to have.[131] In the end, Hamilton apparently found something more important than reason to guide his actions. His second in the duel, Nathaniel Pendleton, tried to convince him to fire at Burr, but Hamilton replied that his decision was "the effect of a *religious scruple,* and does not admit of reasoning. It is useless to say more on the subject, as my purpose is definitely fixed."[132]

But what religious scruple had Hamilton found? Close friend Oliver Wolcott told his wife that "Genl Hamilton has *of late* expressed his conviction of the truths of the Christian Religion" (emphasis mine).[133] Wolcott distinguished his newfound belief in Christianity from his previous religious position. Hamilton's son reported that during this period, his father had told a boyhood friend, "I have examined carefully the evidence of the Christian religion; and, if I was sitting as a juror upon its authenticity, I should unhesitatingly give my verdict in its favor." He said of Christianity to another person, "I have studied it, and I can prove its truth as clearly as any proposition ever submitted to the mind of man."[134]

Hamilton's words and actions in the final week of his life are particularly revealing. He led his wife and children in the Episcopal family worship service on the Sunday before he died. Further, in the two letters he wrote to his wife in the final days before the duel, he confessed that he was a Christian, twice spoke of his humility before God, asked that God's will be done, and placed his hope for the next life on "redeeming grace and divine mercy" rather than on confidence in any works he had done.[135] Here was the language of a Christian: reliance upon "redeeming grace" from God. Hamilton was no longer a theistic rationalist using generic religious language and counting on his own morality.

Of course, he would need to rely on that grace and mercy, as he was mortally wounded by Burr. On his deathbed, he requested that Bishop Benjamin Moore administer communion to him. Moore, wanting to "avoid every appearance of precipitancy in performing one of the most solemn offices of our religion" to one who had never joined the church or publicly declared faith in Christ, refused.[136] Hamilton then sent for Dr. John Mason for the same purpose, but Mason refused because it was against church policy to administer communion privately "to any person under any circumstances." Mason assured Hamilton that communion was only a sign and that "the absence of the sign does not exclude from the mercies signified."[137] Mason then shared the Gospel with Hamilton and reported his response. Mason wrote:

> In the sight of God all men are on a level, as *all have sinned, and come short of his glory*; and that they must apply to him for pardon and life, *as sinners*, whose only refuge is in his *grace reigning by righteousness through our Lord Jesus Christ.* "I perceive it to be so," said he; "I am a sinner: I look to his mercy." I then adverted to "the infinite merit of the Redeemer," as the *propitiation for sin*, the sole ground of our acceptance with God; the sole channel of his favour to us; and cited the following passages of scripture:—"*There is no other name given under heaven among men, whereby we must be saved, but the name of Jesus. He is able to save them to the uttermost who come unto God by him, seeing he ever liveth to make intercession for them. The blood of Jesus Christ cleanseth from all sin.*" . . . He assented, with strong emotion, to these representations.[138]

Mason went on to discuss the grace "which brings salvation," and Hamilton interrupted him to affirm that "it is *rich* grace." Then, according to Mason, "the General . . . looking up towards heaven, said, with emphasis, 'I have a tender reliance on the mercy of the Almighty, through the merits of the Lord Jesus Christ.'"[139] In identifying himself as a "sinner," emphasizing "grace," and appealing specifically to "the Lord Jesus Christ," Hamilton illustrated the difference in language between a theistic rationalist and a Christian. It is also instructive to note that Mason more than once mentioned that Hamilton displayed religious emotion—which also separated the Christian Hamilton from his former theistic rationalism.

Because Mason would not perform the desired service, Hamilton called for Moore to return. He did, and the two men discussed the subject of communion. Moore then asked Hamilton the standard questions preceding Episcopal communion, including: "Do you sincerely repent of your sins past? Have you a lively faith in God's mercy through Christ, with a thankful remembrance of the death of Christ?" Moore reported that Hamilton "lifted up his hands and said, 'With the utmost sincerity of heart I can answer those questions in the affirmative.'" Being convinced of Hamilton's sincerity, Moore administered communion to him, which was received with "great devotion." The minister saw him again the next morning and reported that "with his last faultering words, he expressed a strong confidence in the mercy of God through the intercession of the Redeemer."[140] There is no reason to disbelieve these accounts of Hamilton's death. Indeed, as Chernow has concluded, "It is not certain that Hamilton was as eloquent on his deathbed as his friends later attested, but their accounts corroborate one another and are remarkably consistent."[141]

Hamilton's deathbed confession is discussed at length here to highlight some of the differences between theistic rationalism and Christianity. In Christianity, the central issue is the person and work of Christ. It is his work as redeemer and God's grace to the undeserving that are pivotal, rather than good works or virtuous and moral living. Although theistic rationalism avoided specific doctrines and was coldly calculating, disdaining "enthusiasm" in religion, Hamilton affirmed exclusive doctrines and did so with great emotional fervor. As a theistic rationalist, he avoided mentioning Jesus in his writings, but now he could not help but focus on Him when he embraced Christianity. Perhaps Hamilton's story also reveals something of the practical limits of cold, impersonal, rational religion and something of Christianity's warmth, vibrancy, and enduring power.

Although Alexander Hamilton became a Christian in his waning days, his life and beliefs did not evince Christian faith during the time in which he contributed to the Founding of America. Arguably, his greatest contribution to that Founding was his work as George Washington's secretary of the Treasury and the prime mover of the Washington administration. The next chapter will demonstrate that, contrary to popular opinion, Washington embraced fundamentally the same theistic rationalist beliefs as Hamilton had through most of his life.

7

The Theistic Rationalism of George Washington

> That road to heaven which to them shall seem . . . least liable to exception.
>
> George Washington

FIRST IN WAR, FIRST IN PEACE, and first to be claimed by both sides of the Founders' religion argument, George Washington is the one most ardently embraced by Christian America advocates. Because of the central and symbolic role he played in the Revolution, in the framing of the Constitution, and as the first president and "father of his country," it is vital to the Christian America cause to identify Washington as a Christian. One prominent adherent of that camp told me, "If George Washington was not a Christian, then I'm not a Christian!" Well, George Washington was not a Christian but a theistic rationalist.

In common with nearly everyone in eighteenth-century America, Washington believed in a creator God. He referred to God as the "parent of the human race," as man's "Maker," and as "the Divine Author of life."[1] As that belief was almost universally held in his day and expressed in dozens of his works, further evidence of this will not be presented here. Washington's view of the afterlife was very generic and also basically in accord with that of most every religion in America. He expressed "the hope of future happiness" and believed in "the immortality of the soul." He generally referred to taking "departure for the land of Spirits" or for "the world of Spirits." He apparently believed the afterlife to be a personal existence, as he spoke of the "plant of friendship" being "translated to a happier clime" after death.[2] Washington's difference with Christianity, as will be seen, concerned the basis upon which one entered the afterlife.

As a theistic rationalist, Washington believed in an active, intervening God who was interested in and who impacted human affairs. Richard Brookhiser has noted that, in contrast to the God of the deists, "Washington's God was no watchmaker, who wound the world up and retired, but an active agent and force."[3] Perhaps no one of the period referred more often to the Providence of God or was more diligent in expressing gratitude to Him.

When speaking of God's intervention, Washington employed a number of terms for "God." In that context, he referred to "Heaven," "the supreme being," "the Supreme Ruler of the Universe," "Almighty Being," "invisible hand," "a Gracious Providence," "the Supreme Ruler of nations," "Sovereign Arbiter of Nations," "great disposer of human Events," and "interposing Hand of Heaven,"[4] among others. For Washington, regardless of how one conceived of God or wished to address Him, the Supreme Being was active and involved in the affairs of man.

Washington believed in particular Providence, not just the deist notion of general providence. His God was involved in the universe, with nations, and with individuals. He affirmed all three levels of God's involvement in a single statement in his first inaugural address, when he appealed to "that Almighty Being who rules over the Universe; who presides in the Councils of Nations; and whose providential aids can supply every human defect."[5] Several pages would be needed to document the relevant material, so no attempt will be made here to recount Washington's references to God's ongoing activity in the universe or on behalf of America. Suffice it to say that I have counted fifty-seven separate letters, addresses, or public documents in which he appealed to or recognized the hand of God on the nation's behalf. Documenting Washington's references to God's personal involvement in his own life and the lives of other individuals is a more manageable and important proposition. Washington identified God as the "Great Author of every public and *private* good" and heaven as "the source of all public and *private* blessings" (emphases mine). In a more personal vein, he said that "Providence has a joint claim to my humble and grateful thanks, for its protection and direction of me." Also, in his recounting of a well-known incident to his brother, Washington reported, "By the miraculous care of Providence, that protected me beyond all human expectation; I had 4 Bullets through my Coat, and two Horses shot under me, and yet escaped unhurt."[6] In both cases, Washington expressed the belief that Providence had personally protected him, not simply a belief in a general, overarching notion of providence. Paul Boller, author of a classic book on Washington's religion, concluded that the first president believed that the "finger of Providence" was ordering his life, a conviction that "stimulated and energized" him.[7]

Washington's firm belief in Providence was the basis of his belief in the efficacy of prayer. For deists, there was no longer any God "out there" to whom to appeal—or if there was, He was either not interested or unable to intercede. But Washington believed in prayer. He regularly reported engaging in prayer; he asked his soldiers to pray; he asked Congress to join him in prayer; he called upon the nation to join him in prayer; and he included prayer in addresses on his way into the presidency and on his way out. On various occasions, he reported praying "humbly," "fervently," and "earnestly."[8] Ironically, as will be shown, the two best-known prayers of Washington are both spurious. An unknown person inserted pietistic words into Washington's "Circular to the States" to make it into what is called "Washington's Prayer," and the evidence clearly shows that his famous prayer in the snow at Valley Forge is a fictitious event. That does not change the fact that Washington believed in a present God and that he therefore believed prayer to be a rational activity.

Washington also promoted church attendance and went to church himself fairly consistently. As a general, he "directed that divine Service should be performed . . . every Sunday," and he "require[d] and expect[ed], of all Officers, and Soldiers, not engaged on actual duty, a punctual attendance on divine Service."[9] At home in Virginia, Washington went to church an average of once per month, but that was often enough for him to be a vestryman in his parish. In his study of Washington's diary, Boller discovered that prior to 1774, Washington often "transacted business on Sundays, visited friends and relatives, traveled, and sometimes went fox-hunting instead of going to church." His attendance increased to two or three times per month during the crisis with Britain, and he attended almost every Sunday as president.[10] The rector of a church that Washington attended while president confirmed his "regular attendance in our church," and in a parting letter to the churches he went to as president, Washington spoke of a "high sense of duty in my attendance on public worship." As he was in all matters as president, he was cognizant of his example and wished to model what he considered proper behavior. It seems clear that Washington attended church fairly regularly when he was in the public eye, and it was likely that his example would have been noted. When he returned to Mount Vernon, he returned to his habit of attending about once per month.[11] His attendance record seems to indicate a sense of public duty more than heartfelt piety, which is just what one would expect of a theistic rationalist.

Just as he apparently felt a duty to promote church attendance in others by his own example, Washington, though not a Christian himself, promoted "Christian" behavior in others. As a general, he instructed his soldiers "to live, and act, as becomes a Christian Soldier"; he urged them to show "a true Christian Spirit"; and he encouraged them to pursue the "distinguished Character of [a] Christian." As president, he encouraged Catholics to be "animated alone by the pure spirit of Christianity" and Episcopalians to develop a "more christian-like spirit."[12] It is clear from the context of these pleas that Washington's understanding of the term *Christianity* or *Christian* was that of his fellow theistic rationalists. That is, to be Christian was to be good and moral. This also becomes clear when one looks at Washington's ongoing support for efforts to "civilize and Christianize" Native Americans. From 1775 to 1792, he supported a number of these efforts. He spoke of "converting the Indians to Christianity and consequently to civilization" and of converting them "for the protection of the Union."[13] For Washington, as a theistic rationalist, Christianity was useful for promoting good morals and producing good citizens. In the case of "savages," it would "civilize" them for the benefit of American society. A deist would not have promoted morality under the auspices of Christianity but rather would have made a direct appeal to reason or to nature or to "religion" in general. Having been raised in Christendom and having borrowed some Christian ideas, he was comfortable with some of Christianity's terminology. As Brookhiser put it, "Washington sought to borrow what was useful in Christianity for the United States."[14]

Another reflection of Christian influence upon Washington was his apparent belief in a God who performed miracles. In a letter to the Jewish congregations of Savannah, he identified "the same wonder-working Deity" who long since delivered the Hebrews "from their Egyptian Oppressors" with the God "whose providential agency" had aided the United States.[15] Although this was a public letter in which he may have simply been trying to relate to the Jewish congregations, there is little reason to doubt his sincerity. He could have used innumerable adjectives to draw parallels between the God of the Jews and the God who had aided America, but he chose to emphasize a God who did miracles. He could also have suggested that God accomplished the delivery of both the Jews and America without the use of miracles. One should also remember that he had earlier attributed his survival on the battlefield to "the miraculous care of Providence." Certainly, one who disbelieved in a miracle-working God might casually refer to such an escape as "miraculous," but Washington specified that Providence was responsible for the miraculous event in his life.

Washington's view of the Bible is difficult to pinpoint. His only references to revelation in a general sense are found in two letters. He intimated belief in some written revelation in a letter to a Frenchman, in which he wrote of "the principles of reason and religion (natural and *revealed*)" (emphasis mine). In the next sentence, he referenced "the Scripture." In the 1783 "Circular to the States," Washington said that "above all, the pure and benign light of Revelation" was responsible for "the blessings of society."[16] These passages suggest that he recognized the validity of some written revelation. Certain questions surround the value of drawing conclusions from the "Circular," however, which will be addressed later. Notwithstanding the "Circular" statement, Boller noted that there are "astonishingly few references to the Bible in his letters and public statements." As the Bible was the one book available to and read by virtually all eighteenth-century Americans, it was common to appeal to it for examples, illustrations, or authoritative support. Yet most of Washington's few references to the Bible were humorous.[17] Occasionally, he referred to biblical passages without humor, as when he expressed a desire to "encourage . . . that righteousness which exalteth a Nation" or looked to the day in which "the nations learn war no more," unacknowledged references to Proverbs 14:34 and Isaiah 2:4.[18] Most of the nonhumorous references, as in the first example, were made in letters to religious congregations and in the context of concern for national morality. Especially if one includes the statement in the "Circular," Washington appears to have believed in some revelation and considered it a good influence on society, but he did not deem it important enough to use on a regular basis or as authoritative support for his beliefs or arguments. All of this is consistent with the theistic rationalist perspective on revelation.

Washington's view of Jesus is equally difficult to pin down. He seems to have studiously avoided mentioning the name of Jesus. In more than 20,000 pages of his writings, there is only one reference to "Jesus Christ" and one to "the Divine Author of our blessed Religion," but whether even these are legitimately from Washington is debatable. A speech in his name to the chiefs of the Delaware Indians included these words: "You do well to wish to learn our arts and ways of life, and above all, the religion of Jesus Christ."[19] The reference to "the Divine Author" appears in the aforementioned "Circular to the States," and if it was legitimately representative of Washington's thinking, it could indicate his belief in the divinity of Jesus; alternatively, it could simply mean that he considered Jesus preeminently gifted or extraordinarily excellent.

Scholars question whether these two documents accurately depict Washington's position for three reasons. First, neither is written in his own hand. Second, these types of documents were typically written by aides and simply signed by Washington, in which case he may or may not have read them. Concerning the speech to the Indians, Boller argued that "Washington, who must have been pressed for time, seems simply to have signed the document, without making any revisions." On other occasions, he was more circumspect. For example, he crossed out the word *God* from a later speech to Indian leaders and substituted *the Great Spirit above.*[20] It should also be noted that some of Washington's staff writers had "sincere Christian convictions" that may have found their way into his speeches and other documents but escaped his attention or editing. Third, nowhere else did Washington mention the name of Jesus—much less Christ—or express any sentiments remotely similar to those expressed in the closing paragraph of the "Circular."[21] It is almost inconceivable that a sincere believer in the deity of Jesus who accepted him as the Christ would never mention anything about such a belief to friends or family in correspondence; but there is no evidence of Washington ever doing so. His acquaintances and family members did not testify to such personal discussion, either.

Further evidence suggests that Washington did not accept the person or work of Jesus and that his religious views were not consistent with Christianity. That evidence concerns one of his practices regarding worship: he refused to take communion. Nelly Custis, who was Martha Washington's granddaughter and lived at Mount Vernon and attended church with the Washingtons, said, "On communion Sundays, he left the church with me, after the blessing, and returned home, and we sent the carriage back for my grandmother." Similarly, Bishop William White, who officiated at Christ Church in Philadelphia, which Washington attended, stated, "Truth requires me to say, that General Washington never received the communion, in the churches of which I am parochial minister."[22] Finally, Dr. James Abercrombie, who was assistant rector at Christ Church, observed that "on Sacrament Sundays, Gen'l Washington immediately after the Desk and Pulpit services, went out with the greater part of the congregation, always leaving Mrs. Washington with the communicants." Abercrombie reported:

I considered it my duty, in a sermon on Public Worship, to state the unhappy tendency of *example,* particularly of those in elevated stations, who invariably turned their backs upon the celebration of the Lord's Supper. I acknowledge the remark was intended for the President, and, as such, he received it. A few days after, in conversation with, I believe, a Senator of the U.S., he told me he had dined the day before with the President, who, in the course of the conversation at the table, said, that on the preceding Sunday, he had received a very just reproof from the pulpit, for always leaving the church before the administration of the Sacrament; that he honored the preacher for his integrity and candour; that he had never considered the influence of his example; that he would never again give cause for the repetition of the reproof. . . . Accordingly, he afterwards never came on the morning of Sacrament Sunday, tho' at other times, a constant attendant in the morning.[23]

Washington was adamant about not taking communion, so much so that, cognizant of his example, he stopped attending church on Sacrament

Sundays. Why would one who believed in the person and sacrifice of Jesus Christ so adamantly refuse to engage in the celebration of that event as instituted and commanded by Jesus? He did not leave an explanation; nor did Nelly. Washington's obstinacy in this regard calls into question the idea that the two documents discussed earlier reflect his beliefs about Jesus, and it distances him from identification with Christianity.

Before turning from Washington's relationship to Christianity, some of the apocryphal claims of "zealous filiopietists" need to be addressed. Boller has noted that Washington has been hailed as "'a Christian hero and states-man,' 'Christ's faithful soldier and servant,' 'the founder of a Christian re-public,' 'the great high-priest of the nation;' and at one time it was even suggested that he be duly canonized as the first official saint of the church to which he belonged."[24] In fact, a sort of "cult of personality" emerged a few months after Washington's death. The publication in early 1800 of Mason Locke "Parson" Weems's *Life of Washington* was primarily responsible. That work is the origin of a number of myths, such as the famous cherry tree story. More important for present purposes are the stories Weems in-vented or embellished in order to build Washington's religious reputation.

Weems reported that young George's father taught him about the exis-tence and power of God, as opposed to chance, by planting cabbage seeds to spell out GEORGE WASHINGTON. When retelling the story of Washing-ton escaping unscathed from a "famous Indian warrior," Weems editorial-ized that "there was some invisible hand, which turned aside his bullets."[25] Much is made of this "proof" of Washington's special relationship to God by Christian America adherents, but they are curiously unwilling to posit a similar special relationship between God and Adolf Hitler, who also "mi-raculously" escaped harm in an assassination attempt and then claimed God's special protection.

Certainly, the most famous of Weems's religious stories was the account of Isaac Potts discovering Washington on his knees praying in the snows of Valley Forge. A famous painting depicts this scene of piety on the part of General Washington. What has become known as his "Gethsemane" has been immortalized in bronze on a government building in New York; it is also the basis of a Potts house shrine, as well as the Washington Memorial Chapel and the congressional private chapel. The postal service even is-sued a stamp commemorating the event in 1928. The only problem is that the event did not occur. The account is suspicious on the surface because, according to Bishop White and Nelly Custis, Washington never knelt dur-ing prayer. That fact is particularly noteworthy and was specifically men-tioned by the two witnesses because it was the custom in Washington's denomination to kneel. It seems unlikely that he would do in the snows of Valley Forge what he refused to do in church in the presence of his kneeling peers. More decisive, however, is the fact that historians have discovered that Isaac Potts owned, but did not live on, a farm near Valley Forge until the Revolution was nearly over; and he was nowhere near Valley Forge in the winter of 1777.[26]

Besides fabricating events, Weems also showed a great ability to embellish them. In particular, his creative account of Washington's death quickly became celebrated and was immortalized in another famous painting. In his account, Weems assumed the position of a narrator who knew the thoughts and motives of the actors in a scene. In setting up the death scene, he either intentionally or unintentionally equated Washington with Christ when he said, "Washington, who so often conquered himself, is now about to conquer the last enemy." Coming from a parson, this was clearly a reference to the biblical account of Jesus conquering the "last enemy"—death.[27] Weems reported that Washington asked everyone to leave him alone "with his God," and "there, by himself, like Moses alone on the top of Pisgah, he seeks the face of God."[28] Then, according to an omniscient Weems, with "angel fervour did he adore that *Almighty Love.*" Further channeling the thoughts of Washington, Weems reported that the many gifts Washington had received from God "overwhelmed his soul with gratitude unutterable, exalted to infinite heights his ideas of eternal love, and bade him without fear resign his departing spirit into the arms of his Redeemer God, whose mercies are over all his works. . . . How fervently does he pray that the *unsuffering kingdom of God may come.*"[29] According to Weems, Washington felt he was about to die and said, "Father of mercies! take me to thyself," and then expired. Not content with the heroic death, Weems continued his dramatic account:

> Swift on angels' wings the brightening saint ascended; while voices more than human were heard (*in Fancy's ear*) warbling through the happy regions, and hymning the great procession towards the gates of heaven. His glorious coming was seen far off, and myriads of mighty angels hastened forth, with golden harps, to welcome the honoured stranger. High in front of the shouting hosts, were seen the beauteous forms of FRANKLIN . . . [and others].[30]

One might well ask how he knew all of this if, as Weems claimed, Washington had asked everyone to leave him alone!

According to those actually present at Washington's death, there is not a stitch of truth in Weems's account. His doctor, his secretary Tobias Lear, and Martha were with him to the end. Washington did not call for a clergyman (as would be customary for a member of his denomination) or say anything religious.[31] In fact, the author of the earliest work on his religious opinions felt it necessary to explain away the fact that Washington said nothing religious on his deathbed. He argued that those in attendance "were not such as would most readily encourage the expression of his religious feelings, or carefully record them when uttered." Such an explanation is preposterous, as Washington's stature and fame would have caused all in attendance to hang on to his every word and attempt to record his last pronouncements for posterity. In addition, that same author mentioned the fact that Martha never left his side and rested her head on her Bible throughout[32]—surely, she would not have been reticent to repeat any religious comments uttered by her dying husband! Weems's account of Washington's death is, like much of the Christian America camp's version of history, much more entertaining than the truth—and equally inaccurate.

One other example related to the fabrication of Washington's piety must be noted. Washington's (perhaps spurious) "Circular to the States" was turned into "Washington's Prayer" by inserting "Almighty God" at the beginning and "Through Jesus Christ Our Lord" at the end. The resultant "prayer" was then inscribed on a bronze tablet in St. Paul's Chapel in New York.[33] It seems that an exaggeration of Washington's piety is vital to some beyond the Christian America camp. It is, nonetheless, an exaggeration.

A curious aspect of Washington's religious expression was the impersonal nature of some of his references to Providence. Generally, the personality of Providence was not in question, as he often used anthropomorphic language (speaking of the "hand" or "finger" or "smiles" of Providence) or personal pronouns (referring to "his," "who," "whose/whom," or even "her" or "she").[34] Occasionally, however, he used the impersonal pronoun "it" to refer to Providence. He seemed not to be cognizant of the inconsistency, as on two occasions he mixed his usage of "who" and "it" in the same or successive sentences.[35] A possible explanation is that the personal references may have been to God Himself and the impersonal ones to His power or activity in the world. Washington rarely mentioned "fate" or "fortune," and it is clear that he did not consider them synonyms for Providence, as did a number of deists. Though he, like Gouverneur Morris, did not work out a consistent pronoun use for Providence, he always used masculine personal pronouns when referring to God under any other title than Providence. Washington's references to God were not personal in the sense of warmth or intimate relationship. He always used "God-words" in describing God's being, attributes, or actions rather than intimate terms such as "father" or "savior." As Boller put it, "Washington had a faith that was essentially of the mind, not of the heart."[36] One might say the same for all of the theistic rationalists, for whom the mind was the determining factor in their relationship to God.

Washington shared this emphasis on the mind and reason with deists and with his fellow theistic rationalists. Indeed, in addition to the influence of Christianity, his religious views were shaped by the ideas of the Enlightenment. For example, Washington identified science as a primary factor in the "advancement of true religion," and he rejoiced "that in this Land the light of truth and reason has triumphed over the power of bigotry and superstition."[37] In the eighteenth century, religious "bigotry" was a standard term used to describe having specific doctrinal commitments. Such statements could easily have been made by deists.

Washington also stressed the same attributes of God as did deism—power, wisdom, and benevolence.[38] He regularly referred to God as "All-powerful," "the Omnipotent Being," "the Almighty," "All Wise," and as one whose actions were "all ways wise." He was confident that the ways of God were always "for gracious purposes" and that God was filled with "goodness" and was "kind," "benign," and "beneficent."[39] Along with the deists, Washington emphasized that God and His ways were "inscrutable" and virtually impossible to comprehend.[40] The deist view of God appeared to be rather simple, but that was only what man could know of God; deists stressed that there was much about God that was unknowable. For Washington and the theistic rationalists, what man could know about God was that He represented what one would expect of the best of *men*—but with greater power.

Of course, Christians also believed that God was powerful, wise, and benevolent. However, they emphasized other key attributes as well, such as holiness, justice, and jealousy. The deists rejected many characteristics and actions of the biblical God as inconsistent with their view of him. For instance, they denied the wrath and vengeance of God as being unworthy of a wise and benevolent Supreme Being. In this, Washington, other theistic rationalists, and deists were of one mind.

In contrast to Christians, Washington had a commitment to religious toleration born of the belief that there are many roads leading to God. He emphasized, particularly in his many letters to religious groups, that all people ought to be able to worship God "according to the dictates of their consciences." He often expressed the wish that various sects would find and emphasize common ground. Thus, he wrote, "It always affords me satisfaction, when I find a concurrence in sentiment and practice between all conscientious men in acknowledgments of homage to the great Governor of the Universe."[41] With regard to various Christian denominations in particular, Washington said, "It would ill become me to conceal the joy I have felt in perceiving the fraternal affection which appears to encrease [*sic*] every day among the friends of genuine religion. It affords edifying prospects indeed to see Christians of different denominations dwell together in more charity, and conduct themselves in respect to each other with a more christianlike spirit."[42] He expressed approval of efforts to bring all denominations together: "I was in hopes, that the enlightened and liberal policy, which has marked the present age, would at least have reconciled *Christians* of every denomination so far, that we should never again see their religious disputes carried to such a pitch as to endanger the peace of Society."[43] He was pleased with the progress that had been made toward this end. In fact, he boasted to the Jews in America that "the liberal sentiment towards each other which marks every political and religious denomination of men in this country stands unrivalled in the history of nations."[44]

Like his fellow theistic rationalists, Washington could afford to promote toleration and to advocate removal of barriers between sects because he had no heartfelt attachment to any particular sect himself. Because all roads to God were equally valid in his opinion, he could say to all Americans in his Farewell Address, "With slight shades of difference, you have the same Religion."[45] Speaking specifically of his lack of identification with Christianity and of his belief that the Christian road was a valid one, Washington wrote: "Being no bigot myself to any mode of worship, I am disposed to indulge the professors of Christianity in the church, that road to Heaven, which to *them* shall seem the most direct plainest easiest and least liable to exception" (emphasis mine).[46] By "no bigot" to "any mode of worship," Washington meant that he was not committed to any religious sect. He always spoke of Christians in the third person, as can be seen here and in two quotes cited earlier in which he used "themselves" and "their" when speaking of Christians. He expressed his appreciation to "the Different Denominations" of Philadelphia for their "harmony and brotherly love" and prayed that for *all* of them, "the future reward of good and faithful Servants may be your's [*sic*]." In writing to various religious groups and congregations, he suggested that all people—Protestant, Jewish, and Catholic—would, despite their mutually exclusive beliefs, experience "eternal blessings" or "spiritual felicity" or be made "everlastingly happy" and receive "eternal happiness."[47] To say that Jews would receive "eternal blessings" and be made "everlastingly happy" along with Protestants and Catholics was inconsistent with a particular belief in any of those systems. He even identified his God with the "Great spirit" of the Cherokees.[48] These sentiments were expressed in public letters and might have merely been attempts to curry favor with religious groups, but there is reason to believe that they actually reflected Washington's true beliefs.

For Washington and the theistic rationalists, all concepts of God led back to the same being. That is why he could call on all the people of America to unite in prayer to "that great and glorious Being" of which he spoke in his Thanksgiving Proclamation. In his view, the prayers of Jews, Protestants, Catholics, and Indians all rose to the same being. Washington sometimes expressed this idea more subtly. He claimed to be an "impartial Patron of genuine, vital religion." Being *impartial* requires the existence of more than one party, which suggests that, in his view, several religions were genuine. More significantly, Washington rejoiced that in America, "the light of truth and reason" had triumphed over religious "bigotry." As was noted previously, religious bigotry was defined in the eighteenth century as devotion to one's particular religion. So, if "truth" had triumphed over bigotry, the "truth" according to Washington was that no particular religion was exclusively right. Indeed, in the same sentence, he rejoiced that "every person may here worship God according to the dictates of his own heart."[49] Thus, according to Washington, the "light of truth" allowed *every* person to pursue God in his or her *own* way. And for that to be the case, all paths had to lead to God.

To fully grasp Washington's beliefs in this area, one must look at his membership in Freemasonry. Brookhiser simply concluded that "Washington belonged to another religious body besides the Episcopal Church—the Freemasons."[50] Of course, the Freemasons were not technically a religious group, but they did hold particular religious beliefs. As was mentioned in a previous chapter, Franklin was a Freemason, and he found the Freemasons' beliefs to be consonant with his own. The same was true for Washington. Though some Christian America advocates argue that Washington was not an active Mason but simply joined the group, he was, in fact, a leader. Brookhiser has noted that "in 1793, when Washington laid the cornerstone of the Capitol, Lodge 22 of Alexandria organized the parade, with Washington serving as Grand Master *pro tem* and wearing a Masonic apron knitted for him by Madame Lafayette, whose husband belonged to the lodge of Saint-Jean de la Candeur. This would seem to go beyond the requirements of 'joining.'"[51] Washington was an enthusiastic Freemason who laid the cornerstone of the Capitol with a Masonic trowel. A testament to his extensive involvement is the George Washington Masonic National Memorial in Alexandria, Virginia, which contains the chair in which he presided as master of the Alexandria Lodge and a painting of him in his Masonic regalia.

The significance of Washington's membership in the Freemasons can be seen in a review of Masonic religious beliefs. Freemasonry "holds to a unitary Supreme Being, the so-called Great Architect of the Universe, denies Christ's unique saviorship and atonement, and reduces religion to a moralistic observance of allegedly common ethical principles."[52] In response to a Christian critique, a prominent defender of Masonry wrote:

> Freemasonry . . . transcends the bounds of Christian and Western civilization; it includes the Moslem, the Hindoo, the Buddhist, and the Jew. Without waiting for their respective faiths to come together in a visible federation or unity, they can all meet together in their own and in each other's Lodges throughout the world and pray and worship together to the same one-and-only indivisible God whom all religions acknowledge and venerate.[53]

These beliefs coincide with those that Washington intimated in his writings. In fact, Brookhiser has said that the "difficulty with assessing the intellectual effect of Freemasonry on Washington is that it is redundant, as far as content is concerned. . . . To a man enamored of drama as Washington was, Freemasonry gave symbolic and ceremonial form to goals and ideas he already had."[54] These ideas also coincided with theistic rationalism. Theoretically, one could be a Christian and a Freemason ignorant of its religious teachings, but Washington's expressed beliefs corresponded closely with the anti-Christian teachings of Freemasonry.

In concert with his fellow theistic rationalists, Washington stressed morality as the key to religion. Along with science, he expected morality to produce "true piety" and "the advancement of true religion." Generally, in his writings, "true religion" was connected with morality or virtue. For example, near the end of his Thanksgiving Proclamation, Washington expressed a desire to "promote the knowledge and practice of true religion and virtue."[55] For him, the evidence of "the sanctity of their professions" of religious belief would be "the innocence of their lives and the beneficence of their actions, for no man, who is profligate in his morals, or a bad member of the civil community, can possibly be a true Christian, or a credit to his own religious society." He connected being a good citizen with "genuine, vital religion."[56] Christianity, of course, also promoted morality and expected believers to live virtuously, but morality was not the essence of Christianity. As theistic rationalism taught, morality and virtue were the substance and evidence of true religion for Washington.

Washington also shared the theistic rationalist belief that the purpose of religion was to benefit society by producing good citizens. From the time he led the continental armed forces, he promoted religion for its utilitarian effects of improving morality and its resultant benefits. According to Washington, "The regularity and decorum with which divine service is now performed every Sunday, will reflect great credit on the army in general, tend to improve the morals, and at the same time, to increase the happiness of the soldiery, and must afford the most pure and rational entertainment for every serious and well disposed mind." There was no expressed interest in salvation or even discussion of preparing soldiers who might die to meet their Maker. In a discussion of an establishment bill, Washington explained that he was not against the bill in principle but wished for its death "because I think it will be productive of more quiet to the State." As was noted earlier, he supported efforts to "Christianize" the Indians "for the protection of the Union."[57] Like other theistic rationalists, Washington viewed religion from a utilitarian perspective. He argued more than once that "*Religion* and *Morality* are the essential pillars of Civil society." The best known of such remarks was in his Farewell Address:

> Of all the dispositions and habits which lead to political prosperity, Religion and morality are indispensable supports. In vain would that man claim the tribute of Patriotism, who should labour to subvert these great Pillars of human happiness, these firmest props of the duties of Men and citizens. . . . Let it simply be asked where is the security for property, for reputation, for life, if the sense of religious obligation *desert* the oaths, which are the instruments of investigation in the Courts of Justice? And let us with caution indulge the supposition, that morality can be maintained without religion. Whatever may be conceded to the influence of refined education on minds of peculiar structure, reason and experience both forbid us to expect that National morality can prevail in exclusion of religious principle. 'Tis substantially true, that virtue or morality is a necessary spring of popular government.[58]

Religion and morality supported citizenship duties, provided security for oaths, and constituted a foundation for popular government. Later in the address, Washington asked, "Can it be, that Providence has not connected the permanent felicity of a Nation with its virtue?" Believing that Providence *had* so connected the two, Washington acknowledged churches for their "laudable endeavors to render men sober, honest, and good Citizens, and the obedient subjects of a lawful government."[59] For a theistic rationalist, that was the purpose of religion and, therefore, of churches.

Was George Washington a Christian, as the filiopietists claim? Unlike some of the other key Founders, he never claimed to be a Christian—even by self-determined standards! In fact, Jefferson recounted an incident in which a group of clergymen unsuccessfully tried to "trick" Washington into declaring himself a Christian (or not):

> Dr. Rush tells me that he had it from Asa Green that when the clergy addressed Genl. Washington on his departure from the govmt, it was observed in their consultation that he had never on any occasion said a word to the public which showed a belief in the Xn religion and they thot [sic] they should so pen their address as to force him at length to declare publicly whether he was a Christian or not. They did so. However he observed the old fox was too cunning for them. He answered every article of their address particularly except that, which he passed over without notice.[60]

The "old fox," according to Benjamin Tallmadge, had never been "explicit in his profession of *faith in,* and *dependence on* the finished Atonement of our glorious Redeemer."[61]

James Madison told Jared Sparks that, other than attending services, he did "not suppose that Washington had ever attended to the arguments for Christianity, and for the different systems of religion, or in fact that he had formed definite opinions on the subject."[62] Rev. Samuel Miller asked, "How was it possible . . . for a true Christian, in the full exercise of his mental faculties, to die without one expression of distinctive belief, or Christian hope?"[63] Speaking of Christianity, Jefferson said: "I know that Gouverneur Morris, who pretended to be in his secrets & believed himself to be so, has often told me that Genl. Washington believed no more of that system than he himself did."[64] The clergymen of Washington's church in Philadelphia, whose "reluctant testimony" should carry "a high degree of credibility" and who had nothing to gain by it,[65] testified that Washington was not a Christian. Bishop White said, "I do not believe that any degree of recollection will bring to my mind any fact which would prove General Washington to have been a believer in the Christian revelation; further than as may be hoped from his constant attendance on Christian worship."[66] Dr. Abercrombie, who had publicly chastised Washington for refusing to take communion, mentioned his "regular attendance in our church" but added, "Sir, I cannot consider any man as a real Christian who uniformly disregards an ordinance so solemnly enjoined by the divine Author of our holy religion, and considered as a channel of divine grace."[67] These testimonies, to be sure, are second- and thirdhand reports. Yet they come from sources who knew Washington well and, particularly in the case of the ministers, had no reason to downplay or discount his religious faith.

Some have pointed to the fact that Washington had served as a vestryman in his church in Virginia, arguing that he could not have done so without professing Christianity. If he indeed did that, such a singular and nominal expression of faith would hardly be persuasive. And as Boller noted, "Under the Anglican establishment in Virginia before the Revolution, the duties of a parish vestry were as much civil as religious in nature and it is not possible to deduce any exceptional religious zeal from the mere fact of membership. Even Thomas Jefferson was a vestryman for a while."[68] Steven Keillor observed that prominent Virginia gentlemen were expected to serve as vestrymen and that "vestrymen were often not believers." As Bishop Meade explained at the time, "Even Mr. Jefferson, and [George] Wythe, who did not conceal their disbelief in Christianity, took their parts in the duties of vestrymen . . . for they wished to be men of influence."[69]

George Washington, like the other key Founders, was a theistic rationalist who was not committed to the doctrines of any established sect. He simply had a "conviction that religion was essential as an undergirding of the new State." One of his "primary interests in religion as far as the nation was concerned" was "that citizens should recognize its importance."[70] Religion, regardless of specifics, was vital as a pillar of a free society because of the moralizing effect it had on the people. Personally, Washington believed in a wise and good God to whom all roads led, an active and particular Providence, prayer, some miracles and revelation, and the central part played by morality. Those were the beliefs that seemed to him to be rational.

It should be emphasized that, as has been demonstrated, the first four presidents of the United States were theistic rationalists. For the first quarter of a century under the new Constitution, theistic rationalists established the presidential precedents concerning religion and government. As numerous scholars have stressed, Washington was particularly aware of his precedent-setting role. Determined not to repeat European mistakes and transport religious wars to America, these men sought to establish precedents of toleration without eliminating the importance of real religious commitment on the part of differing adherents. They wrote letters of reassurance and support to congregations of widely varying religious persuasions. They expressed no denominational bias or preference. They gave their support for broad, inclusive acts of civil religion. Among these were public pronouncements, proclamations, and special days set aside to honor and thank God. Some were initiated by these presidents, and some were initiated by Congress, but in each case, appeals were to a very generic notion of God and to aspects of God that all would find to be familiar and comfortable. They signed into law bills calling for public support—even financial support—of religion, including paid congressional chaplains, paid military chaplains, and grants of land specifically set aside for religious purposes. (This topic is discussed in greater detail in chapter 8.) Jefferson and Madison attended church services held in the Capitol Building. Jefferson allowed executive office buildings to be used for services, and he also permitted "executive branch employees under his direct control" to participate in the House church services.[71] In sum, the first four presidents did what they could to publicly promote and encourage religion and morality in the United States without favoring any particular religion. This practice was consistent with the text and original understanding of the First Amendment. It was also activity that came naturally for theistic rationalists.

Having presented the evidence for the existence, origin, and adherents of theistic rationalism, in the final chapter I will address the all-important "so what?" question. What is left to see is the ultimate significance of the fact that theistic rationalism was the belief system of the key Founders and many patriotic preachers and why it is important for us to acknowledge this fact.

8

The Significance of
Theistic Rationalism

A benign religion, professed and practiced in various forms.

Thomas Jefferson

SO WHAT? That is the question that hangs over any academic study, and it serves as the theme for this final chapter. It is my contention that theistic rationalism significantly impacted the political world of eighteenth-century America and that its residual effects extend to the present time. Consequently, awareness and knowledge of that political theology will greatly enhance one's understanding of the history and politics of the Founding era, of American political thought and culture, and of issues in dispute in the twenty-first century.

AMERICAN REVOLUTION

In chronological terms, the first significance of the theistic rationalism of the period was its provision of a theological justification and support for revolution. Chapters 2 and 3 of this book analyzed the political theology expounded from the Revolutionary era pulpits. The fact that the ministers were prominent apologists and recruiters for the American Revolution has been well documented, but this study has shown *how* they did so and *what* they said. Their theistic rationalism allowed preachers to persuade churchgoers familiar with biblical injunctions concerning obedience to, and respect for, authority to support the Revolutionary cause. This book has shown that these devotees of theistic rationalism preached and published liberal democratic theory and reinterpreted Scripture to justify rebellion. There might have been other religious arguments or another way to accomplish this monumental task, but that was the methodology of America's Revolutionary preachers—and their theistic rationalism was certainly up to the task.

FOUNDING DOCUMENTS

A second significance of theistic rationalism was its role as the theological framework underpinning the Founding documents. According to prominent religious historian Sidney Mead, it was the "new religion" (which I call theistic rationalism) that "legitimated the thrust of the Declaration and the constitutional structures of 'the first new nation' in Christendom."[1] It is not within the scope of this study to embark upon a lengthy, detailed analysis of the Declaration of Independence or the Constitution, but some fundamental points must be addressed. Conducting a detailed analysis of the documents in light of an understanding of the theistic rationalism of their authors might be a project worthy of pursuit by a constitutional law scholar in the future.

Much has been made of the religious terminology in the Declaration and of the fact that fundamental political principles were given a religious basis. Conventionally, the argument swirls around whether the language was intended to reflect a Christian consensus or the deism of Jefferson. This study has demonstrated, however, that Jefferson and the other leading committee members, Adams and Franklin, were neither deists nor Christians. The fact that they were theistic rationalists demands a new interpretation and some new conclusions about the religious references in the Declaration.

First, contrary to claims by Christian America devotees, the religious language in the Declaration is neither Christian nor biblical. It contains, as Steven Keillor observed, "no biblical allusions." Jon Butler put it succinctly: "The god who appears in the Declaration is the god of nature rather than the God of Christian scriptural revelation." Michael Zuckert reminded readers that "the Christian God is also the God of nature, of course, but *qua* Christian God, *qua* the God of the covenant of grace, he is the God of super-nature. The Christian events, the incarnation, the resurrection, the economy of salvation—these are miraculous, extraordinary events, not events in or of nature."[2] Robert Kraynak summed it up well:

The Declaration appeals to "the laws of Nature and of Nature's God," which it calls self-evident truths of reason rather than revelations of Scripture. It describes nature's God as the Creator who has endowed all men with unalienable rights to life, liberty, and the pursuit of happiness—rights inherent in the very nature of human beings as creatures of God possessing reason. . . . [But] the notion that God created man to enjoy natural rights and to establish government by consent—the

founding principles of liberal democracy or republican self-government—is not in the Bible. Nor is it in the writings of medieval and
early Reformation theologians nor in the convenantal theology of the
Puritans of colonial America.[3]

Cushing Strout noted that even though the Declaration and the Articles of
Confederation "make conventional references to 'the Supreme Judge of the
World,' reliance on 'Divine Providence,' and respect for the 'Great Governor of the World,'" they "in no way reflect any distinctive Christian gospel."[4] As per examples in previous chapters, these are God-words such as
are typically employed by theistic rationalists. They are not biblical terms
and have no specifically Christian content.

A second observation is that the natural rights philosophy expressed by
key Founders in the Declaration was right in line with what had been taught
from the pulpits of their theistic rationalist brethren for years. In her definitive work, *The New England Clergy and the American Revolution*, Alice
Baldwin claimed, "There is not a right asserted in the Declaration of Independence which had not been discussed by the New England clergy before
1763." She further remarked that these ministers had for years "accepted
and taught them with unquestioning faith and, to a religious people, gave
them the sanction of divine law." The import of these facts was not lost
on Thomas Pangle. Referring to similar findings by Claude Newlin, Pangle
concluded: "It would appear that even among the New England clergy, the
eighteenth century was in America the century of reason and rationalism.
All this must be kept in mind if we are to grasp the true contemporary significance of the Declaration of Independence's emphatic appeal to the God
of Nature rather than to the God of Scripture."[5] This should not surprise
us in the wake of the discussions in chapters 2 and 3, but it should cause us
to consider the inroads made by natural rights philosophy within churches
over the last 200 years. Perhaps the theistic rationalists were successful in
transmitting some of their theology to the American religious mainstream.

A third conclusion to be drawn regarding the Declaration is that the
language of the religious references stresses the rationalism part of the authors' theistic rationalism. As one analyst explained, "In a leap of reason,
it grounded American politics in certain 'self-evident' axioms which rested
on thin air, not on divine revelation. The axioms paralleled the scriptural
assertion that humans were created in God's image, but they did not deign
to rest upon that revelation. They rested on the Enlightenment's scientific,
optimistic, rationalist worldview."[6] Though one might well argue with the
"thin air" remark, the gist of the statement is correct and important. It was

echoed by Robert Kraynak's conclusion that "the Declaration of Independence is primarily a product of the rational religions of the Enlightenment that emphasized God's support for the freedom of self-governing peoples."[7] With their emphasis on the rational element, yet involving a God, the religious references of the Declaration provide quintessential examples of theistic rationalism and its value to artful politicians.

This leads to the fourth conclusion: Jefferson and the others wrote the Declaration "artfully" to appeal both to rationalists and to the more conventionally religious. It has been suggested that the Declaration's religious references consciously reflected "language attractive to both sides and subject to varied interpretations" in order to be acceptable to the religious sensibilities of all who might be part of the Revolutionary movement.[8] As theistic rationalists, the authors were in a perfect position to do this—occupying that middle ground between deism and Christianity. Declaration scholar Pauline Maier has explained that Congress added two references to God to Jefferson's original draft in an attempt to reflect the religious convictions of the people.[9] It is interesting, though, that both additions were God-words—words that were perfectly consonant with Jefferson's theistic rationalism but able to be interpreted in a friendly manner by Christians.

This shows the usefulness of theistic rationalism for statesmen. The theology in the Declaration was "acceptable to a wide spectrum of Christians and Deists." On the one hand, deists "were ready to sign onto a document that emphasized the course of human events without explicit reference to Jesus Christ; the expression 'nature's God' even made it seem that nature had created God and now owned Him." On the other hand, Christians were satisfied by the grounding of rights in the work of an otherwise undefined creator God. One Christian author has warned that "the fact that John Witherspoon and other evangelicals of the day were willing to sign the Declaration should not blind us to its essentially anti-Christian character."[10] I do not necessarily see the Declaration as anti-Christian, but it is clearly non-Christian. Many American Christians have nevertheless read Christian content into the rather generic references to a God.

Understanding that the authors were theistic rationalists could resolve the age-old debate over the language of the Declaration. It is clearly not specifically Christian or biblical, but its "reliance on the protection of divine Providence" is inconsistent with deism, as well. The Declaration is neither the herald of a Christian America nor the deistic expression of a strict secularism. The Declaration is an honest expression of the political theology undergirding the American experiment—theistic rationalism. As Michael Zuckert explained, "Both Locke and Jefferson . . . insisted that modernist liberal politics required the support of religion," and Jefferson demonstrated in the Declaration how to effectively employ such an "alliance between religion and liberal philosophy." Kraynak concluded that it is this "rational-republican religion . . . that makes possible the God-given natural rights of the Declaration of Independence and the republican form of government of the U.S. Constitution."[11]

An understanding of the theistic rationalism of those most influential in the construction of the Constitution also increases our understanding of its principles where religion is concerned. Of course, the most glaring fact about the Constitution with regard to religion is that it does not even mention God, much less anything specifically Christian. Many anti-Federalists opposed it as a "godless Constitution," and in fact, the ratifying conventions of five states expressed regret that the Constitution failed to mention Christianity. This remained a concern of some for a long time. More than a decade later, in arguing against the election of Jefferson, the Reverend John Mitchell Mason reminded readers that the Constitution "*makes no acknowledgement of that God* who gave us our national existence, and saved us from anarchy and internal war." He concluded that "the only way to wipe off the reproach of irreligion, and to avert the descending vengeance, is to prove, by our *national acts,* that the Constitution has not, in this instance, done justice to the public sentiment."[12] Certainly, not all ministers shared Mason's concerns, however. Speaking of the preachers we have discussed, Alice Baldwin concluded:

> It would be hard to measure the value of their service in the war. But of equal value was their help in constitution making. These ministers believed in the theories they preached and intended to see that the unique opportunity before them was not lost. . . . The insistence of the ministers on these and other points seems to have had a decided influence on the course of events. A few years later, when Massachusetts was in the throes of adopting the Federal Constitution, General Lincoln wrote to Washington, "It is very fortunate for us, that the clergy are pretty generally with us. They have in this State a very great influence over the people."[13]

The fact that the Constitution makes no mention of God, much less the Bible, is in itself a telling refutation of the Christian America claim that the document was based on biblical principles and was meant to establish a Christian nation. Without delving more deeply into this claim than is warranted, a few points will serve to cast significant doubt upon it. Aside from not even mentioning God in the text, there was precious little reference to God or the Bible in the Constitutional Convention debates. There were a few casual references to Scripture, but they were offered only to illustrate points already made, not as a basis for principle—despite the Bible's supposed role as the foundation for the whole document and all its parts. Indeed, as Pangle noted, "the Founders . . . scrupulously refrain[ed] from claiming any divine inspiration, or from suggesting any important connection between the Constitution and any *specific* conception of piety *or of divinity*" (emphases mine).[14] None other than John Adams made the same point: "It will never be pretended that any persons employed in that service [framing the U.S. government] had interviews with the gods or were in any degree under the inspiration of Heaven, more than those at work upon ships or houses. . . . Neither the people nor their conventions, committees, or subcommittees considered legislation in any other light than as ordinary arts and sciences, only more important."[15] Adams clearly did not anticipate the creativity of those who today promulgate the Christian America thesis.

In addition to the near silence of the convention notes, the silence of *The Federalist Papers* is also deafening. As an explication of the Constitution and its sources by the "father of the Constitution" and another major contributor to it, what these essays say about the Constitution and its principles is, arguably, definitive. This is particularly true given the nature of Hamilton as assessed by a fellow delegate to the convention: "Col. Hamilton . . . enquires into every part of his subject with the searchings of phylosophy [*sic*] . . . there is no skimming over the surface of a subject with him, he must sink to the bottom to see what foundation it rests on."[16] Comprising eighty-five essays, *The Federalist Papers* would seem to be the perfect place to squeeze in at least some of the biblical evidence and arguments that were supposed to be the "foundation it rests on." However, the word *God* is used only twice, and one of those instances is in reference to the pagan gods of ancient Greece. A few scattered God-words are mentioned ("Almighty" twice and "Providence" three times, for example) but never in connection with any constitutional principle or influence. If there had been any such evidence, one would expect it to be highlighted in essays designed to sway and persuade the intended audience—a religious general public. *The Federalist Papers*, however, are "almost totally silent" in regard to the area claimed by the Christian America camp to be the very basis for the Constitution.[17]

A second constitutional matter to consider is the basic principle of freedom of religion. Most of the delegates to the Constitutional Convention believed that religion "must be left to the conviction and conscience of every man."[18] Consequently, they did not establish a national religion in the Constitution. The theistic rationalism of the key Founders made it natural and easy for them to grant religious liberty. By contrast, it would be difficult for those who believe in the importance of fundamental doctrines and a specific road to Heaven (such as the Puritans in seventeenth-century New England) to allow "false" and "blasphemous" religions to be practiced within their sphere of authority. For the theistic rationalists, however, what was truly vital was not the flourishing of religious truth but the flourishing of morality and society. Since they held to no particular creed but rather to "essentials" to which "all good men" could agree, they had a profound indifference toward specific sects and doctrines.

That is not to say that they were indifferent in regard to religion itself but rather that they believed any religion was as good as another. As all religions with which they were familiar contributed to morality, all could fulfill the primary purpose for religion in society. Consequently, there was no reason to restrict the religions that could be practiced. In a sense, they could *afford* to grant religious liberty in a way that those with exclusive beliefs could not. This does not mean that it would have been *impossible* for Christians or persons committed to specific, exclusive doctrines to allow religious freedom, but the historical record in that regard is rather bleak, whether one turns to ancient Israel, medieval Europe, or Islamic nations in the twenty-first century.

Noted religious historians Perry Miller and Cushing Strout have agreed with this assessment. Miller saw the Founders as "a rational aristocracy, shot through with deistical beliefs, willing to see any number of religions have their freedom because they believed in none of them. As Nathaniel Ward has said, nothing is easier than to tolerate when you do not seriously believe that differences matter."[19] As this study has shown, the Founders were not "deistical," but a substitution of "theistic rationalist" for Miller's "deistical" in this case does not substantively change his observation. Strout similarly argued that these men, "precisely because they could put secular interests ahead of religious differences and were not closely bound to any organized religion, were the only group who, on an intercolonial basis, could speak clearly for a new standard of religious liberty." Strout explained the salience of this point:

Historians of religion today are inclined to patronize this rationalistic religion, which seems so theologically complacent and commonplace. But they have forgotten that its lack of militancy, except on behalf of freedom of conscience, made it possible for revolutionaries to be much more tolerant of traditional religions than the history of persecution might reasonably have justified. Such men were preeminently fitted for the role of conducting the new nation toward a condition of freedom of conscience in which all the contending religions could find their own place, a position they could not have hewn out for themselves because no sect or church had the power to carry a large majority with it.[20]

They were uniquely situated to do this because of their lack of doctrinal identification.

Looking at this issue from one other angle, intriguing questions arise. By promoting religion but not any particular sect, did the Founders actually, in a sense, "establish" their own religion of theistic rationalism? By hailing the importance of religion while putting the imprimatur of the government behind nonsectarianism, were they subconsciously giving advantage to their own belief system? Pangle took this idea so far as to suggest that Jefferson's "real goal" was "conformity based on indifference; not diversity, but the tepid and thoughtless uniformity of Unitarianism in a society where Unitarians no longer have to defend and prove themselves."[21] Of course, Pangle might have taken Jefferson's expressed desire—and prediction—that all Americans would become Unitarians too far; but Jefferson did express such a desire.[22] Sydney Ahlstrom wondered in print whether the American system might not have been "the virtual establishment" of Jefferson's "own theology." Strout could not help but wonder about the same possibility: "The conundrum that Jefferson and Madison left to posterity was one they never appreciated: did their policy . . . seek to 'establish' their own 'enlightened' religion under the guise of 'disestablishment'?"[23]

My primary reason for engaging in this speculation is to emphasize that religious liberty was a natural response to belief in theistic rationalism and that the theistic rationalism of the key Founders may go a long way toward explaining America's exaltation of freedom of religion. A College of Philadelphia mathematics professor determined that the only logical explanations for the religious silences of the Constitution proper (without the First Amendment) were: (1) the delegates were indifferent to religion, or (2) they were all of the same religion and "determined to compel the whole continent to conform" to a single religious standard.[24] Both explanations may be somewhat correct.

As Sidney Mead observed, "The concept of a plurality of [religious] principles . . . implies that all theologies are equally valid, and perhaps equally true,"[25] which was, of course, the theistic rationalist position. The religious liberty offered in America was more than mere toleration or, as we shall see, strict noninvolvement by government in religion. The American system caused the Unitarian (and, possibly, theistic rationalist) Tench Coxe to exult: "Almost every sect and form of Christianity is known here—as also the Hebrew church. None are tolerated. All are admitted, aided by mutual charity and concord, and supported and cherished by the laws."[26] He went on to describe America as a "land of promise for the good men of all denominations." He was pleased to declare, "Mere toleration is a doctrine exploded by our general condition; instead of which have been substituted an unqualified admission, and assertion, 'that their own modes of worship and of faith equally belong to all the worshippers of God, of whatever church, sect, or denomination.'"[27] The key Founders, who believed that all religions were equally valid, that all led to the same God, and that all produced "good men," established a practice in America that perfectly represented their belief system.

Of course, the only mention of religion in the original Constitution was the "no religious test" clause. An incident related to it illustrates the fact that it is much more difficult for those with specific and exclusive beliefs to support religious liberty. At the Massachusetts ratifying convention, the following occurred during discussion of the Constitution's prohibition of religious tests for office:

> By several members it was urged, however, that this article was a departure from the principles of our forefathers, who came here for the preservation of their religion, and that it would admit deists and atheists into the general government. In these efforts to secure religious toleration as a fundamental law of the state and nation the Baptist denomination took an active and a leading part. Not less faithful to this cause were the liberal men among the Congregationalists, while the opposition came almost wholly from the Calvinistic and orthodox churches.[28]

So, among the members present, those in favor of religious liberty were those in the minority who stood to gain (the Baptists) and "the liberal men among the Congregationalists"—that is, the theistic rationalists. Those with firm and uncompromising doctrines, the orthodox and the Calvinists, opposed it.

Daniel Shute, a Baptist, argued at the Massachusetts convention that there were "worthy characters among men of every denomination" in addition to his own—even among "Papists" and those who followed "the dictates of natural religion."[29] He was expressing what mattered to the

Founders: that "worthy characters," or good men or moral men, filled the offices of government. In the ratification debates, the "no religious test" clause was the source of much discussion, though it was added without opposition and virtually without comment in the Constitutional Convention itself. Supporters of the Constitution stressed the framers' intent to allow "wise or good citizens" and men "of abilities and character, of any sect" to hold public office.[30] They believed that there were other means to ensure that good and moral men held office apart from specific and exclusive religious tests.

For instance, Madison explained to Edmund Pendleton that the oaths required of all officeholders would, "as far as it is necessary," "operate" as a religious test:

> If the person swearing believes in the supreme Being who is invoked, and in the penal consequences of offending him, either in this or a future world or both, he will be under the same restraint from perjury as if he had previously subscribed a test requiring this belief. If the person in question be an unbeliever in these points and would notwithstanding take the oath, a previous test could have no effect. He would subscribe it as he would take the oath, without any principle that could be affected by either.[31]

He was not the only one to hold such a view, as evidenced by the South Carolina ratifying convention's proposal to amend the Constitution to insert the word "other" between the words "no" and "religious" in the clause. Washington later identified "religious obligation" as the central factor in oaths.[32] The Founders also believed that the structure of the constitutional system itself would ensure that good men held office and would help to promote morality in officeholders. Publius made such an argument in at least eight of the essays in *The Federalist Papers*.[33]

The *secular* school argues that the Constitution's lack of religious language and prohibition of religious tests prove that the Founders were, at the least, nonreligious and more likely antireligious. They overlook—or choose not to recognize—the religious significance of the oaths. For them, the Establishment Clause of the First Amendment is further proof that the key Founders were hostile to religion. But we have seen, in chapters 4 through 7, that the key Founders were themselves religious and were anything but hostile to religion in a societal context. In fact, "the founders were almost without exception strong supporters of religion" because of its value to society.[34] By promoting the morality needed at the base of liberal democratic society, religion was deemed "a great moral asset to the nation." As Anson Phelps Stokes observed: "The founders saw clearly and definitely that without religion a democratic government could not succeed. . . . The founders saw clearly that religion would be a great aid in maintaining civil government on a high plane."[35] To illustrate, one could turn to the numerous examples of key Founders identifying religion as a pillar of the American system—or to the Northwest Ordinance, which proclaimed that religion and morality were "necessary to good government and the happiness of mankind."[36]

The problem with groups from the secular school, such as People for the American Way and Americans United for Separation of Church and State, is that they do not read the Constitution or the record of the framers. They believe in a "living Constitution" that says simply "what the courts say it says." Consequently, rather than read the Constitution, they read court decisions *about* judges' opinions *about* the Constitution. Because of their belief in a so-called living Constitution, they originally argued that the intent of the framers and the written record of their thinking were irrelevant. They have recently adopted a new strategy, which is to argue backward into the past that the Founders acceded to the modern Court's view of the Establishment Clause. Their method, like that of many in the Christian America camp, is to selectively quote individuals out of context in order to make their case before an ignorant public. The modern Court's understanding of the Establishment Clause as erecting "a wall of separation between church and state" does not stand up to the historical record or to the theistic rationalist emphases of the key Founders.

In the Court's view, neither the national government nor the state or local governments can have anything to do with religion, especially in the sense of giving any kind of support. Because the Constitution is "living," the sphere and application of this interpretation grow and become increasingly intrusive—hence, the radical increase in Establishment Clause cases before the courts. Fortunately for those who care to investigate, James Madison, who authored the First Amendment, explained "the meaning of the words" during debate on the amendment in Congress on August 15, 1789. He said the wording simply meant "that Congress should not establish a religion, and enforce the legal observance of it by law, nor compel men to worship God in any manner contrary to their conscience."[37] That was it. It was not intended to completely separate religion and government, nor to prohibit government support for religion. And it only limited Congress—not the state or local governments.

In fact, Congress funded religious-based and religion-supporting programs during the Founding era. A few examples should suffice to demonstrate this pertinent point. In 1789, Congress adapted the Northwest Ordinance to the Constitution without making any changes to its provision that specifically and intentionally connected schools and the promotion of religion and morality. In 1792, Congress confirmed a grant of land to the Ohio Company that specified a considerable amount of the land would be reserved for the support of religion. And three days before Congress reached final agreement on the language of the Bill of Rights, it passed a law providing salaries for its legislative chaplains. Madison was on the committee involved with the salaries, and he voted for the measure. In March 1791, Congress authorized a paid military chaplain.[38]

In addition to monetary support, the First Congress also approved days of prayer and thanksgiving, actually requesting that Washington proclaim a day to acknowledge "the many signal favors of Almighty God." Ironically, the House version of this resolution passed on the same day that final agreement on the language of the Bill of Rights was reached.[39] Congress also approved the holding of religious services in the House Chamber, the War Office, and the Treasury Building. In keeping with the liberal spirit of the day, services were conducted at various times by "the orthodox," by Quakers, by Roman Catholics, and by Unitarians.[40] As president, Jefferson attended the religious services in the House Chamber more than once. Upon examining the evidence without the taint of the modern Court's view, then, one should find that "the various provisions to encourage religion . . . from the early days of the United States government are cumulative and convincing."[41]

Some have found the "Sundays excepted" phrase in the presentment clause (Article I, Section 7) of the Constitution to be evidence that the framers intended to have a Christian constitution. That may, indeed, be the case. If that were the purpose, however, it seems strange that they did not include a more overt and clear statement to that effect. The burden of proof would seem to rest on those ascribing such significant meaning and purpose to such a mundane phrase. It would have been much simpler and certainly much clearer to simply acknowledge Jesus Christ and their intent to design a government on the basis of his principles. On the surface, the "Sundays excepted" phrase appears to simply be a recognition of the fact that many Americans would attend church instead of conducting business on Sundays. Such a recognition of reality does not indicate a desire or intent to create a Christian constitution. Actually, the phrase was not included in drafts of the Constitution until it was added without comment in mid-August,[42] and the fact that it was added without comment is significant, as some explanation would seem to be required to find great significance in it. There was no discussion of the phrase at the Constitutional Convention and no discussion of it in the state ratifying conventions. Therefore, there is nothing to suggest that it was intended to make a statement in support of the creation of a Christian constitution or nation.

It has also been suggested that there is great significance in the fact that the framers signed the Constitution "in the Year of our Lord 1787." Perhaps it *is* significant. Once again, however, the burden of proof would be on those who find that this is particularly revealing of Christian intent. Absent commentary by the framers or additional information, it would appear to simply be the commonly accepted means of identifying the year. If the intent was to indicate any kind of commitment to that "Lord," specific acknowledgment or at least a mention of Jesus Christ would have made the purpose much clearer. At any rate, there is no evidence from the records of the Constitutional Convention or from those of the state ratifying conventions that any significance beyond identifying the year should be read into the date as recorded.

The American Founders believed that religion, by promoting morality, was a vital and necessary support for a government and society of free people. Imposition of religious belief or practice was unacceptable, but active support for religious efforts was not. Those religious efforts had beneficial societal effects. If the key Founders had been secularists, it is likely that they would have *actually* erected the wall of separation between church and state proclaimed by the Court and imagined by today's secularists. They certainly would not have exhorted future generations to maintain and promote religion, and they would not have established such traditions as celebrating days of thanksgiving and opening legislative sessions with prayer or such practices as providing legislative and military chaplains.

CIVIL RELIGION

A third significance of theistic rationalism is its contribution to American civil religion. Political philosophers have always stressed the value of a civil religion undergirding a political structure. Whether one reads Plato, Machiavelli, or Rousseau—no matter the era—the utility of religion to bolster the political regime is extolled. As has been established, the theistic rationalists shared such a view of religion and its usefulness. As Cushing Strout put it, "Far from being indifferent to religion, these statesmen believed that the liberal state needed its own style of religious expression."[43] Ever the wordsmith, Jefferson, in his first inaugural address, gave an apt description of the civil religion he helped to create. He said that Americans were "enlightened by a benign religion, professed, indeed, and practiced in various forms, yet all of them inculcating honesty, truth, temperance, gratitude, and the love of man; acknowledging and adoring an overruling Providence, which by all its dispensations proves that it delights in the happiness of man here and his greater happiness hereafter."[44] In other words, Americans benefited from just the kind of religion the theistic rationalists preferred. The civil religion successfully created for America by the theistic rationalists still thrives today. It persists rather covertly, however, because it is largely creedless, because it survives under an assumed name, and because it was ostensibly never "established" as the official national religion.

The theistic rationalists' successful blending of elements of Christianity with rationalism was replicated in the civil religion that emerged from their political theology. Because of the desire of most Americans to retain identification with Christianity, this civil religion became identified with Christianity. The common conception of what constitutes Christianity, then, became increasingly political and increasingly generic and inclusive. For example, as one eminent scholar observed, "that the equality of human souls in the sight of God ought to be translated into a political structure of equal political rights has come to be regarded as the most authentic interpretation of the Gospel itself"—despite the fact that there was no political component to the Gospel preached by Christ or the apostles; that "Christ endorses no specific form of government"; and that "Christian freedom . . . is a moral and spiritual concept . . . compatible with obedience to external political authority, even with political oppression." Michael Zuckert has noted this transformation:

> Americans were able to bring their still lively religious sensibilities to the sphere of politics, but in the service of a substantive politics very different from the traditional political teachings of Christianity. The natural rights philosophy, while not itself a Christian philosophy, or even particularly descended from Christian positions, was able to win the support of American Christians and Christianity. Thus began that potent alliance Tocqueville noticed and all American politics has attested to for two centuries in what Robert Bellah and others have spoken of as the American civil religion. The result has been remarkable: a society in which religion has been supportive of an essentially secular political

orientation and in which private and public morality both have derived salutary aid from deep-flowing religious impulses.[45]

This was precisely the goal of the theistic rationalist Founders.

Because political elements were attached to Christianity, patriotism and piety became connected. Ahlstrom observed that a "patriotic spirit . . . soon pervaded every aspect of the country's thought and feeling," and "a mystical theology of the Union" was brought into being. From the beginning, reverence for the nation and piety came to be seen as "intrinsic elements in the religion of Americans." In fact, a concept of "patriotic piety" became the basis for a "belief in the divinely appointed mission of the American nation."[46] The piety involved here, however, was piety in the theistic rationalist sense, not in the Christian sense. It had nothing to do with devotion to Christ. It referred to being good to one's fellow men, being moral, and being a good citizen. It was summed up in the Golden Rule, which, though it is a moral teaching of Jesus, is not the Gospel or the essence of Christianity. As Robert Kraynak and Paul Johnson observed: "What makes such a nation possible is the gradual development of a rationalized Christianity . . . reducing religion to a simple belief in God and morality . . . '[that] was itself the civil and moral creed of republicanism.' It provided a consensus among Protestants, Catholics, Jews, and even nonbelievers because they could accept 'the premise that religion, meaning morality, was essential to democratic institutions.'"[47] Here are found the fundamental elements of theistic rationalism—rationalism, simple belief in God, and religion as morality. Kraynak and Johnson also recognized that, like theistic rationalism itself, the American civil religion that stemmed from it was a "republican civil religion that mixed elements of Evangelical Protestantism and Enlightenment liberalism."[48]

These scholars agreed that this civil religion is the only explanation for the claims of Adams and Washington that the Constitution "presupposes 'a moral and religious people' without specifying the content of that religion." They also saw, as do I, a link between this religion and that of Abraham Lincoln.[49] Lincoln was an heir to the civil religion spawned by theistic rationalism. The reason that scholars have struggled to place his religious beliefs into an accepted "niche" may be that theistic rationalism has not been considered an accepted niche. Although Lincoln did not generally emphasize the rational element, that element of theistic rationalism had faded somewhat from emphasis in American civil religion. It faded because it had done its work so well that it became an unstated given, an inherent assumption. Most of the elements of theistic rationalism were nonetheless present in Lincoln's theology.

Although it is beyond the purview of this study to delve deeply into Lincoln's religious beliefs, a few examples will illustrate his congruence with the American civil religion descending from theistic rationalism. Harry Jaffa, perhaps the preeminent scholar of Lincoln's thought, said that "[Lincoln] never himself professed the Christian (or any other) religion. It is undoubtedly true that Lincoln has become the greatest interpreter of America's religious destiny in part because of his distance from any sectarian religious identification. Every church or synagogue can think of him as one of their own, because he scarcely ever spoke a word inconsistent with such an assumption. By belonging to none, he belonged to all."[50] Though Lincoln believed deeply in a present and active God, all of his references to that God were God-words with no sect-specific content. Despite the fact that he is often recognized as "America's most genuinely religious president,"[51] Lincoln, like the theistic rationalists, spurned doctrines and specific beliefs. He also seemed to share their belief that all religions lead to the same God, as he urged "*all ministers and teachers of all denominations . . .* to observe and keep that day [of humiliation, prayer, and fasting] according to *their several creeds and modes of worship . . .* to the end that the *united prayer* of the nation *may ascend to the Throne of Grace* and bring down plentiful blessings upon our Country" (emphases mine).[52]

Jaffa properly and significantly has written extensively on the link between Lincoln and the Declaration. It is appropriate and accurate to draw such a connection, yet their common religious ground was rooted in theistic rationalism, not Christianity. Lincoln was a major "theologian" of the "American democratic faith" in that he contributed two "civil religion texts" to it: the Gettysburg Address and the second inaugural address.[53] The American civil religion created by the Founders that found great expression in Lincoln persists to this day. It is no accident that each president has felt constrained to make vague references to God in his inaugural address.

Pangle suggested that the Founders attempted to "exploit and transform Christianity in the direction of liberal rationalism" and that people today identify them with some sort of "Christianity" "because they succeeded so well in their project of changing the heart and soul of Christianity." They actually changed the common conception of what counts as Christianity, not Christianity itself, but Pangle's basic point remains valid. As Strout observed, "Large numbers of Americans today, especially among Protestants, would find themselves in considerable agreement with Jefferson and Adams."[54] Prominent sociologist Will Herberg concluded that "American religion is . . . non-theological and non-liturgical; it is . . . associated with the de-emphasis of theology and doctrine. Americans tend to believe that 'ethical behavior and a good life, rather than adherence to a specific creed,

[will] earn a share in the heavenly kingdom.'"[55] In other words, American religion has become just what the theistic rationalist Founders would have preferred. Although Herberg wrote four decades ago and there has since been a resurgence of religious conservatism in the nation, his observation remains valid for most Americans.

An extended quote from Herberg's celebrated study of religion in America will demonstrate the continuing influence of theistic rationalism on American civil religion:

> Americans believe in religion in a way that perhaps no other people do. It may indeed be said that the primary religious affirmation of the American people, in harmony with the American Way of Life, is that religion is a "good thing," a supremely "good thing," for the individual and the community. And "religion" here means not so much any particular religion, but religion as such, religion-in-general. "Our government makes no sense," President Eisenhower recently declared, "unless it is founded in a deeply felt religious faith—*and I don't care what it is.*" [*New York Times,* December 23, 1952; italics in the original.] In saying this, the President was saying something that almost any American could understand and approve. . . . Every American could understand, first, that Mr. Eisenhower's apparent indifferentism . . . was not indifferentism at all, but the expression of the conviction that at bottom the "three great faiths" were really "saying the same thing" in affirming the "spiritual ideals" and "moral values" of the American Way of Life. Every American, moreover, could understand that what Mr. Eisenhower was emphasizing so vehemently was the indispensability of religion as the foundation of society. . . . The object of devotion of this kind of religion, however, is "not God but 'religion.'" . . . This is, by and large, what they mean, and not any commitment to the doctrines or traditions of the historic faiths.[56]

One should note the approbation of religion, its lack of specificity, its political importance, the equal validity of all religions, and the emphasis on morality. Adams, Jefferson, and the others probably could not have imagined that their religion would have such a lasting impact upon the religion of the general public.

Kraynak and Johnson have suggested that this civil religion "survives today in what is loosely called the Judeo-Christian tradition which Americans appeal to when they recite the Pledge of Allegiance to the Flag and pay tribute to the republic as 'one nation under God.'"[57] I would suggest that it also survives in church sanctuaries that display the American flag, in the singing of hymns to the nation in worship services, and in the generic petition "God bless America." The attacks on the World Trade Center and the Pentagon produced some classic examples of American civil religion in action. Countless commentators suggested that all of those who perished went to heaven or to be "with God," particularly those who died in service to their country or their fellow man. Finally, the service attended by the president in the National Cathedral and the prayer service with representatives of every conceivable religion in Yankee Stadium were examples of civil religion that gave classic expression to the theistic rationalist belief that all "religious traditions" are equally valid and that all pray to the same God.

MISCELLANEOUS POLITICAL EFFECTS

Theistic rationalism influenced the American political scene in other ways, as well. Alice Baldwin showed at great length the significant contributions of the ministers to their state constitutions in the New England states.[58] And Michael Zuckert outlined the political effect of the use of Scripture to confirm the teachings of reason (rather than the reverse):

> Once this has been accomplished, the biblical texts are then free to fulfill yet another, and politically very significant, function: the higher or more intense authority of religion now stands behind the cool rationalism of Locke. There can be little doubt that the enlistment of St. Paul in Locke's army had much to do with the fervor Americans of the revolutionary era brought to the political conflicts of the day.[59]

The impact of theistic rationalism on religious liberty was discussed earlier, but it should also be noted that the theistic rationalists' view "was certainly more impartial than any conception then alive in their society. Locke himself did not tolerate atheists or Catholics; Roger Williams's colony excluded Catholics from the franchise; and even Pennsylvania, which alone had not penalized Catholics and whose state constitution was otherwise the most liberal of all, demanded that officeholders accept the whole Bible as divinely inspired."[60] Incidentally, the influence of particular sects was generally greater at the state level than at the national level, for several reasons: because of the role of specific sects in the founding of individual states, because a sect could represent a much greater proportion of a state's population than that of the nation, and because interest in electoral majorities produced greater deference to the religious preferences of the majority.

Two other political aspects merit mention. First, in addition to being emphasized by the theistic rationalists, the connection between religion and morals was widely accepted in eighteenth-century America. Henry May contended that "few doubted that religion was necessary for good order and sound morals." Indeed, the Continental Congress recommended "that states encourage 'true religion and good morals' as 'the only solid foundation of public liberty and happiness.'" As has been stressed throughout this study, men "like Jefferson and Madison" honored religion "for its moral value," but they were not concerned about *which* religion.[61] What has not been emphasized (because it was taken for granted in eighteenth-century America) is *why* they viewed religion as uniquely important to public morality. There were two primary reasons. One was expressed by a pamphleteer during the election of 1800, who stressed the import of a president's religious beliefs for morality due to the influence he wielded. Using sarcasm in reference to Jefferson's religion, he said: "He will *only* be looked upon as a sample of his countrymen. His example will *only* be rendered an hundred times more extensive in its influence. . . . He will *only* become incessantly and unboundedly conspicuous. Fashions will take their birth from his elevation; his opinion will be quoted."[62] Although there is no official religious test for office, Americans have always wanted their president to be an example of morality, at least until Bill Clinton. It is not by chance that no atheist or professedly irreligious man has ever been considered a viable presidential candidate in America. Another commentator on the election of 1800 warned that the election of an irreligious president would "destroy religion, introduce immorality, and loosen all the bonds of society."[63] Note the progression here—the loss of religion results in immorality that destroys society. That was the eighteenth-century view.

The other reason that religion was seen as uniquely important to public morality was that "religious faith and religious faith alone sanctions morals and civic duty by the 'wrath' of God; by the 'tribunal' before which we must all appear on judgment day in the hereafter."[64] The theistic rationalists did not really believe in the so-called wrath of God, but they knew that most Americans did. Religion, therefore, was an effective control on the behavior of the people. Even the theistic rationalists believed in some (only temporary) "punishment" after death, but though some believed in just retribution, most believed punishment would be primarily rehabilitative. Morality founded in religion was their answer to the question of what would make men behave civilly in a free society without an iron-fisted government.

A second general political aspect to be mentioned was the resolution of the "intellectual tension between the theology professed and promulgated by a majority of the sects, and the theology that legitimates the institutional structures of the American democratic way and style of life." As Sidney

Mead explained, "Practically every species of traditional orthodoxy in Christendom is intellectually at war with the basic premises upon which the constitutional and legal structures of the Republic rest."[65] A number of observers have discussed the problem of conflict and/or competition between republican government and "Christianity." Harvey Mansfield has said that "any revealed religion is incompatible with modern natural right," and Walter Berns has argued that the "origin of free government in the modern sense coincides and can *only* coincide with the solution of the religious problem." John West has also discussed this "theological-political problem" effectively and at great length.[66] Robert Kraynak has seen the solution to this problem in what I call theistic rationalism:

> Yet, it is not only the large number of influential figures subscribing to some version of rational religion that forces one to take it seriously. One must also consider the importance of rational religion for modern politics. Speaking broadly, I would argue that liberal democracy in America and England would not be possible without the religions of reason because they played a decisive role in reconciling Christianity with modern liberal democracy. In America, most of the founding generation embraced Deism or Theism; it enabled the intellectual and political leaders of the day to combine belief in God with a rational theory of natural rights, producing the American political creed of *God-given natural rights.*[67]

As was explained previously, the political and religious leaders did such an effective job of reconciling Christianity with modern liberal democracy that, for many, Christianity became identified with liberal democracy. Many also found that theistic rationalism harmonized the two. It also de-emphasized the importance of genuine Christianity in favor of "religion." As I have stressed elsewhere concerning the Founders: "So long as religion supported political harmony, few of them were all that concerned with *what* a person believed."[68]

Today, both popular Christianity and elite religion are in some respects more extreme. Elites have moved from theistic rationalism's middle ground to rank secularism or atheism; the Christian public has become less rationalist and more evangelical ("enthusiastic" in eighteenth-century terminology). As a result, it may be that they view each other across a wider and deeper canyon than was the case in the late eighteenth century. Each group wishes to claim the Founders for its side of the canyon, but the truth is that the key Founders stood on neither side. Rather, they were standing on a bridge largely of their own making. Without such a bridge, perhaps the Constitution—even the Revolution—would not have been possible. Rediscovering the Founders' understanding on their own terms reveals both the wisdom and the fragility of their position. Is it too much to imagine that statesmen of today might fashion a similar bridge that unites the "secular" and the "religious" for political purposes?

FINAL THOUGHTS

In 1797, the Senate of the United States ratified "without protest" a treaty with Tripoli stipulating that "the government of the United States of America is not, in any sense, founded on the Christian religion." The treaty was approved "without a single dissenting vote" and signed by President John Adams.[69] Since treaties are part of "the supreme law of the land," the United States was *officially* not a Christian nation as of 1797. Thus, the Christian America camp is wrong—America was not founded as a Christian nation. Equally wrong, however, are the secularists' claims that the Founders were irreligious or deists or hostile to religion and that they meant to construct a purely secular state with no connection between the government and religion. The framers did not erect a wall of separation between church and state; they promoted religion and considered it a necessary support for a free society.

Attempts by groups such as the Christian Coalition to elect only Christians to office in order to "reclaim our heritage" would not, in fact, have been supported by the very Founders they claim to follow. At least eight prominent members of that illustrious group were not Christians themselves, including the first four presidents. As a group, the framers wrote a Constitution that specifically prohibited religious tests for office. Yet attempts by groups such as the American Civil Liberties Union to segregate and expunge religion from the public sphere would not have been supported by the Founders either. The Founders that they claim to venerate were religious, they supported religion with public speeches *and public money,* and they established a number of the traditions now under attack as "excessive entanglement."

Those who represent the secular school benefit from the simplistic accepted dichotomy concerning the religion of the Founders—that they were either Christians or irreligious secularists. They find it easy to disprove or dismiss with academic snobbery many of the claims of the Christian America position, particularly when most people do not *want* the Christian America claims to be true. In a world of only two options, theirs emerges victorious, which explains why it is the predominant view, particularly among academics. Both sides have looked at the evidence selectively and conveniently in order to support their preconceived political agendas. The truth lies, as is often the case, in the middle. The key Founders were neither Christians nor rank secularists but theistic rationalists.

For the theistic rationalists, each belief and each principle had to meet the standard of rationality. Reason determined what counted as legitimate revelation from God; reason was the standard that had to be met by any potential doctrine; and reason was the final "trump card" that could command rejection of an authority or a tenet. Reason was no longer a supplement to revelation, employed to support and better understand truth as determined by the authoritative Word of God. Rather, the roles were reversed, and revelation was selectively employed to confirm or expand upon what reason determined to be true. Doctrines, ideas, and events stated clearly in the Bible could be—and were—rejected as irrational and, therefore, "unworthy" of the God of the theistic rationalists. Since the theistic rationalists constructed that God, this amounted to being unworthy of *them*.

A dispassionate observer might be struck by what appears to be an astonishing arrogance on their part. Consider John Adams's claim that he would not believe in the Trinity if he were on Mount Sinai and God personally told him it were true. Imagine sitting next to Jefferson as he took a pair of scissors to the New Testament to determine for himself what Jesus *really* said and did, notwithstanding the fact that the New Testament authors were actually *there*—that they lived with Jesus and were taught by Him. Or think about Jefferson's claim to be "a sect by myself" and whether that was a veiled statement suggesting that only he was right. One might reflect on Franklin's assertion that it was "needless" for him to "busy" himself with the question of Jesus's deity—that is, with the question of the nature of God. Or one might ponder the efforts of ministers such as Charles Chauncy to define and confine God to the limits of their "enlightened" minds. As James Jones observed, "The essence of eighteenth century liberalism was that man could judge for himself what was best for man and could make God comply with it."[70]

By making their own reason the final determinant of what counted as legitimate revelation and the final determinant of the meaning of revelation, the theistic rationalists essentially defined away any independent divine influence on their own religion and politics. God effectively lost the ability to define Himself or make demands of them with which they were not comfortable. In other words, they effectively *became* the voice of God to themselves. In a practical sense, God became whoever they preferred Him to be and made only those demands they wished Him to make. They had truly created a god in their own image.

Notes

CHAPTER ONE. THEISTIC RATIONALISM INTRODUCED

1. Thomas L. Pangle, *The Spirit of Modern Republicanism* (Chicago: University of Chicago Press, 1988), 38.

2. Speech at Bob Jones University, May 8, 1999; quotation can be found in Cushing Strout, *The New Heavens and New Earth: Political Religion in America* (New York: Harper & Row, 1974), 59.

3. Pangle, *Spirit*, 21.

4. Sidney E. Mead, *The Old Religion in the Brave New World* (Berkeley: University of California Press, 1977), 24.

5. See, e.g., Lev. 10:1–2; Num. 25:2–5; Deut. 4:24, 7:1–5, 13:1–16; John 14:6; Matt. 7:13–14, 21; John 14:6; Acts 4:12; Gal. 1:8–9; Rom. 13:1–2, 6; John 19:11; Gal. 2:16; Eph. 2:8–9.

6. Stephen A. Marini, "Religion, Politics, and Ratification," in *Religion in a Revolutionary Age*, ed. Ronald Hoffman and Peter J. Albert (Charlottesville: University Press of Virginia, 1994), 196.

7. Henry F. May, *The Enlightenment in America* (New York: Oxford University Press, 1976), xiv; Nathan O. Hatch, *The Sacred Cause of Liberty* (New Haven, Conn.: Yale University Press, 1977), 4.

8. John Corrigan, *The Hidden Balance* (Cambridge: Cambridge University Press, 1987), 112.

9. Sydney E. Ahlstrom, *A Religious History of the American People* (New Haven, Conn.: Yale University Press, 1972), 364; Robert P. Kraynak, *Christian Faith and Modern Democracy* (Notre Dame, Ind.: University of Notre Dame Press, 2001), 64.

10. See Mark A. Noll, Nathan O. Hatch, and George M. Marsden, *The Search for Christian America* (Westchester, Ill.: Crossway Books, 1983), 118; Strout, *New Heavens,* 75; George Willis Cooke, *Unitarianism in America: A History of Its Origin and Development* (Boston: American Unitarian Association, 1902), 38.

11. Cooke, *Unitarianism,* 37.

12. Ahlstrom, *Religious History,* 391, 392.

13. Hatch, *Sacred Cause,* 16.

14. Kraynak, *Christian Faith,* 46–49.

15. Anson Phelps Stokes, *Church and State in the United States* (New York: Harper & Brothers, 1950), 1:285; Patricia U. Bonomi, *Under the Cope of Heaven* (New York: Oxford University Press, 1986), 212; Hatch, *Sacred Cause,* 12.

16. Steven J. Keillor, *This Rebellious House* (Downer's Grove, Ill.: InterVarsity Press, 1996), 87, 88, 90.

17. Basil Willey, *The Eighteenth Century Background: Studies on the Idea of Nature in the Thought of the Period* (Boston: Beacon Press, 1961), 6.

18. Conrad Wright, *The Liberal Christians* (Boston: Beacon Press, 1970), 20; Wright, *The Beginnings of Unitarianism in America* (Hamden, Conn.: Archon Books, 1976), 3; Wright, *Liberal Christians,* 6, 16.

19. Wright, *Liberal Christians,* 3, 5, 6.

20. Stokes, *Church and State,* 1:292.

21. May, *Enlightenment,* xi–xii, xvii, xviii.

22. Kraynak, *Christian Faith,* 125.

23. Ibid.

24. Ibid., 126.

25. Ibid., 127.

26. Mead, *Old Religion,* 28.

27. Ibid., 83.

28. Strout, *New Heavens,* 77–78.

29. Ibid., 79.

30. Ibid., 80.

31. Ahlstrom, *Religious History,* 356.

32. Ibid., 357–358.

33. Ibid., 366.

34. Ibid., 359.

35. Ibid., 368.

36. Pangle, *Spirit,* 2.

37. Ibid., 35.

38. Wright, *Liberal Christians,* 5–6, 5–17; Corrigan, *Hidden Balance,* 33; Edward M. Griffin, *Old Brick: Charles Chauncy of Boston, 1705–1787* (Minneapolis: University of Minnesota Press, 1980), 4; Michael Kammen, *People of Paradox* (New York: Vintage Books, 1972), 176.

39. Strout, *New Heavens,* 48.

40. McMurry S. Richey, "Jonathan Mayhew: American Christian Rationalist," in *A Miscellany of American Christianity,* ed. Stuart C. Henry (Durham, N.C.: Duke University Press, 1963), 292, 304; Ahlstrom, *Religious History,* 357, 366; May, *Enlightenment,* 257; Michael Zuckert, *The Natural Rights Republic* (Notre Dame, Ind.: University of Notre Dame Press, 1996), 199.

41. February 27, 1821, letter to Timothy Pickering, in *The Writings of Thomas Jefferson,* ed. H. A. Washington (Washington, D.C.: Taylor & Maury, 1853–1854), 7:210; September 23, 1800, letter to Benjamin Rush, in *The Papers of Thomas Jefferson,* ed. Julian Boyd, L. H. Butterfield, Charles T. Cullen, and John Catanzariti (Princeton, N.J.: Princeton University Press, 1950–2009), 32:266.

42. October 31, 1819, letter to William Short, in *The Works of Thomas Jefferson,* ed. Paul Leicester Ford (New York: G. P. Putnam's Sons, 1904–1905), 12:242.

43. Carl L. Becker, *The Heavenly City of the Eighteenth-Century Philosophers* (New Haven, Conn.: Yale University Press, 1932), 7–9, 20; William Ebenstein, *Great Political Thinkers,* 4th ed. (Hinsdale, Ill.: Dryden Press, 1969), 217–218; George Sabine, *A History of Political Theory,* 3rd ed. (New York: Holt, Rinehart and Winston, 1961), 248.

44. Ernest L. Fortin, "St. Thomas Aquinas," in *History of Political Philosophy,* 2nd ed., ed. Leo Strauss and Joseph Cropsey (Chicago: University of Chicago Press, 1981), 227, 228, 246; Will Durant, *The Age of Faith,* vol. 4 of *The Story of Civilization* (New York: Simon & Schuster, 1950), 967.

45. Douglass Adair, *Fame and the Founding Fathers* (New York: W. W. Norton, 1974), 145.

46. Harold R. Hutcheson, ed., *Lord Herbert of Cherbury's De Religione Laici* (New Haven, Conn.: Yale University Press, 1944), 55; Kerry S. Walters, *The American Deists* (Lawrence: University Press of Kansas, 1992), 41.

47. Hutcheson, *Lord Herbert*, 55; E. Graham Waring, ed., *Deism and Natural Religion: A Source Book* (New York: Frederick Ungar, 1967), x.

48. Russel Blaine Nye, *The Cultural Life of the New Nation* (New York: Harper & Row, 1960), 64; Edward, Lord Herbert of Cherbury, *De Veritate*, ed. Meyrick H. Carre (Bristol, UK: J. W. Arrowsmith, 1937), 308; Thomas Paine, "Age of Reason, Being an Investigation of True and Fabulous Theology," in *The Life and Writings of Thomas Paine*, ed. Daniel Edwin Wheeler (New York: Vincent Parke, 1908), 6:5–12, 22.

49. Peter Gay, *Deism: An Anthology* (Princeton, N.J.: D. Van Nostrand, 1968), 11–12; Wright, *Liberal Christians*, 5.

50. Jonathan Edwards, "A History of the Work of Redemption," in *The Works of Jonathan Edwards*, ed. John F. Wilson (New Haven, Conn.: Yale University Press, 1989), 9:432.

51. Walters, *American Deists*, 26–33.

52. Ibid.; Paine, "Age of Reason," 6:8–9; John Leland, *A View of the Principal Deistical Writers*, 5th ed. (London: printed for T. Cadell Jun. & W. Davies, 1798), 2:387.

53. Kerry S. Walters, ed., *Elihu Palmer's "Principles of Nature"* (Wolfeboro, N.H.: Longwood Academic, 1990), 35; Elihu Palmer, *Principles of Nature*, in *Elihu Palmer's "Principles of Nature,"* ed. Kerry S. Walters (1806; repr., Wolfeboro, N.H.: Longwood Academic, 1990), 114–115, 231–232.

54. Edwards, "History of the Work," 9:432.

55. Willey, *Eighteenth Century Background*, 7.

56. M. E. Bradford, *A Worthy Company* (Marlborough, N.H.: Plymouth Rock Foundation, 1982), v–vi.

57. Russell Kirk, *The Roots of American Order* (Washington, D.C.: Regnery Gateway, 1991), 337.

58. Bonomi, *Under the Cope*, 104.

59. Keillor, *This Rebellious House*, 81, 84, 87–88.

60. May, *Enlightenment*, xviii; Wright, *Beginnings*, 6; Marini, "Religion, Politics," 195; David Robinson, *The Unitarians and the Universalists* (Westport, Conn.: Greenwood Press, 1985), 11.

61. Mead, *Old Religion*, 28; Ahlstrom, *Religious History*, 353; Kraynak, *Christian Faith*, 126.

62. Melvin H. Buxbaum, *Benjamin Franklin and the Zealous Presbyterians* (University Park: Pennsylvania State University Press, 1975), 82; Nye, *Cultural Life*, 195; Gustav Adolf Koch, *Republican Religion: The American Revolution and the Cult of Reason* (Gloucester, Mass.: Peter Smith, 1964), 185.

63. Earl Morse Wilbur, *A History of Unitarianism* (Boston: Beacon Press, 1945), 384.

64. Jonathan Mayhew quoted in Alden Bradford, *Memoir of the Life and Writings of Rev. Jonathan Mayhew, D.D.* (Boston: C. C. Little, 1838), 102.

CHAPTER TWO. "DIVINE" SOURCES OF
THEISTIC RATIONALISM

1. March 26, 1691, letter from Anthony Ashley Cooper to John Locke, in *The Life, Unpublished Letters, and Philosophical Regimen of Anthony, Earl of Shaftesbury*, ed. Benjamin Rand (London: Swan Sonnenschein, 1900), 290.

2. Melvin H. Buxbaum, *Benjamin Franklin and the Zealous Presbyterians* (University Park: Pennsylvania State University Press, 1975), 86; Thomas L. Pangle, *The Spirit of Modern Republicanism* (Chicago: University of Chicago Press, 1988), 25.

3. Stanley Green, *Shaftesbury's Philosophy of Religion and Ethics* (Athens: Ohio University Press, 1967), xvii–xviii.

4. Benjamin Franklin, "On the Providence of God in the Government of the World," in *Benjamin Franklin, Writings*, ed. J. A. Leo Lemay (New York: Library of America, 1987), 163.

5. Grean, *Shaftesbury's Philosophy*, 37, 46, 48; Basil Willey, *The Eighteenth Century Background: Studies on the Idea of Nature in the Thought of the Period* (Boston: Beacon Press, 1961), 67, 65.

6. Grean, *Shaftesbury's Philosophy*, 47; Anthony Ashley Cooper, Earl of Shaftesbury, *Characteristics of Men, Manners, Opinions, Times*, ed. John M. Robertson (New York: Bobbs-Merrill, 1964), 2:91; Cooper, *Characteristics*, 2:97–98; Grean, *Shaftesbury's Philosophy*, 51; Benjamin Franklin, "Articles of Belief and Acts of Religion," in *Literature of the Early Republic*, ed. Edwin H. Cady (New York: Holt, Rinehart and Winston, 1965), 328–334.

7. Grean, *Shaftesbury's Philosophy*, 63, 64, 67, 68; Franklin, "Articles," 328–331.

8. Willey, *Eighteenth Century Background*, 67–71; Franklin, "Articles," 332–334.

9. Willey, *Eighteenth Century Background*, 71; Grean, *Shaftesbury's Philosophy*, 71; Franklin, "Articles," 328–331.

10. Grean, *Shaftesbury's Philosophy*, 62; Cooper, *Characteristics*, 2:54.

11. Franklin, "On the Providence of God," 165–168.

12. Willey, *Eighteenth Century Background*, 71.

13. Allen Jayne, *Jefferson's Declaration of Independence: Origins, Philosophy, and Theology* (Lexington: University Press of Kentucky, 1998); August 22, 1813, letter from Thomas Jefferson to John Adams, in *The Adams-Jefferson Letters*, ed. Lester J. Cappon (Chapel Hill: University of North Carolina Press, 1959), 2:369; June 25, 1819, letter to Ezra Stiles, in Thomas Jefferson, *The Writings of Thomas Jefferson*, ed. H. A. Washington (Washington, D.C.: Taylor & Maury, 1853–1854), 7:127.

14. Will and Ariel Durant, *The Age of Voltaire: Part 9 of The Story of Civilization* (New York: Simon & Schuster, 1965), 122; Conyers Middleton, *A Letter from Rome* (London, 1741), iii; Middleton, *The Miscellaneous Works of Conyers Middleton* (London, 1755), 1:lxxxii; Middleton, *Letter from Rome*, lxxxvii.

15. Middleton, *Miscellaneous Works*, 1:lxxxiii–lxxxiv, 1:x.

16. Conyers Middleton, *A Letter to Dr. Waterland; Containing Some Remarks on His Vindication of Scripture* (London, 1731), 44–45.

17. Ibid., 46; Durant and Durant, *Age of Voltaire*, 122.

18. Peter Gay, *Deism: An Anthology* (Princeton, N.J.: D. Van Nostrand, 1968), 140–141.

19. Willey, *Eighteenth Century Background,* 169.

20. Norman Cousins, *The Republic of Reason* (San Francisco: Harper & Row, 1988), 164–165.

21. E.g., April 21, 1803, letter from Jefferson to Benjamin Rush, in *The Works of Thomas Jefferson,* ed. Paul Leicester Ford (New York: G. P. Putnam's Sons, 1904–1905), 9:457; March 9, 1790, letter from Franklin to Ezra Stiles, in *The Works of Benjamin Franklin,* ed. Jared Sparks (Boston: Tappan & Whittemore, 1837–1844), 10:424; February 2, 1816, letter from Adams to Jefferson, in *Adams-Jefferson Letters,* 2:461; Thomas Jefferson, "Syllabus of an Estimate of the Merit of the Doctrines of Jesus, Compared with Those of Others," in *Works of Thomas Jefferson,* 9:462; August 22, 1813, letter from Jefferson to Adams, in *Adams-Jefferson Letters,* 2:369.

22. August 22, 1813, letter from Jefferson to Adams, in *Adams-Jefferson Letters,* 2:369, 368; July 18, 1813, letter from Adams to Jefferson, in *Adams-Jefferson Letters,* 2:361; see July 16, 1813, letter from Adams to Jefferson, in *Adams-Jefferson Letters,* 2:359–360; July 18, 1813, letter from Adams to Jefferson, in *Adams-Jefferson Letters,* 2:361–362; July 22, 1813, letter from Adams to Jefferson, in *Adams-Jefferson Letters,* 2:362–363; August 9, 1813, letter from Adams to Jefferson, in *Adams-Jefferson Letters,* 2:364.

23. July 22, 1813, letter from Adams to Jefferson, in *Adams-Jefferson Letters,* 2:363; December 3, 1813, letter from Adams to Jefferson, in *Adams-Jefferson Letters,* 2:405; April 9, 1803, letter to Joseph Priestley, in *Works of Thomas Jefferson,* 9:459; January 29, 1804, letter to Priestley, in *Works of Thomas Jefferson,* 10:70.

24. E.g., February 1814 letter from Adams to Jefferson, in *Adams-Jefferson Letters,* 2:427–429; July 22, 1813, letter from Adams to Jefferson, in *Adams-Jefferson Letters,* 2:363; March 21, 1801, letter to Priestley, in *Works of Thomas Jefferson,* 9:217.

25. Paul K. Conkin, "Priestley and Jefferson: Unitarianism as a Religion for a New Revolutionary Age," in *Religion in a Revolutionary Age,* ed. Ronald Hoffman and Peter J. Albert (Charlottesville: University Press of Virginia, 1994), 291.

26. Ibid., 301, 302–303.

27. Joseph Priestley, *Memoirs* (London: E. Hemsted, 1806), 1:190; Conkin, "Priestley and Jefferson," 302–303; Willey, *Eighteenth Century Background,* 204; Earl Morse Wilbur, *A History of Unitarianism* (Boston: Beacon Press, 1945), 396; July 19, 1822, letter from Jefferson to Benjamin Waterhouse, in *Works of Thomas Jefferson,* 12:244; Anne Holt, *A Life of Joseph Priestley* (London: Oxford University Press, 1931), 187.

28. Gustav Adolf Koch, *Republican Reason: The American Revolution and the Cult of Reason* (Gloucester, Mass.: Peter Smith, 1964), 226.

29. Joseph Priestley, *An History of the Corruptions of Christianity* (Birmingham, UK: Percy and Jones, 1782), 1:278–79; Willey, *Eighteenth Century Background,* 186–187.

30. Priestley, *History of the Corruptions,* 1:286.

31. Joseph Priestley, *Letters to a Philosophical Unbeliever* (Birmingham, UK: Pearson and Rollason, 1787), 1:33; Conkin, "Priestley and Jefferson," 297.

32. Priestley, *Letters*, 1:xix; Joseph Priestley, *Institutes of Natural and Revealed Religion* (Birmingham, UK: Pearson and Rollason, 1782), 2:3–4.

33. Priestley, *Letters*, 1:xiv–xv.

34. Willey, *Eighteenth Century Background*, 189.

35. Joseph Priestley, *Lectures on History and General Policy* (Birmingham, UK: Pearson and Rollason, 1788), 527–528.

36. E.g., Joseph Priestley, *Disquisitions Relating to Matter and Spirit* (London, 1777), 152–153; Joseph Priestley, "Considerations in Evidence That the Apostolic and Primitive Church Was Unitarian," in Priestley, *A History of the Corruptions of Christianity* (London: British and Foreign Unitarian Association, 1871), 321; Priestley, *Letters*, 1:318, 356.

37. Priestley, *Letters*, 1:xvii–xviii; November 23, 1825, letter from Madison to Doctor C. Caldwell, in *Letters and Other Writings of James Madison*, ed. William Rives (New York: R Worthington, 1884), 3:505.

38. Priestley, *Letters*, 1:vi–xii, xiii.

39. Priestley, *Institutes*, 2:52–53.

40. David Robinson, *The Unitarians and the Universalists* (Westport, Conn.: Greenwood Press, 1985), 22; Priestley, *Letters*, 1:182.

41. Conkin, "Priestley and Jefferson," 295; Priestley, *Letters*, 1:109.

42. Priestley, *Letters*, 1:109–110.

43. Ibid., 1:110–111.

44. Willey, *Eighteenth Century Background*, 189.

45. Priestley, *History of the Corruptions*, 1:xiv.

46. Robinson, *Unitarians*, 22.

47. Priestley, *History of the Corruptions*, 2:441.

48. Willey, *Eighteenth Century Background*, 175, 188.

49. Priestley, *Letters*, 2:33; Priestley, *History of the Corruptions*, 1:146, 321.

50. Willey, *Eighteenth Century Background*, 192, 176.

51. Priestley, "Considerations," 320; Willey, *Eighteenth Century Background*, 181.

52. Conrad Wright, *The Beginnings of Unitarianism in America* (Hamden, Conn.: Archon Books, 1976), 202; Priestley, *History of the Corruptions*, 1:141–142; George Willis Cooke, *Unitarianism in America: A History of Its Origin and Development* (Boston: American Unitarian Association, 1902), 83; Priestley, *History of the Corruptions*, 1:146.

53. Colin Wells, *The Devil & Doctor Dwight* (Chapel Hill: University of North Carolina Press, 2002), 106; Priestley, "Considerations," 321; Conkin, "Priestley and Jefferson," 299.

54. Willey, *Eighteenth Century Background*, 186–187; Priestley, *History of the Corruptions*, 1:153.

55. Conkin, "Priestley and Jefferson," 298; Priestley, *History of the Corruptions*, 1:152–153.

56. Priestley, *History of the Corruptions*, 1:153.

57. Willey, *Eighteenth Century Background*, 184; Priestley, *History of the Corruptions*, 1:281.

58. Priestley, *Letters*, 1:xix.

59. Priestley, *History of the Corruptions*, 1:172–177; Willey, *Eighteenth Century Background*, 191.

60. Conkin, "Priestley and Jefferson," 295–296.

61. Joseph Priestley, *Discourses Relating to the Evidences of Revealed Religion* (Philadelphia: John Thompson, 1796), 359–360.

62. Priestley, "Considerations," 321.

63. Priestley, *History of the Corruptions*, 2:440; ibid., 1:177; Priestley, *Letters*, 1:34.

64. Priestley, *History of the Corruptions*, 1:279.

65. Joseph Priestley, *An Essay on the First Principles of Government, and on the Nature of Political, Civil, and Religious Liberty* (London, 1771), 117, 14.

66. Priestley, *Essay*, 120, 110, 114–115.

67. Priestley, "Considerations," 336.

68. Ibid., 336, Priestley, *History of the Corruptions*, 1:154.

69. Priestley, *History of the Corruptions*, 1:326; Priestley, *Letters*, 1:xiv; Priestley, *Memoirs*, 1:75.

70. John Adams, August 27, 1774, "Diary" entry, in *The Works of John Adams*, ed. Charles Francis Adams (Boston: Little, Brown, 1850–1856), 2:356; James L. McAllister, "John Witherspoon: Academic Advocate for American Freedom," in *A Miscellany of American Christianity*, ed. Stuart C. Henry (Durham, N.C.: Duke University Press, 1963), 191.

71. McAllister, "John Witherspoon," 191–193.

72. James J. Walsh, *Education of the Founding Fathers of the Republic: Scholasticism in the Colonial Colleges* (New York: Fordham University Press, 1935), 162–163; Jack Scott, "Introduction," in John Witherspoon, *Lectures on Moral Philosophy*, ed. Jack Scott (Newark: University of Delaware Press, 1982), 33, 51; McAllister, "John Witherspoon," 192, 224.

73. James H. Smylie, "Madison and Witherspoon: Theological Roots of American Political Thought," *Princeton University Library Chronicle* 22 (Spring 1961): 118–132.

74. Ibid., 49–50; Garrett Ward Sheldon, *The Political Philosophy of James Madison* (Baltimore, Md.: Johns Hopkins University Press, 2001), 14–15.

75. McAllister, "John Witherspoon," 220.

76. Ibid., 194, 220; Henry F. May, *The Enlightenment in America* (New York: Oxford University Press, 1976), 63; Scott, "Introduction," 51, 52.

77. Mark A. Noll, Nathan O. Hatch, and George M. Marsden, *The Search for Christian America* (Westchester, Ill.: Crossway Books, 1983), 88–89; Elizabeth Flower and Murray G. Murphey, *A History of Philosophy in America* (New York: G. P. Putnam's Sons, 1977), 1:233; McAllister, "John Witherspoon," 222.

78. Scott, "Introduction," 38–39; Smylie, "Madison and Witherspoon," 119–120; Federalist No. 55.

79. Stephen A. Marini, "Religion, Politics, and Ratification," in *Religion in a Revolutionary Age*, ed. Ronald Hoffman and Peter J. Albert (Charlottesville: University Press of Virginia, 1994), 203.

80. Noll, Hatch, and Marsden, *Search*, 93.

81. John Witherspoon, *Lectures on Moral Philosophy*, ed. Jack Scott (Newark: University of Delaware Press, 1982), 64, 73, 92, 125, 150; Marini, "Religion, Politics," 203.

82. Witherspoon, *Lectures*, 92, 97, 98.

83. Ibid., 103; see also Scott's notes on p. 107.

84. Scott, "Introduction," 39–40.

85. Witherspoon, *Lectures,* 187, 64.

86. Ibid., 65.

87. McAllister, "John Witherspoon," 218.

88. Noll, Hatch, and Marsden, *Search,* 90–91.

89. Scott, "Introduction," 50; Flower and Murphey, *History of Philosophy,* 1:234.

90. Witherspoon, *Lectures,* 64, 66.

91. Ibid., 87.

92. Ibid., 92.

93. E.g., ibid., 125, 126; Flower and Murphey, *History of Philosophy,* 1:234.

94. May, *Enlightenment,* 63.

95. Noll, Hatch, and Marsden, *Search,* 93; Scott, "Introduction," 40.

96. David Martin, "General Tendencies and Historical Filters," *Annual Review of Social Science of Religion* 3 (1979): 10.

97. Noll, Hatch, and Marsden, *Search,* 93.

98. May, *Enlightenment,* 62.

99. Witherspoon, *Lectures,* 109, 159, 160.

100. Ibid., 78.

101. McAllister, "John Witherspoon," 198–199.

102. John Witherspoon, *Treatises on Justification and Regeneration* (Glasgow, Scotland: William Collins, 1830), 91, 262–273.

103. Marini, "Religion, Politics," 204; May, *Enlightenment,* 64; Scott, "Introduction," 41.

104. E.g., Witherspoon, *Lectures,* 140–141.

105. See McAllister, "John Witherspoon," 110–111, 122, 145–146, 160, 199–201.

106. Ibid., 205–206.

107. Noll, Hatch, and Marsden, *Search,* 92.

108. July 18, 1813, letter from Adams to Jefferson, in *Adams-Jefferson Letters,* 2:362; May, *Enlightenment,* 25; Ralph L. Ketcham, "James Madison and Religion," in *James Madison on Religious Liberty,* ed. Robert S. Alley (Buffalo, N.Y.: Prometheus Books, 1985), 177; Scott, "Introduction," 35.

109. John T. Noonan, *The Lustre of Our Country* (Berkeley: University of California Press, 1998), 86; November 20, 1825, letter to Frederick Beasley, in James Madison, *The Writings of James Madison,* ed. Gaillard Hunt (New York: G. P. Putnam's sons, 1900–1910), 9:230; Ketcham, "James Madison," 177, 180.

110. Cooke, *Unitarianism,* 45; May, *Enlightenment,* 38; Mary Latimer Gambrell, *Ministerial Training in Eighteenth-Century New England* (New York: Columbia University Press, 1937), 38; Wright, *Beginnings of Unitarianism,* 201; Conrad Wright, *The Liberal Christians* (Boston: Beacon Press, 1970), 6; Robert J. Wilson III, *The Benevolent Deity: Ebenezer Gay and the Rise of Rational Religion in New England, 1696–1787* (Philadelphia: University of Pennsylvania Press, 1984), 65.

111. E. Graham Waring, ed., *Deism and Natural Religion: A Source Book* (New York: Frederick Ungar, 1967), 44; Samuel Clarke, *Discourse Concerning the Unchangeable Obligations of Natural Religion, and the Truth and Certainty of the Christian Revelation* (London: W. Botham, 1706), 250–258, 344–345; Robinson, *Unitarians,* 15.

112. Clarke, *Discourse,* 241; ibid., 244; May, *Enlightenment,* 11.

113. Robinson, *Unitarians*, 15.

114. McMurry S. Richey, "Jonathan Mayhew: American Christian Rationalist," in *A Miscellany of American Christianity*, ed. Stuart C. Henry (Durham, N.C.: Duke University Press, 1963), 303–304; Willey, *Eighteenth Century Background*, 59.

115. Cooke, *Unitarianism*, 45; May, *Enlightenment*, 11–12.

116. Leslie Stephen, *History of English Thought in the Eighteenth Century* (London: G. P. Putnam's Sons, 1876), 1:123; Clarke, *Discourse*, 147–148.

117. Ketcham, "James Madison," 178.

118. Clarke, *Discourse*, 346, 388–389.

119. Ibid., 265–266.

120. Ibid., 290.

121. Ezio Vailati, "Introduction," in Samuel Clarke, *A Demonstration of the Being and Attributes of God and Other Writings*, ed. Ezio Vailati (Cambridge: Cambridge University Press, 1998), xii; Willey, *Eighteenth Century Background*, 60.

122. Clarke, *Discourse*, 301; Samuel Clarke, *A Demonstration of the Being and Attributes of God and Other Writings*, ed. Ezio Vailati (Cambridge: Cambridge University Press, 1998), xiii–xiv, xxiii.

123. Clarke, *Discourse*, 306–310, 323, 326–331.

124. Vailati, "Introduction," xi–xii; Wright, *Beginnings of Unitarianism*, 201.

125. Levi Paine, *A Critical History of the Evolution of Trinitarianism* (Boston: Houghton Mifflin, 1900), 99–100.

126. Clarke, *Discourse*, 291, 296–297; May, *Enlightenment*, 15.

127. Clarke, *Discourse*, 301; Clarke, *Demonstration*, xiii; Clarke, *Discourse*, 266; Richey, "Jonathan Mayhew," 304.

128. Clarke, *Discourse*, 141, 155, 290, 326, 337; Richey, "Jonathan Mayhew," 304; Clarke, *Discourse*, 141.

129. Charles H. Lippy, *Seasonable Revolutionary: The Mind of Charles Chauncy* (Chicago: Nelson-Hall, 1981), 100; Cushing Strout, *The New Heavens and New Earth: Political Religion in America* (New York: Harper & Row, 1974), 48–49.

130. Douglass Adair and John A. Schutz, eds., *Peter Oliver's Origin and Progress of the American Revolution: A Tory View* (San Marino, Calif.: Huntington Library, 1963), quoted in Lippy, *Seasonable Revolutionary*, ix.

131. Lippy, *Seasonable Revolutionary*, 11; Wright, *Liberal Christians*, 6; Edward M. Griffin, *Old Brick: Charles Chauncy of Boston, 1705–1787* (Minneapolis: University of Minnesota Press, 1980), 4.

132. Lippy, *Seasonable Revolutionary*, 130.

133. James W. Jones, *The Shattered Synthesis* (New Haven, Conn.: Yale University Press, 1973), 171.

134. Griffin, *Old Brick*, 5, 110; June 14, 1771, letter from Chauncy to Ezra Stiles, in Ezra Stiles, *Extracts from the Itineraries and Other Miscellanies of Ezra Stiles*, ed. Franklin Bowditch Dexter (New Haven, Conn.: Yale University Press, 1916), 451; Lippy, *Seasonable Revolutionary*, 122.

135. Griffin, *Old Brick*, 8, 4.

136. John Corrigan, *The Hidden Balance* (Cambridge: Cambridge University Press, 1987), 33, 40, 47.

137. Lippy, *Seasonable Revolutionary*, 114, 129; Robinson, *Unitarians*, 13.

138. Charles Chauncy quoted in Alan Heimert and Perry Miller, eds., *The Great*

Awakening: Documents Illustrating the Crisis and Its Consequences (Indianapolis, Ind.: Bobbs-Merrill, 1967), 232; Griffin, *Old Brick*, 4, 109–110, 175.

139. Charles Chauncy, *The Mystery Hid from Ages and Generations, Made Manifest by the Gospel-Revelation; or, The Salvation of All Men* (London, 1784), vi.

140. Jones, *Shattered Synthesis*, 166, 192.

141. Lippy, *Seasonable Revolutionary*, 114.

142. Ibid., 113.

143. Joseph Haroutunian, *Piety versus Moralism: The Passing of the New England Theology* (New York: H. Holt, 1932), 145.

144. Jones, *Shattered Synthesis*, 168–169.

145. Ibid., 167.

146. Charles Chauncy, *The Benevolence of the Deity* (Boston: Powars & Willis, 1784), 33–34.

147. Jones, *Shattered Synthesis*, 168.

148. Griffin, *Old Brick*, 4, 109; Jones, *Shattered Synthesis*, 181; Corrigan, *Hidden Balance*, 16–18.

149. Lippy, *Seasonable Revolutionary*, 117–118.

150. Ibid., 117; Jones, *Shattered Synthesis*, 171; Griffin, *Old Brick*, 121–125.

151. Robinson, *Unitarians*, 19.

152. Chauncy, *Mystery Hid*, 15; ibid., 1.

153. Chauncy, *Benevolence of the Deity*, viii.

154. Chauncy, *Mystery Hid*, 319–320.

155. Griffin, *Old Brick*, 121–125; Robinson, *Unitarians*, 19–20; Jones, *Shattered Synthesis*, 171, 194; Chauncy, *Mystery Hid*, 9.

156. Griffin, *Old Brick*, 121–125.

157. Jones, *Shattered Synthesis*, 194–195.

158. Lippy, *Seasonable Revolutionary*, 27, 85.

159. Charles Chauncy, *Twelve Sermons . . . with Interspersed Notes* (Boston: D. and J. Kneeland for Thomas Leverett, 1765), 339, quoted in Lippy, *Seasonable Revolutionary*, 85.

160. Corrigan, *Hidden Balance*, 48; Robinson, *Unitarians*, 8; Jones, *Shattered Synthesis*, 168, 170; Chauncy, *Twelve Sermons*, 203, quoted in Jones, *Shattered Synthesis*, 177.

161. Robinson, *Unitarians*, 13.

162. Strout, *New Heavens*, 48–49.

163. Charles Chauncy, "Civil Magistrates Must Be Just" [1747], in Ellis Sandoz, ed., *Political Sermons of the American Founding Era* (Indianapolis, Ind.: Liberty Press, 1991), 145; Corrigan, *Hidden Balance*, 75–76; Chauncy, "Civil Magistrates," 153.

164. Cooke, *Unitarianism*, 61.

165. Richey, "Jonathan Mayhew," 297–298; Cooke, *Unitarianism*, 45; Perry Miller, *Jonathan Edwards* (New York: W. Sloane Associates, 1949), 322; Charles Graves, *A History of Unitarianism* (Boston: American Unitarian Association, 1934), 14.

166. John Wingate Thornton, ed., *The Pulpit of the American Revolution: or the Political Sermons of the Period of 1776* (Boston: Gould and Lincoln, 1860), 43.

167. April 5, 1818, letter from John Adams to William Tudor, in *Works of John*

Adams, 10:301; February 13, 1818, letter from Adams to H. Niles, in *Works of John Adams,* 10:288.

168. Thornton, *Pulpit,* facing title page.

169. Ibid., 44–45; Alice M. Baldwin, *The New England Clergy and the American Revolution* (New York: Frederick Ungar, 1958), 92.

170. Baldwin, *New England Clergy,* 9; December 2, 1815, letter from John Adams to Dr. J. Morse, in *Works of John Adams,* 10:188; Robert Treat Paine quoted in Thornton, *Pulpit,* 43; John Adams, "Novanglus," in *Works of John Adams,* 4:29; John Adams, "A Dissertation on the Canon and Feudal Law," in *Works of John Adams,* 3:464; February 13, 1818, letter from John Adams to H. Niles, in *Works of John Adams,* 10:287–288.

171. John Adams, March 17, 1756, entry in "Diary of John Adams," in *Diary and Autobiography of John Adams,* ed. L. H. Butterfield (New York: Atheneum, 1964), 1:14–15.

172. Cooke, *Unitarianism,* 62–63.

173. Richey, "Jonathan Mayhew," 292, 300, 304; Cooke, *Unitarianism,* 45; Thornton, *Pulpit,* 46; Richey, "Jonathan Mayhew," 294; Corrigan, *Hidden Balance,* 40.

174. Richey, "Jonathan Mayhew," 292, 304; Wright, *Beginnings of Unitarianism,* 123.

175. Richey, "Jonathan Mayhew," 312, 317; Robinson, *Unitarians,* 15; Jonathan Mayhew, *Christian Sobriety* (Boston: Richard and Samuel Draper, 1763), 50.

176. Jonathan Mayhew, *Seven Sermons* (1750), reprinted as *Sermons,* ed. Edwin S. Gaustad (New York: Arno Press, 1969), 35–36.

177. Richey, "Jonathan Mayhew," 318.

178. Ibid., 309, 315, 310.

179. Jones, *Shattered Synthesis,* 147; Corrigan, *Hidden Balance,* 44; Jonathan Mayhew, *Sermons upon the Following Subjects* (Boston: Richard Draper, 1755), 418n; Jonathan Mayhew, "A Discourse Concerning Unlimited Submission and Non-resistance to the Higher Powers," in Mayhew, *Seven Sermons,* 42.

180. Mayhew, *Seven Sermons,* 75, 88.

181. Jones, *Shattered Synthesis,* 149.

182. Mayhew, *Seven Sermons,* 101; Richey, "Jonathan Mayhew," 323.

183. Jones, *Shattered Synthesis,* 145; Richey, "Jonathan Mayhew," 318.

184. Jonathan Mayhew, *The Expected Dissolution of All Things: A Motive to Universal Holiness* (Boston, 1755), 59, quoted in Jones, *Shattered Synthesis,* 149.

185. Jonathan Mayhew, *Two Sermons on the Nature, Extent, and Perfection of the Divine Goodness* (Boston: D. and J. Kneeland, 1763), 58.

186. Jones, *Shattered Synthesis,* 145, 146, 148, 149.

187. Mayhew, *Two Sermons,* 19.

188. Jones, *Shattered Synthesis,* 150.

189. Graves, *History of Unitarianism,* 14; Wilbur, *History of Unitarianism,* 387–388; Richey, "Jonathan Mayhew," 296.

190. Mayhew, *Christian Sobriety,* 50; Richey, "Jonathan Mayhew," 323, 324; Jones, *Shattered Synthesis,* 148.

191. Richey, "Jonathan Mayhew," 294; Jones, *Shattered Synthesis,* 144; Claude M. Newlin, *Philosophy and Religion in Colonial America* (New York: Philosophical

Library, 1962), 197; John Adams, March 17, 1756, entry in "Diary," 1:14–15; Cooke, *Unitarianism*, 63.

192. Mayhew, *Seven Sermons*, 38; Wright, *Beginnings of Unitarianism*, 218–219; Richey, "Jonathan Mayhew," 296.

193. Mayhew, *Christian Sobriety*, 90, 65.

194. Mayhew, *Sermons upon the Following Subjects*, 103.

195. Ibid., 105.

196. Ibid., 103.

197. Ibid., 83; Jones, *Shattered Synthesis*, 160; Richey, "Jonathan Mayhew," 297, 317, 320.

198. Mayhew, *Seven Sermons*, 148, 152.

199. Wright, *Beginnings of Unitarianism*, 122; Jones, *Shattered Synthesis*, 155; Mayhew, *Sermons upon the Following Subjects*, 173n.

200. Mayhew, *Sermons upon the Following Subjects*, 157–158, 107, 104.

201. Corrigan, *Hidden Balance*, 45; Jones, *Shattered Synthesis*, 155–156; Mayhew, *Sermons upon the Following Subjects*, 167; Corrigan, *Hidden Balance*, 36; Jones, *Shattered Synthesis*, 160, 161.

202. Mayhew, *Two Sermons*, 21.

203. Mayhew, *Seven Sermons*, 154.

204. Richey, "Jonathan Mayhew," 321.

205. Corrigan, *Hidden Balance*, 62–63; Jonathan Mayhew, folder 11 of *Bortman Collection*, 5, quoted in Corrigan, *Hidden Balance*, 80.

206. Richey, "Jonathan Mayhew," 318; Strout, *New Heavens*, 55; folder 11 of *Bortman Collection*, 6, quoted in Corrigan, *Hidden Balance*, 80.

207. Mayhew, "Discourse Concerning Unlimited Submission," 13–15.

208. Ibid., 15.

209. Ibid., 21, 24, 29.

210. Ibid., 36n.

CHAPTER THREE. THEISTIC RATIONALISM IN THE REVOLUTIONARY PULPIT

1. Mark A. Noll, Nathan O. Hatch, and George M. Marsden, *The Search for Christian America* (Westchester, Ill.: Crossway Books, 1983), 118.

2. Mark Noll, *Christians in the American Revolution* (Washington, D.C.: Christian University Press, 1977), 172.

3. Ibid.; Nathaniel Niles, "Two Discourses on Liberty" (1774), quoted in Cushing Strout, *The New Heavens and New Earth* (New York: Harper & Row, 1974), 62; Noll, Hatch, and Marsden, *Search*, 118.

4. Strout, *New Heavens*, 63.

5. Alice M. Baldwin, *The New England Clergy and the American Revolution* (New York: Frederick Ungar, 1958), 3; Mary Latimer Gambrell, *Ministerial Training in Eighteenth-Century New England* (New York: Columbia University Press, 1937), 52.

6. William Buell Sprague, *Annals of the American Pulpit . . .*, 9 vols. (New York, 1857–1869), vols. 1 and 2; William Allen, *An American Biographical and Historical Dictionary*, 2nd ed. (Boston, 1832); John Eliot, *A Biographical Dictionary . . .*, 2nd ed. (Boston, 1809); and Franklin B. Dexter, *Biographical Sketches of*

the Graduates of Yale College with Annals of the College History, 6 vols. (New York, 1885–1912), vol. 1, all cited in Gambrell, *Ministerial Training*, 52.

7. Gambrell, *Ministerial Training*, 38.

8. Ibid., 37, 40–41.

9. George Whitefield, *A Continuation of the Reverend Mr. Whitefield's Journal . . . The Seventh Journal* (London, 1741), 55, quoted in Conrad Wright, *The Beginnings of Unitarianism in America* (Hamden, Conn.: Archon Books, 1976), 41; Earl Morse Wilbur, *A History of Unitarianism* (Boston: Beacon Press, 1945), 384; George Willis Cooke, *Unitarianism in America: A History of Its Origin and Development* (Boston: American Unitarian Association, 1902), 41; Whitefield, *Continuation*, 28, 29, quoted in Wright, *Beginnings of Unitarianism*, 41.

10. Cooke, *Unitarianism*, 35–36.

11. Gambrell, *Ministerial Training*, 57, 58; John Corrigan, *The Hidden Balance* (Cambridge: Cambridge University Press, 1987); Robert J. Wilson III, *The Benevolent Deity: Ebenezer Gay and the Rise of Rational Religion in New England, 1696–1787* (Philadelphia: University of Pennsylvania Press, 1984), 65.

12. McMurry S. Richey, "Jonathan Mayhew: American Christian Rationalist," in *A Miscellany of American Christianity*, ed. Stuart C. Henry (Durham, N.C.: Duke University Press, 1963), 299; Claude M. Newlin, *Philosophy and Religion in Colonial America* (New York: Philosophical Library, 1962), 198, 199–211.

13. Gambrell, *Ministerial Training*, 62; Wilson, *Benevolent Deity*, 63.

14. Josiah Quincy, *The History of Harvard University* (Cambridge: John Owen, 1840), 2:52; William Henry Channing, *Memoir of William Ellery Channing* (Boston: Crosby, Nichols, 1854), 1:60, 61.

15. Gambrell, *Ministerial Training*, 62–63, 64.

16. Wilson, *Benevolent Deity*, 65; Gambrell, *Ministerial Training*, 77; Lyman Beecher, *Autobiography, Correspondence, etc., of Lyman Beecher, D.D.*, ed. Charles Beecher (New York: Harper, 1864), 1:43.

17. Gambrell, *Ministerial Training*, 63.

18. Edmund S. Morgan, "The American Revolution Considered as an Intellectual Movement," in *Paths of American Thought*, ed. Arthur M. Schlesinger Jr. and Morton White (Boston: Houghton Mifflin, 1963), 15; Wright, *Beginnings of Unitarianism*, 147.

19. Basil Willey, *The Eighteenth Century Background: Studies on the Idea of Nature in the Thought of the Period* (Boston: Beacon Press, 1961), 181.

20. Cooke, *Unitarianism*, 44; Wright, *Beginnings of Unitarianism*, 281–291.

21. Russel B. Nye and Norman S. Grabo, eds., *The Revolution and the Early Republic*, vol. 2, *American Thought and Writing* (Boston: Houghton Mifflin, 1965), 262; Gustav Adolf Koch, *Republican Religion: The American Revolution and the Cult of Reason* (Gloucester, Mass.: Peter Smith, 1964), 238.

22. Whitefield, *Continuation*, 38, quoted in Wright, *Beginnings of Unitarianism*, 42.

23. Wright, *Beginnings of Unitarianism*, 42.

24. Charles Chauncy, *Seasonable Thoughts on the State of Religion in New England* (Boston: Rogers and Fowle, 1743), 166.

25. Henry F. May, *The Enlightenment in America* (New York: Oxford University Press, 1976), 138.

26. Timothy Dwight, "The Present Dangers of Infidelity," from *A Discourse on Some Events*, 1801, quoted in Nye and Grabo, *Revolution*, 265.

27. Ibid.
28. Ibid., 267, 269–270, 271.
29. Cooke, *Unitarianism,* 56.
30. May, *Enlightenment,* 57.
31. Richey, "Jonathan Mayhew," 299.
32. Cooke, *Unitarianism,* 57, 50; Joseph Bellamy, in *Historical Magazine,* n.s., 9, no. 227 (April 1871), quoted in Cooke, *Unitarianism,* 45; Bellamy, "A Letter to Scripturista," in *The Works of Joseph Bellamy* (Boston: Doctrinal Tract and Book Society, 1853), 1:610; Wilbur, *History of Unitarianism,* 389.
33. Wilbur, *History of Unitarianism,* 384–385; Alden Bradford, *Memoir of the Life and Writings of Rev. Jonathan Mayhew* (Boston: C. C. Little, 1838), 24; William Buell Sprague, *Annals of the American Unitarian Pulpit* (New York: Robert Carter & Brothers, 1865), 1–14, 22–32, 37–50, 65–68; C. A. Bartol, *The West Church and Its Ministers* (Boston: Crosby, Nichols, 1856), 136.
34. Cooke, *Unitarianism,* 56; Wright, *Beginnings of Unitarianism,* 201, 202, 209; May, *Enlightenment,* 15.
35. Newlin, *Philosophy,* 212.
36. Wright, *Beginnings of Unitarianism,* 218, 220, 222.
37. Ibid., 185.
38. *A Concert of Prayer Propounded to the Citizens of the United States of America* (Exeter, N.H.: Lamson & Ranlet, 1787), 4, 9, quoted in Nathan O. Hatch, *The Sacred Cause of Liberty* (New Haven, Conn.: Yale University Press, 1977), 2.
39. Hatch, *Sacred Cause,* 97; Patricia U. Bonomi, *Under the Cope of Heaven* (New York: Oxford University Press, 1986), 212.
40. Bonomi, *Under the Cope,* 209, 212, 214.
41. Ibid., 209–210.
42. Ibid., 210.
43. July 23, 1775, letter from John Adams to Abigail Adams, in *Familiar Letters of John Adams and His Wife Abigail Adams during the Revolution,* ed. Charles Francis Adams (New York: Hurd and Houghton, 1876), 84; Anson Phelps Stokes, *Church and State in the United States* (New York: Harper & Brothers, 1950), 1:280.
44. Hatch, *Sacred Cause,* 3, 62, 63.
45. Strout, *New Heaven,* 62, 63.
46. Baldwin, *New England Clergy,* xii, 168, 169, 170.
47. Daniel Leonard, "Massachusettensis," in *Novanglus, and Massachusettensis; or Political Essays, Published in the Years 1774 and 1775* (Boston: Hews and Goss, 1819), 151.
48. Baldwin, *New England Clergy,* 171.
49. Bonomi, *Under the Cope,* 216.
50. Ibid., 211.
51. John E. Semonche, *Keeping the Faith: A Cultural History of the U.S. Supreme Court* (New York: Rowman & Littlefield, 1998), 14.
52. Charles Turner, "1773 Election Sermon," in *They Preached Liberty,* ed. Franklin P. Cole (Indianapolis, Ind.: Liberty Press), 51.
53. Jonathan Boucher, *A View of the Causes and Consequences of the American Revolution* (1797; repr., New York: Russell & Russell, 1967), 505.

54. Phillips Payson, "1778 Election Sermon," in *The Pulpit of the American Revolution*, ed. John Wingate Thornton (New York: Da Capo Press, 1970), 330.

55. Samuel West, "1776 Election Sermon," in Thornton, *Pulpit*, 276–278.

56. Harry V. Jaffa, *A New Birth of Freedom* (Lanham, Md.: Rowman & Littlefield, 2000), 135, 144–146.

57. Ibid., 144, 145.

58. Steven M. Dworetz, *The Unvarnished Doctrine: Locke, Liberalism, and the American Revolution* (Durham, N.C.: Duke University Press, 1990), 156, 155.

59. Samuel Seabury, *St. Peter's Exhortation to Fear God and Honor the King, Explained and Inculcated* (New York: H. Gaine, 1777), 15, quoted in Nancy L. Rhoden, *Revolutionary Anglicanism* (New York: New York University Press, 1999), 68–69.

60. Seabury, *St. Peter's*, 12, quoted in Rhoden, *Revolutionary*, 76; Boucher, *View*, 508.

61. John Calvin, "On Civil Government," bk. 4, chap. 20 of *Institutes of the Christian Religion*, in *Luther and Calvin on Secular Authority*, trans. and ed. Harro Hopfl (Cambridge: Cambridge University Press, 1991), 76, 79.

62. Ibid., 76, 78, 80, 75.

63. Ibid., 82.

64. Ibid., 82–83.

65. Dworetz, *Unvarnished Doctrine*, 172.

66. Samuel Cooke, "1770 Election Sermon," in Thornton, *Pulpit*, 159, 162, 171.

67. West, "1776 Election Sermon," 272.

68. Ibid., 275, 285, 312, 321.

69. Simeon Howard, "1780 Election Sermon," in Thornton, *Pulpit*, 372; John Tucker, "Election Day Sermon of 1771," in *American Political Writing during the Founding Era 1760–1805*, ed. Charles Hyneman and Donald Lutz (Indianapolis, Ind.: Liberty Fund, 1983), 161.

70. Gad Hitchcock, "1774 Election Sermon," in Hyneman and Lutz, *American Political Writing*, 285.

71. Samuel Cooper, "A Sermon on the Day of the Commencement of the Constitution," in *Political Sermons of the American Founding Era*, ed. Ellis Sandoz (Indianapolis, Ind.: Liberty Press, 1991), 637.

72. Ibid., 639.

73. Dworetz, *Unvarnished Doctrine*, 183.

74. E.g., Jack Scott, "Introduction," in John Witherspoon, *Lectures on Moral Philosophy*, ed. Jack Scott (Newark: University of Delaware Press, 1982), 47; Morgan, "American Revolution," 14; Stokes, *Church and State*, 1:279; Richey, "Jonathan Mayhew," 298; Baldwin, *New England Clergy*, 7–8; Bonomi, *Under the Cope*, 212; Dean Hammer, *The Puritan Tradition in Revolutionary, Federalist, and Whig Political Theory* (New York: Peter Lang, 1998), 100–101; Conrad Wright, *The Liberal Christians* (Boston: Beacon Press, 1970), 11.

75. Baldwin, *New England Clergy*, 7–8; Hammer, *Puritan*, 100–101.

76. Michael P. Zuckert, *The Natural Rights Republic* (Notre Dame, Ind.: University of Notre Dame Press, 1996), 150, 159.

77. Ibid., 195; Hammer, *Puritan*, 101.

78. Dworetz, *Unvarnished Doctrine*, 32, 182–183; 138–148; 32, 135, 182.

79. Zuckert, *Natural Rights,* 172.

80. Ibid., 176.

81. Ibid., 176–178, 178–179, 180–181.

82. Ibid., 199.

83. Cooke, "1770 Election Sermon," 158; Howard, "1780 Election Sermon," 362–363; Tucker, "Election Day Sermon," 165; Hitchcock, "1774 Election Sermon," 292.

84. Moses Mather, "America's Appeal to the Impartial World," in Sandoz, *Political Sermons,* 446.

85. Zabdiel Adams, "1782 Election Sermon," in Hyneman and Lutz, *American Political Writing,* 553.

86. West, "1776 Election Sermon," 267–268, 270, 271.

87. Walter Berns, "Religion and the Founding Principle," in *The Moral Foundations of the American Republic,* 3rd ed., ed. Robert H. Horwitz (Charlottesville: University Press of Virginia, 1986), 215.

88. West, "1776 Election Sermon," 270, 279; Cooke, "1770 Election Sermon," 158.

89. Cooke, "1770 Election Sermon," 162.

90. Ibid., 163, 186; Howard, "1780 Election Sermon," 362; Tucker, "Election Day Sermon," 162; Cooper, "Sermon," 637.

91. West, "1776 Election Sermon," 305; Tucker, "Election Day Sermon," 162; Mather, "America's Appeal," 447.

92. Cooke, "1770 Election Sermon," 159; Mather, "America's Appeal," 474.

93. West, "1776 Election Sermon," 276.

94. Tucker, "Election Day Sermon," 162.

95. Ezra Stiles, "1783 Election Sermon," in Thornton, *Pulpit,* 402; Hitchcock, "1774 Election Sermon," 283; Adams, "1782 Election Sermon," 540, 549, 544.

96. Bonomi, *Under the Cope,* 212; Hitchcock, "1774 Election Sermon," 289; West, "1776 Election Sermon," 285, 283, 312, 279.

97. John Locke, *Two Treatises of Government,* ed. Peter Laslett (Cambridge: Cambridge University Press, 1988) [Second Treatise, chap. 2, sec. 6], 271.

98. Payson, "1778 Election Sermon," 330, 343, 350; Stiles, "1783 Election Sermon," 419; Samuel Langdon, "The Republic of the Israelites an Example to the American States," in Sandoz, *Political Sermons, 959.*

99. Howard, "1780 Election Sermon," 364, 386; Adams, "1782 Election Sermon," 543.

100. Mather, "America's Appeal," 486.

101. Tucker, "Election Day Sermon," 161.

102. Ibid., 162.

103. Ibid., 163.

104. Ibid., 161.

105. Hitchcock, "1774 Election Sermon," 288, 292.

106. West, "1776 Election Sermon," 286.

107. Ibid., 275, 274.

108. Ibid., 275.

109. Cooke, "1770 Election Sermon," 157, 159.

110. Samuel Langdon, "1775 Election Sermon," in Thornton, *Pulpit,* 240, 250.

111. Howard, "1780 Election Sermon," 384.

112. Adams, "1782 Election Sermon," 544.

113. Stiles, "1783 Election Sermon," 423; Hitchcock, "1774 Election Sermon," 289; Mather, "America's Appeal," 446; Cooper, "Sermon," 637.

114. Howard, "1780 Election Sermon," 373; Hitchcock, "1774 Election Sermon," 289.

115. Mather, "America's Appeal," 451, 452; West, "1776 Election Sermon," 276; Tucker, "Election Day Sermon," 162.

116. Cooper, "Sermon," 634–635; Stiles, "1783 Election Sermon," 402.

117. Cooke, "1770 Election Sermon," 159; Howard, "1780 Election Sermon," 364; Langdon, "Republic," 959.

118. Payson, "1778 Election Sermon," 343, 350; Langdon, "1775 Election Sermon," 250; Cooke, "1770 Election Sermon," 162.

119. Cooke, "1770 Election Sermon," 159, 164, 161; Langdon, "1775 Election Sermon," 240.

120. West, "1776 Election Sermon," 267, 294, 270, 273, 277, 282, 283, 276, 274.

121. Payson, "1778 Election Sermon," 330; Tucker, "Election Day Sermon," 161, 164, 165.

122. Cooper, "Sermon," 637, 643; Adams, "1782 Election Sermon," 550; Mather, "America's Appeal," 486, 448.

123. Langdon, "1775 Election Sermon," 250; West, "1776 Election Sermon," 304; Tucker, "Election Day Sermon," 162; Adams, "1782 Election Sermon," 549; Mather, "America's Appeal," 486.

124. West, "1776 Election Sermon," 270; Mather, "America's Appeal," 456; Howard, "1780 Election Sermon," 373–374.

125. Adams, "1782 Election Sermon," 558.

126. West, "1776 Election Sermon," 274; Payson, "1778 Election Sermon," 330; Tucker, "Election Day Sermon," 159; Payson, "1778 Election Sermon," 339; Cooke, "1770 Election Sermon," 166.

127. Payson, "1778 Election Sermon," 330; Tucker, "Election Day Sermon," 159.

128. West, "1776 Election Sermon," 278, 285; Stiles, "1783 Election Sermon," 421–422.

129. Adams, "1782 Election Sermon," 543.

130. West, "1776 Election Sermon," 279.

131. Mather, "America's Appeal," 450; West, "1776 Election Sermon," 280; Stiles, "1783 Election Sermon," 414.

132. Payson, "1778 Election Sermon," 335, 349; Howard, "1780 Election Sermon," 364; Stiles, "1783 Election Sermon," 420, 510, 421, 510; Payson, "1778 Election Sermon," 330.

133. Cooke, "1770 Election Sermon," 159; Langdon, "1775 Election Sermon," 244; Payson, "1778 Election Sermon," 331.

134. Langdon, "1775 Election Sermon," 239; Howard, "1780 Election Sermon," 360–361, 365.

135. Langdon, "Republic," 947; Howard, "1780 Election Sermon," 360; Langdon, "Republic," 951; Cooper, "Sermon," 634–635.

136. Cooper, "Sermon," 635.

137. Langdon, "Republic," 948, 952, 955; Howard, "1780 Election Sermon," 361.

138. Howard, "1780 Election Sermon," 365.

139. Ibid., 360, 361; Langdon, "Republic," 946–947.

140. Adams, "1782 Election Sermon," 540.

141. Tucker, "Election Day Sermon," 171.

142. West, "1776 Election Sermon," 284, 292, 281, 290, 296, 291.

143. Zuckert, *Natural Rights*, 177.

144. West, "1776 Election Sermon," 278, 274–275.

145. Ibid., 284.

146. Tucker, "Election Day Sermon," 164; Hitchcock, "1774 Election Sermon," 289; Mather, "America's Appeal," 456; West, "1776 Election Sermon," 281; 286–287, 282; 279–280.

147. Langdon, "1775 Election Sermon," 250; West, "1776 Election Sermon," 278, 285.

148. Stiles, "1783 Election Sermon," 414.

149. Locke, *Two Treatises*, 404.

150. Noll, *Christians*, 168.

CHAPTER FOUR. THE THEISTIC RATIONALISM OF JOHN ADAMS

1. See, e.g., Jeffrey Cohen and David Nice, *The Presidency* (Boston: McGraw-Hill, 2003), ix, 15; Robert C. Hartnett, "The Religion of the Founding Fathers," in *Wellsprings of the American Spirit,* ed. F. Ernest Johnson (New York: Institute for Religious and Social Studies, 1948), 49.

2. July 8, 1820, letter to Samuel Miller, in John Adams, *The Works of John Adams,* ed. Charles Francis Adams (Boston: Little, Brown, 1850–1856), 10:389–390.

3. E.g., December 3, 1813, letter to Thomas Jefferson, in *The Adams-Jefferson Letters,* ed. Lester J. Cappon (Chapel Hill: University of North Carolina Press, 1959), 2:406; December 25, 1813, letter to Jefferson, in *Adams-Jefferson Letters,* 2:412; June 28, 1812, letter to Jefferson, in *Adams-Jefferson Letters,* 2:309; September 14, 1813, letter to Jefferson, in *Adams-Jefferson Letters,* 2:374; May 3, 1816, letter to Jefferson, in *Adams-Jefferson Letters,* 2:471; March 2, 1756, entry, in John Adams, *Diary and Autobiography of John Adams,* ed. L. H. Butterfield (New York: Atheneum, 1964), 1:11.

4. May 1, 1756, entry, in *Diary,* 1:24.

5. June 28, 1812, letter to Jefferson, in *Adams-Jefferson Letters,* 2:309.

6. March 2, 1816, letter to Jefferson, in *Adams-Jefferson Letters,* 2:465; May 3, 1816, letter to Jefferson, in *Adams-Jefferson Letters,* 2:471.

7. August 9, 1816, letter to Jefferson, in *Adams-Jefferson Letters,* 2:486; September 14, 1813, letter to Jefferson, in *Adams-Jefferson Letters,* 3:374; December 3, 1813, letter to Jefferson, in *Adams-Jefferson Letters,* 2:406; June 28, 1812, letter to Jefferson, in *Adams-Jefferson Letters,* 3:310; Norman Cousins, ed., *The Republic of Reason* (San Francisco: Harper & Row, 1988), 75.

8. March 2, 1756, entry, in *Diary,* 1:11.

9. November 29, 1812, letter to Benjamin Rush, in *The Spur of Fame: Dialogues of John Adams and Benjamin Rush, 1805–1813,* ed. John A. Schutz and Douglass Adair (San Marino, Calif.: Huntington Library, 1966), 255.

10. August 29, 1756, letter to Richard Cranch, in *Papers of John Adams,* ed. Robert J. Taylor (Cambridge, Mass.: Belknap Press of Harvard University Press, 1977–2010), 1:16.

11. "Novanglus" [1774], in *Works of John Adams*, 4:22; "Discourses on Davila" [1790–1791], in *Works of John Adams*, 6:395; "To the Officers of the First Brigade of the Third Division of the Militia of Massachusetts," October 11, 1798, in *Works of John Adams*, 9:228; July 23, 1806, letter to Benjamin Rush, in Rush, *Spur of Fame*, 61–62.

12. July 13, 1815, letter to F. A. Van der Kemp, in *Works of John Adams*, 10:168; December 27, 1816, letter to F. A. Van der Kemp, in *Works of John Adams*, 10:235; January 21, 1810, letter to Benjamin Rush, in *Works of John Adams*, 9:627; "A Dissertation on the Canon and Feudal Law," in *Works of John Adams*, 3:452; "Diary" entry on February 22, 1756, in *Works of John Adams*, 2:6–7.

13. February 2, 1807, letter to Benjamin Rush, in Rush, *Spur of Fame*, 75–76; December 25, 1813, letter to Jefferson, in *Adams-Jefferson Letters*, 2:412; John Adams, "A Defence of the Constitutions of Government of the United States of America," in *Works of John Adams*, 6:61.

14. E.g., December 25, 1813, letter to Jefferson, in *Adams-Jefferson Letters*, 2:413; December 3, 1813, letter to Jefferson, in *Adams-Jefferson Letters*, 2:405.

15. March 2, 1756, entry, in *Diary*, 1:11.

16. December 27, 1816, letter to F. A. Van der Kemp, in *Works of John Adams*, 10:235.

17. July 8, 1820, letter to Samuel Miller, in *Works of John Adams*, 10:390; December 27, 1816, letter to F. A. Van der Kemp, in *Works of John Adams*, 10:234; February 2, 1816, letter to Jefferson, in *Adams-Jefferson Letters*, 2:462.

18. February 13, 1756, entry, in *Diary*, 1:6.

19. March 17, 1756, entry, in *Diary*, 1:14–15; Henry F. May, *The Enlightenment in America* (New York: Oxford University Press, 1976), 280.

20. April 25, 1756, entry, in *Diary*, 1:22.

21. January 21, 1810, letter to Benjamin Rush, in *Works of John Adams*, 9:627.

22. "Novanglus," in *Works of John Adams*, 4:55.

23. Ibid., 56.

24. June 28, 1813, letter to Jefferson, in *Adams-Jefferson Letters*, 2:339–340.

25. Ibid., 2:340.

26. January 23, 1825, letter to Jefferson, in *Adams-Jefferson Letters*, 2:608; February 2, 1816, letter to Jefferson, in *Adams-Jefferson Letters*, 2:461; November 14, 1813, letter to Jefferson, in *Adams-Jefferson Letters*, 2:397.

27. November 4, 1816, letter to Jefferson, in *Adams-Jefferson Letters*, 2:494.

28. May 3, 1816, letter to Jefferson, in *Adams-Jefferson Letters*, 2:470–471; December 27, 1816, letter to F. A. Van der Kemp, in *Works of John Adams*, 10:236.

29. August 9, 1816, letter to Jefferson, in *Adams-Jefferson Letters*, 2:486.

30. Ibid., 2:487.

31. February[–March 3], 1814, letter to Jefferson, in *Adams-Jefferson Letters*, 2:428; July 8, 1820, letter to Samuel Miller, in *Works of John Adams*, 10:390.

32. July 13, 1815, letter to F. A. Van der Kemp, in *Works of John Adams*, 10:170.

33. July 8, 1820, letter to Samuel Miller, in *Works of John Adams*, 10:390; August 9, 1816, letter to Jefferson, in *Adams-Jefferson Letters*, 2:486; "Diary" entry on February 16, 1756, in *Works of John Adams*, 2:5; December 25, 1813, letter to Jefferson, in *Adams-Jefferson Letters*, 2:413; July 8, 1820, letter to Samuel Miller, in *Works of John Adams*, 10:390.

34. May 3, 1816, letter to Jefferson, in *Adams-Jefferson Letters*, 2:471.

35. July 23, 1806, letter to Benjamin Rush, in Rush, *Spur of Fame*, 65.

36. July 16, 1814, letter to Jefferson, in *Adams-Jefferson Letters*, 2:435.

37. February 2, 1816, letter to Jefferson, in *Adams-Jefferson Letters*, 2:462.

38. Adams, *Diary and Autobiography*, 3:262.

39. July 8, 1820, letter to Samuel Miller, in *Works of John Adams*, 10:389.

40. April 22, 1761, letter to Samuel Quincy, in *Papers of John Adams*, 1:49.

41. April 19, 1817, letter to Jefferson, in *Adams-Jefferson Letters*, 2:509.

42. December 21, 1819, letter to Jefferson, in *Adams-Jefferson Letters*, 2:551.

43. September 14, 1813, letter to Jefferson, in *Adams-Jefferson Letters*, 2:373–374.

44. March 10, 1823, letter to Jefferson, in *Adams-Jefferson Letters*, 2:590.

45. July 16, 1813, letter to Jefferson, in *Adams-Jefferson Letters*, 2:360.

46. July 13, 1815, letter to F. A. Van der Kemp, in *Works of John Adams*, 10:168; March 2, 1816, letter to Jefferson, in *Adams-Jefferson Letters*, 2:464–465.

47. February 18, 1756, entry, in *Diary*, 1:8.

48. July 13, 1815, letter to F. A. Van der Kemp, in *Works of John Adams*, 10:170.

49. November 4, 1816, letter to Jefferson, in *Adams-Jefferson Letters*, 2:494; July 16, 1813, letter to Jefferson, in *Adams-Jefferson Letters*, 2:360.

50. December 27, 1816, letter to F. A. Van der Kemp, in *Works of John Adams*, 10:234.

51. July 8, 1820, letter to Samuel Miller, in *Works of John Adams*, 10:390.

52. Adams, *Diary and Autobiography*, 3:262; October 18, 1756, letter to Richard Cranch, in *Papers of John Adams*, 1:17.

53. July 18, 1813, letter to Jefferson, in *Adams-Jefferson Letters*, 2:361.

54. April 18, 1808, letter to Benjamin Rush, in Rush, *Spur of Fame*, 106.

55. Letter no. 13 to John Taylor (1814), in *Works of John Adams*, 6:474.

56. December 25, 1813, letter to Jefferson, in *Adams-Jefferson Letters*, 2:412.

57. Ibid.

58. March 2, 1816, letter to Jefferson, in *Adams-Jefferson Letters*, 2:465.

59. January 21, 1810, letter to Benjamin Rush, in *Works of John Adams*, 9:627.

60. December 3, 1813, letter to Jefferson, in *Adams-Jefferson Letters*, 2:406.

61. December 25, 1813, letter to Jefferson, in *Adams-Jefferson Letters*, 2:411.

62. Paul K. Conkin, "Priestley and Jefferson: Unitarianism as a Religion for a New Revolutionary Age," in *Religion in a Revolutionary Age,* ed. Ronald Hoffman and Peter J. Albert (Charlottesville: University Press of Virginia, 1994), 304; United First Parish Church, "A Brief History," July 21, 2003, available at http://www.ufpc.org/history.htm.

63. December 21, 1809, letter to Benjamin Rush, in John Adams, Alexander Biddle, Thomas Jefferson, and Benjamin Rush, *Old Family Letters: Copied from the Originals for Alexander Biddle* (Philadelphia: J. B. Lippincott, 1892), A:248–249.

64. September 14, 1813, letter to Jefferson, in *Adams-Jefferson Letters*, 2:373.

65. February [–March], 1814, letter to Jefferson, in *Adams-Jefferson Letters*, 2:429; November 14, 1813, letter to Jefferson, in *Adams-Jefferson Letters*, 2:395–396; January 23, 1825, letter to Jefferson, in *Adams-Jefferson Letters*, 2:608.

66. September 24, 1821, letter to Jefferson, in *Adams-Jefferson Letters*, 2:576.

67. December 25, 1813, letter to Jefferson, in *Adams-Jefferson Letters*, 2:412; July 13, 1815, letter to F. A. Van der Kemp, in *Works of John Adams*, 10:169–170.

68. February 2, 1807, letter to Benjamin Rush, in Rush, *Spur of Fame*, 76.

69. June 21, 1776, letter to Zabdiel Adams, in *Works of John Adams*, 9:401.

70. December 21, 1819, letter to Jefferson, in *Adams-Jefferson Letters*, 2:550; August 28, 1811, letter to Rush, in *Works of John Adams*, 9:636; February 16, 1809, letter to F. A. Van der Kemp, in *Works of John Adams*, 9:610.

71. "To the Officers of the First Brigade of the Third Division of the Militia of Massachusetts," October 11, 1798, in *Works of John Adams*, 9:229.

72. August 14, 1796, entry, in *Diary*, 3:240–241.

CHAPTER FIVE. THE THEISTIC RATIONALISM OF THOMAS JEFFERSON AND BENJAMIN FRANKLIN

1. Stephen A. Marini, "Religion, Politics, and Ratification," in *Religion in a Revolutionary Age*, ed. Ronald Hoffman and Peter J. Albert (Charlottesville: University Press of Virginia, 1994), 196.

2. July 16, 1814, letter to Jefferson, in *The Adams-Jefferson Letters*, ed. Lester J. Cappon (Chapel Hill: University of North Carolina Press, 1959), 2:435; July 16, 1813, letter to Jefferson, in *Adams-Jefferson Letters*, 2:360.

3. July 18, 1813, letter to Jefferson, in *Adams-Jefferson Letters*, 2:362.

4. August 22, 1813, letter to Adams, in *Adams-Jefferson Letters*, 2:368.

5. E.g., Kerry S. Walters, *The American Deists* (Lawrence: University Press of Kansas, 1992), 14, 15–16, 22, 27, 31; Russel Blaine Nye, *The Cultural Life of the New Nation* (New York: Harper & Row, 1960), 211.

6. Walters, *American Deists*, 27.

7. E.g., June 13, 1814, letter to Thomas Law, in Thomas Jefferson, *The Writings of Thomas Jefferson*, ed. H. A. Washington (Washington, D.C.: Taylor & Maury, 1853–1854), 6:348; February 27, 1821, letter to Timothy Pickering, in *Writings of Thomas Jefferson*, 7:211; October 14, 1816, letter to John Adams, in *Adams-Jefferson Letters*, 2:492; April 11, 1823, letter to Adams, in *Adams-Jefferson Letters*, 2:592–594.

8. E.g., Heb. 1:2; Col. 1:16; 1 Cor. 8:6.

9. Benjamin Franklin, "Autobiography," in *The Works of Benjamin Franklin*, ed. Jared Sparks (Boston: Tappan & Whittemore, 1837–1844), 1:103.

10. Benjamin Franklin, "Articles of Belief and Acts of Religion" (1728), in *The Papers of Benjamin Franklin*, ed. Leonard W. Labaree (New Haven, Conn.: Yale University Press, 1959–2006), 1:101, 104–105.

11. Franklin, "Autobiography," 1:119; March 9, 1790, letter to Ezra Stiles, in *Works of Benjamin Franklin*, 10:423; July 17, 1771, letter to Jane Mecom, in *Papers of Benjamin Franklin*, 18:185.

12. Benjamin Franklin, "On the Providence of God in the Government of the World" (1732), in *Papers of Benjamin Franklin*, 1:265–266.

13. Franklin, "Articles of Belief," 1:103, 105–106.

14. July 28, 1743, letter to Jane Mecom, in *Papers of Benjamin Franklin*, 2:385; June 6, 1753, letter to Joseph Huey, in *Papers of Benjamin Franklin*, 4:505; Franklin, "Autobiography," 1:119; March 9, 1790, letter to Ezra Stiles, in *Works of Benjamin Franklin*, 10:423; Franklin, "Doctrine to Be Preached," in *Papers of Benjamin Franklin*, 1:213.

15. July 15, 1763, letter to John Page, in *The Works of Thomas Jefferson*, ed. Paul Leicester Ford (New York: G. P. Putnam's Sons, 1904–1905), 1:443; April 11,

1823, letter to John Adams, in *Adams-Jefferson Letters,* 2:592; October 17, 1808, letter to the members of the Baltimore Baptist Association, in *Writings of Thomas Jefferson,* 8:138, 137.

16. Thomas Jefferson, *Jefferson's Notes, on the State of Virginia* (Baltimore, Md.: W. Pechin, 1800), 164.

17. Ibid.

18. December 5, 1801, letter to the Reverend Isaac Story, in *The Papers of Thomas Jefferson,* ed. Julian P. Boyd, L. H. Butterfield, Charles T. Cullen, and John Catanzariti (Princeton, N.J.: Princeton University Press, 1950–2009), 36:30; August 10, 1787, letter to Peter Carr, in *Papers of Thomas Jefferson,* 12:16.

19. October 17, 1808, letter to the members of the Baltimore Baptist Association, in *Writings of Thomas Jefferson,* 8:138; November 13, 1818, letter to Adams, in *Adams-Jefferson Letters,* 2:529; September 26, 1814, letter to Miles King, in *Writings of Thomas Jefferson,* 6:388.

20. Franklin, "Autobiography," 1:74–75.

21. Ibid., 1:75–76.

22. E.g., Franklin, "Autobiography," 1:76, 1:119; March 9, 1790, letter to Ezra Stiles in *Works of Benjamin Franklin,* 10:423.

23. November 9, 1779, letter to Benjamin Vaughan, in *Papers of Benjamin Franklin,* 31:59; Benjamin Franklin, "The Lord's Prayer Revised," in *Works of Benjamin Franklin,* 1:77n–79n.

24. Franklin, "On the Providence," 1:266; Franklin, "Articles of Belief," 1:103; Benjamin Franklin, "Proposals Relating to the Education of Youth in Pensilvania [*sic*]" [1749], in *Papers of Benjamin Franklin,* 3:416; Franklin, "Poor Richard" (1734), in *Papers of Benjamin Franklin,* 1:350.

25. Franklin, "Autobiography," 1:114; February 24, 1786, letter to Jonathan Shipley, in *Works of Benjamin Franklin,* 10:251; Franklin, "Poor Richard" [1746], in *Papers of Benjamin Franklin,* 3:66 (translation by Labaree).

26. December 13, 1757, letter to an unknown person, in *Papers of Benjamin Franklin,* 7:294.

27. Franklin, "Articles of Belief," 1:103–105; February 24, 1786, letter to Jonathan Shipley, in *Works of Benjamin Franklin,* 10:252; March 9, 1790, letter to Ezra Stiles, in *Works of Benjamin Franklin,* 10:423.

28. August 19, 1784, letter to William Strahan, in *Works of Benjamin Franklin,* 10:129.

29. Benjamin Franklin, "A Comparison of the Conduct of the Ancient Jews and of the Anti-Federalists in the United States of America," in *Works of Benjamin Franklin,* 5:162.

30. 1788 letter to John Langdon, in *Benjamin Franklin, Writings,* ed. J. A. Leo Lemay (New York: Library of America, 1987), 1170.

31. Franklin quoted in Max Farrand, ed., *The Records of the Federal Convention of 1787* (New Haven, Conn.: Yale University Press, 1966), 1:451.

32. Ibid.; Herbert J. Storing, "The Federal Convention of 1787," in *The American Founding,* ed. Ralph A. Rossum and Gary L. McDowell (Port Washington, N.Y.: Kennikat Press, 1981), 24.

33. Franklin, "On the Providence," 1:267.

34. Ibid., 1:267–268.

35. Ibid., 1:266, 268.

36. Ibid., 1:268.

37. Ibid., 1:269.

38. Ibid.

39. E.g., Franklin, "Autobiography," 1:119; Franklin, "Doctrine to Be Preached," 1:213; Franklin, "Lord's Prayer Revised," 1:77n–79n; Franklin, "Autobiography," 1:104, 111; Franklin, "Articles of Belief," 1:104–105, 107–109.

40. Farrand, *Records,* 1:451–452.

41. Storing, "Federal Convention," 24.

42. Farrand, *Records,* 3:471–473.

43. Jared Sparks's Journal Notes of Visit with Madison (April 19, 1830), in Farrand, *Records,* 3:479; April 8, 1831, letter from Madison to Sparks, in Farrand, *Records,* 3:499; January 6, 1834, letter from Madison to Thomas S. Grimke, in Farrand, *Records,* 3:531.

44. Franklin quoted in Jared Sparks, *The Life of Benjamin Franklin* (Boston: Whittemore, Niles, and Hall, 1857), 515.

45. A Friend to *Real* Religion [anonymous], "A Vindication of the Religion of Mr. Jefferson, and a Statement of His Services in the Cause of Religious Liberty," attached to Jefferson, *Jefferson's Notes,* 18.

46. Kerry S. Walters, *Rational Infidels: The American Deists* (Durango, Colo.: Longwood Academic, 1992), 166–167.

47. September 26, 1814, letter to Miles King, in *Writings of Thomas Jefferson,* 6:387–388.

48. December 5, 1801, letter to the Reverend Isaac Story, in *Papers of Thomas Jefferson,* 36:30.

49. January 24, 1814, letter to Adams, in *Adams-Jefferson Letters,* 2:421; October 12, 1813, letter to Adams, in *Adams-Jefferson Letters,* 2:385.

50. August 4, 1820, letter to William Short, in *Writings of Thomas Jefferson,* 7:166.

51. E.g., ibid., and October 31, 1819, letter to William Short, in *Works of Thomas Jefferson,* 12:142; July 19, 1822, letter to Benjamin Waterhouse, in *Works of Thomas Jefferson,* 12:244; April 11, 1823, letter to Adams, in *Adams-Jefferson Letters,* 2:594, 593.

52. January 9, 1816, letter to Charles Thomson, in *Works of Thomas Jefferson,* 11:498.

53. April 11, 1823, letter to John Adams, in *Adams-Jefferson Letters,* 2:591.

54. January 24, 1814, letter to John Adams, in *Adams-Jefferson Letters,* 2:421.

55. October 12, 1813, letter to John Adams, in *Adams-Jefferson Letters,* 2:384.

56. E.g., January 24, 1814, letter to John Adams in *Adams-Jefferson Letters,* 2:421; April 25, 1816, letter to F. A. Van der Kemp, in *Writings of Thomas Jefferson,* 6:594; October 31, 1819, letter to William Short, in *Works of Thomas Jefferson,* 12:141.

57. October 31, 1819, letter to William Short, in *Works of Thomas Jefferson,* 12:142; August 4, 1820, letter to William Short, in *Writings of Thomas Jefferson,* 7:166.

58. January 24, 1814, letter to John Adams, in *Adams-Jefferson Letters,* 2:421; October 31, 1819, letter to William Short, in *Works of Thomas Jefferson,* 12:142; April 25, 1816, letter to F. A. Van der Kemp, in *Writings of Thomas Jefferson,* 6:594; April 13, 1820, letter to William Short, in *Writings of Thomas Jefferson,* 7:156.

59. August 4, 1820, letter to William Short, in *Writings of Thomas Jefferson,* 7:166.

60. Ibid., 7:165–166; April 13, 1820, letter to William Short, in *Writings of Thomas Jefferson,* 7:156; August 4, 1820, letter to William Short, in *Writings of Thomas Jefferson,* 7:168; August 10, 1787, letter to Peter Carr, in *Papers of Thomas Jefferson,* 12:17.

61. April 13, 1820, letter to William Short, in *Writings of Thomas Jefferson,* 7:156.

62. Ibid.

63. April 9, 1803, letter to Joseph Priestley, in *Works of Thomas Jefferson,* 9:458.

64. Thomas Jefferson, "Syllabus of an Estimate of the Merit of the Doctrines of Jesus, Compared with Those of Others," in *Works of Thomas Jefferson,* 9:462; August 4, 1820, letter to William Short, in *Writings of Thomas Jefferson,* 7:167.

65. August 4, 1820, letter to William Short, in *Writings of Thomas Jefferson,* 7:167.

66. Jefferson, "Syllabus," 9:462.

67. October 31, 1819, letter to William Short, in *Works of Thomas Jefferson,* 12:142.

68. January 9, 1816, letter to Charles Thomson, in *Works of Thomas Jefferson,* 11:499; October 31, 1819, letter to William Short, in *Works of Thomas Jefferson,* 12:142.

69. April 9, 1803, letter to Joseph Priestley, in *Works of Thomas Jefferson,* 9:458.

70. December 8, 1822, letter to James Smith, in *Writings of Thomas Jefferson,* 7:270; February 27, 1821, letter to Timothy Pickering, in *Writings of Thomas Jefferson,* 7:210.

71. September 26, 1814, letter to Miles King, in *Writings of Thomas Jefferson,* 6:387.

72. August 10, 1787, letter to Peter Carr, in *Papers of Thomas Jefferson,* 12:15–16.

73. Ibid., 12:15, 16, 17.

74. August 4, 1820, letter to William Short, in *Writings of Thomas Jefferson,* 7:165.

75. Franklin, "Autobiography," 1:76–77.

76. E.g., Benjamin Franklin, "Compassion and Regard for the Sick" [March 25, 1731], in *Benjamin Franklin, Writings,* 169–170; Franklin, "Dialogue between Two Presbyterians," in *Papers of Benjamin Franklin,* 2:30; April 13, 1738, letter to Josiah and Abiah Franklin, in *Papers of Benjamin Franklin,* 2:204; Franklin, "Autobiography," 1:115; 1745 letter to John Franklin, in *Papers of Benjamin Franklin,* 3:27; November 8, 1764, letter to Sarah Franklin, in *Papers of Benjamin Franklin,* 11:449.

77. Franklin, "Articles of Belief," 1:105–106.

78. Franklin, "On the Providence," 1:265.

79. Franklin, "A Parable against Persecution," in *Papers of Benjamin Franklin,* 6:122–123; Sparks, *Life of Benjamin Franklin,* 251–252.

80. Franklin quoted in Sparks, *Life of Benjamin Franklin,* 173; Franklin, "Lord's Prayer Revised," 1:79n; August 21, 1784, letter to Joseph Priestley in *Works of Benjamin Franklin,* 10:134.

81. E.g., January 9, 1816, letter to Charles Thomson, in *Works of Thomas Jefferson,* 11:498; April 21, 1803, letter to Benjamin Rush, in *Works of Thomas Jefferson,* 9:457n.

82. April 21, 1803, letter to Benjamin Rush, in *Works of Thomas Jefferson,* 9:457n; October 12, 1813, letter to Adams, in *Adams-Jefferson Letters,* 2:384.

83. November 4, 1820, letter to Jared Sparks, in *Writings of Thomas Jefferson,* 7:185; April 21, 1803, letter to Benjamin Rush, in *Works of Thomas Jefferson,* 9:457n; October 12, 1813, letter to Adams, in *Adams-Jefferson Letters* 2:384; January 9, 1816, letter to Charles Thomson, in *Works of Thomas Jefferson,* 11:498; April 21, 1803, letter to Rush, in *Works of Thomas Jefferson,* 9:457n; September 23, 1800, letter to Rush, in *Papers of Thomas Jefferson,* 32:167.

84. October 31, 1819, letter to William Short, in *Works of Thomas Jefferson,* 12:142, 142n.

85. Franklin, "Proposals," 3:413; Franklin, "Compassion," 170; Alfred Owen Aldridge, *Benjamin Franklin and Nature's God* (Durham, N.C.: Duke University Press, 1967), 270; Franklin, "Lord's Prayer Revised," 1:78.

86. Franklin, "Autobiography," 1:139; Sparks, *Life of Benjamin Franklin,* 517; March 9, 1790, letter to Ezra Stiles, in *Works of Benjamin Franklin,* 10:424.

87. Franklin, "Dialogue," 2:32.

88. June 11, 1760, letter to Miss Mary Stevenson, in *Papers of Benjamin Franklin,* 9:121; Franklin, "Autobiography," 1:103, 119; March 9, 1790, letter to Ezra Stiles, in *Works of Benjamin Franklin,* 10:423; Franklin, "Doctrine to Be Preached," 1:213; Franklin, "Articles of Belief," 1:103–105, 105.

89. Sparks, *Life of Benjamin Franklin,* 516–517.

90. Franklin, "Autobiography," 1:76–77, 125.

91. Melvin H. Buxbaum, *Benjamin Franklin and the Zealous Presbyterians* (University Park: Pennsylvania State University Press, 1975), 95, 99, 102.

92. Franklin, "Dialogue," 2:29.

93. Ibid., 30.

94. Ibid., 33.

95. April 13, 1738, letter to Josiah and Abiah Franklin, in *Papers of Benjamin Franklin,* 2:204.

96. June 6, 1753, letter to Joseph Huey, in *Papers of Benjamin Franklin,* 4:505–506.

97. Acts 4:12; John 14:6.

98. Franklin, "Proposals," 3:413; December 13, 1757, letter to an unknown person, in *Papers of Benjamin Franklin,* 7:295.

99. Franklin, "Autobiography," 1:104, 136.

100. Ibid., 1:120–121.

101. Franklin quoted in Sparks, *Life of Benjamin Franklin,* 352; November 8, 1764, letter to his daughter Sarah Franklin, in *Papers of Benjamin Franklin,* 11:449–450; Franklin, "Autobiography," 1:103–104, 126.

102. Aldridge, *Benjamin Franklin,* 270, 271.

103. April 25, 1816, letter to F. A. Van der Kemp, in *Writings of Thomas Jefferson,* 6:594; October 31, 1819, letter to William Short, in *Works of Thomas Jefferson,* 12:142; April 9, 1803, letter to Joseph Priestley, in *Works of Thomas Jefferson,* 9:458, 459.

104. September 18, 1813, letter to William Canby, in *Writings of Thomas Jefferson*, 6:210; November 4, 1820, letter to Jared Sparks, in *Writings of Thomas Jefferson*, 7:185; April 13, 1820, letter to William Short, in *Writings of Thomas Jefferson*, 7:156.

105. September 27, 1809, letter to James Fishback, in *Writings of Thomas Jefferson*, 5:471; April 19, 1803, letter to Edward Dowse, in *Writings of Thomas Jefferson*, 4:477.

106. January 19, 1810, letter to Samuel Kercheval, in *Writings of Thomas Jefferson*, 5:492; January 9, 1816, letter to Charles Thomson, in *Works of Thomas Jefferson*, 11:499; April 13, 1820, letter to William Short, in *Writings of Thomas Jefferson*, 7:155; June 25, 1819, letter to Ezra Stiles, in *Writings of Thomas Jefferson*, 7:127.

107. Jefferson, "Syllabus," 9:460–461.

108. April 9, 1803, letter to Joseph Priestley, in *Works of Thomas Jefferson*, 9:458; January 29, 1815, letter to Charles Clas, in *Writings of Thomas Jefferson*, 6:413.

109. April 13, 1820, letter to William Short, in *Writings of Thomas Jefferson*, 7:155–156.

110. Jefferson, "Syllabus," 9:461–462; April 9, 1803, letter to Joseph Priestley, in *Works of Thomas Jefferson*, 9:458.

111. August 15, 1820, letter to John Adams, in *Adams-Jefferson Letters*, 2:568; June 25, 1819, letter to Ezra Stiles, in *Writings of Thomas Jefferson*, 7:127–128.

112. April 9, 1803, letter to Joseph Priestley, in *Works of Thomas Jefferson*, 9:458; April 21, 1803, letter to Benjamin Rush, in *Works of Thomas Jefferson*, 8:457n.

113. August 4, 1820, letter to William Short, in *Writings of Thomas Jefferson*, 7:167.

114. October 31, 1819, letter to William Short, in *Works of Thomas Jefferson*, 12:142.

115. E.g., John 8:58–59; John 10:30–31; John 10:38–39; John 17:5, 21, 24.

116. Jefferson, "Syllabus," 9:462.

117. August 4, 1820, letter to William Short, in *Writings of Thomas Jefferson*, 7:164.

118. April 25, 1816, letter to F. A. Van der Kemp, in *Writings of Thomas Jefferson*, 6:594.

119. August 4, 1820, letter to William Short, in *Writings of Thomas Jefferson*, 7:164.

120. November 4, 1820, letter to Jared Sparks, in *Writings of Thomas Jefferson*, 7:186; April 11, 1823, letter to John Adams, in *Adams-Jefferson Letters*, 2:594; April 9, 1803, letter to Joseph Priestley, in *Works of Thomas Jefferson*, 9:458; Jefferson, "Syllabus," 9:462.

121. February 27, 1821, letter to Timothy Pickering, in *Writings of Thomas Jefferson*, 7:210.

122. April 11, 1823, letter to John Adams, in *Adams-Jefferson Letters*, 2:594.

123. Aldridge, *Benjamin Franklin*, 269; April 13, 1738, letter to Josiah and Abiah Franklin, in *Papers of Benjamin Franklin*, 2:204.

124. March 9, 1790, letter to Ezra Stiles, in *Works of Benjamin Franklin*, 10:424.

125. Buxbaum, *Benjamin Franklin*, 140; Franklin, "Dialogue," 2:54–55; Buxbaum, *Benjamin Franklin*, 99–101.

126. Franklin quoted in Aldridge, *Benjamin Franklin,* 170; Franklin, "Compassion," 169; Franklin, "Autobiography," 1:107; Buxbaum, *Benjamin Franklin,* 108.

127. March 9, 1790, letter to Ezra Stiles, in *Works of Benjamin Franklin,* 10:424.

128. June 13, 1814, letter to Thomas Law, in *Writings of Thomas Jefferson,* 6:350; September 18, 1813, letter to William Canby, in *Writings of Thomas Jefferson,* 6:210; September 26, 1814, letter to Miles King, in *Writings of Thomas Jefferson,* 6:388.

129. July 15, 1763, letter to John Page, in *Papers of Thomas Jefferson,* 1:10; December 5, 1801, letter to Isaac Story, in *Papers of Thomas Jefferson,* 36:30.

130. April 11, 1823, letter to John Adams, in *Adams-Jefferson Letters,* 2:594; November 13, 1818, letter to John Adams, in *Adams-Jefferson Letters,* 2:529.

131. Franklin quoted in Sparks, *Life of Benjamin Franklin,* 597.

132. May 23, 1785, letter to George Whatley, in *Benjamin Franklin, Writings,* 1106.

133. February 22, 1756, letter to Elizabeth Hubbart, in *Papers of Benjamin Franklin,* 6:407.

134. July 28, 1743, letter to Jane Mecom, in *Papers of Benjamin Franklin,* 2:385.

135. June 6, 1753, letter to Joseph Huey, in *Papers of Benjamin Franklin,* 4:505.

136. May 23, 1785, letter to George Whatley, in *Benjamin Franklin, Writings,* 1106.

137. March 9, 1790, letter to Ezra Stiles, in *Works of Benjamin Franklin,* 10:424.

138. Franklin, "Autobiography," 1:105.

139. Benjamin Franklin, "On Wine" [1779], in *Benjamin Franklin, Writings,* 939.

140. August 10, 1787, letter to Peter Carr, in *Papers of Thomas Jefferson,* 12:15; August 6, 1816, letter to Mrs. M. Harrison Smith, in *Writings of Thomas Jefferson,* 7:28; August 1, 1816, letter to John Adams, in *Adams-Jefferson Letters,* 2:484.

141. June 5, 1822, letter to Rev. Thomas Whittemore, in *Writings of Thomas Jefferson,* 7:245.

142. June 26, 1822, letter to Benjamin Waterhouse, in *Works of Thomas Jefferson,* 12:243.

143. June 25, 1819, letter to Ezra Stiles, in *Writings of Thomas Jefferson,* 7:128.

144. November 2, 1822, letter to Thomas Cooper, in *Works of Thomas Jefferson,* 12:272.

145. Jefferson, *Jefferson's Notes,* 162.

146. Ibid., 160.

147. September 26, 1814, letter to Miles King, in *Writings of Thomas Jefferson,* 6:388.

148. Ibid.

149. June 25, 1819, letter to Ezra Stiles, in *Writings of Thomas Jefferson,* 7:128.

150. November 2, 1822, letter to Thomas Cooper, in *Works of Thomas Jefferson,* 12:271.

151. September 18, 1813, letter to William Canby, in *Writings of Thomas Jefferson,* 6:210.

152. December 8, 1822, letter to James Smith, in *Writings of Thomas Jefferson,* 7:270; September 27, 1809, letter to James Fishback, in *Writings of Thomas Jefferson,* 5:471.

153. January 21, 1809, letter to Thomas Leiper, in *Works of Thomas Jefferson,* 11:89.

154. Ibid.

155. May 5, 1817, letter to John Adams, in *Adams-Jefferson Letters*, 2:512.

156. Jefferson, *Jefferson's Notes*, 162; December 8, 1822, letter to James Smith, in *Writings of Thomas Jefferson*, 7:269.

157. March 9, 1790, letter to Ezra Stiles, in *Works of Benjamin Franklin*, 10:424; Franklin, "Autobiography," 1:103.

158. July 28, 1743, letter to Jane Mecom, in *Papers of Benjamin Franklin*, 2:385; March 9, 1790, letter to Ezra Stiles, in *Works of Benjamin Franklin*, 10:425.

159. March 9, 1790, letter to Ezra Stiles, in *Works of Benjamin Franklin*, 10:425; Franklin, "Dialogue," 2:33.

160. Franklin, "Autobiography," 1:137.

161. Benjamin Franklin, "Poor Richard" [1743], in *Papers of Benjamin Franklin*, 2:373; Franklin, "Dialogue," 2:33; Franklin, "Autobiography," 1:117; April 13, 1738, letter to Josiah and Abiah Franklin, in *Papers of Benjamin Franklin*, 2:203.

162. Franklin quoted in Sparks, *Life of Benjamin Franklin*, 352.

163. Buxbaum, *Benjamin Franklin*, 95.

164. Benjamin Franklin, "Information to Those Who Would Remove to America" [1784], in *Works of Benjamin Franklin*, 2:477; Franklin, "A Parable against Persecution," in *Papers of Benjamin Franklin*, 6:122–123.

165. November 25, 1788, letter to Elizabeth Partridge, in *Works of Benjamin Franklin*, 10:366.

166. Franklin, "Autobiography," 1:119, 114.

167. Buxbaum, *Benjamin Franklin*, 89–90.

168. Ibid., 90; April 13, 1738, letter to Josiah and Abiah Franklin, in *Papers of Benjamin Franklin*, 2:204.

169. Franklin, "On the Providence," 1:265; Franklin, "Proposals," 3:416n.

170. Buxbaum, *Benjamin Franklin*, 98, 110.

171. Ibid., 82.

172. March 9, 1790, letter to Ezra Stiles, in *Works of Benjamin Franklin*, 10:425.

173. April 21, 1803, letter to Benjamin Rush, in *Works of Thomas Jefferson*, 9:457n; December 8, 1822, letter to James Smith, in *Writings of Thomas Jefferson*, 7:270; April 19, 1803, letter to Edward Dowse, in *Writings of Thomas Jefferson*, 4:477–478; April 13, 1820, letter to William Short, in *Writings of Thomas Jefferson*, 7:155.

174. Thomas Jefferson, undated memorandum, in *Works of Thomas Jefferson*, 9:459; April 26, 1803, letter to Levi Lincoln in *Works of Thomas Jefferson*, 9:459; August 22, 1813, letter to John Adams, in *Adams-Jefferson Letters*, 2:369.

175. April 25, 1816, letter to F. A. Van der Kemp, in *Writings of Thomas Jefferson*, 6:594.

176. January 11, 1817, letter to John Adams, in *Adams-Jefferson Letters*, 2:506.

177. February 21, 1825, letter to Thomas Jefferson Smith, in *Our Sacred Honor*, ed. William J. Bennett (New York: Simon & Schuster, 1997), 413.

178. August 4, 1820, letter to William Short, in *Writings of Thomas Jefferson*, 7:166.

179. Daniel Boorstin, *The Lost World of Thomas Jefferson* (Boston: Beacon Press, 1948), 152.

CHAPTER SIX. THE THEISTIC RATIONALISM OF THE KEY FRAMERS

1. John E. Semonche, *Keeping the Faith: A Cultural History of the U.S. Supreme Court* (New York: Rowman & Littlefield, 1998), 27.

2. April 8, 1831, letter to Jared Sparks, in Max Farrand, ed., *The Records of the Federal Convention of 1787* (New Haven, Conn.: Yale University Press, 1966), 3:499.

3. December 22, 1814, letter to Timothy Pickering, in Jared Sparks, ed., *The Life of Gouverneur Morris, with Selections from His Correspondence and Miscellaneous Papers* (Boston: Gray & Bowen, 1832), 3:323.

4. February 24, 1815, letter from Morris to William Hill Wells, in Sparks, *Life of Gouverneur Morris*, 3:339.

5. Mark David Hall, *The Political and Legal Philosophy of James Wilson, 1742–1798* (Columbia: University of Missouri Press, 1997), 1; Max Farrand quoted in James Wilson, *Selected Political Essays of James Wilson*, ed. Randolph G. Adams (New York: Alfred A. Knopf, 1930), 19; Richard J. Ellis, ed., *Founding the American Presidency* (Lanham, Md.: Rowman & Littlefield, 1999), xii; Hall, *Political and Legal*, 196.

6. Alexander Hamilton, "Address of the Annapolis Convention," in *The Papers of Alexander Hamilton*, ed. Harold C. Syrett (New York: Columbia University Press, 1961–1987), 3:686–689.

7. John Patrick Diggins, *The Lost Soul of American Politics* (New York: Basic Books, 1984), 37; M. E. Bradford, *A Worthy Company* (Marlborough, N.H.: Plymouth Rock Foundation, 1982), v; Charles Page Smith, *James Wilson: Founding Father* (Chapel Hill: University of North Carolina Press, 1956), 16–17, 319.

8. Norman Cousins, ed., *The Republic of Reason: Personal Philosophies of the Founding Fathers* (San Francisco: Harper & Row, 1988), 296; Cushing Strout, *The New Heavens and New Earth: Political Religion in America* (New York: Harper & Row, 1974), 79; Robert P. Kraynak, *Christian Faith and Modern Democracy* (Notre Dame, Ind.: University of Notre Dame Press, 2001), 127.

9. Douglass Adair, *Fame and the Founding Fathers*, ed. Trevor Colbourn (New York: W. W. Norton, 1974), 145–149.

10. James Wilson, "Lectures on Law," in *The Works of James Wilson*, ed. James DeWitt Andrews (Chicago: Callaghan, 1896), 1:49.

11. E.g., ibid., 1:64, 93, 94, 96, 93; 2:49, 92, 95, 122; 1:274.

12. Ibid., 1:99.

13. February 12, 1814, letter to Lewis B. Sturges, in Sparks, *Life of Gouverneur Morris*, 3:302; Gouverneur Morris, "Speech to New York Congress," 1776, in Sparks, *Life of Gouverneur Morris*, 1:106; July 22, 1806, letter to John Parish, in Sparks, *Life of Gouverneur Morris*, 3:236; Morris, "Diary," August 19, 1796, in Sparks, *Life of Gouverneur Morris*, 1:435.

14. June 23, 1813, letter to Egbert Benson, in Sparks, *Life of Gouverneur Morris*, 3:294; February 12, 1814, letter to Lewis B. Sturges, in Sparks, *Life of Gouverneur Morris*, 3:303; June 22, 1815, letter to Joseph Kingsberry, in Sparks, *Life of Gouverneur Morris*, 3:340; October 17, 1814, letter to Timothy Pickering, in Sparks, *Life of Gouverneur Morris*, 3:313.

15. February 28, 1790, diary entry, in Gouverneur Morris, *A Diary of the French Revolution*, ed. Beatrix Cary Davenport (Boston: Houghton Mifflin, 1939), 1:430; April 17, 1778, letter to mother, in Sparks, *Life of Gouverneur Morris*, 1:157; June 23, 1793, letter to Mrs. Euphemia Ogden, in Sparks, *Life of Gouverneur Morris*, 3:44; November 1, 1801, letter to the Countess of Hohenthal, in Sparks, *Life of Gouverneur Morris*, 3:155.

16. E.g., July 22, 1806, letter to John Parish, in Sparks, *Life of Gouverneur Morris*, 3:236; June 23, 1813, letter to Egbert Benson, in Sparks, *Life of Gouverneur Morris*, 3:294; February 12, 1814, letter to Lewis Sturges, in Sparks, *Life of Gouverneur Morris*, 3:303; February 12, 1814, letter to Lewis Sturges in Sparks, *Life of Gouverneur Morris*, 3:302; November 1, 1801, letter to the Countess of Hohenthal, in Sparks, *Life of Gouverneur Morris*, 3:155; June 22, 1815, letter to Joseph Kingsberry, in Sparks, *Life of Gouverneur Morris*, 3:340.

17. June 23, 1793, letter to Euphemia Ogden in Sparks, *Life of Gouverneur Morris*, 3:49; Morris quoted in Howard Swiggett, *The Extraordinary Mr. Morris* (Garden City, N.Y.: Doubleday, 1952), 232; April 27, 1805, letter to Madame de Stael, in Sparks, *Life of Gouverneur Morris*, 3:219; December 19, 1815, letter to Joseph Kingsberry, in Sparks, *Life of Gouverneur Morris*, 3:342; Robert C. Hartnett, "The Religion of the Founding Fathers," in *Wellsprings of the American Spirit*, ed. F. Ernest Johnson (New York: Harper & Brothers, 1948), 59.

18. James Madison, "Memorial and Remonstrance" [1785], in *The Writings of James Madison*, ed. Gaillard Hunt (New York: G. P. Putnam's Sons, 1900–1910), 2:187; Madison, "Message to Congress," December 15, 1815, in Marvin Meyers, ed., *The Mind of the Founder: Sources of the Political Thought of James Madison* (Hanover, N.H.: University Press of New England, 1973), 305.

19. Madison, "Memorial and Remonstrance," 2:191; Federalist No. 37, in Alexander Hamilton, James Madison, and John Jay, *The Federalist Papers*, ed. Clinton Rossiter (New York: New American Library, 1961; reprinted in 1999), 198–199; "First Inaugural Address," March 4, 1809, in *Inaugural Addresses of the Presidents of the United States* (Washington, D.C.: U.S. Government Printing Office, 1989), 28.

20. James Madison, "War Message to Congress," June 1, 1812, in *Writings of James Madison*, 8:200; "Second Inaugural Address," March 4, 1813, in *Inaugural Addresses*, 29; June 10, 1773, letter to William Bradford, in James Madison, *The Papers of James Madison*, ed. Robert A. Rutland and William M. E. Rachal (Chicago: University of Chicago Press, 1962–1991), 1:89.

21. John C. Miller, *Alexander Hamilton and the Growth of the Nation* (New York: Harper & Row, 1959), 285; Alexander Hamilton, "The Farmer Refuted," February 5, 1775, in *Papers of Alexander Hamilton*, 1:87; "To the *Royal Danish-American Gazette*," September 6, 1772, in *Papers of Alexander Hamilton*, 1:37; Hamilton, "The Stand," April 19, 1798, in *The Works of Alexander Hamilton*, ed. Henry Cabot Lodge (New York: Knickerbocker Press, 1904), 6:310.

22. April 12, 1804, letter from Hamilton to unknown friend, in *Works of Alexander Hamilton*, 10:456.

23. July 22, 1806, letter from G. Morris to John Parish, in Sparks, *Life of Gouverneur Morris*, 3:235.

24. Madison, "Memorial and Remonstrance," 2:187.

25. Wilson, "Lectures," 1:124.

26. Ibid., 1:99; 2:297.

27. Ibid., 1:101, 216, 99; 1:218.

28. E.g., October 17, 1814, letter to Timothy Pickering, in Sparks, *Life of Gouverneur Morris,* 3:313; June 23, 1793, letter to Mrs. Euphemia Ogden, in Sparks, *Life of Gouverneur Morris,* 3:44; November 1, 1801, letter to the Countess of Hohenthal, in Sparks, *Life of Gouverneur Morris,* 3:155; June 23, 1793, letter to Mrs. Euphemia Ogden, in Sparks, *Life of Gouverneur Morris,* 3:44; July 22, 1806, letter to John Parish, in Sparks, *Life of Gouverneur Morris,* 3:235; March 3, 1814, letter to William Hill Wells, in Sparks, *Life of Gouverneur Morris,* 3:305.

29. November 20, 1825, letter to Frederick Beasley, in *Writings of James Madison,* 9:230.

30. E.g., "To the *Royal Danish-American Gazette,*" 1:35–37; Hamilton, "Farmer Refuted," 1:87; April 12, 1804, letter to an unknown friend, in *Works of Alexander Hamilton,* 10:456; Miller, *Alexander Hamilton,* 14.

31. Wilson, "Lectures," 1:56, 108, 223, 250–251, 266, 212.

32. Ibid., 1:276.

33. Ibid., 1:270, 275, 307; 1:93.

34. E.g., November 20, 1825, letter to Frederick Beasley, in *Writings of James Madison,* 9:230–231; *Madison,* "Memorial and Remonstrance," 9:190; James Madison, "Detached Memoranda," ed. Elizabeth Fleet, *William and Mary Quarterly,* 3rd ser., vol. 3, no. 4 (October 1946): 559; November 23, 1825, letter to Doctor C. Caldwell, in *Letters and Other Writings of James Madison,* ed. William Rives (New York: R. Worthington, 1884), 3:505.

35. Franklin Steiner, *The Religious Beliefs of Our Presidents: From Washington to FDR* (Amherst, N.Y.: Prometheus Books, 1995), 93; Ralph L. Ketcham, "James Madison and Religion—A New Hypothesis," in *James Madison on Religious Liberty,* ed. Robert S. Alley (Buffalo, N.Y.: Prometheus Books, 1985), 177–178.

36. "To the *Royal Danish-American Gazette,*" 1:37; Hamilton, "Farmer Refuted," 1:86–88.

37. Miller, *Alexander Hamilton,* 14, 121, 285.

38. Hamilton, "Farmer Refuted," 1:113.

39. John C. Hamilton, *History of the Republic of the United States of America, as Traced in the Writings of Alexander Hamilton* (Philadelphia: J. B. Lippincott, 1864), 7:790.

40. Wilson, "Lectures," 1:117, 98, 99, 214, 95, 221.

41. Ron Chernow, *Alexander Hamilton* (New York: Penguin Books, 2004), 659.

42. Madison, "Detached Memoranda," 560; Daniel Boorstin, "The Founding Fathers and the Courage to Doubt," in *James Madison on Religious Liberty,* ed. Robert S. Alley (Buffalo, N.Y.: Prometheus Books, 1985), 210; October 28, 1787, letter to Edmund Pendleton, in *Writings of James Madison,* 5:44–45; Madison, "Detached Memoranda," 561.

43. June 23, 1793, letter to Mrs. Euphemia Ogden, in Sparks, *Life of Gouverneur Morris,* 3:305; March 3, 1814, letter to William Hill Wells, in Sparks, *Life of Gouverneur Morris,* 3:304.

44. March 3, 1814, letter to William Hill Wells, in Sparks, *Life of Gouverneur Morris,* 3:305.

45. Henry F. May, *The Enlightenment in America* (New York: Oxford University Press, 1976), 125.

46. See, for example, October 2, 1790, diary entry, in Morris, *Diary of the French Revolution,* 2:9; October 7, 1790, diary entry, in Morris, *Diary of the French Revolution,* 2:14; March 29, 1791, diary entry, in Morris, *Diary of the French Revolution,* 2:150; October 18, 1789, diary entry, in Morris, *Diary of the French Revolution,* 1:264.

47. Ketcham, "James Madison," 184.

48. May 29, 1785, letter to James Monroe, in *Writings of James Madison,* 2:145; December 3, 1821, letter to F. L. Schaeffer, in *Letters and Other Writings of James Madison,* 3:242; John T. Noonan, *The Lustre of Our Country* (Berkeley: University of California Press, 1998), 86.

49. January 9, 1785, letter to Thomas Jefferson, in *Writings of James Madison,* 2:114; Madison, "Detached Memoranda," 556; "Speeches in the Virginia Convention" [June 12, 1788], in *Writings of James Madison,* 5:176; Federalist No. 10, 52.

50. August 1820 letter to Jacob de la Motta, in *Writings of James Madison,* 9:30.

51. Madison, "Detached Memoranda," 554.

52. January 22, 1786, letter to Thomas Jefferson, in *Papers of James Madison,* 8:474; April 1, 1774, letter to William Bradford, in *Writings of James Madison,* 1:24; Madison, "Memorial and Remonstrance," 2:186.

53. Madison, "Memorial and Remonstrance," 2:184.

54. Madison, "Detached Memoranda," 556, 559; "Essay" in *National Gazette,* March 27, 1792, in Alley, *James Madison,* 77; Madison, "Journal of the Virginia Convention" [1776], in *Writings of James Madison,* 1:40.

55. Adair, *Fame,* 144, 148; April 1779 letter from Hamilton to John Laurens, in *Papers of Alexander Hamilton,* 2:37; Adair, *Fame,* 148; Allan McLane Hamilton, *The Intimate Life of Alexander Hamilton* (New York: Charles Scribner's Sons, 1910), 334.

56. Miller, *Alexander Hamilton,* 104; Alexander Hamilton, "Second Letter from Phocion," April 1784, in *Papers of Alexander Hamilton,* 3:553, 554.

57. Hamilton, "Second Letter from Phocion," 3:554; Alexander Hamilton, "Remarks on the Quebec Bill: Part Two," June 22, 1775, in *Papers of Alexander Hamilton,* 1:173.

58. Hamilton, "Remarks," 1:171–172; Alexander Hamilton, "A Full Vindication of the Measures of Congress, &c.," December 15, 1774, in *Papers of Alexander Hamilton,* 1:68; Alexander Hamilton, "Report on the Subject of Manufactures," December 5, 1791, in *Alexander Hamilton, Writings,* ed. Joanne B. Freeman (New York: Library of America, 2001), 662.

59. Charles Page Smith, *James Wilson: Founding Father* (Chapel Hill: University of North Carolina Press, 1956), 319; Wilson, "Lectures," 1:95; 1:110; 1:118, 111–112, 258, 124; 2:425.

60. March 3, 1814, letter to William Hill Wells, in Sparks, *Life of Gouverneur Morris,* 3:305; April 5, 1813, letter to David B. Ogden, in Sparks, *Life of Gouverneur Morris,* 3:286; October 25, 1804, letter to John Parish, in Sparks, *Life of Gouverneur Morris,* 3:214.

61. November 9, 1789, diary entry, Gouverneur Morris, *The Diary and Letters of Gouverneur Morris,* ed. Anne Cary Morris (New York: Charles Scribner's Sons, 1888), 1:221; June 28, 1792, letter to Lord George Gordon, in Sparks, *Life of Gouverneur Morris,* 3:31.

62. December 3, 1821, letter to F. L. Schaeffer, in *Letters and Other Writings of James Madison,* 3:242; Ketcham, "James Madison," 182; Madison, "Journal of the Virginia Convention," 1:40; October 28, 1787, letter to Edmund Pendleton, in *Writings of James Madison,* 5:44–45.

63. Minutes of January 1, 1795, in Thomas Hart Benton and John C. Rives, eds., *Abridgment of the Debates of Congress, from 1789 to 1856* (New York: D. Appleton, 1857), 557.

64. August 1820 letter to Jacob de la Motta, in *Letters and Other Writings of James Madison,* 3:179; March 19, 1823, letter to Edward Everett, in *Writings of James Madison,* 9:127.

65. November 20, 1825, letter to Frederick Beasley, in *Writings of James Madison,* 9:230.

66. See Vincent Phillip Munoz, "Religious Liberty and American Constitutionalism" (Ph.D. diss., Claremont Graduate University, 2001), and March 19, 1823, letter to Edward Everett, in *Writings of James Madison,* 9:126.

67. See, for example, Alexander Hamilton, "Memorandum on the French Revolution," in *Writings of Alexander Hamilton,* 834, 835; Hamilton, "The Stand," no. 2, and "The Stand," no. 3, in *Papers of Alexander Hamilton,* 21:391, 404–405; Hamilton, "Fragment," in *Works of Alexander Hamilton,* 8:425–427.

68. July 30, 1796, letter to George Washington, in *Alexander Hamilton, Writings,* 862–864.

69. A. M. Hamilton, *Intimate Life,* 334.

70. J. C. Hamilton, *History of the Republic,* 7:790.

71. Hamilton, "Stand," no. 3, 21:402, 404, 405; Hamilton, "Fragment," 8:426–427.

72. January 2, 1800, letter to Tobias Lear, in *Works of Alexander Hamilton,* 10:357.

73. Mark D. Hall, "James Wilson: Presbyterian, Anglican, Thomist, or Deist? Does It Matter?" in *The Founders on God and Government,* ed. Daniel L. Dreisbach, Mark D. Hall, and Jeffry H. Morrison (Lanham, Md.: Rowman & Littlefield, 2004), 187–188.

74. Wilson, "Lectures," 1:60.

75. June 28, 1792, letter from Morris to Lord George Gordon, in Sparks, *Life of Gouverneur Morris,* 3:32; Swiggett, *Extraordinary,* 336–337.

76. Thomas Jefferson, "The Anas" [February 1, 1800], in *The Works of Thomas Jefferson,* ed. Paul Leicester Ford (New York: G. P. Putnam's Sons, 1904–1905), 1:353.

77. Henry F. May, *The Enlightenment in America* (New York: Oxford University Press, 1976), 96; Ketcham, "James Madison," 176, 184; Bishop Meade, *Old Churches, Ministers and Families of Virginia* (Philadelphia: J. B. Lippincott, 1857), 2:99; September 25, 1773, letter to William Bradford, in *Papers of James Madison,* 1:96; Ketcham, "James Madison," 181.

78. September 25, 1773, letter to William Bradford, in *Papers of James Madison,* 1:96.

79. December 1, 1773, letter to William Bradford, in *Papers of James Madison,* 1:101; Spring 1833 letter to Jasper Adams, in Alley, *James Madison,* 87; Madison, "Memorial and Remonstrance," 2:189; Ketcham, "James Madison," 184; Noonan, *Lustre of Our Country,* 88.

80. E.g., Garrett Ward Sheldon, *The Political Philosophy of James Madison* (Baltimore, Md.: Johns Hopkins University Press, 2001), and James H. Smylie, "Madison and Witherspoon: Theological Roots of American Political Thought," *Princeton University Library Chronicle* 22 (Spring 1961): 118–132.

81. Sheldon, *Political Philosophy*, 24.

82. Clinton Rossiter, *The Political Thought of the American Revolution* (New York: Harcourt, Brace & World, 1963), 102.

83. Sheldon, *Political Philosophy*, 25.

84. Adair, *Fame*, 144, 146.

85. Ibid., 146–147.

86. July 6, 1780, letter to General Anthony Wayne, in *Papers of Alexander Hamilton*, 2:354; John Rodgers quoted in Isaac A. Cornelison, *The Relationship of Religion to the Civil Government, in the United States of America: A State without a Church, but Not without a Religion* (New York: G. P. Putnam's Sons, 1895), 204; Alexander Hamilton, "The Reynolds Pamphlet" [July 1797], in *Works of Alexander Hamilton*, 7:378, 369–411.

87. May 21, 1778, letter from Morris to George Washington, in *The Writings of George Washington*, ed. John C. Fitzpatrick (Washington, D.C.: U.S. Government Printing Office, 1931–1944), 11:483n; September 25, 1773, letter to William Bradford, in *Papers of James Madison*, 1:96; November 20, 1825, letter to Frederick Beasley, in *Writings of James Madison*, 9:230; Adair, *Fame*, 145; Madison, "Memorial and Remonstrance," 2:187; Madison, "Detached Memoranda," 556.

88. Wilson, "Lectures," 1:489.

89. November 23, 1825, letter to Doctor C. Caldwell, in *Letters and Other Writings of James Madison*, 3:504; Madison, "Memorial and Remonstrance," 2:189.

90. E.g., Madison, "Detached Memoranda," 556; September 25, 1773, letter to William Bradford, in *Papers of James Madison*, 1:96.

91. Meade, *Old Churches*, 2:99–100; Ketcham, "James Madison," 182.

92. Wilson, "Lectures," 1:106; 1:93; 2:491.

93. E.g., ibid., 1:93 (2 Tim. 1:10); 1:214 (Ps.139:14); 1:253 (Gen. 2:18).

94. Ibid., 1:489; 1:92; 1:123; 2:317.

95. Ibid., 2:483–484.

96. Ibid., 1:106.

97. Ibid., 1:121, 123; 1:122.

98. Ibid., 1:122.

99. March 3, 1814, letter to William Hill Wells, in Sparks, *Life of Gouverneur Morris*, 3:304; June 23, 1793, letter to Mrs. Euphemia Ogden, in Sparks, *Life of Gouverneur Morris*, 3:44; June 28, 1792, letter to Lord George Gordon, in Sparks, *Life of Gouverneur Morris*, 3:31.

100. Ketcham, "James Madison," 177.

101. Ibid., 177–178.

102. November 20, 1785, letter to Frederick Beasley, in *Writings of James Madison*, 9:230–231; November 9, 1772, letter to William Bradford, in *Writings of James Madison*, 1:10; Madison, "Detached Memoranda," 560–561; Madison, "Journal of the Virginia Convention," 1:40.

103. Meade, *Old Churches*, 2:99; Madison, "Memorial and Remonstrance," 2:191; "First Inaugural Address" in *Inaugural Addresses*, 28.

104. "To the *Royal Danish-American Gazette*," 1:36–37; Robert Troup quoted in Nathan Schachner, ed., "Alexander Hamilton Viewed by His Friends: The Narratives of Robert Troup and Hercules Mulligan," *William and Mary Quarterly*, 3d ser., vol. 4 (1947): 213, in Adair, *Fame*, 146.

105. September 1825 letter from William Steele to Jonathan D. Steele, in Farrand, *Records*, 3:472; January 6, 1834, letter from James Madison to Thomas S. Grimke, in Farrand, *Records*, 3:531.

106. J. C. Hamilton, *History of the Republic*, 7:790.

107. Hamilton, "Stand," 7:275, quoted in George Adams Boyd, *Elias Boudinot: Patriot and Statesman* (Princeton, N.J.: Princeton University Press, 1952), 23–24; "To the *Royal Danish-American Gazette*," 1:36–37.

108. Alexander Hamilton, "Fragment on the French Revolution" (c. 1796), in *Alexander Hamilton and the Founding of the Nation*, ed. Richard B. Morris (New York: Dial Press, 1957), 422; Hamilton, "Farmer Refuted," 1:87.

109. July 4, 1804, letter to Mrs. Hamilton, in *Papers of Alexander Hamilton*, 26:293; "Last Will and Testament of Alexander Hamilton," July 9, 1804, in *Papers of Alexander Hamilton*, 26:305.

110. November 9, 1772, letter to William Bradford, in *Writings of James Madison*, 1:10.

111. Wilson, "Lectures," 1:489.

112. Quoted in Swiggett, *Extraordinary*, 225, 331.

113. Swiggett, *Extraordinary*, 192, 162, 179, 190.

114. Ibid., 80, 220, 182.

115. Ibid., 238, 179; Morris quoted in Swiggett, *Extraordinary*, 218; Swiggett, *Extraordinary*, 209, 181, 183, 220, 238.

116. Swiggett, *Extraordinary*, 290, 297, 317, 320–323, 362, 211, 216, 222, 314, 315, 356.

117. Jefferson, "Anas" 1:353.

118. For a more complete and detailed explanation, see Gregg L. Frazer, "Alexander Hamilton, Theistic Rationalist," in *The Forgotten Founders on Religion and Public Life*, ed. Daniel L. Dreisbach, Mark David Hall, and Jeffry H. Morrison (Notre Dame, Ind.: University of Notre Dame Press, 2009), 109–112.

119. Broadus Mitchell, *Alexander Hamilton: A Concise Biography* (New York: Oxford University Press, 1976), 105; Adair, *Fame*, 148.

120. April 10, 1797, letter to William Smith, in Adair, *Fame*, 148n10.

121. E.g., several essays under the title "The Stand" in 1798 and "The War in Europe" in 1799, in *Works of Alexander Hamilton*, 7.

122. Adair, *Fame*, 152n18.

123. Ibid., 157; Hamilton quoted in A. M. Hamilton, *Intimate Life*, 335; April 1802 letter to James Bayard, in *Works of Alexander Hamilton*, 10:432–436.

124. Stephen A. Marini, "Religion, Politics, and Ratification," in *Religion in a Revolutionary Age*, ed. Ronald Hoffman and Peter J. Albert (Charlottesville: University Press of Virginia, 1994), 203–204.

125. Ketcham, "James Madison," 176.

126. Steiner, *Religious Beliefs*, 91.

127. 1833 letter to Jasper Adams in Alley, *James Madison*, 87–88.

128. J. C. Hamilton, *History of the Republic*, 7:499, 790; Adair, *Fame*, 155.

129. Adair, *Fame*, 157.

130. April 12, 1804, letter to an unknown friend, in *Works of Alexander Hamilton*, 10:456.

131. July 10, 1804, letter to Elizabeth Hamilton, in *Papers of Alexander Hamilton*, 26:308; Alexander Hamilton, "Statement on Impending Duel with Aaron Burr," June 28–July 10, 1804, in *Papers of Alexander Hamilton*, 26:278–280.

132. Quoted in J. C. Hamilton, *History of the Republic*, 7:826.

133. Oliver Wolcott, July 12, 1804, letter to his wife, in A. M. Hamilton, *Intimate Life*, 406.

134. Quoted in J. C. Hamilton, *History of the Republic*, 7:790.

135. Ibid., 823, cited in Adair, *Fame*, 158; July 4 and 10, 1804, letters to Elizabeth Hamilton, in *Papers of Alexander Hamilton*, 26:293, 308.

136. Bishop Benjamin Moore, July 12, 1804, letter to the editor of the *Evening Post*, in *A Collection of the Facts and Documents, Relative to the Death of Major-General Alexander Hamilton*, ed. William Coleman (Boston: Houghton Mifflin, 1904), 50.

137. Dr. John Mason, July 18, 1804, letter to the editor of the *Evening Post*, in Coleman, *Collection*, 54.

138. Ibid., 54–55.

139. Ibid., 55.

140. Moore, July 12, 1804, letter to the *Evening Post*, 51–52.

141. Chernow, *Hamilton*, 706.

CHAPTER SEVEN. THE THEISTIC RATIONALISM OF GEORGE WASHINGTON

1. "First Inaugural Address," April 30, 1789, in *The Writings of George Washington*, ed. John C. Fitzpatrick (Washington, D.C.: U.S. Government Printing Office, 1931–1944), 30:296; September 1789 letter to the Annual Meeting of Quakers, in *Writings of George Washington*, 30:416n54; March 3, 1797, letter to the Clergy of Different Denominations Residing in and near the City of Philadelphia, in *Writings of George Washington*, 35:417.

2. March 2, 1797, letter to the Rector, Church Wardens, and Vestrymen of the United Episcopal Churches of Christ Church and St. Peter's of Philadelphia, in *Writings of George Washington*, 35:411; August 31, 1788, letter to Annis Boudinot Stockton, in *Writings of George Washington*, 30:76; March 25, 1799, letter to the Secretary of War, in *Writings of George Washington*, 37:158; January 10, 1788, letter to Henry Knox, in *Writings of George Washington*, 29:378; January 5, 1784, letter to Jonathan Trumbull, in *Writings of George Washington*, 27:294.

3. Richard Brookhiser, *Founding Father: Rediscovering George Washington* (New York: Free Press, 1996), 146.

4. E.g., "General Orders," July 9, 1776, in *Writings of George Washington*, 5:245; "General Orders," February 15, 1783, in *Writings of George Washington*, 26:135; November 27, 1783, letter to the Reformed German Congregation of New York, in *Writings of George Washington*, 27:249; "First Inaugural Address," in *Writings of George Washington*, 30:293; "First Annual Address to Congress," January 8, 1790, in *Writings of George Washington*, 30:491; "Sixth Annual Address to

Congress," November 19, 1794, in *Writings of George Washington*, 34:37; "Eighth Annual Address to Congress," December 7, 1796, in *Writings of George Washington*, 35:320; February 20, 1784, letter to Henry Knox, in *Writings of George Washington*, 27:341; August 26, 1792, letter to the Attorney General, in *Writings of George Washington*, 32:136; November 15, 1781, letter to Thomas McKean, in *Writings of George Washington*, 23:343.

5. "First Inaugural Address," in *Writings of George Washington*, 30:293.

6. Ibid.; May 26, 1789, letter to the General Assembly of Presbyterian Churches, in *Writings of George Washington*, 30:336n12; May 30, 1778, letter to Landon Carter, in *Writings of George Washington*, 11:492; July 18, 1755, letter to John Augustine Washington, in *Writings of George Washington*, 1:152.

7. Paul F. Boller, *George Washington & Religion* (Dallas, Tex.: Southern Methodist University Press, 1963), 107, 100.

8. E.g., "Talk to the Cherokee Nation," August 29, 1796, in *Writings of George Washington*, 35:198; July 31, 1788, letter to James McHenry, in *Writings of George Washington*, 30:30; March 3, 1797, letter to the Philadelphia clergy, in *Writings of George Washington*, 35:417; "General Orders," July 4, 1775, in *Writings of George Washington*, 3:309; "Sixth Annual Address to Congress," November 19, 1794, in *Writings of George Washington*, 34:37; "Thanksgiving Proclamation," October 3, 1789, in *Writings of George Washington*, 30:427–428; "First Inaugural Address," April 30, 1789, in *Writings of George Washington*, 30:293; "Farewell Address," September 19, 1796, in *Writings of George Washington*, 35:238; "Thanksgiving Proclamation," in *Writings of George Washington*, 30:427–428; "First Inaugural Address," in *Writings of George Washington*, 30:295–296; "Fifth Annual Address to Congress," December 3, 1793, in *Writings of George Washington*, 33:164; "Eighth Annual Message," December 7, 1796, in *Writings of George Washington*, 35:320; "Farewell Address," in *Writings of George Washington*, 35:238; July 31, 1788, letter to James McHenry, in *Writings of George Washington*, 30:30.

9. "General Orders," February 15, 1783, in *Writings of George Washington*, 26:135; "General Orders," July 4, 1775, in *Writings of George Washington*, 3:309.

10. Boller, *George Washington*, 26–30.

11. James Abercrombie to Origen Bacheler, November 29, 1831, *Magazine of American History* 13 (June 1885): 597; March 2, 1797, letter to the Rector, Church Wardens, and Vestrymen of the United Episcopal Churches of Christ Church and St. Peter's of Philadelphia, in *Writings of George Washington*, 35:410; Boller, *George Washington*, 30.

12. "General Orders," July 9, 1776, in *Writings of George Washington*, 5:245; "Instructions to Colonel Benedict Arnold," September 14, 1775, in *Writings of George Washington*, 3:492; "General Orders," May 2, 1778, in *Writings of George Washington*, 11:343; March 15, 1790, letter to the Roman Catholics in the United States of America, in *Writings of George Washington*, 31:22n47; undated letter to the Bishops, Clergy, and Laity of the Protestant Episcopal Church in New York, New Jersey, Pennsylvania, Delaware, Maryland, Virginia, and North Carolina, in *Writings of George Washington*, 30:383.

13. E.g., September 30, 1775, letter to the President of Congress, in *Writings of George Washington*, 3:526; January 25, 1785, letter to Sir James Jay, in *Writings of George Washington*, 28:41; April 10, 1792, letter to Rev. John Carroll, in *Writings*

of *George Washington,* 32:20; May 2, 1788, letter to Rev. John Ettwein, in *Writings of George Washington,* 29:489; July 10, 1789, letter to the Society of United Brethren for Propagating the Gospel among the Heathen, in *Writings of George Washington,* 30:355; August 15, 1789, letter to the Moravian Society for Propagating the Gospel, in *The Papers of George Washington: Presidential Series,* ed. W. W. Abbot (Charlottesville: University Press of Virginia, 1989), 3:466.

14. Brookhiser, *Founding Father,* 149.

15. May 1790 letter to the Savannah, Ga., Hebrew Congregation, in *The Papers of George Washington: Presidential Series,* ed. Dorothy Twohig (Charlottesville: University Press of Virginia, 1996), 5:448.

16. April 25, 1788, letter to the Marquis de Chastellux, in *The Writings of George Washington,* ed. Worthington Chauncey Ford (New York: G. P. Putnam's Sons, 1891), 11:247–248; "Circular to the States," June 8, 1783, in *Writings of George Washington,* 26:485.

17. Boller, *George Washington,* 40, 41–43.

18. April 21, 1789, letter to the Ministers, Church Wardens, and Vestry-men of the German Lutheran Congregation, in *Writings of George Washington,* 30:289; April 25, 1788, letter to the Marquis de Chastellux, in *Writings of George Washington,* ed. Ford, 11:248.

19. May 12, 1779, "Speech to the Delaware Chiefs," in *Writings of George Washington,* 15:55.

20. Boller, *George Washington,* 69.

21. Ibid., 70–76.

22. Eleanor Parke Custis to Jared Sparks, February 26, 1833, in *The Writings of George Washington,* ed. Jared Sparks (New York: Harper & Brothers, 1848), 12:406; William White to Colonel Hugh Mercer, August 15, 1835, in Bird Wilson, *Memoir of the Life of the Right Reverend William White* (Philadelphia: C. H. Kay, 1839), 197.

23. Abercrombie to Bacheler, 597.

24. Boller, *George Washington,* 5.

25. Mason L. Weems, *The Life of Washington,* ed. Marcus Cunliffe (Cambridge, Mass.: Harvard University Press, 1962), 12, 13–16, 42.

26. Ibid., 181–182; Boller, *George Washington,* 3–11, 33, 10.

27. Weems, *Life,* 166; 1 Cor. 15:26, 55–57.

28. Weems, *Life,* 166.

29. Ibid., 167.

30. Ibid., 168.

31. Boller, *George Washington,* 113.

32. E. C. McGuire, *The Religious Opinions and Character of Washington* (New York: Harper & Brothers, 1836), 343, 344.

33. Boller, *George Washington,* 72.

34. E.g., May 10, 1789, letter to the United Baptist Churches in Virginia, in *George Washington: A Collection,* ed. W. B. Allen (Indianapolis, Ind.: Liberty Fund, 1988), 532; March 15, 1790, letter to the Roman Catholics in the United States of America, in Allen, *Collection,* 547; July 20, 1788, letter to Jonathan Trumbull, in *Writings of George Washington,* 30:22; March 26, 1781, letter to John Armstrong, in *Writings of George Washington,* 21:378; November 15, 1781, letter to Thomas McKean, in *Writings of George Washington,* 23:343; August 20, 1778, letter to

Thomas Nelson, in *Writings of George Washington,* 12:343; October 19, 1777, letter to Israel Putnam, in *Writings of George Washington,* 9:401; July 13, 1798, letter to the President of the United States, in *Writings of George Washington,* 36:328; October 17, 1789, letter to the Legislature of the State of Connecticut, in *Writings of George Washington,* 30:453; October 12, 1783, letter to Chevalier de Chastellux, in *Writings of George Washington,* 27:189; November 8, 1777, letter to Brigadier General Thomas Nelson, in *Writings of George Washington,* 10:28.

35. March 9, 1781, letter to Rev. William Gordon, in *Writings of George Washington,* 21:332; May 30, 1778, letter to Landon Carter, in *Writings of George Washington,* 11:492; May 19, 1780, letter to Lund Washington, in *Writings of George Washington,* 18:392; August 15, 1798, letter to Rev. Jonathan Boucher, in *Writings of George Washington,* 36:413–414.

36. Boller, *George Washington,* 94, 109.

37. Richard V. Pierard and Robert D. Linder, *Civil Religion & the Presidency* (Grand Rapids, Mich.: Zondervan Publishing House, 1988), 72; "Reply to an Address from Ministers and Elders Representing the Massachusetts and New Hampshire Churches . . . ," October 28, 1789, in *The Republic of Reason,* ed. Norman Cousins (San Francisco: Harper & Row, 1988), 60; January 27, 1793, letter to the Members of the New Church in Baltimore, in *Writings of George Washington,* 32:315.

38. Boller, *George Washington,* 94–96.

39. E.g., February 20, 1784, letter to Henry Knox, in *Writings of George Washington,* 27:341; July 31, 1788, letter to the Secretary of War, in *Writings of George Washington,* 31:30; "After Orders" for May 5, 1778, in *Writings of George Washington,* 11:354; March 13, 1778, letter to Rev. Israel Evans, in *Writings of George Washington,* 11:78; August 26, 1792, letter to the Attorney General, in *Writings of George Washington,* 32:136; March 1, 1778, letter to Bryan Fairfax, in *Writings of George Washington,* 11:3; May 15, 1784, letter to Jonathan Trumbull, in *Writings of George Washington,* 27:399; October 12, 1783, letter to Chevalier de Chastellux, in *Writings of George Washington,* 27:189; July 13, 1798, letter to the President of the United States, in *Writings of George Washington,* 36:328–329; April 3, 1797, letter to the General Assembly of Rhode Island, in *Writings of George Washington,* 35:431; October 17, 1789, letter to the Legislature of the State of Connecticut, in *Writings of George Washington,* 30:453.

40. E.g., March 1, 1778, letter to Bryan Fairfax, in *Writings of George Washington,* 11:3; July 20, 1788, letter to Jonathan Trumbull, in *Writings of George Washington,* 30:22; August 31, 1797, letter to Thaddeus Kosciuszko, in *Writings of George Washington,* 36:22.

41. E.g., May 10, 1789, letter to the United Baptist Churches in Virginia, in Allen, *Collection,* 532; May 26, 1789, letter to the General Assembly of Presbyterian Churches, in *Writings of George Washington,* 30:336n12; September 1789 letter to the Annual Meeting of Quakers, in *Writings of George Washington,* 30:416n54; May 29, 1789, letter to the Bishops of the Methodist Episcopal Church, in *Writings of George Washington,* 30:339.

42. Undated letter to the Bishops, Clergy, and Laity of the Protestant Episcopal Church in New York, New Jersey, Pennsylvania, Delaware, Maryland, Virginia, and North Carolina, in *Writings of George Washington,* 30:383.

43. October 20, 1792, letter to Sir Edward Newenham, in *Writings of George Washington,* 32:190.

44. January 1790 letter to the Hebrew Congregations, in Allen, *Collection,* 545.

45. "Farewell Address," September 19, 1796, in *Writings of George Washington,* 35:220.

46. August 15, 1787, letter to the Marquis de Lafayette, in *Writings of George Washington,* 29:259.

47. E.g., March 3, 1797, letter to the Clergy of Different Denominations Residing in and near the City of Philadelphia, in *Writings of George Washington,* 35:416–417; January 1790 letter to the Hebrew Congregations, in Allen, *Collection,* 546; March 15, 1790, letter to the Roman Catholics in the United States of America, in *Writings of George Washington,* 31:22n47; August 18, 1790, letter to the Hebrew Congregation in Newport, in *The Papers of George Washington: Presidential Series,* ed. Mark A. Mastromarino (Charlottesville: University Press of Virginia, 1996), 6:285; November 16, 1782, letter to the Minister, Elders, and Deacons of the Reformed Protestant Dutch Church in Kingston, in *Writings of George Washington,* 25:347.

48. "Talk to the Cherokee Nation," August 29, 1796, in *Writings of George Washington,* 35:198.

49. "Thanksgiving Proclamation," October 3, 1789, in *Writings of George Washington,* 30:427; May 29, 1789, letter to the Bishops of the Methodist Episcopal Church, in *Writings of George Washington,* 30:339; January 27, 1793, letter to the Members of the New Church in Baltimore, in *Writings of George Washington,* 32:315.

50. Brookhiser, *Founding Father,* 149.

51. Ibid.

52. John Warwick Montgomery, *The Shaping of America* (Minneapolis, Minn.: Bethany House Publishers, 1976), 54, 56.

53. Vindex [pseud.], *Light Invisible: The Freemason's Answer to Darkness Visible* (London: Regency Press, 1952), 137–138.

54. Brookhiser, *Founding Father,* 150, 151.

55. "Reply to an Address from Ministers and Elders," October 28, 1789, in Cousins, *Republic of Reason,* 60; "Thanksgiving Proclamation," October 3, 1789, in *Writings of George Washington,* 30:428.

56. May 1789 letter to the General Assembly of Presbyterian Churches, in *Writings of George Washington,* 30:336n12; May 29, 1789, letter to the Bishops of the Methodist Episcopal Church, in *Writings of George Washington,* 30:339.

57. "General Orders" for March 22, 1783, in *Writings of George Washington,* 26:250; October 3, 1785, letter to George Mason, in *Writings of George Washington,* 28:285; July 10, 1789, letter to the Society of United Brethren for Propagating the Gospel among the Heathen, in *Writings of George Washington,* 30:355.

58. March 3, 1797, letter to the Clergy of Different Denominations Residing in and near the City of Philadelphia, in *Writings of George Washington,* 35:416; "Farewell Address," September 19, 1796, in *Writings of George Washington,* 35:229.

59. "Farewell Address," September 19, 1796, in *Writings of George Washington,* 35:231; May 1789 letter to the General Assembly of Presbyterian Churches, in *Writings of George Washington,* 30:336n12.

60. Thomas Jefferson, *The Works of Thomas Jefferson,* ed. Paul Leicester Ford (New York: G. P. Putnam's Sons, 1904–1905), 1:352.

61. Benjamin Tallmadge in Charles Swain Hall, *Benjamin Tallmadge, Revolutionary Soldier and American Businessman* (New York: Columbia University Press, 1943), 167.

62. "CC" Proctor, ed., "After-Dinner Anecdotes of James Madison, Excerpts from Jared Sparks' Journal for 1829–31," *Virginia Magazine of History and Biography* 60 (April 1952): 263.

63. Samuel Miller, *The Life of Samuel Miller* (Philadelphia: Claxton, Remsen, and Haffelfinger, 1869), 123.

64. Jefferson, *Works of Thomas Jefferson,* 1:353.

65. Boller, *George Washington,* 34.

66. William White to Rev. B. C. C. Parker, December 21, 1832, in Wilson, *Memoir,* 193.

67. James Abercrombie to Origen Bacheler, November 29, 1831, *Magazine of American History,* XIII (June, 1885), 597.

68. Boller, *George Washington,* 26.

69. Steven J. Keillor, *This Rebellious House* (Downer's Grove, Ill.: InterVarsity Press, 1996), 85; Bishop Meade, *Old Churches, Ministers and Families of Virginia* (Philadelphia: J. B. Lippincott, 1900), 1:191.

70. Anson Phelps Stokes, *Church and State in the United States* (New York: Harper & Brothers, 1950), 1:310.

71. James H. Hutson, *Religion and the Founding of the American Republic* (Washington, D.C.: Library of Congress, 1998), 84–96.

CHAPTER EIGHT. THE SIGNIFICANCE OF THEISTIC RATIONALISM

1. Sidney E. Mead, *The Old Religion in the Brave New World* (Berkeley: University of California Press, 1977), 29.

2. Steven J. Keillor, *This Rebellious House* (Downer's Grove, Ill.: InterVarsity Press, 1996), 91; Jon Butler, *Awash in a Sea of Faith* (Cambridge, Mass.: Harvard University Press, 1990), 196; Michael P. Zuckert, *The Natural Rights Republic* (Notre Dame, Ind.: University of Notre Dame Press, 1996), 128.

3. Robert P. Kraynak, *Christian Faith and Modern Democracy* (Notre Dame, Ind.: University of Notre Dame Press, 2001), 127–128.

4. Cushing Strout, *The New Heavens and New Earth: Political Religion in America* (New York: Harper & Row, 1974), 50.

5. Alice M. Baldwin, *The New England Clergy and the American Revolution* (New York: Frederick Ungar, 1958), 170, 172; Thomas L. Pangle, *The Spirit of Modern Republicanism* (Chicago: University of Chicago Press, 1988), 24.

6. Keillor, *This Rebellious House,* 91.

7. Kraynak, *Christian Faith,* 128.

8. Marvin Olasky, *Fighting for Liberty and Virtue: Political and Cultural Wars in Eighteenth-Century America* (Washington, D.C.: Regnery Publishing, 1995), 155–156.

9. Pauline Maier, *American Scripture: Making the Declaration of Independence* (New York: Alfred A. Knopf, 1997), 148–149.

10. John T. Noonan Jr. and Edward McGlynn Gaffney Jr., *Religious Freedom: History, Cases, and Other Materials on the Interaction of Religion and Government*

(New York: Foundation Press, 2001), 189; Olasky, *Fighting for Liberty,* 156; C. Gregg Singer, *A Theological Interpretation of American History* (Nutley, N.J.: Craig Press, 1976), 40.

11. Zuckert, *Natural Rights,* 201; Kraynak, *Christian Faith,* 128.

12. William Warren Sweet, *Religion in the Development of American Culture, 1765–1840* (New York: Charles Scribner's Sons, 1952), 86; John Mitchell Mason, "The Voice of Warning to Christians, on the Ensuing Election of a President of the United States," in *The Complete Works of John M. Mason, D.D.,* ed. Ebenezer Mason (New York: Baker and Scribner, 1849), 5:570, 571.

13. Baldwin, *New England Clergy,* 172.

14. Pangle, *Spirit of Modern Republicanism,* 79.

15. John Adams, "A Defence of the Constitution of Government of the United States of America," in *The Political Writings of John Adams,* ed. George A. Peek Jr. (Indianapolis, Ind.: Bobbs-Merrill, 1954), 117.

16. William Pierce, "Characters in the Convention of the States Held at Philadelphia, May 1787," in *Documents Illustrative of the Formation of the Union of the American States,* ed. Charles C. Tansill (Washington, D.C.: Government Printing Office, 1927), 98–99.

17. Pangle, *Spirit of Modern Republicanism,* 78.

18. Russel Blaine Nye, *The Cultural Life of the New Nation* (New York: Harper & Row, 1960), 203.

19. Perry Miller, "The Contribution of the Protestant Churches to the Religious Liberty in Colonial America," *Harvard Review* 2, no. 2 (Winter-Spring 1964): 67.

20. Strout, *New Heavens,* 88, 82–83.

21. Pangle, *Spirit of Modern Republicanism,* 83.

22. E.g., June 26, 1822, letter from Jefferson to Benjamin Waterhouse, in *The Works of Thomas Jefferson,* ed. Paul Leicester Ford (New York: G. P. Putnam's Sons, 1904–1905), 12:243.

23. Sydney E. Ahlstrom, *A Religious History of the American People* (New Haven, Conn.: Yale University Press, 1972), 367–368; Strout, *New Heavens,* 86.

24. Edwin Gaustad, "Religious Tests, Constitutions, and 'Christian Nation,'" in *Religion in a Revolutionary Age,* ed. Ronald Hoffman and Peter J. Albert (Charlottesville: University Press of Virginia, 1994), 224.

25. Mead, *Old Religion,* 23.

26. Tench Coxe quoted in Anson Phelps Stokes, *Church and State in the United States* (New York: Harper & Brothers, 1950), 1:275.

27. Ibid.

28. George Willis Cooke, *Unitarianism in America: A History of Its Origin and Development* (Boston: American Unitarian Association, 1902), 86–87.

29. Daniel Shute [January 30, 1788], in *Debates, Resolutions and Other Proceedings of the Convention of the Commonwealth of Massachusetts* (Boston: Oliver & Munroe and Joshua Cushing, 1808), 156–157.

30. E.g., Tench Coxe, Oliver Ellsworth, and Edmund Randolph quoted in *The Founders' Constitution,* ed. Philip B. Kurland and Ralph Lerner (Indianapolis, Ind.: Liberty Fund, 1987), 639, 640, 644.

31. James Madison, October 28, 1787, letter to Edmund Pendleton quoted in Kurland and Lerner, *Founders' Constitution,* 639.

32. Kurland and Lerner, *Founders' Constitution*, 644; George Washington, *Farewell Address*, in *George Washington: A Collection*, ed. W. B. Allen (Indianapolis, Ind.: Liberty Fund, 1988), 521.

33. E.g., Federalist No. 27, 35, 36, 53, 57, 62, 63, and 72.

34. Stokes, *Church and State*, 1:514.

35. Ibid., 1:515.

36. Quoted in *The Sacred Rights of Conscience*, ed. Daniel L. Dreisbach and Mark David Hall (Indianapolis, Ind.: Liberty Fund, 2009), 238.

37. James Madison [August 15, 1789], in Thomas Hart Benton and John C. Rives, eds., *Abridgment of the Debates of Congress, from 1789 to 1856* (New York: D. Appleton, 1857), 137.

38. Noonan and Gaffney, *Religious Freedom*, 215, 639, 645.

39. Ibid., 201–202.

40. Stokes, *Church and State*, 1:499.

41. Ibid., 1:515.

42. Max Farrand, ed., *The Records of the Federal Convention of 1787* (New Haven, Conn.: Yale University Press, 1966), 2:167, 181; 2:295.

43. Strout, *New Heavens*, 87.

44. Thomas Jefferson, "First Inaugural Address," March 4, 1801, in *Inaugural Addresses of the Presidents of the United States* (Washington, D.C.: U.S. Government Printing Office, 1989), 15.

45. Harry V. Jaffa, *A New Birth of Freedom* (Lanham, Md.: Rowman & Littlefield, 2000), 151; Kraynak, *Christian Faith*, 52, 53; Zuckert, *Natural Rights*, 200.

46. Ahlstrom, *Religious History*, 383, 379.

47. Kraynak, *Christian Faith*, 129.

48. Ibid., 128.

49. Ibid., 129.

50. Jaffa, *New Birth*, 352.

51. Richard V. Pierard and Robert D. Linder, *Civil Religion & the Presidency* (Grand Rapids, Mich.: Academic Books, 1988), 89.

52. Abraham Lincoln, "Proclamation of a National Fast Day," August 12, 1861, in *The Collected Works of Abraham Lincoln*, ed. Roy P. Basler (New Brunswick, N.J.: Rutgers University Press, 1953), 4:482.

53. Pierard and Linder, *Civil Religion*, 97, 112.

54. Pangle, *Spirit of Modern Republicanism*, 21; Strout, *New Heavens*, 82.

55. Will Herberg, *Protestant-Catholic-Jew* (Garden City, N.Y.: Doubleday, 1960), 83.

56. Ibid., 84.

57. Kraynak, *Christian Faith*, 128.

58. Baldwin, *New England Clergy*, 134–153.

59. Zuckert, *Natural Rights*, 178.

60. Strout, *New Heavens*, 88.

61. Henry F. May, *The Enlightenment in America* (New York: Oxford University Press, 1976), 16; Strout, *New Heavens*, 67; Pangle, *Spirit of Modern Republicanism*, 81–82.

62. A Layman, *The Claims of Thomas Jefferson to the Presidency, Examined at the Bar of Christianity* (Philadelphia: Asbury Dickins, 1800), 45.

63. Rev. William Linn, *Serious Consideration on the Election of a President: Addressed to the Citizens of the United States* (New York: John Furman, 1800), 24, quoted in Philip Hamburger, *Separation of Church and State* (Cambridge, Mass.: Harvard University Press, 2002), 114.

64. Pangle, *Spirit of Modern Republicanism,* 84.

65. Mead, *Old Religion,* 2, 3.

66. Harvey Mansfield quoted in Walter Berns, "Religion and the Founding Principle," in *The Moral Foundations of the American Republic,* 3rd ed., ed. Robert H. Horwitz (Charlottesville: University Press of Virginia, 1986), 220; Berns, "Religion," 223; John G. West Jr., *The Politics of Revelation and Reason* (Lawrence: University Press of Kansas, 1996).

67. Kraynak, *Christian Faith,* 127.

68. Mark A. Noll, Nathan O. Hatch, and George M. Marsden, *The Search for Christian America* (Westchester, Ill: Crossway Books, 1983), 107.

69. Nye, *Cultural Life,* 203n; Stokes, *Church and State,* 1:497; Paul A. Rahe, *Republics Ancient and Modern* (Chapel Hill: University of North Carolina Press, 1992), 753.

70. James W. Jones, *The Shattered Synthesis* (New Haven, Conn.: Yale University Press, 1973), 196.

Bibliography

Abercrombie, James. "Letter to Origen Bacheler, November 29, 1831." *Magazine of American History* 13 (June 1885): 596–597.

Adair, Douglass. *Fame and the Founding Fathers.* New York: W. W. Norton, 1974.

Adams, John. *Diary and Autobiography of John Adams.* 4 vols. Edited by L. H. Butterfield. New York: Atheneum, 1964.

———. *Familiar Letters of John Adams and His Wife Abigail Adams during the Revolution.* Edited by Charles Francis Adams. New York: Hurd and Houghton, 1876.

———. *Papers of John Adams.* 15 vols. Edited by Robert J. Taylor. Cambridge, Mass.: Belknap Press of Harvard University Press, 1977–2010.

———. *The Political Writings of John Adams.* Edited by George A. Peek Jr. Indianapolis, Ind.: Bobbs-Merrill, 1954.

———. *The Works of John Adams.* 10 vols. Edited by Charles Francis Adams. Boston: Little, Brown, 1850–1856.

Adams, John, Alexander Biddle, Thomas Jefferson, and Benjamin Rush. *Old Family Letters: Copied from the Originals for Alexander Biddle.* 2 vols. Philadelphia: J. B. Lippincott, 1892.

Ahlstrom, Sydney E. *A Religious History of the American People.* New Haven, Conn.: Yale University Press, 1972.

Aldridge, Alfred Owen. *Benjamin Franklin and Nature's God.* Durham, N.C.: Duke University Press, 1967.

Allen, W. B., ed. *George Washington: A Collection.* Indianapolis, Ind.: Liberty Fund, 1988.

Alley, Robert S., ed. *James Madison on Religious Liberty.* Buffalo, N.Y.: Prometheus Books, 1985.

Baldwin, Alice M. *The New England Clergy and the American Revolution.* New York: Frederick Ungar, 1958.

Bartol, C. A. *The West Church and Its Ministers.* Boston: Crosby, Nichols, 1856.

Becker, Carl L. *The Heavenly City of the Eighteenth-Century Philosophers.* New Haven, Conn.: Yale University Press, 1932.

Beecher, Lyman. *Autobiography, Correspondence, etc., of Lyman Beecher, D.D.* Vol. 1. Edited by Charles Beecher. New York: Harper, 1864.

Bellamy, Joseph. *The Works of Joseph Bellamy.* 2 vols. Boston: Doctrinal Tract and Book Society, 1853.

Bennett, William J., ed. *Our Sacred Honor.* New York: Simon & Schuster, 1997.

Benton, Thomas Hart, and John C. Rives, eds. *Abridgment of the Debates of Congress, from 1789 to 1856.* New York: D. Appleton, 1857.

Berns, Walter. "Religion and the Founding Principle." In *The Moral Foundations of the American Republic,* 3rd ed., edited by Robert H. Horwitz. Charlottesville: University Press of Virginia, 1986.

Boller, Paul F. *George Washington & Religion.* Dallas, Tex.: Southern Methodist University Press, 1963.

Bonomi, Patricia U. *Under the Cope of Heaven.* New York: Oxford University Press, 1986.

Boorstin, Daniel. "The Founding Fathers and the Courage to Doubt." In *James Madison on Religious Liberty,* edited by Robert S. Alley. Buffalo, N.Y.: Prometheus Books, 1985.

———. *The Lost World of Thomas Jefferson.* Boston: Beacon Press, 1948.

Boucher, Jonathan. *A View of the Causes and Consequences of the American Revolution.* New York: Russell & Russell, 1967. Reprint of 1797 original.

Boyd, George Adams. *Elias Boudinot: Patriot and Statesman.* Princeton, N.J.: Princeton University Press, 1952.

Bradford, Alden. *Memoir of the Life and Writings of Rev. Jonathan Mayhew, D.D.* Boston: C. C. Little, 1838.

Bradford, M. E. *A Worthy Company.* Marlborough, N.H.: Plymouth Rock Foundation, 1982.

Brookhiser, Richard. *Founding Father: Rediscovering George Washington.* New York: Free Press, 1996.

Butler, Jon. *Awash in a Sea of Faith.* Cambridge, Mass.: Harvard University Press, 1990.

Buxbaum, Melvin H. *Benjamin Franklin and the Zealous Presbyterians.* University Park: Pennsylvania State University Press, 1975.

Cady, Edwin H., ed. *Literature of the Early Republic.* New York: Holt, Rinehart and Winston, 1965.

Calvin, John. "On Civil Government." Bk. 4, chap. 20 of *Institutes of the Christian Religion.* In *Luther and Calvin on Secular Authority,* edited by Harro Hopfl. Cambridge: Cambridge University Press, 1991.

Cappon, Lester J., ed. *The Adams-Jefferson Letters.* 2 vols. Chapel Hill: University of North Carolina Press, 1959.

Channing, William Henry. *Memoir of William Ellery Channing.* 3 vols. Boston: Crosby, Nichols, 1854.

Chauncy, Charles. *The Benevolence of the Deity.* Boston: Powars & Willis, 1784.

———. "Civil Magistrates Must Be Just." [1747]. In *Political Sermons of the American Founding Era,* edited by Ellis Sandoz. Indianapolis, Ind.: Liberty Press, 1991.

———. *The Mystery Hid from Ages and Generations, Made Manifest by the Gospel-Revelation; or, The Salvation of All Men.* London: 1784.

———. *Seasonable Thoughts on the State of Religion in New England.* Boston: Rogers and Fowle, 1743.

———. *Twelve Sermons . . . with Interspersed Notes.* Boston: D. and J. Kneeland for Thomas Leverett, 1765.

Chernow, Ron. *Alexander Hamilton.* New York: Penguin Books, 2004.

Clarke, Samuel. *A Demonstration of the Being and Attributes of God and Other Writings*. Edited by Ezio Vailati. Cambridge: Cambridge University Press, 1998.

——. *Discourse Concerning the Unchangeable Obligations of Natural Religion, and the Truth and Certainty of the Christian Revelation*. London: W. Botham, 1706.

Cohen, Jeffrey, and David Nice. *The Presidency*. Boston: McGraw-Hill, 2003.

Cole, Franklin P., ed. *They Preached Liberty*. Indianapolis, Ind.: Liberty Press, 1977.

Coleman, William, ed. *A Collection of the Facts and Documents, Relative to the Death of Major-General Alexander Hamilton*. Boston: Houghton Mifflin, 1904.

Conkin, Paul K. "Priestley and Jefferson: Unitarianism as a Religion for a New Revolutionary Age." In *Religion in a Revolutionary Age,* edited by Ronald Hoffman and Peter J. Albert. Charlottesville: University Press of Virginia, 1994.

Cooke, George Willis. *Unitarianism in America: A History of Its Origin and Development*. Boston: American Unitarian Association, 1902.

Cooper, Anthony Ashley, Earl of Shaftesbury. *Characteristics of Men, Manners, Opinions, Times*. Edited by John M. Robertson. New York: Bobbs-Merrill, 1964.

Cornelison, Isaac A. *The Relationship of Religion to the Civil Government, in the United States of America: A State without a Church, but Not without a Religion*. New York: Putnam, 1895.

Corrigan, John. *The Hidden Balance*. Cambridge: Cambridge University Press, 1987.

Cousins, Norman, ed. *The Republic of Reason: The Personal Philosophies of the Founding Fathers*. San Francisco: Harper & Row, 1988. Published under the title *In God We Trust* in 1958, with same pagination.

Debates, Resolutions and Other Proceedings of the Convention of the Commonwealth of Massachusetts. Boston: Oliver & Munroe and Joshua Cushing, 1808.

Diggins, John Patrick. *The Lost Soul of American Politics*. New York: Basic Books, 1984.

Dreisbach, Daniel L., and Mark David Hall, eds. *The Sacred Rights of Conscience*. Indianapolis, Ind.: Liberty Fund, 2009.

Durant, Will. *The Age of Faith*. Pt. 4 of *The Story of Civilization*. New York: Simon & Schuster, 1950.

Durant, Will, and Ariel Durant. *The Age of Voltaire*. Pt. 9 of *The Story of Civilization*. New York: Simon & Schuster, 1965.

Dworetz, Steven M. *The Unvarnished Doctrine: Locke, Liberalism, and the American Revolution*. Durham, N.C.: Duke University Press, 1990.

Ebenstein, William. *Great Political Thinkers*. 4th ed. Hinsdale, Ill.: Dryden Press, 1969.

Edwards, Jonathan. "A History of the Work of Redemption." In *The Works of Jonathan Edwards,* edited by John F. Wilson. New Haven, Conn.: Yale University Press, 1989.

Ellis, Richard J., ed. *Founding the American Presidency*. Lanham, Md.: Rowman & Littlefield, 1999.

Farrand, Max, ed. *The Records of the Federal Convention of 1787.* 3 vols. New Haven, Conn.: Yale University Press, 1966.

Flower, Elizabeth, and Murray G. Murphey. *A History of Philosophy in America.* 2 vols. New York: G. P. Putnam's Sons, 1977.

Fortin, Ernest L. "St. Thomas Aquinas." In *History of Political Philosophy*, 2nd ed., edited by Leo Strauss and Joseph Cropsey. Chicago: University of Chicago Press, 1981.

Franklin, Benjamin. *Benjamin Franklin, Writings.* Edited by J. A. Leo Lemay. New York: Library of America, 1987.

———. *The Papers of Benjamin Franklin.* 39 vols. Edited by Leonard W. Labaree. New Haven, Conn.: Yale University Press, 1959–2006.

———. *The Works of Benjamin Franklin.* 10 vols. Edited by Jared Sparks. Boston: Tappan & Whittemore, 1836–1840.

Frazer, Gregg L. "Alexander Hamilton, Theistic Rationalist." In *The Forgotten Founders on Religion and Public Life*, edited by Daniel L. Dreisbach, Mark David Hall, and Jeffry H. Morrison. Notre Dame, Ind.: University of Notre Dame Press, 2009.

Friend to *Real* Religion, A [Anonymous]. "A Vindication of the Religion of Mr. Jefferson, and a Statement of His Services in the Cause of Religious Liberty." Attached to Thomas Jefferson, *Jefferson's Notes, on the State of Virginia.* Baltimore, Md.: W. Pechin, 1800.

Gambrell, Mary Latimer. *Ministerial Training in Eighteenth-Century New England.* New York: Columbia University Press, 1937.

Gaustad, Edwin. "Religious Tests, Constitutions, and 'Christian Nation.'" In *Religion in a Revolutionary Age*, edited by Ronald Hoffman and Peter J. Albert. Charlottesville: University Press of Virginia, 1994.

Gay, Peter. *Deism: An Anthology.* Princeton, N.J.: D. Van Nostrand, 1968.

Graves, Charles. *A History of Unitarianism.* Boston: American Unitarian Association, 1934.

Grean, Stanley. *Shaftesbury's Philosophy of Religion and Ethics.* Athens: Ohio University Press, 1967.

Griffin, Edward M. *Old Brick: Charles Chauncy of Boston, 1705–1787.* Minneapolis: University of Minnesota Press, 1980.

Hall, Charles Swain. *Benjamin Tallmadge, Revolutionary Soldier and American Businessman.* New York: Columbia University Press, 1943.

Hall, Mark David. "James Wilson: Presbyterian, Anglican, Thomist, or Deist? Does It Matter?" In *The Founders on God and Government*, edited by Daniel L. Dreisbach, Mark D. Hall, and Jeffry H. Morrison. Lanham, Md.: Rowman & Littlefield, 2004.

———. *The Political and Legal Philosophy of James Wilson, 1742–1798.* Columbia: University of Missouri Press, 1997.

Hamburger, Philip. *Separation of Church and State.* Cambridge, Mass.: Harvard University Press, 2002.

Hamilton, Alexander. *The Papers of Alexander Hamilton.* 27 vols. Edited by Harold C. Syrett and Jacob E. Cooke. New York: Columbia University Press, 1961–1987.

———. *The Works of Alexander Hamilton.* 12 vols. Edited by Henry Cabot Lodge. New York: Knickerbocker Press, 1904.

Hamilton, Alexander, James Madison, and John Jay. *The Federalist Papers.* Edited by Clinton Rossiter. New York: New American Library, 1999. Reprint of 1961 edition.

Hamilton, Allan McLane. *The Intimate Life of Alexander Hamilton.* New York: Charles Scribner's Sons, 1910.

Hamilton, John C. *History of the Republic of the United States of America, as Traced in the Writings of Alexander Hamilton.* 7 vols. Philadelphia: J. B. Lippincott, 1864.

Hammer, Dean. *The Puritan Tradition in Revolutionary, Federalist, and Whig Political Theory.* New York: Peter Lang, 1998.

Haroutunian, Joseph. *Piety versus Moralism: The Passing of the New England Theology.* New York: H. Holt, 1932.

Hartnett, Robert C. "The Religion of the Founding Fathers." In *Wellsprings of the American Spirit,* edited by F. Ernest Johnson. New York: Institute for Religious and Social Studies, 1948.

Hatch, Nathan O. *The Sacred Cause of Liberty.* New Haven, Conn.: Yale University Press, 1977.

Heimert, Alan, and Perry Miller, eds. *The Great Awakening: Documents Illustrating the Crisis and Its Consequences.* Indianapolis, Ind.: Bobbs-Merrill, 1967.

Herberg, Will. *Protestant-Catholic-Jew.* Garden City, N.Y.: Doubleday, 1960.

Hoffman, Ronald, and Peter J. Albert, eds. *Religion in a Revolutionary Age.* Charlottesville: University Press of Virginia, 1994.

Holt, Anne. *A Life of Joseph Priestley.* London: Oxford University Press, 1931.

Hutcheson, Harold R., ed. *Lord Herbert of Cherbury's De Religione Laici.* New Haven, Conn.: Yale University Press, 1944.

Hutson, James H. *Religion and the Founding of the American Republic.* Washington, D.C.: Library of Congress, 1998.

Hyneman, Charles, and Donald Lutz, eds. *American Political Writing during the Founding Era, 1760–1805.* Indianapolis, Ind.: Liberty Fund, 1983.

Inaugural Addresses of the Presidents of the United States. Washington, D.C.: U.S. Government Printing Office, 1989.

Jaffa, Harry V. *A New Birth of Freedom.* Lanham, Md.: Rowman & Littlefield, 2000.

Jayne, Allen. *Jefferson's Declaration of Independence: Origins, Philosophy, and Theology.* Lexington: University Press of Kentucky, 1998.

Jefferson, Thomas. *Jefferson's Notes, on the State of Virginia.* Baltimore, Md.: W. Pechin, 1800.

———. *The Papers of Thomas Jefferson.* 37 vols. Edited by Julian Boyd, L. H. Butterfield, Charles T. Cullen, and John Catanzariti (Princeton, N.J.: Princeton University Press, 1950–2009.

———. *The Works of Thomas Jefferson.* 12 vols. Edited by Paul Leicester Ford. New York: G. P. Putnam's Sons, 1904–1905.

———. *The Writings of Thomas Jefferson.* 9 vols. Edited by H. A. Washington. Washington, D.C.: Taylor & Maury, 1853–1854.

Jones, James W. *The Shattered Synthesis.* New Haven, Conn.: Yale University Press, 1973.

Kammen, Michael. *People of Paradox.* New York: Vintage Books, 1972.

Keillor, Steven J. *This Rebellious House.* Downer's Grove, Ill.: InterVarsity Press, 1996.

Ketcham, Ralph L. "James Madison and Religion—A New Hypothesis." In *James Madison on Religious Liberty,* edited by Robert S. Alley. Buffalo, N.Y.: Prometheus Books, 1985.

Kirk, Russell. *The Roots of American Order.* Washington, D.C.: Regnery Gateway, 1991.

Koch, Gustav Adolf. *Republican Religion: The American Revolution and the Cult of Reason.* Gloucester, Mass.: Peter Smith, 1964.

Kraynak, Robert P. *Christian Faith and Modern Democracy.* Notre Dame, Ind.: University of Notre Dame Press, 2001.

Kurland, Philip B., and Ralph Lerner, eds. *The Founders' Constitution.* Indianapolis, Ind.: Liberty Fund, 1987.

Layman, A. [Anonymous]. *The Claims of Thomas Jefferson to the Presidency, Examined at the Bar of Christianity.* Philadelphia: Asbury Dickins, 1800.

Leland, John. *A View of the Principal Deistical Writers.* Vol. 2. London: W. Richardson and S. Clark, 1764.

Leonard, Daniel. "Massachusettensis." In *Novanglus, and Massachusettensis; or Political Essays, Published in the Years 1774 and 1775.* Boston: Hews and Goss, 1819.

Lincoln, Abraham. *The Collected Works of Abraham Lincoln.* 9 vols. Edited by Roy P. Basler. New Brunswick, N.J.: Rutgers University Press, 1953–1955.

Lippy, Charles H. *Seasonable Revolutionary: The Mind of Charles Chauncy.* Chicago: Nelson-Hall, 1981.

Locke, John. *Two Treatises on Government.* Edited by Peter Laslett. Cambridge: Cambridge University Press, 1988.

Madison, James. "After-Dinner Anecdotes of James Madison, Excerpts from Jared Sparks' Journal for 1829–31." *Virginia Magazine of History and Biography* 60 (April 1952): 263.

———. "Detached Memoranda." Edited by Elizabeth Fleet. *William and Mary Quarterly,* 3rd ser., vol. 3, no. 4 (October 1946): 534–568.

———. *Letters and Other Writings of James Madison.* 4 vols. Edited by William Rives. New York: R Worthington, 1884.

———. *The Papers of James Madison.* 17 vols. Edited by Robert A. Rutland and William M. E. Rachal. Chicago: University of Chicago Press, 1962–1991.

———. *The Writings of James Madison.* 9 vols. Edited by Gaillard Hunt. New York: G. P. Putnam's Sons, 1900–1910.

Maier, Pauline. *American Scripture: Making the Declaration of Independence.* New York: Alfred A. Knopf, 1997.

Marini, Stephen A. "Religion, Politics, and Ratification." In *Religion in a Revolutionary Age,* edited by Ronald Hoffman and Peter J. Albert. Charlottesville: University Press of Virginia, 1994.

Martin, David. "General Tendencies and Historical Filters." *Annual Review of Social Science of Religion* 3 (1979): 1–16.

Mason, John Mitchell. "The Voice of Warning, to Christians, on the Ensuing Election of a President of the United States." In *The Complete Works of John M. Mason, D.D.,* edited by Ebenezer Mason. New York: Baker and Scribner, 1849.

May, Henry F. *The Enlightenment in America.* New York: Oxford University Press, 1976.

Mayhew, Jonathan. *Christian Sobriety.* Boston: Richard and Samuel Draper, 1763.

———. "A Discourse Concerning Unlimited Submission and Non-resistance to the Higher Powers." In *Seven Sermons* (1750), reprinted as *Sermons,* edited by Edwin S. Gaustad. New York: Arno Press, 1969.

———. *Sermons upon the Following Subjects.* Boston: Richard Draper, 1755.

———. *Seven Sermons* (1750), reprinted as *Sermons.* Edited by Edwin S. Gaustad. New York: Arno Press, 1969.

———. *Two Sermons on the Nature, Extent, and Perfection of the Divine Goodness.* Boston: D. and J. Kneeland, 1763.

McAllister, James L. "John Witherspoon: Academic Advocate for American Freedom." In *A Miscellany of American Christianity,* edited by Stuart C. Henry. Durham, N.C.: Duke University Press, 1963.

McGuire, E. C. *The Religious Opinions and Character of Washington.* New York: Harper & Brothers, 1836.

Mead, Sidney E. *The Old Religion in the Brave New World.* Berkeley: University of California Press, 1977.

Meade, Bishop William. *Old Churches, Ministers and Families of Virginia.* 2 vols. Philadelphia: J. B. Lippincott, 1900.

Meyers, Marvin, ed. *The Mind of the Founder: Sources of the Political Thought of James Madison.* Hanover, N.H.: University Press of New England, 1973.

Middleton, Conyers. *A Letter from Rome.* London, 1741.

———. *A Letter to Dr. Waterland; Containing Some Remarks on His Vindication of Scripture.* London, 1731.

———. *The Miscellaneous Works of Conyers Middleton.* Vol. 1. London, 1755.

Miller, John C. *Alexander Hamilton and the Growth of the Nation.* New York: Harper & Row, 1959.

Miller, Perry. "The Contribution of the Protestant Churches to the Religious Liberty in Colonial America." *Harvard Review* 2, no. 2 (Winter–Spring 1964): 60–69.

———. *Jonathan Edwards.* New York: W. Sloane Associates, 1949.

Miller, Samuel. *The Life of Samuel Miller.* Philadelphia: Claxton, Remsen, and Haffelfinger, 1869.

Mitchell, Broadus. *Alexander Hamilton: A Concise Biography.* New York: Oxford University Press, 1976.

Montgomery, John Warwick. *The Shaping of America.* Minneapolis, Minn.: Bethany House Publishers, 1976.

Morgan, Edmund S. "The American Revolution Considered as an Intellectual Movement." In *Paths of American Thought,* edited by Arthur M. Schlesinger Jr. and Morton White. Boston: Houghton Mifflin, 1963.

Morris, Gouverneur. *The Diary and Letters of Gouverneur Morris.* Edited by Anne Cary Morris. New York: Charles Scribner's Sons, 1888.

————. *A Diary of the French Revolution.* 2 vols. Edited by Beatrix Cary Davenport. Boston: Houghton Mifflin, 1939.

Morris, Richard B., ed. *Alexander Hamilton and the Founding of the Nation.* New York: Dial Press, 1957.

Munoz, Vincent Phillip. "Religious Liberty and American Constitutionalism." Ph.D. diss., Claremont Graduate University, 2001.

Newlin, Claude M. *Philosophy and Religion in Colonial America.* New York: Philosophical Library, 1962.

Noll, Mark. *Christians in the American Revolution.* Washington, D.C.: Christian University Press, 1977.

Noll, Mark A., Nathan O. Hatch, and George M. Marsden. *The Search for Christian America.* Westchester, Ill.: Crossway Books, 1983.

Noonan, John T. *The Lustre of Our Country.* Berkeley: University of California Press, 1998.

Noonan, John T., Jr., and Edward McGlynn Gaffney Jr. *Religious Freedom: History, Cases, and Other Materials on the Interaction of Religion and Government.* New York: Foundation Press, 2001.

Nye, Russel Blaine. *The Cultural Life of the New Nation.* New York: Harper & Row, 1960.

Nye, Russel B., and Norman S. Grabo, eds. *The Revolution and the Early Republic.* Vol. 2 of *American Thought and Writing.* Boston: Houghton Mifflin, 1965.

Olasky, Marvin. *Fighting for Liberty and Virtue: Political and Cultural Wars in Eighteenth-Century America.* Washington, D.C.: Regnery Publishing, 1995.

Paine, Levi. *A Critical History of the Evolution of Trinitarianism.* Boston: Houghton Mifflin, 1900.

Paine, Thomas. "The Age of Reason, Being an Investigation of Time and Fabulous Theology." In *The Life and Writings of Thomas Paine,* vol. 6, edited by Daniel Edwin Wheeler. New York: Vincent Parke, 1908.

Palmer, Elihu. *Principles of Nature.* In *Elihu Palmer's "Principles of Nature,"* edited by Kerry S. Walters. Wolfeboro, N.H.: Longwood Academic, 1990. Reprint of 1806 edition.

Pangle, Thomas L. *The Spirit of Modern Republicanism.* Chicago: University of Chicago Press, 1988.

Pierard, Richard V., and Robert D. Linder. *Civil Religion & the Presidency.* Grand Rapids, Mich.: Academie Books, 1988.

Pierce, William. "Characters in the Convention of the States Held at Philadelphia, May 1787." In *Documents Illustrative of the Formation of the Union of the*

American States, edited by Charles C. Tansill. Washington, D.C.: Government Printing Office, 1927.

Priestley, Joseph. "Considerations in Evidence That the Apostolic and Primitive Church Was Unitarian." In *A History of the Corruptions of Christianity.* London: British and Foreign Unitarian Association, 1871.

———. *Discourses Relating to the Evidences of Revealed Religion.* Philadelphia: John Thompson, 1796.

———. *Disquisitions Relating to Matter and Spirit.* London, 1777.

———. *An Essay on the First Principles of Government, and on the Nature of Political, Civil, and Religious Liberty.* London, 1771.

———. *An History of the Corruptions of Christianity.* Birmingham, UK: Percy and Jones, 1782.

———. *Institutes of Natural and Revealed Religion.* Birmingham, UK: Pearson and Rollason, 1782.

———. *Lectures on History and General Policy.* Birmingham, UK: Pearson and Rollason, 1788.

———. *Letters to a Philosophical Unbeliever.* Birmingham, UK: Pearson and Rollason, 1787.

———. *Memoirs.* 2 vols. London: E. Hemsted, 1806.

Quincy, Josiah. *The History of Harvard University.* 2 vols. Cambridge, Mass.: John Owen, 1840.

Rahe, Paul A. *Republics Ancient and Modern.* Chapel Hill: University of North Carolina Press, 1992.

Rand, Benjamin, ed. *The Life, Unpublished Letters, and Philosophical Regimen of Anthony, Earl of Shaftesbury.* London: Swan Sonnenschein, 1900.

Rhoden, Nancy L. *Revolutionary Anglicanism.* New York: New York University Press, 1999.

Richey, McMurry S. "Jonathan Mayhew: American Christian Rationalist." In *A Miscellany of American Christianity,* edited by Stuart C. Henry. Durham, N.C.: Duke University Press, 1963.

Robinson, David. *The Unitarians and the Universalists.* Westport, Conn.: Greenwood Press, 1985.

Rossiter, Clinton. *The Political Thought of the American Revolution.* New York: Harcourt, Brace & World, 1963.

Sabine, George. *A History of Political Theory.* 3rd ed. New York: Holt, Rinehart and Winston, 1961.

Sandoz, Ellis, ed. *Political Sermons of the American Founding Era.* Indianapolis, Ind.: Liberty Press, 1991.

Schachner, Nathan, ed. "Alexander Hamilton Viewed by His Friends: The Narratives of Robert Troup and Hercules Mulligan." *William and Mary Quarterly,* 3rd ser. vol. 4 (April 1947): 203–225.

Schutz, John A., and Douglass Adair, eds. *The Spur of Fame: Dialogues of John Adams and Benjamin Rush, 1805–1813.* San Marino, Calif.: Huntington Library, 1966.

Semonche, John E. *Keeping the Faith: A Cultural History of the U.S. Supreme Court.* New York: Rowman & Littlefield, 1998.

Sheldon, Garrett Ward. *The Political Philosophy of James Madison.* Baltimore, Md.: Johns Hopkins University Press, 2001.

Singer, C. Gregg. *A Theological Interpretation of American History.* Nutley, N.J.: Craig Press, 1976.

Smith, Charles Page. *James Wilson: Founding Father.* Chapel Hill: University of North Carolina Press, 1956.

Smylie, James H. "Madison and Witherspoon: Theological Roots of American Political Thought." *Princeton University Library Chronicle* 22 (Spring 1961): 118–132.

Sparks, Jared. *The Life of Benjamin Franklin.* Boston: Whittemore, Niles, and Hall, 1857.

———. *The Life of Gouverneur Morris, with Selections from His Correspondence and Miscellaneous Papers.* 3 vols. Boston: Gray & Bowen, 1832.

Sprague, William Buell. *Annals of the American Pulpit. . . .* 9 vols. New York: Robert Carter & Brothers, 1857–1869.

———. *Annals of the American Unitarian Pulpit.* New York: Robert Carter & Brothers, 1865.

Steiner, Franklin. *The Religious Beliefs of Our Presidents: From Washington to FDR.* Amherst, N.Y.: Prometheus Books, 1995.

Stephen, Leslie. *History of English Thought in the Eighteenth Century.* 2 vols. London: G. P. Putnam's Sons, 1876.

Stiles, Ezra. *Extracts from the Itineraries and Other Miscellanies of Ezra Stiles.* Edited by Franklin Bowditch Dexter. New Haven, Conn.: Yale University Press, 1916.

Stokes, Anson Phelps. *Church and State in the United States.* 3 vols. New York: Harper & Brothers, 1950.

Storing, Herbert J. "The Federal Convention of 1787." In *The American Founding,* edited by Ralph A. Rossum and Gary L. McDowell. Port Washington, N.Y.: Kennikat Press, 1981.

Strout, Cushing. *The New Heavens and New Earth: Political Religion in America.* New York: Harper & Row, 1974.

Sweet, William Warren. *Religion in the Development of American Culture, 1765–1840.* New York: Charles Scribner's Sons, 1952.

Swiggett, Howard. *The Extraordinary Mr. Morris.* Garden City, N.Y.: Doubleday, 1952.

Thornton, John Wingate, ed. *The Pulpit of the American Revolution: or The Political Sermons of the Period of 1776.* Boston: Gould and Lincoln, 1860.

Vindex [pseud.]. *Light Invisible: The Freemason's Answer to Darkness Visible.* London: Regency Press, 1952.

Walsh, James J. *Education of the Founding Fathers of the Republic: Scholasticism in the Colonial Colleges.* New York: Fordham University Press, 1935.

Walters, Kerry S. *The American Deists.* Lawrence: University Press of Kansas, 1992.

———. *Elihu Palmer's "Principles of Nature"* Wolfeboro, N.H.: Longwood Academic, 1990.

———. *Rational Infidels: The American Deists*. Durango, Colo.: Longwood Academic, 1992.

Waring, E. Graham, ed. *Deism and Natural Religion: A Source Book*. New York: Frederick Ungar, 1967.

Washington, George. *The Papers of George Washington: Presidential Series*. 15 vols. Edited by Dorothy Twohig and W. W. Abbot. Charlottesville: University Press of Virginia, 1987–2009.

———. *The Writings of George Washington*. 39 vols. Edited by John C. Fitzpatrick. Washington, D.C.: U.S. Government Printing Office, 1931–1944.

———. *The Writings of George Washington*. 14 vols. Edited by Worthington Chauncey Ford. New York: G. P. Putnam's Sons, 1889–1893.

———. *The Writings of George Washington*. 12 vols. Edited by Jared Sparks. New York: Harper & Brothers, 1834–1840.

Weems, Mason L. *The Life of Washington*. Edited by Marcus Cunliffe. Cambridge, Mass.: Harvard University Press, 1962.

Wells, Colin. *The Devil & Doctor Dwight*. Chapel Hill: University of North Carolina Press, 2002.

West, John G., Jr. *The Politics of Revelation and Reason*. Lawrence: University Press of Kansas, 1996.

Whitefield, George. *A Continuation of the Reverend Mr. Whitefield's Journal . . . The Seventh Journal*. London, 1741.

Wilbur, Earl Morse. *A History of Unitarianism*. Boston: Beacon Press, 1945.

Willey, Basil. *The Eighteenth Century Background: Studies on the Idea of Nature in the Thought of the Period*. Boston: Beacon Press, 1961.

Wilson, Bird. *Memoir of the Life of the Right Reverend William White*. Philadelphia: C. H. Kay, 1839.

Wilson, James. *Selected Political Essays of James Wilson*. Edited by Randolph G. Adams. New York: Alfred A. Knopf, 1930.

———. *The Works of James Wilson*. 2 vols. Edited by James DeWitt Andrews. Chicago: Callaghan, 1896.

Wilson, Robert J., III. *The Benevolent Deity: Ebenezer Gay and the Rise of Rational Religion in New England, 1696–1787*. Philadelphia: University of Pennsylvania Press, 1984.

Witherspoon, John. *Lectures on Moral Philosophy*. Edited by Jack Scott. Newark: University of Delaware Press, 1982.

———. *Treatises on Justification and Regeneration*. Glasgow, Scotland: William Collins, 1830.

Wright, Conrad. *The Beginnings of Unitarianism in America*. Hamden, Conn.: Archon Books, 1976.

———. *The Liberal Christians*. Boston: Beacon Press, 1970.

Zuckert, Michael. *The Natural Rights Republic*. Notre Dame, Ind.: University of Notre Dame Press, 1996.

INDEX